❧ SOVIET ATTITUDES
TOWARD AMERICAN WRITING

✌✌✌ SOVIET ATTITUDES TOWARD AMERICAN WRITING

BY DEMING BROWN

PRINCETON, NEW JERSEY
PRINCETON UNIVERSITY PRESS
1962

Publication of this book has been aided by
the Ford Foundation program to support
publication, through university presses,
of works in the humanities and social sciences.

❖

DEMING BROWN has studied at the University of Washington,
Cornell University, and Columbia University, and holds
degrees both in American Literature and in Slavic Literature.
He is currently Professor of Slavic Languages and
Literature at the University of Michigan, and was Chairman
of the Department from 1957 to 1961. In gathering materials
for this book, he twice visited the Soviet Union. He is a
co-author (with Glenora W. Brown) of A GUIDE TO SOVIET
RUSSIAN TRANSLATIONS OF AMERICAN LITERATURE, New York,
1954, and contributes regularly to scholarly journals.

Printed in the United States of America
by Princeton University Press, Princeton, New Jersey

For Gerry, Kate, and Sarah

⤳⤳⤳ IN THE Soviet Union the relationship between literature and politics is direct and intimate. Even literature that refrains from specific political appeals—or attempts to avoid politics altogether—is subject to evaluation of a political nature. Literary activity in the United States, by contrast, is much less civic in its orientation. The writer and the critic are at liberty to accept or reject political responsibility and to seek their own values in literature.

This does not mean that American literature is apolitical. On the contrary, it has often been deeply concerned with political questions. But it is varied and unpredictable, whereas Soviet literature is politically uniform and disciplined. The American writer functions under no explicit ideological mandate and his only clear social obligation is to avoid slander and obscenity. He need not be concerned, if he does not wish to be, with the direction in which American civilization is moving, and he need not make explicit social or moral judgments. The Soviet writer, on the other hand, has inherited from pre-revolutionary Russian literature a sense of social duty and a deep concern for the national destiny. This civic frame of mind has become intensified in the Soviet period through four decades of constant indoctrination, so that the Soviet writer and critic are instinctively and perpetually aware of the political implications of literature. This book, then, is an account of an autonomous, heterogeneous American literature as it is interpreted by representatives of a literature that is organized and directed as an active weapon of a monolithic state.

The book is based on Soviet works of literary history and criticism, articles in journals and newspapers, critical prefaces to Soviet editions of American works, and conversations with Soviet literary specialists. It concentrates on American literature of the twentieth century, although there is an occasional reference to nineteenth-century works. Since the account concerns the criticism of imaginative literature, it excludes journalists such as John Reed and Lincoln Steffens, who have been widely published in the Soviet Union. The Soviet sources to be cited appeared originally in Russian or in English translation. Sources in the other languages of the USSR have not been used.

A note is necessary on the always vexatious problem of transliteration. For the purpose of providing the reader with easy access to the materials on which this work is based, all titles and proper names in the notes that come from sources in Russian have been transliterated directly from the Cyrillic original. In the process, a number of American names which appeared in the sources in transliterated Russian have had to be re-transliterated back into English, with resulting distortions. (Sherwood Anderson's *Winesburg, Ohio*, for example, comes out *Vainsburg, Ogaio*.) The situation is further complicated by the fact that the Russians have frequently been inconsistent in their own transliteration of English spellings. (Upton Sinclair appears sometimes as "Epton" and other times as "Upton," and Theodore Dreiser appears as both "Dreizer" and "Draizer.") Also, American proper names have occasionally been distorted by Russian case endings. English-language sources have likewise been inconsistent in their transliterations from the Russian. As a result, for example, the Soviet critic whose name is transliterated by the system used in this book as Ivan Kashkin sometimes appears in the notes as "Kashkeen," because the latter spelling appeared in the English-language source that is being cited. Finally, Soviet critics have frequently signed their own works inconsistently, so that one and the same critic can appear sometimes as "Abel Startsev" and at other times as "A. Startsev." It is probable that the critic who often signs himself as "A.S." is in fact the same man. Although all of these inconsistencies are regrettable, strict bibliographical accuracy requires that they be retained.

Portions of this book have previously appeared, in different form, in *American Literature, American Quarterly, Comparative Literature,* and the *Russian Review.* I am grateful to the editors of these journals for permission to use that material.

I am also indebted to the Rockefeller Foundation, the Fund for the Advancement of Education, the Inter-University Committee on Travel Grants, the Graduate School of Northwestern University, and the Horace H. Rackham School of Graduate Studies of the University of Michigan for the liberal financial support which has made the research for this book possible.

A number of persons have generously given me advice and encouragement in the various stages of the writing of this book. By far the greatest assistance has come from Glenora W. Brown. The initial enthusiasm and sustained support of Ernest J. Simmons were invaluable. My former colleague at Northwestern University, Wallace W. Douglas, gave the manuscript a severe and extremely helpful reading at a crucial stage, and Walter B. Rideout, also of Northwestern, has assisted me with his expert knowledge of American literature. Miss R. Miriam Brokaw and Mrs. James Holly Hanford of Princeton University Press have been wise and most gracious editors.

DEMING BROWN

ANN ARBOR, MICHIGAN

April 1962

❧ CONTENTS

SOVIET ATTITUDES

TOWARD AMERICAN WRITING

INTRODUCTION

✿✿✿ THE MAIN PURPOSE of this study is to bring to light a fund of Soviet critical opinion about twentieth-century American writing, and to evaluate that criticism in terms of aesthetic theory and political ideology. Chapters I and II provide a general account of the publication and critical reception of American literature in the Soviet Union in the 1920's and 1930's. The chronological narrative is then interrupted for three chapters devoted to specific problems that arose in the thirties: (1) Soviet reaction to the American "proletarian" literature of the thirties; (2) critical discussions of the works of John Dos Passos—a major episode in the formation of the Soviet attitude toward the contemporary literature of the West; and (3) Soviet criticism of a group of prominent American writers whose response to the social crises of the thirties made them attractive to the Russians but whose attachment to Western aesthetic modes made them ideologically displeasing.

With Chapters VI and VII the chronological narrative resumes and covers the period from the beginning of World War II to the terminal year 1960. In the next five chapters there is a series of "case studies" of the criticism of contemporary American writers who have been read widely in Soviet Russia. These chapters provide a detailed picture of the ideological, aesthetic, and political content of Soviet criticism. The concluding chapter is a summary of the general characteristics, strengths, and weaknesses of Soviet criticism of American literature.

The opinions cited in this study, most of them originally printed in Russian and therefore unavailable to American readers, are of special interest first of all because they come from a nation whose cultural heritage and present-day way of life differ greatly from those of the United States. For this reason Soviet Russian criticism offers an interpretation of American literary phenomena that is in many respects unique. Soviet culture represents, however, not only a passive contrast to that of the United States, but an active challenge. The

Soviet measurement of contemporary American literature is an evaluation made by an avowed cultural opponent, and it deserves the attention that is normally paid to an ambitious and aggressive antagonist. But Soviet criticism is more than just an instrument of national rivalry. It is the product of a total ideological system that includes specific assumptions about the nature and function of art. Soviet notions of aesthetics provide a point of view on American literature that is of interest in and for itself. To the extent that these notions are valid and relevant, they provide a fresh and valuable perspective from which to examine American writing of the twentieth century.

Another purpose of the present study is to determine the extent to which considerations of Soviet domestic and foreign policy, as distinct from cultural ideology and aesthetic theory, have affected the treatment of American literature. The Communist Party of the Soviet Union regards literature primarily as a social weapon, intimately and dynamically involved in the processes of history and capable of exerting a powerful influence on the course of public affairs. Literature and its criticism are a highly valued means of shaping public opinion in the Soviet Union, and for this reason literary activity is closely coordinated with the implementation of state policies. Portions of this study therefore trace (1) the evolution of those domestic policies of the Communist Party that have affected literary theory and criticism in general and (2) events in the realm of international affairs that have influenced the "literary foreign policy" of the USSR.

It is in fact impossible to understand Soviet pronouncements about American literature without paying close attention to the constantly changing political atmosphere in which they were made. Soviet literary critics are acutely conscious of the immediate, short-range political aims of the Soviet government at any given time. They are likewise intensely aware of the long-range, historic goals of the Soviet system. These aims and goals are always prominent in their thinking about literature, and this consciousness heavily colors their judgment of American works. Very often the fortunes

[4]

of American writers in Soviet criticism have been closely tied to the swing of the political pendulum, and aesthetic considerations have had little to do with the matter.

This study will also attempt to suggest the image of American culture that has been created among the Soviet public through the translation and criticism of American literature. (The question of the influence of American literature on Soviet writing is a large and separate one that deserves a detailed investigation of its own.) A knowledge of what American works have been published in various stages of Soviet development provides a valuable indication of the pattern and quality of understanding of the United States that has been available to Soviet readers. In Soviet practice, however, works of contemporary foreign literature are not simply allowed to speak for themselves. They are accompanied by comments, either in the form of prefaces or separate critical articles and reviews, designed to provide the reader with political, ideological, and cultural orientation. Literary criticism in the Soviet Union is in fact a form of propaganda whose function is to supplement and sometimes to "correct" the impression which the reader is likely to derive from a given work. To a great extent the Soviet reader's image of American literature has been shaped not only by selective publishing but also by a criticism that is systematically biased. A function of the present study is to determine the extent of this bias, as an indication of the accuracy and comprehensiveness with which contemporary American literature is presented to the Soviet reader.

Finally, this book aims to present evidence of the degree of effectiveness of contemporary American literature in conveying an understanding of the culture of the United States to the Russian people. Here it must be emphasized that any conclusions in this respect cannot be very substantial. It is much easier to discover which American works have been published and what the critics have written about them than to determine the Soviet reader's impressions of those works and the culture they represent. Literature is merely one of numerous influences that compete in forming Soviet public opinion, and that opinion itself is complex, varied and elusive.

Several different kinds of information and interpretation, all of them interdependent, form the basis of the present study. The greater portion is devoted to an account of Soviet criticism of American literature and an evaluation of this criticism. However, facts and figures about the Soviet publication of American works are distributed throughout, since this information is essential to an understanding of official policies toward American writing. Publication figures give an indication of just which contemporary American works the Russians were most likely to be reading in any given period. More importantly, they show what the publishing industry thought was the most appropriate and useful American literature for Russian readers in the separate stages of Soviet development. It should be kept in mind that in the USSR the publishing industry is completely controlled by the state and that in this nation of insatiable readers the Communist Party is acutely aware of the propaganda value of literature. The decision whether or not to publish a book is a political one, involving careful consideration not only of the broad ideological principles involved, but also of the immediate effects which publication will have on the attainment of the current goals and the implementation of the current plans of the Party. Publication figures, then, suggest the image of the United States and her culture which Soviet authorities were attempting to foster at any given time. They also provide an indication of the kind of official taste and mentality that operated in the Soviet approach to American literature.

As an indication of the true preferences of Soviet readers, however, publication figures are of limited usefulness. Censorship has always interfered with the selection of titles for publication. Also, except for a brief period in the 1920's, there has been no free publishing market in the USSR, and supply and demand have not functioned in the same way as they do in the United States. There has always been a shortage of books in the Soviet Union; the Russian public is hungry for all sorts of literature and is more likely than the public of other countries to read everything that is made available.

Nevertheless, publication figures do partially reflect the readers' choice, since the publishing houses are responsive, to a
degree, to the tastes of Soviet citizens. It is advantageous for
a Soviet publisher to print large editions of books that have
won popular favor, and it is likewise disadvantageous to continue printing a book if the public is unwilling to buy it. We
can be sure that if a work of American literature has been
issued repeatedly in the Soviet Union, the public likes it.
But the small printing of a book, or failure to print it at all,
does not necessarily indicate that Soviet readers do not or
would not like it. It is reasonably certain, for example, that
the works of Thomas Wolfe, F. Scott Fitzgerald, James T.
Farrell, and Thornton Wilder would find many enthusiastic
readers in the Soviet Union. Yet they have never been published there.

The impact of American literature in the Soviet Union
depends not only on how many and what kinds of individual
works have been published, but also on whether or not they
have been translated fully and accurately. Expurgated or
altered versions of works can be even more misleading than
erroneous or malicious comments about them. (American authors have no copyright protection in the USSR and are
completely at the mercy of the publishers.) A thorough examination of the Soviet translations of three novels—Upton
Sinclair's *Oil!*, Sinclair Lewis' *Kingsblood Royal*, and Jack
London's *The Iron Heel*—plus a less detailed inspection of a
dozen assorted translations of shorter American works, leads
to the conclusion that the Russians attempt, within certain
limitations, to publish complete and accurate versions of the
works they elect to translate. It is in the choice of works to be
translated, rather than in the process of translation itself,
that the practice of censorship operates most severely.

A few examples from the translation of *Kingsblood Royal*
illustrate the Soviet practice in this respect. The most serious
misrepresentations in the Soviet version were alterations and
omissions of a political and ideological character. (Lewis'
few disparaging references to the Soviet Union and communism—including humorous allusions to Lenin and Marx

—were all eliminated. His simile "black as the heart of a dictator" was translated as "black as the soul of a tyrant.") Everything that portrayed religion and the church in a favorable light was eliminated. (All Biblical references were cut, and a few short passages showing clerics as defenders of popular justice were omitted.) In a few places the translation raised the emotional and social pitch. ("Colored help" was rendered as "colored slaves.") The novel was made slightly less complex in a social sense. (There were several small cuts designed to eliminate the impression that antagonisms exist within Negro society.) Numerous errors crept in because of the translator's ignorance of American social institutions. (The Junior League was rendered as the "Students' Union of Youth"!) A few of Lewis' vividly erotic expressions were slightly muffled. Finally, there were a small number of purely linguistic errors. (The proper name "Evan" was mistaken for the adverb "even" and this resulted in a mistranslation.)

The above chronicle of alterations, however, may suggest a more serious misrepresentation than actually occurred. Reprehensible as the political and ideological changes may have been, they were relatively few. The linguistic and cultural errors were likewise not numerous and quite harmless. True, the Soviet translator working in anticipation of the censor, or perhaps the censor himself, tampered with the text of the novel. But the novel actually appeared in Russian substantially the way it was written, and Soviet readers, despite the expurgations, were able to form an impression of it that was only slightly inaccurate. The point is that Soviet authorities felt they could publish Lewis' work with minor cuts and retouching. Had more been required, the book would simply not have been translated.

Concerning the degree of accuracy with which American works were represented, two other common Soviet practices require mention. One was the separate publication of politically pointed excerpts from larger American works. Such excerpts, usually disparaging some aspect of American life, were selected for their socially dramatic shock effect and used as anti-American propaganda. Although they often gave a distorted impression of the work as a whole, they were clearly labeled as excerpts and in this sense were not a misrepresentation. The other practice was that of adding interpretive prefaces to translations of American works. To the extent that both practices permitted a kind of editorial intervention between the American author and his Soviet reader, they resulted in distortion.

Because Soviet publishers and critics work under the pressure of a central political authority, many of their acts and judgments that seem on the surface to be whimsical, capricious, or purely accidental become comprehensible when considered in the light of political coercion and controls. The Party and government, however, have not always been able to regulate literature absolutely and, even in those periods when such direction was possible, they have not always chosen to keep a completely tight rein. Varying degrees of discipline have been exerted over literary theory and publication, and these variations have had important effects on the general literary climate from time to time. Specifically, they have affected the choice of American works for publication and the attitude which Soviet critics have been able to express toward them. For this reason the present study indicates the extent of supervision that was exerted over the critics and publishing houses in the various periods of Soviet development.

Soviet criticism is in the main a tightly organized, disciplined body of thought and prejudice. In a very real sense there has been no "independent" Soviet criticism since the late 1920's. Originality and heterodoxy have cropped up occasionally, but in the end the forces of Party-imposed uniformity have always produced critical opinions that were virtually unanimous. Any variations or published disagreements among the critics have always been reconciled, sooner or later, within the terms of a single Party line. Since the critics agree on essential matters, it is nearly always possible to generalize about Soviet opinion of a single author or mode of literature and to refer to the critics as if they were a single individual.

Soviet policies governing the production, publication, and

evaluation of literature have been influenced directly and profoundly by events which, in the West, would be considered nonliterary or, at best, peripheral to literature. Nevertheless, aesthetic doctrine also plays an important role. Canonized in the name of "Marxism-Leninism," this body of theory was designed primarily to guide the creation of a new Soviet socialist art, but it also serves as a basis for the criticism of foreign works. Although Soviet doctrine has become uniform in its basic propositions, there have been variations in emphasis over the four decades in which it has developed. The hammering out of a Soviet aesthetics has been a painful process, and its cost in spiritual and intellectual frustration has been high. As an aid for interpreting the attitudes of critics toward individual American works in separate periods, notes on the general history of Soviet critical theory are provided in the present study.

Soviet critics deny the legitimacy of many strains of literature that have become prominent in twentieth-century America. Their interest and approval are in fact confined to two general classifications, which they call "critical realism" and "socialist realism." In the Soviet conception these two "realisms" have much in common. Both of them concentrate on recording the contemporary scene with accuracy and attention to detail, avoiding romantic coloration and subjective prejudice. Ordinary life is portrayed, with particular emphasis on social experience. Both types of literature include prose, poetry, and the drama, and although no specific narrative techniques are prescribed, an emphasis on the rational cognition of reality is considered essential. Tolstoy and Balzac, for example, are considered models of realism. Both kinds of realism portray the negative as well as the positive aspects of life and, while attempting to show things as they are, assume a notion of things as they should be. Discrepancies between the ideal and the actual, in fact, constitute the moral and ideological burden of both kinds of writing. The essential difference between the two is in the quality and degree of the writer's discontent with the world around him, his conception of human nature, and his vision of the future.

Critical realism is considered to be the natural product of the capitalist order of things. The writer expresses a kind of "loyal opposition," since he examines the prevailing atmosphere and trends of society from the viewpoint of one who shares in its myths and believes in its highest goals. He discloses injustice and ugliness, displays anger and indignation over the shortcomings he perceives, and implicitly pleads for humaneness and sanity. His criticism, however, is directed not against the foundations and best standards of his society, but rather against the forces which, he feels, are eroding, perverting, or betraying them. The value of critical realism, in the Soviet view, is in its display of the malfunctioning of capitalist society and its portrayal of the unhappiness, frustration, and inhumanity that result from its operations. The usefulness of critical realism (utility is always a major criterion in the Soviet judgment of literature) is in pointing out the inadequacies of life under capitalism, arousing discontent, and starting the ferment of revolt.

The essence of critical realism is negation, and the critical realist is not obligated to advocate cures for the ills he portrays or to suggest solutions to the problems he formulates. From the Soviet point of view, he is really incapable of doing these things, for he believes, or at least does not sufficiently disbelieve, in the fundamental assumptions on which the society about which he is writing is based. Dissatisfied with the world as it is, he lacks faith in the ability of humanity to organize the world in a better fashion. In short, he does not conceive of, or at least cannot bring himself to advocate, the Communist solution of revolutionary overthrow of the capitalist order. As a consequence, he often expresses bewilderment, bitterness, and disillusionment. His criticism leads to fatalism, brooding about the past, and irony, rather than to confidence, hope, and the espousal of active, constructive programs. His works feature frustrated, ineffectual, socially alienated, or destructive heroes, and he is incapable of creating positive, hopeful characters who are dedicated to the social good and oriented toward the future. Nevertheless, Soviet theory endorses critical realism as the most powerful and valuable kind of writing the capitalist world has produced. It is far preferable, for example, to what the Russians call the school of "tender realism" of William Dean Howells and Henry James, who employed the methods of realism to *affirm* the capitalist society in which they lived. Howells, incidentally, has never been published in the Soviet Union, and James is represented by only two short anthology pieces.

The term "socialist realism" is a Soviet invention. As Soviet theory defines it, the function of socialist realism is to point the way to the society of the future. Its underlying assumption is that the world is dynamic, that change is the dominant order of things, and that literature must not only reflect this change but also stimulate it. In the current state of civilization, according to this belief, the social and moral values of capitalism represent an evil that is strong but doomed, and the purpose of the writer is not so much to document that evil as to demonstrate that it is being eradicated by the militant forces of socialism. Socialist realism is therefore a revolutionary kind of art not in its technical devices but in its message.

Socialist realism must be affirmative in essence: confident and optimistic, expressing a rational faith in the ability of mankind to reshape the world and create a life of harmony, justice, and abundance. Evil and darkness are depicted, but only for the purpose of instructing the reader in methods of combating them. The tone of the individual work must be one of assurance; there is no room for bewilderment and irony. Confidence in the relentless progress of history prevents the writer from bemoaning the inadequacies of the past and present and enables him to perceive the indications of a bright new future in the life around him. The function of characterization in works of socialist realism is to show how individuals are educated to believe in and work for the goal of communism, and psychological interest centers on the relationship of the individual to the collective. The most prominent characters are active, resolute idealists—"positive heroes" whose purpose is to inspire the reader by their example of courage, wisdom, and social dedication.

By its very definition socialist realism is more appropriate for Soviet writers, who presumably see the evidence of social progress all about them, than it is for writers in the capitalist world. Nevertheless, the Russians argue, there are opportunities for writers under capitalism. Although historical conditions are not as "advanced" in the United States as they are in the Soviet Union, American writers need not confine themselves to critical realism. For the seeds of the future are to be found everywhere, and a writer who is equipped with revolutionary insight can discern them in the American scene. Accordingly, Soviet critics have consistently looked for socialist realism in American writing.

In the Soviet period the Russians have heavily favored prose fiction among American works, and for this reason the present study concentrates almost exclusively on prose. Soviet readers are poorly acquainted with America's poetic accomplishment of the last four decades. Their favorite American poet has always been Walt Whitman, whose verses were widely translated even before the Revolution. Poe and Longfellow, who were also well known in pre-Revolutionary times, are still read extensively. Among twentieth-century poets, however, the only two who have achieved even a modest popularity are Langston Hughes and Carl Sandburg. The Soviet liking for Hughes is explained by the spirit of social protest and the prominence of Negro folk motifs in his verses. Sandburg is regarded as a kind of latter-day Whitman because of his expansiveness, urbanism, and assertions of faith in democracy and belief in the popular masses.

The Russians have scorned the most advanced poets of this period on the ground that their verse is obscure, subjective, and devoted to esoteric formal experimentation, and therefore decadent and undemocratic. The only serious critic of contemporary American poetry has been Ivan Kashkin, who published a series of articles on the subject in the thirties and collaborated on an anthology of translated American verse in 1939. Kashkin divided the poets into two main groups— "realists" such as Sandburg, Edwin Arlington Robinson, Edgar Lee Masters, and Robert Frost, and "decadents" such as e.e. cummings, Marianne Moore, John Gould Fletcher, Hilda Doolittle, and William Carlos Williams. Although the "realists" in general received mild praise from Kashkin because of their serious attention to the world about them, he deplored their frequent pessimism and despair and their fondness for writing in a minor key. Kashkin admired the technical prowess of the "decadents" but argued that they were spiritually aimless. Despite their formal accomplishments, they isolated themselves from meaningful social problems and therefore had nothing important to write about. Although Kashkin was severely critical of the ideological content of most modern American poetry, he wrote about it with care and dignity. The occasional references of other Soviet critics to contemporary American poetry, however, have been merely doctrinaire and abusive. T. S. Eliot, for example, has been the subject of journalistic vituperation but has never been translated or seriously investigated as a poet.

Similarly, the Russians have been largely indifferent to American literary criticism, since much of it, like the poetry of this period, has concentrated on technical problems. The Soviet *bete noire* of the twenties and thirties was the New Humanism, whose aristocratic emphasis on discipline and moral tradition, the Russians insisted, betrayed an absolutist frame of mind. The New Humanists' suspicion of scientific knowledge and reliance on religious intuition represented, to Soviet critics, "black reaction" and fascism. The Russians have also been singularly unresponsive to the major trend of emphasis on the study of literary forms and close textual analysis. As exemplified by John Crowe Ransom, Richard P. Blackmur, Cleanth Brooks, Allen Tate, and others, the New Criticism has been indifferent to the social relevance of literature, and the Russians have likewise damned this socially detached view as aristocratic. "Formalism," they insisted, is just as detrimental to criticism as it is to literature itself.

Because they are interested primarily in the social role and obligations of literature and because they regard culture as a product of the struggle of economic classes, Soviet critics consider Vernon Louis Parrington the ultimate authority on

the history of American writing. American Communist critics, on the other hand, have made little impression on the
Russians, and although Soviet critics have treated them with
solicitude, they have obviously never found sufficient talent
among them to accord them great stature. Other Americans
who specialize in social analysis and cultural history, such as
Van Wyck Brooks, Waldo Frank, Malcolm Cowley, and
Alfred Kazin, have been favorably mentioned on occasion,
but none of them has been genuinely accepted. H. L. Mencken,
whom a few specialists read attentively in the twenties and
thirties, was finally dismissed as a Nietzschean individualist.
Psychoanalysis, which has profoundly influenced American
criticism, is anathema in the Soviet Union, as is political
liberalism. Consequently our most gifted critics—Edmund
Wilson, F. O. Matthiessen, and Lionel Trilling among them
—have not been permitted a Soviet audience. For opinions of
American writing, Russian readers must rely on indigenous
Soviet judgments.

The ideological uniformity of Soviet criticism and its dis-
regard of many legitimate literary interests have produced
a narrowness of scope that is lamentable in many respects.
But its rigid dogmatism, which permits few subtleties and
uncertainties, has given it a set of firm and stable standards.
The Soviet critic is held fast by a doctrinal anchor. If this
situation constricts him it nevertheless gives him the advantage of knowing what he is supposed to believe. Because
of its quality of social dedication and its fixed set of moral
criteria, and because it persistently asks the same ideological
questions, Soviet criticism of American literature is interesting and relevant for students of both cultures.

CHAPTER I

THE NINETEEN TWENTIES

⌇⌇⌇ AT THE TIME of the October Revolution, the Russian conception of the United States was haphazard and fragmentary. For a good many Russians, America was a land of youth, growth, and democracy, but many felt that she was also a crudely materialistic nation, whose culture was, for the most part, either secondhand or superficial.

For decades, Russians had been devoted to the novels of James Fenimore Cooper; every schoolboy knew *Tom Sawyer* and *Huckleberry Finn*, and millions had wept over the fate of Uncle Tom and Little Eva. Around the turn of the century, the poets had discovered Poe, Longfellow, and Whitman, and had translated them with loving care. Ten years before the Revolution, Jack London's wilderness tales had caused a sensation among Russian readers. The Russians knew, therefore, that America had created a literature.

They were also romantically aware of her huge physical expanse, her vast areas of virgin territory, her tremendous productivity, and her mammoth cities. For over a century the United States had provided a beacon of freedom for oppressed Europeans, and hundreds of thousands of refugees from the regime of the Tsars had found a haven in America. But the United States was not solely a symbol of wealth, freedom, and opportunity, for the Russians shared the general European suspicion that the very turbulence of America's growth had brought about social and moral evil. Two generations of Russian radical commentators, from Alexander Herzen to Maxim Gorky, had fairly consistently depicted the United States as a grasping, undisciplined, adolescent giant, whose terrible energy destroyed human souls at the same time that it built skyscrapers and dammed rivers.

For the average Russian in 1917, however, the image of the United States was little more than an unstable collection of random, sometimes anachronistic, often contradictory, impressions. When in that year the United States asserted herself as a world power by sending her troops to European trenches, Russian soldiers were already deserting those trenches in droves. In the chaos of the Revolution which followed, there was no time for refined speculations. Russians, depending on their political sympathies, looked upon the United States either as a potential ally and desperate, remote refuge from Civil War, or as a hostile force threatening the Revolution itself. The average Russian was preoccupied with the problem of staying alive, but if he thought of America at all, he was forced to rely on an uneasy mixture of sentiment, myth, and wartime rumor.

In the next few years, a tiny minority of those who were hostile to the Bolshevik regime made their way to the United States and learned for themselves the character of this exotic country across the seas. For the multitudes who remained in their homeland to remake their lives as Soviet citizens, America became, simultaneously, an ogre, a technological paradise, and a pitiful swamp of social insanity.

Soviet propaganda soon indicted the United States and its Allies with the charge of intervention on the side of counter-revolution. America was identified, in terms of official doctrine, with the forces of decadent capitalism, organically hostile to the Soviet power. This crystallized a prejudice which had been incipient long before the Revolution: America was bourgeois; her culture was rotten and rested on false foundations. At the same time, the United States was to be emulated, for her industry led the world and her technicians had mastered the secret of material abundance. For the next four decades, Soviet attitudes toward the United States displayed these two chief tendencies: ideological hostility toward America on the one hand, and a grudging admiration of her productive efficiency on the other.

It took some years, however, for Soviet attitudes to harden into doctrine. The United States government remained officially aloof by withholding diplomatic recognition for sixteen years, and American society regarded the new regime with a mixture of dread, perplexity, and contempt. Meanwhile, the Russians were examining American political, social, economic, and cultural phenomena with heightened interest and in much greater detail than ever before. Impelled by a new revolutionary world-consciousness, Soviet intellectuals labored to fit America, with all its paradoxes and contradictions, into a cohesive, Marxist-Leninist picture of twentieth-century civilization as a whole. In the process, the Russian understanding of American culture became more comprehensive than it was before the Revolution, but, at the same time, more doctrinaire.

Fortunately, the Soviet regime chose not to rely solely on its own indigenous propaganda in promoting its conception of the United States. It soon fostered the publication of a quantity and variety of American literature much greater than that which had been available before the Revolution. Despite a censorship which has excluded many works that militate against the official Soviet interpretation, America, to some extent, was permitted to speak for herself through her literature.[1]

While the Revolution brought a new eagerness to learn about the outside world, and while Soviet intellectuals, as early as 1919, proclaimed the need for a program of translating foreign literature,[2] Russia could not at once afford the luxury of new literary vistas. In the lean years of War Communism, 1918-1921, book publication in general was at an extremely low ebb.[3] During this period of chaos, Soviet pub-

---

[1] See Glenora W. Brown and Deming B. Brown, *A Guide to Soviet Russian Translations of American Literature*, King's Crown Press, New York, 1954.

[2] In 1917 a group of academicians, literary scholars, and writers banded together under the leadership of Maxim Gorky to form an organization called *Vsemirnaya literatura* (World Literature), with the intention of publishing 4,000 freshly translated foreign works. In the course of the next seven years, it succeeded in issuing 120 titles. The selection of American works was conservative—London, Poe, Sinclair, Twain, and Whitman. Accounts of the organization can be found in R. Culle [Kulle], "American Writers and Literature in Soviet Russia," *Russki golos*, November 6, 1927, p. 4; N. Ashukin, " 'Vsemirnaya literatura,' " *Literaturnaya entsiklopediya*, Moscow, 1929, II, 325-26; and K. Chukovski, "Kak ya polyubil anglo-amerikanskuyu literaturu," *Internatsionalnaya literatura*, Nos. 9-10 (1941), p. 236.

[3] Book production in pre-Revolutionary Russia had reached its peak in

lishing houses relied for their American quota on writers whose appeal had already been proved. Of the eight American authors printed in book form, six—Longfellow, Mark Twain, Whitman, London, Bret Harte, and Upton Sinclair —had been well known in Tsarist Russia. Through them, the public could only perpetuate its outdated impression of America. But there was some difference. In this era of crisis, the publishing industry, like all other sectors of the economy, was put to the service of the Revolution, and both the foreign and the domestic literature which it issued tended to stress revolutionary themes. Many of the works of Whitman, London, Sinclair, and Longfellow which were printed at this time expressed sentiments of social protest or revolt. Albert Edwards' *Comrade Yetta* was translated with an obviously hortatory purpose. Russia was still staggering under a burden of civil war, intervention, and the first stages of reconstruction.

During the period of the New Economic Policy (NEP), 1921-1928, Russia developed into a nation of insatiable readers, many of them newly literate. A rehabilitated and expanding publishing industry, partly state-owned and partly private, brought forth a flood of books, both native and translated. In these seven years, at least 91 different American authors, 80 of them entirely new to Soviet readers, appeared in Russian print. Under War Communism there had been 38 printings of American books, totaling 350,000 copies; during the NEP there were over 900 printings, totaling 10,500,-000 copies. Whole new areas of American thought, new regional and cultural landscapes, heretofore undiscovered facets of the American character, and many new points of view regarding the American scene were disclosed. The farm, the factory, and the office; the small town and the big city; the North and South and Middle West; the soldier, the flapper, the capitalist, and the union organizer—all seen from

---

1912-13. The output had declined fairly steadily until 1921, when it was less than half that of 1913. See *Book Publishing in Soviet Russia: An Official Survey Based upon the Data of the All-Union Book Department*, Helen Lambert Shadick, tr., Public Affairs Press, Washington, D.C., 1948, p. 2.

the perspective of the twenties—came before the Russian reader for the first time. Dozens of unfamiliar writers, past and contemporary—realists, humorists, satirists, decadents, sentimentalists, romancers, provincials, Bohemians, Freudians, and Marxists—became accessible. The selection of American books was more eclectic than it had ever been before in Russia, and much more so than it was to be in succeeding years.

This unique catholicity was the result of several features peculiar to the NEP. In an effort to raise the mass cultural level, the Soviet government strongly encouraged the production of books. But native Soviet literature, especially fiction, grew slowly in comparison to the rapidly increasing number of readers, and translated literature became a substitute. On the other hand, Soviet authorities also desired to make Russians world-conscious, and new foreign literature provided an ideal device. None of these factors, however, either alone or in combination, could have promoted such a wide and heterogeneous circulation of American literature had not Soviet cultural policy been fairly liberal at the time. The new regime, retreating from its initial vindictive intolerance of bourgeois culture, had decided for the moment to permit the circulation of literature of dubious ideology.

The atmosphere was one of watchful forbearance. Blatantly anti-Soviet books were excluded, and preference was shown for works which criticized bourgeois civilization. In the absence of the doctrinal rigidity which was to characterize Soviet literary policy in later years, however, Russian readers were offered a comparatively broad selection of American books.

The three most popular American writers in the Russia of the twenties were Jack London, O. Henry, and Upton Sinclair, and each represents a type of literature that became widely admired. During the NEP and, to a lesser extent, in later periods, Soviet publishers looked to America for romantic narratives of adventure in remote settings, animal stories, and nature tales. London was the most prominent author of such fiction, but the Russian taste in the twenties ranged from Cooper to Zane Grey. Russians were curious about life in the Wild West, the Far North, and the primitive forests, and while this interest was in large measure simply a product of the universal love for the exotic, it was undoubtedly also based on romantic misconceptions about American civilization, in which many Russians assumed that the frontier atmosphere of the nineteenth century still obtained in large sections of the United States. In drawing from that segment of American literature which depicted life on the periphery of civilization, or which showed our culture in its early periods, Soviet publishers tended to create an inaccurate picture of contemporary America. Other strains of our literature soon became dominant in the Soviet Union, however, so that the reader could distinguish between fact and anachronism a little more easily. Nevertheless, fondness for this kind of literature has continued to the present.

O. Henry appeared in Russia in 1923, and ushered in the works of dozens of Americans who were diverting because of their humor, local color, or sheer narrative charm. This group, like that which I have associated with London, is a motley one, since it includes such diverse writers as Irvin S. Cobb, Ben Hecht, and Kathleen Norris. But its members do have decisive characteristics in common. Most of them worked closely within the framework of American society and focused on the center of our civilization rather than its outskirts. They tended to write about twentieth-century America, and to reflect her standards more fully than others. Also, their chief function was to amuse rather than to edify. On the whole, they brought to the Russian reader of the twenties the kind of literature his American counterpart was reading at the same time. This was the only period in all of Russian history when the average reader could come in contact, wholesale, with the books which the masses of middle-class Americans were currently reading. To a great extent this literature was superficial, ephemeral, and generally mediocre. And the experience was short-lived, for with the beginning of the Five Year Plans, Russian publishers ceased employing the criterion of success in the American popular market in selecting books for translation. But this brief exposure must have given many Russians an entirely new understanding of the popular literature of contemporary America.

Upton Sinclair represents a group of writers whose orientation was basically sociological and political and who displayed a left-wing, although not necessarily a Marxist, bias toward the problems of American life. Their number includes muckrakers, novelists, and poets of protest, political and social satirists, and writers whose chief distinction is a preoccupation with some minority group. Sinclair's survey of America's troubles was the most comprehensive, but there were others of similar scope, such as Robert Herrick, Charles Norris, and David Graham Phillips. Still others were more specialized, and concentrated on the proletariat, either by emphasizing the class struggle or by exploring the life of tramps and vagabonds. At this time there also began the publication of works by and about American Negroes. All of these writers were either specifically or implicitly critical of life in America, and the Soviet regime created increasingly favorable conditions for the dissemination of literature exposing the negative sides of capitalist civilization. Publishing houses under the NEP (and even more so under the Five Year Plans) stressed the anticapitalist criterion above all else in selecting American works.

A fourth type of contemporary American literature began to appear in translation in 1924, with the publication of novels by Sherwood Anderson, John Dos Passos, and Sinclair Lewis. Their works gave Russia its first opportunity to know the best of current American writing and helped somewhat to dispel the hazy, romantic, and generally erroneous conception of the United States that still lingered in the middle years of the NEP. In contrast to the transitory fiction of such authors as Edna Ferber and Anita Loos, their books made a lasting impression on the Soviet reader. Together with more politically tendentious authors who were to appear in the next three decades, this group has continued to dominate Soviet publication to the present. The continued preference for these writers in the thirties, forties, and fifties indicates a Soviet tendency to appreciate the best of American literature in an era when many other avenues to cultural understanding were closed.

Even the briefest of outlines would not be complete without mention of the sustained and, in some respects, increased enthusiasm for nineteenth-century American literature which obtained during these years. Mark Twain had been a favorite for decades, and now his reputation grew steadily. Poe, Whitman, Cooper, Harte, Longfellow, and Mrs. Stowe continued to be published. A volume of Artemus Ward appeared, together with such turn-of-the-century writers as Ambrose Bierce, Frank Norris, and Stephen Crane, and Melville's *Typee* came out in a children's edition. The NEP had released great quantities of exploratory energy.

There was much intellectual ferment in the Russia of the twenties. No one was certain what course the new regime would take. The lines of political power, although fairly well established in form, were far from clear in actuality. Cultural policy was debated sometimes exuberantly, sometimes bitterly, and always with great heat. In literary matters, differences of opinion could be prolonged indefinitely and with relative impunity for all parties concerned. As yet there was no central artistic authority, for even the Communist Party leadership was openly divided about cultural affairs.

Soviet culture was on the defensive. Despite its pioneering enthusiasm, its experimental spirit, and its air of limitless potentiality, it also exhibited a timid awareness of its lack of prestige in the world. Soviet spokesmen repeatedly affirmed that bourgeois culture was in decay, but they realized that as yet they could only dream of matching its monuments. As they contemplated the task of displacing the culture of centuries, they were extremely unsure of themselves. Only at the very end of the decade, with the victory of the Stalin faction and the consolidation of a monolithic Communist Party, did a concerted cultural offensive begin.

Gradually, however, it became clear that Marxism, in one form or another, would gain complete hegemony over the

Soviet arts. The problem was to determine which version of Marxist aesthetics would most closely conform to the demands of Soviet actuality. The area of most acute concern was Soviet literature itself, and criticism of the literature of the capitalist West became an auxiliary concern whose chief function was to instruct Soviet writers by providing a basis of comparison.

From the very beginning, some Soviet critics of American literature were Marxists. Others, without being Marxists, shared the prejudices of the Revolution, and looked at the literature of capitalist countries with nearly the same eyes. On the other hand, a number of critics in these early years wrote as if they were unaware of Bolshevik political, social, and economic categories, while still others confined their remarks to purely aesthetic judgments. By the end of the twenties, however, a Marxist homogeneity had overtaken nearly all of Soviet criticism. Many critics at first had approached American literature with humility and a great deal of uncertainty. Often their book reviews had shown a reluctance to go beyond the text in hand, and amounted to little more than synopses. By the close of the decade, Soviet criticism adopted its own peculiar tone of sophistication, and naive curiosity was replaced by doctrinaire certainty. At last the critics had been told what to look for in American literature, and those who had not learned their lessons had ceased to write.

A profile of America as seen through the eyes of Soviet critics in the early and middle twenties would look something like this: the United States, emerging from an "imperialist" World War with heightened prestige among capitalist nations, had embarked upon an era of thunderous construction. The key to American development was "technique," the ability to get things done with the utmost speed and efficiency. Furious tempos, however, and the employment of more and bigger machines, served only for the aimless accumulation of luxuries. Mesmerized by a drive to produce in ever-increasing quantities, and goaded by a fiercely competitive system of private enterprise, Americans had lost sight of the purpose of work. Business had become an end in itself.

The image of a highly mechanized, vastly productive society was a fascinating one. From the very start of the reconstruction period, official Soviet slogans had centered on the theme of industrialization. It is understandable why America could capture the Russian popular imagination in the twenties and why, for example, a translation of Henry Ford's autobiography could run to four editions in 1924. Yet Americomania, if we are to judge from published Soviet sources, was confined to admiration of our "technique" and of our relative abundance of goods and services. Even in these early years the United States was depicted as a Babylon, whose awesome feats of construction were matched by an equally colossal maldistribution of income. Soviet spokesmen assured the Russian public that violent class contrasts nullified most of America's technological progress. The entire economic system was organized for the benefit of the few financial giants who held the purse strings. Under them toiled skilled laborers, white collar workers, and small business employees, deluded creatures who either performed monotonous, narrowly specialized tasks or dashed about frantically in cars, subways, and elevators in the conviction that "time is money." At the base of the economic and social structure was the expanding proletariat, whose backbreaking, hand-to-mouth existence was constantly threatened by unemployment. The avaricious capitalist gorged himself on luxuries; his nervous underlings competed savagely for the leavings of his table; and the proletariat starved.

Soviet propagandists at first made little attempt to hide the fact that America's streets were filled with automobiles and that her factories hummed with energy. In the face of such an admission, the accusation of mass poverty could not be entirely convincing. Other aspects of the indictment, however, probably made it more persuasive. For the United States was also depicted as a land of moral and spiritual impoverishment, whose standards had been grievously twisted in the pursuit of the almighty dollar. Unbridled corruption, wide-

spread racial persecution, hypocrisy, and Philistinism pervaded American life. Like the rest of the "decadent" capitalist
West, our society was becoming ossified. Criticism was being suppressed, social inequality increasing. The country was
writhing in a nightmare of Scopes trials and Klan uprisings.
The murderers Leopold and Loeb, sons of millionaires, were
given soft jobs in a prison library, where they "delighted
their fellow inmates with elegant philosophical composi-
tions,"[4] while Sacco and Vanzetti were condemned to death.
Under such depressing circumstances the common man, "unable to snatch his share in the labor market of life, to become
a businessman, a merchant, a sly agent or a highly skilled
specialist, is doomed by the force of the senseless tempo of
life to vagabondage, to the role of a swindler, a burglar, the
scum of society, or a pitiful common workman, eking out an
existence by means of sporadic and extremely heavy labor."[5]

This fantastic vision of a rigidly stratified, brutal American
society, rife with class injustice and devoid of freedom and
opportunity, was obviously compounded of ten parts Marxist
ideology, one part truth. Despite its accurate highlights (the
moneyed privilege of Leopold and Loeb *did* help to save their
lives, Sacco and Vanzetti may indeed have been unjustly
condemned, the lot of the American working man *was* hard),
this portrayal of a nation consisting of arrogant masters and
cringing slaves, of a people dominated by soulless materialism and abounding bigotry, was the product, on the one
hand, of sheer Soviet ignorance of life in the United States
and, on the other hand, of the heady self-delusions of a newly
embraced Marxist doctrine. In retrospect the America of the
twenties seems indeed to have been heedless of its social and
economic responsibilities, giddy in its pursuit of material
wealth, callow and provincial. But the organic strength of
America—abundantly evident in her capacity for loud and
free self-criticism, her ideal of social justice, her political

---

[4] Vladimir Mayakovski, "Amerika," *Krasnaya nov,* No. 2 (1926), p.
172.

[5] R. Kulle [Culle], "O sovremennoi amerikanskoi literature," *Zvezda,*
No. 6 (1926), p. 230.

flexibility, and the relative mobility of her economic classes—was a source of viability to which Soviet observers were willfully blind.

In the Soviet interpretation, the chief attribute of the American mind was its shallowness. One critic observed, "The American bourgeois does not like to meditate. The tempo of the life which surrounds him irresistibly urges him on and on. Both in politics and in the realm of art and science —everywhere—there is business. To stop, to linger in one place, on one thought or fact, is too great a luxury. He must hurry. Time is the dollar!"[6] Much of the current output of American literature, the critics argued, was tailored to appeal to such a personality. The bourgeois reader desired to be amused, not instructed. Accordingly, American writers were turning out a spate of light, diverting fiction, depending heavily on intricate plot and extraordinary situations for its interest. Adventure, crime, and detective stories abounded. In general, popular literature was written with high technical competence. In a social sense, however, it was superficial, since it avoided or glossed over the uglier features of the contemporary scene and drew the reader's attention away from the most profound and burning problems of the day.

This Soviet portrayal of the American "bourgeois" mind and literary tastes was, like a good many Soviet notions about American culture, little more than a caricature. It is true that in the twenties vast quantities of trivial writing were produced and willingly consumed—as they are in any literate nation at any time. It is also true that, by and large, the American middle class in the twenties was neither as contemplative nor as worried over social questions as it was to become in later decades. But the image of an America composed of cynically pandering writers and frivolously acquiescent readers was no more accurate than the notion of an America composed of silk-hatted plutocrats and sunken-cheeked proletarians. The writers of the twenties, in fact, were exploring every aspect of the United States more critically, and were

[6] L. Polonskaya, "S. G. Adams. *Razgul*," *Krasnaya nov*, No. 7 (1928), p. 239.

challenging bourgeois complacency more insistently, than ever before.

The liberation of American literature from the Genteel Tradition had begun to take place before World War I. From its early stirrings in Dreiser's realism and in Veblen's damnation of our commercial civilization, the urge to explore dark and heretofore forbidden aspects of life in the United States, to question, and to condemn, had become at least as strong by 1920 as the impulse to affirm and celebrate. Puritanism, the morals of the market place, bigotry, and the smug parochialism of the uncultured provinces were all under attack. Above all—as H. L. Mencken's ferocious satire, Edgar Lee Masters' *Spoon River Anthology*, Ellen Glasgow's novels of Southern disillusionment, and Sherwood Anderson's *Winesburg, Ohio* amply testified—writers no longer assumed America's inevitable righteousness and certain progress. Profoundly dissatisfied, American writers had already begun a detailed reappraisal of the national way of life that was unprecedented in its severity and scope. These writers were "bourgeois," and it was to a "bourgeois" audience that they expressed their misgivings, disappointment, and fears.

In the twenties the literature of the United States became more lively and vital, more varied in its themes and modes, than it had ever been before. With the publication of *Main Street* in 1920 Sinclair Lewis ended his apprenticeship and launched the brilliant series of satires that won him the Nobel Prize ten years later. Dreiser's greatest novel, *An American Tragedy*, was published in 1925. Other accomplished novelists whose reputations had been established in the previous decade —such as Willa Cather, Edith Wharton, and Ellen Glasgow —continued their sensitive interpretations of individual sectors of society. These and many others who had come into prominence before the war—playwright Eugene O'Neill, poets Robert Frost, Edwin Arlington Robinson, and Carl Sandburg, muckraker Lincoln Steffens, critic Van Wyck Brooks—were joined in the twenties by a gifted new generation who infused even greater strength and originality into an already powerful modern literature. In the hands of these young writers the language of Americans became a more versatile literary instrument, and the standards of literary craftsmanship rose. The writing of the best of them—F. Scott Fitzgerald, e. e. cummings, Thornton Wilder, Ernest Hemingway, John Dos Passos, and William Faulkner—was so resourceful that it is now recognized as a major contribution to the art of prose fiction.

An intensive and painful examination of American ideals and experience was under way. The reevaluation was not so specifically social and economic as it was to become in the next decade; rather it was aesthetic, moral and psychological. By reporting on the multiple facets of life and culture in the USA with greater accuracy than ever before, fragmenting it, and scrutinizing each component skeptically, the new writers invited Americans to see themselves as they actually were and to discard their illusions. Now it was possible to proclaim a truth that convention had muffled: this country, which had greeted the twentieth century with such faith and exuberance, had become ugly. In a land of increasing opulence men were not so free, nor the opportunities for their spiritual growth so abundant, as they were thought to have been. The traditional symbols of felicity in America—wealth and public esteem—were false, since money could not buy immunity from the prevailing vulgarity and the price of public acceptance was conformity to mediocre norms.

The new freedom to write about sex and to explore the subconscious disclosed hidden sources of tension and tragedy beneath the surface of life. In treating of emotions and appetites that American literature had largely avoided, writers discovered that humans in general, and Americans in particular, are more complicated than they seem to be, more isolated from one another, more bewildered and lonely than they themselves realize. Much of this writing was intensely personal, subjective, and self-pitying, and its tone of disillusionment often approached nihilism. Also, the spirit of aesthetic experimentation and concern for stylistic innovation led frequently to a preoccupation with craftsmanship for its own sake. But the attempt to define more precisely what

Americans are really like, to analyze their myths and correct their illusions about themselves, created a much more accurate, detailed, and critical image of the national institutions and character than literature had heretofore given.

Although American literature's most famous achievement in the twenties was in prose fiction, there was also a flowering of poetry and a significant growth in the drama. This was the decade in which the first collection of Ezra Pound's *Cantos* was published and in which T. S. Eliot, an even more influential expatriate, published *The Waste Land*. Edna St. Vincent Millay, Wallace Stevens, Allen Tate, Robinson Jeffers, Stephen Vincent Benet, Archibald MacLeish, John Crowe Ransom, William Carlos Williams, Hart Crane, and many other poets were at work in the twenties. Eugene O'Neill enjoyed his most productive period in these years, and other playwrights, such as Elmer Rice, became prominent. The scene was livened by H. L. Mencken, who continued to delight the "booboisie" by insulting it, and by such fashionable but ephemeral writers as James Branch Cabell and Carl van Vechten, sophisticated aesthetes who cultivated an urbane, highly mannered prose. Americans at the time did not always recognize the best that was being written for them and about them, but the renaissance proceeded.

Few of the poets of the twenties have ever been widely read in the Soviet Union, and none of them were recognized by the Russians until the next decade. Other important writers have not been translated to this day: Fitzgerald, for example, was carelessly classified as a "bourgeois aesthete" unworthy of Soviet attention; Mencken, cummings, and Wilder were snubbed for political and ideological reasons that became clear in the thirties. Edith Wharton and Willa Cather did not attract sufficient attention to be translated. One novel of Ellen Glasgow was published but promptly forgotten. Cabell, whose romantic, whimsical fantasies enjoyed an enormous vogue in the United States, was ignored entirely. Omissions such as these prevented the Russian reader from understanding the total variety of contemporary American literature. However, a great many of the writers of the twenties who were to achieve lasting fame—Dreiser, Anderson, Lewis, O'Neill, Sinclair, Hemingway, and Dos Passos—were extensively translated into Russian. Their Soviet reputations will be traced in later chapters.

An indication of the Soviet critics' general ideological outlook on the American literature of the twenties is provided in their comments on a number of prominent but lesser novelists whose works were translated fairly widely in that decade— T. S. Stribling, Joseph Hergesheimer, Ben Hecht, Edna Ferber, Zona Gale, Fannie Hurst, Floyd Dell, and Martha Ostenso. First, however, a few words about the ideological climate of American literature as Soviet critics interpreted it. According to Marxist theory, literature, like any other cultural manifestation, tends to express the ideology of the economic class that dominates the society in which it is produced. It followed that American literature was therefore predominantly bourgeois. But a process of ideological rupture was taking place within the ranks of the bourgeoisie. As capitalism matured, increasing numbers of individuals were bound to lose economic and social status. The petty bourgeoisie, in particular, became anxious and insecure as they faced the prospect of being pressed down into the ranks of the proletariat. From an ideological standpoint, therefore, American literature was far from homogeneous, since the intelligentsia varied widely in degree of allegiance to the standards of the dominant class. Some maintained an attitude of dilettante iconoclasm, and chose to criticize relatively minor propositions in the bourgeois system of beliefs. Others, more profoundly concerned over the trend of society, either pleaded for reforms within the existing order or expressed impotent disillusionment. Finally, there were those who not only rejected the basic assumptions of bourgeois society, but also actively sought their replacement. These were potential revolutionaries.

In the middle twenties, when Russians were buying *Tarzan* and its sequels in tens of thousands of copies, the critics did not simply content themselves with deriding such literature. They also pointed out the existence of much worthier

American books, although they slighted much of the best of current literature. And in the latter half of the decade, they established a fairly definite hierarchy of American works. At the bottom of the scale was James Oliver Curwood (extremely popular among Soviet *readers* from 1925 to 1928), together with a host of others now long since forgotten even in the United States. These authors were considered to be devoid of value, aesthetically and socially. Superior to them were the local-colorists and novelists of manners—graceful storytellers with a keen eye for native behavior and surroundings. Occasionally a limited degree of social criticism cropped up among them, the Russians felt. Edna Ferber contrasted a vigorous, healthy rural existence with the poisonous life of the corrupt metropolis.[7] Zona Gale disclosed the dreary, narrow-minded, self-satisfied character of the middle class in the provinces.[8] These writers, together with others such as Fannie Hurst and Martha Ostenso, constituted something of a feminist movement in literature, agitating for the rights of women in a society which discouraged equality between the sexes.[9] But they were often sentimental, and none of them questioned the fundamentals of the economic and social order.

A more accurate picture, the critics felt, was provided by Ben Hecht, Floyd Dell, Joseph Hergesheimer, and T. S. Stribling. Their books exposed areas of deep suffering, moral decay, psychological maladjustment, and social inequality. Hecht focused on the disaffected urban "petty bourgeois intelligentsia," creatures in revolt against the tormenting tensions of the big city, which crushed and warped the personality.[10] Insulted, debauched, pathologically erotic, his fanatically individualistic heroes cut themselves off from the world and sought solace in aimless aestheticism or bitter

[7] Kulle, "O sovremennoi . . . ," *op.cit.*, p. 236.
[8] Diar, "Noviye amerikanskiye perevody," *Na literaturnom postu*, Nos. 13-14 (1928), p. 111.
[9] R. Kulle, "Po stranitsam mirovoi literatury," *Sibirskiye ogni*, No. 2 (1928), p. 208.
[10] R. Kulle, "Realisty sovremennoi amerikanskoi prozy," *Sibirskiye ogni*, No. 3 (1929), pp. 164-165.

[33]

nihilism.[11] As a portrayal of the futility of this kind of flight from reality, and as a picture of the demoralization of the American intelligentsia, his novels had great social significance,[12] but the author himself was a victim of the decadence he so graphically painted. With his exaggerated interest in sexual motivation, his Bohemianism, and his preoccupation with human failure, he was capable only of "opposing a negative with a negation,"[13] since his impotent hatred of the bourgeoisie had not been replaced by active sympathy for the proletariat.[14] On the other hand, the critics felt that Floyd Dell, who had likewise been strongly influenced by Bohemianism, had relied excessively on Freudianism,[15] and had been preoccupied with disillusionment, hopelessness, and jazz-age confusion, had now taken up more socially constructive themes.[16] An excellent psychologist,[17] he was in "transition from a petty bourgeois psychology to a proletarian one, and from inert decorative romanticism to a full-blooded, socially significant realism." This was particularly true of his novel, *Runaway*.[18] Stribling's novel *Birthright*, with its treatment of the frustrations that beset educated Negroes in the South, was praised for its examination of the psychology of a persecuted race and of the moral degeneration of the "southern exploiters."[19] The writings of Hergesheimer, the critics found, were packed with colorful and highly informative detail concerning American economic and social life,[20] illustrating the

[11] Diar, "Noviye . . . ," *op.cit.*, pp. 112-113.

[12] Ya. Nikolayev, "Ben Khekt. *Igra v zhizn,*" *Na literaturnom postu*, No. 19 (1927), p. 81; Kulle, "Realisty . . . ," *op.cit.*, p. 165.

[13] S. Dinamov, "Ben Khekt. *Geni naiznanku,*" *Pechat i revolyutsiya*, No. 6 (1927), p. 236.

[14] Diar, "Noviye . . . ," *op.cit.*, p. 113.

[15] S. Dinamov, "Epton Sinkler," *Pechat i revolyutsiya*, No. 5 (1928), p. 126.

[16] S. Dinamov, "Floid Dell. *Prichudy starika,*" *Pechat i revolyutsiya*, No. 2 (1928), p. 203.

[17] Yu. Danilin, "Teodor Dreizer, *Nyu york*; Floid Dell, *Prichudy starika*; D. Stivens, *Drovosek Benyan,*" *Oktyabr*, No. 1 (1928), p. 244.

[18] Diar, "Noviye . . . ," *op.cit.*, pp. 113-114.

[19] S. K., "T. Stribling. *Drama krovi,*" *Na literaturnom postu*, Nos. 17-18 (1927), pp. 91-92.

[20] R. Kulle, "O sovremennoi amerikanskoi proze," *Oktyabr*, No. 9 (1929), p. 147.

"deformity of the social order."[21] All four of these writers interested the critics because each supported the Soviet contention that America was riddled with anxieties, class hatred, and spiritual and moral decay. Each of them was deficient, however, in one or more fundamental respects. Hecht was a prisoner of his own disillusionment. Dell was still in transition, and had not yet adopted a completely "proletarian" psychology. The sword which Stribling had raised over the heads of the "inhumane exploiters" in the South remained in mid-air. And Hergesheimer, despite his "illumination of the dark and decadent sides of contemporary bourgeois society," was too strongly inclined to retreat to the past for his subject matter, or to concentrate on the exotic.

In the opinion of the critics, the writers in this group, and especially Hecht and Dell, were distinguished chiefly by the spontaneity of their reaction to the immediate moral and psychological tensions of the day. Each was a kind of barometer, indicating the response of the dissatisfied, skeptical bourgeois intelligentsia to changes in the American social atmosphere. But like their lesser contemporaries, all of them were engrossed in random symptoms of social disharmony, and this prevented them from comprehending the malaise of the whole. Theirs was a passive protest. As one critic remarked, ". . . we more often meet confusion, disillusionment, and doubt in the durability of the ideals and fundamentals of contemporary life than its criticism in the form of sharp, triumphant satire."[22]

This observation was perfectly correct, as far as it went. Very few American writers of that time—and none of the most talented ones—were interested in promoting, through satire or any other means, an economic and social revolution modeled on the Russian experience. The literature of the twenties was one of bewildered complaint, of cultural, moral, and psychological reassessment, and even the typical "radical" writer of the generation that came to flower in those years was likely to be first of all a Bohemian, second a Freudian,

21 Kulle, "Po stranitsam . . . ," op.cit., p. 210.
22 Kulle, "O sovremennoi . . . ," op.cit., p. 236.

and only incidentally and vaguely a socialist. Insofar as it dealt explicitly with social and economic problems, the literature of the twenties expressed far greater concern over the ethical standards and myths of a commercial civilization, over the excessive uniformity which the age of technology had imposed on the lives of Americans, than over the question of who should own the means of production. But these characteristics, which had absolutely no bearing on the aesthetic value of the works produced, were already being singled out by Soviet critics as the most important shortcomings of contemporary American literature.

In its compulsion to judge the worth of a work of literature in terms of the degree to which it advocated the overthrow of the capitalist order, Soviet criticism was already displaying the bias which to this day vitiates its aesthetic and social perceptivity. Did it really matter that Hergesheimer chose to dwell retrospectively on a bygone society, so long as his observations were accurate and evocative and were stated with insight and grace? Were the artistic faults of Ben Hecht really attributable to the niche he occupied in the American class structure, or were they not characteristic, rather, of his own individual personality as a writer? Did the measure of Stribling's prowess as a novelist consist in his persuasiveness (or lack of it) in advocating Communist revolution as a solution to the race question? Should not the main question really have been how well he understood and was able to express the psychology of a Negro trying to make his way in a hostile white world? The Marxist imperative of seeking the essence of a work of literature in its immediate political and economic content was already driving out many of the legitimate interests of criticism.

In the early thirties one of the chief aims of Soviet criticism was to promote an ideological revolution in American and other Western literatures. By comparison, the criticism of the twenties was less pointed in its goals. It is true that the critics hopefully sought a revolutionary strain in the writing of the first postwar decade. But the prospect was a relatively remote

[36]

one. One critic remarked in 1925, "In the capitalistic countries there are not and cannot be the conditions for the flowering of proletarian literature. The advance guard is busy
with only the most fundamental thing—the struggle with the
exploiters."[23] For the time being, the critic's task was to examine the process of ideological decomposition and, if possible, to sift out elements of incipient revolution.

Toward the end of the decade, some efforts were made to
encourage the development of revolutionary writing abroad.
An International Union of Revolutionary Writers (IURW)
was organized in the Soviet Union in 1925. At first, its efforts were confined largely to European countries, and, according to Soviet testimony, "bore too passive a character."[24]
For all practical purposes, American literature was virtually
ignored by this organization. The ideological offensive was
only beginning.

[23] A. Z., "Maikl Gold. *Proklyaty agitator i drugiye rasskazy,*" *Oktyabr,*
Nos. 3-4 (1925), p. 241.
[24] Yan Mateika, "Mezhdunarodnoye obyedineniye revolyutsionnykh
pisatelei," *Literaturnaya entsiklopediya,* Moscow, 1934, VII, 84.

CHAPTER II

THE NINETEEN THIRTIES

꒰꒰꒰ THE DECADE of the 1930's was awesome, bitter, and tumultuous for both the Russian people and the peoples of the West. As this period began, the Soviet Union was embarking on the first of the Five Year Plans—an upheaval at once more sudden, painful, and profound than any that had preceded it in Russian history. The West at this time was suffering the economic agony and social bewilderment of the great Depression. By the middle thirties a sinister response to both the increasing power of Soviet communism and to the Western Depression appeared: international fascism. As the decade came to a close, the Communist and capitalist nations alike had armed for the inevitable showdown with fascism, and the most devastating war the world had ever known was already in its initial stages. Within the next two years the Soviet Union had formed a working coalition with the greatest capitalist powers to eradicate the common enemy.

A Soviet Russian in 1930 would never have believed that such a coalition was possible. Twelve years of persistent indoctrination had taught him that the world was being polarized into two camps—socialism and capitalism—which, by the very nature of things, could never be reconciled. The sacrifices currently demanded of him for the completion of the Five Year Plan were necessitated in large measure, he was told, by the urgent danger of a capitalist encirclement of the Soviet Union. Russia was building factories so that her people might have a new and glorious life, but the Soviet citizen was also being urged to believe that these factories were desperately needed for defense. As yet the political distinction between democracy and fascism was vague and immaterial; for the Russians, the USSR was the unique socialist country, an island of righteousness in a hostile and predatory sea of capitalist reaction.

Soviet propaganda has always striven to express itself in neat and simple equations. The Depression in the West, for all its complexity, was universal and dramatic, and its very intensity invited crude formularization. It is impossible to determine precisely how the Kremlin evaluated the Depression in the early thirties, but it is clear that the victorious Stalin faction was more concerned with the effort to "build socialism in one country" than it was with fomenting an immediate world revolution, and it is probable that the Kremlin did not feel that such a revolution was imminent. Nevertheless, the Soviet press at this time contained dire predictions of the impending collapse of capitalism in the West. The Soviet citizen was being urged to believe, simultaneously, three things: (1) his present grim, austere existence under the Five Year Plan was but the prelude to a beautiful socialist future; (2) that future was threatened by the armed might of a vindictive international capitalism; and (3) international capitalism itself, bled white by the Depression, was faced with a revolutionary crisis unprecedented in its intensity.

The third proposition—that the capitalist world was *in extremis*—is of most interest to us here. In 1929 the policy of the Comintern had swerved sharply to the left, and, as the Depression became more severe, the Communist parties of the West stepped up their revolutionary activities. The origin of this new tactic is cloudy, and there is reason to doubt the sincerity of the Kremlin in endorsing it.[1] Nevertheless, Soviet domestic propaganda agreed with that of the Comintern in presenting the following view of recent history: since the World War, the capitalist nations had been in a state of general crisis. The most ominous event had been the October Revolution, which, in the immediate postwar years (or the "first stage" of the general crisis), threatened to engulf the capitalist world.[2] There had then been a "second stage," a period of prosperity and "temporary stabilization" extending

[1] See F. Borkenau, *World Communism: A History of the Communist International*, W. W. Norton, New York, 1939, pp. 337-40 and Max Beloff, *The Foreign Policy of Soviet Russia, 1929-1941*, Oxford University Press, New York, 1947, I, 9-14.

[2] Iv. Anisimov, "Borba za revolyutsionny vykhod iz krizisa i pisateli zapada, poryvayushchiye s kapitalizmom," *Krizis kapitalizma i soyuzniki proletariata v literature zapada*, GIKhL, Moscow-Leningrad, 1933, p. 6.

roughly from 1922 to 1928, in which the danger of revolution had abated for a time. Despite the illusion of security it created, this was merely a breathing spell for capitalism in which "the over-all situation changed little," for "the fundamental contradictions of bourgeois society continued to develop, and became sharper."[3] Now, in the "third stage," capitalism was being shaken to its foundations. The impact of the Depression had been tremendous. Economic dislocation was proceeding rapidly and thoroughly, the bourgeoisie was in panic, the ranks of the proletariat were swelling, the class struggle was gaining unprecedented ferocity, and the final crash of the dying social order could be expected momentarily.

America fit clearly and prominently into this picture. This "citadel of world capitalism" had been the first to suffer the blows of the Depression: poverty was spreading, small farmers were being dispossessed, unemployment had forced millions of workers into the streets, and thousands of others were out on strike. In fact, the class struggle was taking on its most dramatic form precisely in the United States, and "revolutionary enthusiasm" was increasing.[4] American culture was also in a crisis. The "sunset of capitalism" had shocked the nation into a reexamination of its traditional values, and many time-honored assumptions were being newly scrutinized in fear and anxiety.[5] This did not mean that America was yet ready to repudiate her bourgeois heritage, for the old prejudices were still deeply imbedded in the national consciousness. But, the Russians argued, the pressure of economic and social events was rapidly forcing America's most intelligent and responsible cultural spokesmen to recognize that the prevailing ideas and institutions were hopelessly inadequate in the face of the threatening catastrophe.

[3] A. Startsev, "Vseobshchi krizis kapitalizma i novaya volna soyuznikov proletariata v literature Ameriki," *Marksistsko-Leninskoye iskusstvoznaniye,* Nos. 5-6. (1932), p. 39.

[4] *ibid.,* p. 39; Ivan Anisimov, "Zarnitsy velikoi grozy," *Oktyabr,* No. 9 (1932), p. 173; A. Yelistratova [Elistratova], "Literatura sovremennoi Ameriki," *Internatsionalnaya literatura,* No. 5 (1933), p. 99.

[5] Ye. Lann, "Amerikanskaya literatura v 1931 godu," *Proletarski avangard,* No. 5 (1932), p. 242.

For years the Russians had been repeatedly accusing America of ideological poverty. In 1929, for example, a critic pointed out that in the United States the theoretical sciences had chronically lagged behind the empirical disciplines.[6] As the Depression deepened, however, the Russians found that America was painfully developing a capacity for ideological self-examination: "For a very long time theory has been the 'bottleneck' of American culture. Money-making, empiricism, and one-sided practicality have been blossoming on American soil. Restriction to a narrow professional framework, a disdainful outlook on general theoretical questions, questions of world-view, have been considered 'good form' among the mass of American intellectuals. The situation has changed basically only under the influence of the crisis. In the process of today's general reconsideration of ideological values, the American intelligentsia is hastening with redoubled avidity to revise and supplement its theoretical baggage."[7] This reorientation was a direct reflection of the accelerating class struggle. The bourgeoisie, sensing that its dominant position in American culture was in danger, had set up new ideological barricades. As described by Soviet critics, the most formidable of these was the New Humanism—an attempt of the bourgeoisie to justify its continued existence as a class by asserting the need of civilization for a strong cultural aristocracy.[8] The Russians also found, however, that for the most part the ideological defenses of the American bourgeoisie in this time of trouble consisted of rather pathetic variations on traditional themes—optimism, the cult of the bold, powerful personality who rises to success in business against seemingly impossible odds, a reiteration of the commercial virtues of cunning and enterprise, and, above all, self-reliance.[9]

[6] N. Eishiskina, "Osnovniye tendentsii sovremennoi kritiki v Soyedinyonnikh Shtatakh," *Pechat i revolyutsiya*, No. 11 (1929), p. 88.

[7] Yelistratova, *op.cit.*, p. 99.

[8] Startsev, *op.cit.*; S. Dinamov, "Amerikanski fashizm i literatura," *Literatura i iskusstvo*, No. 4 (1931), pp. 79-87; S. Dinamov, "Teodor Draizer i revolyutsiya," *Krizis kapitalizma i soyuzniki proletariata v literature zapada*, GIKhL, Moscow-Leningrad, 1933, p. 80.

[9] Lann, *op.cit.*, p. 242.

A more interesting, varied, and significant response to the Depression, the Russians felt, was that of the American petty bourgeois intelligentsia, a large, growing, and motley group of individuals who could no longer subscribe fully to bourgeois beliefs. Their theories ranged throughout the ideological spectrum, approaching fascism at one extreme and communism at the other, but their chief characteristic was ideological instability. Emotionally tied to the bourgeois order, but deeply puzzled by the economic and social changes that were so rapidly and drastically affecting their lives, these individuals were constantly groping for an explanation of their predicament, vacillating, and shifting their allegiance from one panacea to another. The general trend of their thought was leftward, however, so that Soviet observers interpreted the very instability of this class as an indication of cultural progress. More and more frequently, the Russians argued, the sharpening crisis would force the intellectual leaders of the American petty bourgeoisie to a Marxian analysis of their country's ills.

The end result of America's cultural reawakening in the early thirties, the Russians insisted, would be the hegemony of Marxist theory in all spheres of intellectual activity. Soviet critics at this time frequently referred to the "radicalization of the American intelligentsia," and contended that the leading thinkers of America were "going to the proletariat." In plainer terms, this meant that they were accepting the intellectual leadership of the American Communist Party, which styled itself as both the source and the repository of all constructive proletarian thought.

For these reasons, the Russians felt, the most active and important sector in the American literature of the early thirties was the petty bourgeois. Here were concentrated the crucial doubts and sharpest protests of the vast lower middle class—the Americans on whom the psychic blows of the Depression had rained most cruelly, and who were now experiencing the deepest ideological anguish. According to the critic Startsev, petty bourgeois literature in the United States had recently experienced an "extremely strong exfoliation," in the course of which one part of it had fallen into a condition of "complete ideological marasmus," another had been "thrust into the embrace of reaction," and the third (and most advanced) part had "turned to the proletariat."[10] Nearly all of the American writers who figured prominently in Soviet criticism of the thirties (and most of those with whom the present study is concerned) fell into the petty bourgeois category. For the works of this group dramatized America's troubles most vividly, and gave the Russians their greatest hopes for the development of a genuine revolutionary literature in the United States.

The concept of an American petty bourgeoisie, however, was much less precise, accurate, and relevant when applied to literature than when applied to political, social, and economic affairs. In the first place, Soviet critics assumed a much more direct relationship between literature and politics than actually existed in the United States. The class allegiance of American writers was vaguer and less self-conscious than the Russians supposed it to be. In the second place, the term "petty bourgeois" came to be applied indiscriminately to a wide variety of literary phenomena which had little relationship to each other and often had no tangible class association. The idea of a petty bourgeois mentality was stretched to include and explain peculiarities of writers that could have been much better explained in aesthetic, psychological, or philosophical terms, or in terms of national tradition. As a result of this heavy reliance on a class notion, Soviet critics excluded from their judgments of American literature a great many important considerations. Their understanding of the American literary currents which they called petty bourgeois was mechanical and vastly oversimplified.

Before 1930, Soviet critics approached American literature as interested but uninvolved spectators; in the next three years, their tone changed to one of deep concern, paternal didacticism, and persistent exhortation. Convinced that America was on the eve of a cultural revolution, the Russians did all they could to guide and channel that revolution along

10 Startsev, *op.cit.*, p. 40.

Soviet lines. Criticism itself, however, was only one of the means they employed in the effort to reshape American literature, for theirs was a genuine cultural offensive, broadly international in scope, and highly political in its aims and methods. At its height, Soviet intervention in American literary affairs involved international conferences, a network of writers' clubs, and organized attempts to integrate writers into the purely political activities of the American Communist Party. To a great extent these meetings, organizations, and activities were indigenous to the United States and might have developed without Soviet encouragement, and it is clear that in many instances Soviet guidance was both unsolicited and resented. Nevertheless, the Russians were under the impression that their aid was vital and welcome, and for a limited period they assumed the role of politico-literary mentor with great ardor.

The chief agency through which the Russians attempted to influence foreign literature was the IURW.[11] Organized in 1925, the union had remained largely dormant until 1927, when it held its first international conference, drew up a political platform, made provision for the establishment of constituent national sections, and founded a journal, *Vestnik Inostrannoi Literatury* (Messenger of World Literature). The general aim of the organization was to foster the development of an international proletarian literature by bringing about a rapprochement between proletarian writers and those whom it described as petty bourgeois revolutionary writers. Politically, the union was pledged to fight against such phenomena as fascism, imperialist war, and the "white terror." In Soviet eyes, however, there were a number of defects in the organization between 1927 and 1930. Although it had been conceived as a world union, it remained essentially European;[12] the national sections had developed unevenly, so that the Russian, German, and Hungarian organizations

[11] The organization was originally called the International Bureau of Revolutionary Literature.

[12] Yan Mateika, "Mezhdunarodnoye obyedineniye revolyutsionnykh pisatelei," *Literaturnaya entsiklopediya,* VII, 85.

were by far the strongest (the American was considered ideologically weak) ;[13] the fight to stamp out right and left deviations had not been entirely won; and *Vestnik Inostrannoi Literatury* had merely "recorded the achievements of international revolutionary literature, instead of stimulating them."[14]
Significantly, this journal was published only in the Russian
language. Perhaps the most revealing complaint was that
many proletarian writers within the organization were "first
of all writers, and only then Communists, and not, as it should
be, the opposite."[15] The "world crisis" demanded more militancy and more orthodoxy.

The second conference of the IURW was held at Kharkov
in November 1930, and opened a period of sharp intervention
in American literary affairs. Attended by delegates (85 percent of them Communists) from 22 nations, the conference
reiterated the previous political aims of the union, while placing particular emphasis upon the obligation of all its members
to defend the USSR against its enemies. In literary matters,
the conference endorsed the hazily defined creative method of
dialectical materialism, which was currently being urged upon
Soviet writers, and reaffirmed the theoretical basis for an international revolutionary literature by proclaiming that a
proletarian culture could be created even in countries still
dominated by capitalism. The most urgent task of the organization, however, remained that of winning over allies from
the ranks of the disaffected petty bourgeoisie and thus, under
the impetus of the Depression, of creating a mass revolutionary movement in literature. The increased militancy of
the union was indicated in the decision to change the name
of its journal to *Literature of the World Revolution*, and the
increased scope of the union's activities was reflected in the
new policy of issuing the journal in separate Russian, French,
German, and English editions.

Following the Kharkov conference, the union rapidly in-

[13] Yan Mateika, "Zadachi mezhdunarodnovo byuro revolyutsionnoi literatury," *Literatura i iskusstvo*, No. 2 (1930), pp. 105-9.
[14] Mateika, "Mezhdunarodnoye . . . ," *op.cit.*, p. 84.
[15] Mateika, "Zadachi . . . ," *op.cit.*, p. 107.

creased its activities in the United States. Its American section centered on the John Reed Clubs, which had existed only in New York City prior to the conference, but which now expanded to many cities throughout the nation. *The New Masses*, a journal which had existed since 1926 under strong Communist Party influence, now became the central organ of the American section, and spawned a number of lesser magazines, all devoted to the promotion of revolutionary literature, under such proletarian appellations as *Left Front, Anvil,* and *Blast.* For the next three years, the Russians watched closely as the American section strove to recruit and train writers from the ranks of working men, and to enlist the allegiance of intellectuals who had been disillusioned by the Depression. It is impossible to determine the degree of Soviet control over the American section, but the Soviet attitude was clearly supervisory. Detailed critiques of current American left-wing literary activity, written by Russians, appeared in the journals, and their tone was frequently one of sharp reprimand. The editorial policies of the magazines were subjected to the closest scrutiny, and individual authors were given meticulous advice on how to improve the ideological content of their writings.

During this period of close intervention, strong efforts were made to instill in the Russian people themselves a sense of participation in an international cultural movement. They were urged to feel that revolutionary literature was a worldwide, unified, cooperative enterprise of the proletariat, for which the Soviet people, as citizens of the only socialist country, held a special responsibility. Accordingly, in Soviet domestic journals there was much commentary on contemporary foreign literature, with particular emphasis on the activities and policies of the IURW, and on the works of its individual members.

Soviet publication of American literature supplemented this new cultural foreign policy. With the inauguration of the First Five Year Plan the circulation of American books had begun to drop. In 1929 the number of American authors in new Russian printings was only half that of 1928, and the number continued steadily to dwindle, until in 1932 the works of only nine Americans were published in book form, as compared to fifty-two in 1927. Even more striking is the contrast in number of printings: in 1927 there were 177; in 1932 there were 14. Soviet publishing continued to follow its searching, experimental pattern, but its choice of fiction ceased having any correlation with American best-seller lists. The period of relative catholicity in publication of American books had come to an end. A great many American writers disappeared from the Russian scene as a result of the new policies; well over half of those who had been known in the twenties were no longer printed in the thirties. Among the most prominent of those who ceased to appear were Konrad Bercovici, Rex Beach, Maxwell Bodenheim, Irvin S. Cobb, James Oliver Curwood, Edna Ferber, Zona Gale, Zane Grey, Ben Hecht, Joseph Hergesheimer, Fannie Hurst, and Charles Norris. A good share of these writers would undoubtedly have been forgotten in any case, just as they lost prominence in America, but others would probably have held their readers had their books been available.

Here it should be emphasized that under the First Five Year Plan, Soviet literature itself experienced a fundamental transformation. Toward the end of 1928, writers were instructed to create, and publishers were ordered to print, works in direct support of the drastically accelerated program of industrialization and collectivization. Further, the proportion of nonliterary works—technical books on agriculture, industry, and science, and books of political, economic, and social indoctrination—increased rapidly. With the entire publishing apparatus mobilized in the service of the Plan, the translation of foreign works not likely to contribute politically, psychologically, or ideologically to its fulfillment was discouraged. Also, private publishing houses had been closed down at the end of the NEP. These firms, judging from their output in the twenties, had enjoyed relative freedom in choosing foreign works, and had exercised it widely. When they ceased to exist, a certain speculative drive in Russian publishing died with them.

[47]

The most substantial cause for the change in Soviet publication, however, was political and ideological. As the NEP gave way to the Five Year Plans, the Party assumed increasingly active control over all publishing. Marxism as a critical tool became more widely used and highly developed, and as its principles became clearly defined along the lines which the Party wished to establish, the demands on Western literature grew more exacting. Fewer and fewer current American works of the type that had been acceptable, or at least tolerated, in the twenties, were now looked upon with favor by the Party.

Meanwhile, American literature itself was changing, for the Depression brought about a marked increase in works of political, economic, and social discontent. Some of this writing was clearly Marxist in orientation, some was partly derived from Marxist theory, and much of it was merely protest literature of no particular ideological parentage. All of it had in common a strong inclination to indict contemporary institutions and to plead the necessity for radical alterations in the existing order if further economic and social suffering were to be prevented. All of it painted contemporary America in dismal colors, and suggested that the capitalist world was in distress.

This type of literature displaced the popular bourgeois writers who had been so prominent in Russia in the twenties. By 1931, the relatively small amount of American literature issued in Russia was clearly weighed in favor of left-wing writing. Of the eleven authors published in book form in that year, seven—John Dos Passos, Michael Gold, Charles Harrison, Robert Herrick, David Gordon, Upton Sinclair, and Jim Tully—can be considered writers of social protest. In 1932, all but two of the nine authors published were in this category. During 1933 and 1934, books by the following fourteen authors were published: Thomas Bailey Aldrich, Sherwood Anderson, Pearl Buck, Dos Passos, Theodore Dreiser, Ernest Hemingway, Langston Hughes, Jack London, Longfellow, Sinclair, Agnes Smedley, John Spivak, Sophie Treadwell, and Mark Twain. Not all of these can be associated with left-wing writing, but the pattern is clear.

The period of sharpest intervention in American literary affairs ended in 1933, when the IURW liberalized its attitude toward petty bourgeois and fellow-traveling writers. Although the major aim of the organization—to create a world-wide revolutionary literature—remained the same, the emphasis on the purely proletarian nature of the movement was somewhat relaxed, and the tendency toward direct, literal supervision of foreign literary production was checked. Undoubtedly the most important cause of this decision was the change in Soviet domestic literary policy which took place in 1932. Dissatisfied with the results of its increasingly rigid and intolerant insistence on narrowly utilitarian literature, the Party redefined its attitude and declared an amnesty toward Soviet writers who were generally sympathetic toward the regime but who had been unable completely to embrace official ideology. This by no means signified a relaxation of Party controls over Soviet writers, but it did result in greater tolerance toward temporary deviations. At the same time, the new policy officially terminated the trend toward "proletarian hegemony" in the Soviet arts. While these changes were designed to affect Soviet literature, it is clear that the new outlook also resulted in a greater willingness to accept foreign writers on their own terms, and hence in a liberalization of the policies of the IURW.

The decreased aggressiveness of the IURW was paralleled by a decrease in the ideological purism governing Soviet selection of American writings for translation. In 1932, *Literature of the World Revolution* was replaced by a new organ named, much less portentously, *International Literature*. At the outset the editors of the new journal proclaimed that the Russian edition would print not only "the most characteristic works of foreign revolutionary writers," but also "the works of world writers who are not connected with revolutionary literature, if these works have exceptional artistic significance."[16] The literary standards of the new magazine were

16 "Dnevnik sekretariata MORPa," *Internatsionalnaya literatura*, No. 1 (1933), p. 157.

high. While there was no mistaking its left-wing orientation and its hostility to "bourgeois culture," it presented in the next decade an excellent cross section of the best of American literature, past and contemporary. A whole issue of the Russian edition in 1933 was devoted to American writing. In the following years, dozens of representative Americans who had not heretofore been published in Russia came to the Soviet reader through its pages. Among them were Willa Cather, Carl Sandburg, William Faulkner, William Saroyan, Robert Frost, Sidney Howard, Edwin Arlington Robinson, Archibald MacLeish, Vachel Lindsay, Frank Stockton, Manuel Komroff, and Irwin Shaw. The magazine also published much literary criticism, and regularly reviewed current American books. Further, it served as a testing ground, and the appearance of several of our writers in book form in Russia was undoubtedly a consequence of enthusiastic response to their original publication in *International Literature*. This was by no means the only Soviet magazine which performed a similar function in the thirties, but it was the most effective. Its planned and systematic presentation of American works undoubtedly did much to stimulate Soviet interest in our culture.

Another cause of the increase in Russian publication of American literature in the middle thirties was the creation of a Popular Front against fascism. In January 1933, Adolph Hitler became *Reichskanzler* of Germany, and within the next two years his threat to the Soviet Union became unmistakable. By the middle of the decade, the USSR had modified its policy of revolutionary hostility toward the capitalist democracies and the new orientation gradually influenced the Soviet attitude toward Western culture.

From 1934 until the signing of the nonaggression pact with Germany in 1939, the Soviet Union diligently sought allies against fascism, and was willing to collaborate, for the moment, with any political forces in the West that it felt would contribute to the struggle. Since the opposition to fascism included many left-of-center parties which the Comintern had heretofore fought against long and bitterly, certain political readjustments were required. In the effort to accommodate its newly sought friends (notably, the parties of social democracy), the Comintern abandoned its ideological purism in limited areas and discarded its militant hostility toward the non-Communist left. Although international communism remained the standard-bearer of world revolution, its tactics had become defensive.

The one truth upon which the opponents of fascism could agree was its cultural barbarity—its contempt for the standards of decency and humanitarian ideals upon which Western civilization had been built. Accordingly, Soviet propaganda described the Popular Front as a union of the forces of civilization against the forces of cultural eclipse, and implied that within the world of capitalism, which only very recently had been described as decadent, there existed healthy elements worthy of being defended. This was by no means a wholesale reevaluation of capitalist culture, but as a result of the new policy, Soviet utterances showed increased respect for the living Western democratic heritage.

At an international congress of writers held in Paris in June 1935 (the first such congress since 1930), Soviet delegates enthusiastically joined those of 37 other nations in forming an International Association for the Defense of Culture. On its presidium were Americans Sinclair Lewis and Waldo Frank, whose only political distinction was their profound distaste for fascism. The political heterogeneity of the conference, and the diversity of its intellectual backgrounds, were further underlined by the presence of such figures as Heinrich Mann, E. M. Forster, Aldous Huxley, André Malraux, and André Gide. United by the single aim of protecting civilization against further Fascist inroads, the congress resolved upon a series of measures designed to stimulate cultural exchange among all nations and individuals who remained hostile to fascism. Shortly after the congress, the IURW was dissolved, and Soviet support was thrown to the International Association for the Defense of Culture. Gradually the Soviet Union withdrew from its position as leader of a cultural revolution and assumed the role of partner among beleaguered equals.

What is important here is the fact that the necessity of cooperating with the enemies of fascism brought a new friendliness into Soviet pronouncements about American culture. In the anger and alarm of American intellectuals at the expanding power of Hitler, and particularly in the widespread anti-Franco sentiment in America, the Russians found strength which they had previously chosen to ignore. The formation of the League of American Writers in 1935 and its subsequent congresses in 1937 and 1939, were hailed as deeply significant events, evidencing a newly developed sense of political responsibility and solidarity among the American intelligentsia.[17] The "historic friendship" between the peoples of Russia and the United States was rediscovered, and testimonials of mutual national esteem by American and Soviet authors were printed in *International Literature* by the dozen.[18] The old prejudices endured: Soviet critics continued to favor literature that dwelt on the Depression and, as late as 1937, could still refer to the "coming social revolution."[19] On the other hand, the "crisis" which had seemed so imminent to them in the early thirties, and which had encouraged them to urge American writers to immediate revolutionism, lost prominence in their thinking, so that they were now pleased with literature of social protest that was only implicitly revolutionary.

In keeping with this somewhat liberalized attitude, Soviet publishers stepped up the production of books by Americans. The decline in publication which had begun with the First

[17] A. Yelistratova, "Vtoroi kongress amerikanskikh pisatelei," *Internatsionalnaya literatura*, Nos. 2-3 (1938), p. 358; "Tretyemu kongressu ligi amerikanskikh pisatelei," *Internatsionalnaya literatura*, Nos. 7-8 (1939), pp. 270-71; Al. Abramov, "Peredovaya literatura sovremennoi Ameriki," *Internatsionalnaya literatura*, Nos. 7-8 (1939), p. 272.

[18] "Antifashistskiye pisateli mira," *Internatsionalnaya literatura*, No. 11 (1937), pp. 176-231 and No. 12 (1937), pp. 117-34; "Pereklichka cherez okean," *Internatsionalnaya literatura*, Nos. 7-8 (1939), pp. 214-18, 231-36, 284-88, 310-14, 340-43, 366-68.

[19] A. Startsev, "The Civil War and the Contemporary American Historical Novel," *International Literature*, No. 9 (1937), p. 70.

Five Year Plan continued through 1934, but in 1935 the number of authors represented, number of editions, and number of copies printed rose sharply. In 1937, the number of copies—2,350,000—was ten times greater than it had been in 1934.

A greater variety of American books was also made available. The publishers continued to favor left-wing writers, but by no means did they confine themselves to contemporary literature of social protest. The well-established liking for Twain, London, and O. Henry was perpetuated by frequent new printings, and other favorites of long standing, such as Cooper, Bret Harte, Mrs. Stowe, Whitman, and Longfellow, continued to be published in numerous editions. Several other excellent American writers were translated for the first time. Stephen Crane was published, Pearl Buck's novels became very popular, a volume of Ring Lardner came out, and several anthologies, representing the best American prose and poetry, were issued.

Among twentieth-century writers, the school of critical realism became as prominent as the school of immediate social protest. In number of books circulated and frequency of new printings, such authors as Erskine Caldwell, Dreiser, Mrs. Buck, Dos Passos, John Steinbeck, and Hemingway far exceeded such writers as Jack Conroy and Michael Gold. Most of the protest writers, with the notable exception of Upton Sinclair, were represented by only one or two works, and few of these achieved more than a single printing. The only reason for considering them prominent is the size of their group, which shows that the publishing houses were continuing the search for new American left-wing writers who would be appealing to Soviet readers, as well as ideologically acceptable.

For the most part, the individual American writers who became genuinely popular in Russia in the thirties cannot be identified as proletarian. Most of these critical realists did display some measure of left-wing bias, but their chief traits were psychological profundity, faithfulness in observation of human relationships, breadth of social understanding, and, above all, the ability to write well. These qualities, rather than exact conformity to Soviet ideological demands, perpetuated the Russian interest in such men as Anderson, Waldo Frank, and Lewis, and established the liking for Hemingway, Steinbeck, Caldwell, and Richard Wright. On the whole during this period, the Soviet public was given an opportunity to read much of the best contemporary American literature and showed a preference for it.

But the Popular Front was an uneasy partnership, and one in which the Russians could never join wholeheartedly. Soviet cooperation with the non-Communist left was carried on in a spirit of suspicion and truculence, and the shift in immediate political objectives left the main body of Communist doctrine undisturbed. The nations of the world, scared and confused, were jockeying for position in a struggle which only naked power could resolve, and under the circumstances cultural exchange was a weak and nearly superfluous weapon. Clearly the Soviet leaders recognized this fact. The cries for an international literature of upheaval were toned down, it is true, and the effort to create an open, organized, subversive literary movement of world-wide dimensions was terminated. But the gestures which the Russians made in the direction of cultural cooperation were small indeed; it is evident that they felt they would probably have to go it alone and were preparing for such an eventuality. In the course of the year 1937, *International Literature* ceased to be a forum of world literature, and became a showcase for Soviet culture. Its Russian edition continued to print translations of foreign works, and to report on the left-wing literary activity that was taking place outside the Soviet Union. But the foreign language editions became, quite frankly and obviously, organs of propaganda designed chiefly to display the glories of Soviet life and the wisdom of Soviet policies. The international literary movement was shrinking, and was losing its last traces of political significance.

The Nazi-Soviet pact of August 1939 sealed the doom of the Popular Front, and for the next two years the Soviet attitude toward the culture of the capitalist democracies resumed its traditional hostility. Until the German invasion of the USSR in June 1941, Soviet propaganda described World War II as a conflict between imperialist rivals within the capitalist world, and the United States, although officially neutral, was stamped as a participant because of her manifest sympathy for the Allied cause. Once again the class struggle became the chief theme in Soviet comments about America, and once more the number of American books published declined sharply. In 1938 over a million copies of books by 22 American authors were published in Russian translation; by 1940, the number had dwindled to 275,000, representing 12 Americans. For the second time within the Soviet period, Russia had sunk into extreme cultural isolationism.

In the two decades after the Revolution, Soviet intellectual life became centrally directed and increasingly disciplined. Literary publication and criticism became more and more dependent on the ideology and day-to-day policies of the Communist Party. Both the translation and the criticism of American works were governed by a growing sensitivity to the demands of Soviet foreign policy, to the official Party view of the capitalist world, and to the image of the United States which the Party strove to create in the minds of Russian readers. In the twenties the critics attempted to make a detached, although ideologically critical, evaluation of current American literature. But in the thirties, inspired by the vision and goal of an ideologically uniform, revolutionary world literature, the critics commented on American writing with a greater sense of involvement and concern. The next three chapters will show how the Soviet attitudes of the thirties were applied to specific American writers and schools.

CHAPTER III

PROLETARIAN LITERATURE

↶↶↶ PROLETARIAN LITERATURE in the United States in the thirties was a spontaneous response to the Depression. It was not exclusively a Communist, or even a Marxist, phenomenon. What unified it was not a specific political program, but rather an attitude of social protest which, as the decade progressed, was to be shared by untutored worker-writers and sophisticated aesthetes alike.

The movement included authentic proletarians—writers of working-class origin who strove to speak for their class—and proletarians-by-adoption—writers with nonproletarian backgrounds whose interest in the lower classes was essentially philanthropic. Some members of both groups came very close to total approval from Soviet critics, and they were, in Soviet terms, the "true" proletarians, or, as they were oftener referred to later in the decade, "revolutionary writers." Others, who were equally engrossed in the social problems arising from the Depression, and whom most Americans of that time considered to be left-wingers, failed in varying degrees to measure up to Soviet demands, and so were infrequently, if ever, accorded these titles. An example is James T. Farrell, whom the Russians boycotted entirely.

In the early thirties the Russians had high hopes of channeling the politically unorganized and culturally heterogeneous proletarian trend into a disciplined, unified school of revolutionary writing. Then, as always, their favored instrument was the American Communist Party, which could exert direct, though often covert, influence over those writers who joined it. But the chief agency for overtly organizing literary effort was the IURW which, through its American section, was designed to attract fellow travelers into a mass literary movement.[1] The concept of proletarian art, however, was raw and rudimentary, and the only stable element in it was its

[1] A. Yelistratova, *"New Masses, 1931," International Literature*, No. 1 (1932), p. 107.

political content. Although it had been debated in Russia for over a decade and was, by Party fiat, the governing theory of Soviet literature from 1929 to 1932, its principles were still hypothetical and were accepted by most Soviet writers only nominally and under great pressure. Its assumption that an autonomous proletarian culture, based upon the dominance of a new social class and largely independent of the cultural heritage of the past, could be built quickly for the purpose of performing specific revolutionary tasks, was now being tested in practice in the drive for a Five Year Plan literature. But in attempting to create such a body of literature, Soviet authorities proposed to employ art as an aid for the construction of socialism in a country which had already experienced its political revolution. The situation in America was totally different. Not only had the revolution not arrived, but, despite the tacit Soviet dismissal of their importance, the cultural traditions and current literary conventions of the United States, vastly different from the Russian, promised to offer strong resistance against any efforts to impose a partially formulated, untried Soviet pattern on American writing. For their part, the American advocates of proletarian literature, gathering around *The New Masses*, were even more poorly equipped in aesthetic theory than the Russians. And in their revolutionary enthusiasm they looked to the Russians for guidance, unaware of the fact that here was a situation of the blind leading the blind.

The advice which the Russians did offer was almost exclusively political, a running exhortation to carry out the decisions of the IURW in detail. Problems of literary creation were considered subordinate to the task of organizing the new movement and disciplining it ideologically. Even here the Russian experience, incomplete and remote from American actuality, could be of little assistance. Nevertheless, the Americans, lacking any other model and anxious to prove themselves loyal revolutionaries, tried to emulate Soviet practice wherever possible. New authors from the ranks of authentic working men were assiduously recruited. Every attempt was made to involve writers in political action and to engage them in the practical, everyday tasks of the workers' movement, in much the same fashion as the writers of the USSR were currently taking part in "socialist construction." Utilitarian literature of immediate political relevance was prized above all else. Writers were urged to join in labor strikes, civil rights conflicts, and political campaigns, and to report their first-hand observations—the closer, the more active their participation in events at the popular level, the better. The one tactic which could not be employed in America on any significant scale was coercion. Whereas Soviet writers, particularly from 1929 to 1932, could be forced through a variety of means to take up topics dear to the Party, the American section of the IURW, which controlled only the John Reed Clubs, *The New Masses* and a few lesser publications, had to rely much more heavily on persuasion.

In 1933, responding to the mounting sentiment for a Popular Front against fascism and chastened, no doubt, by the manifest failure of the attempt to regiment Russian literature during the First Five Year Plan, the IURW gradually abandoned its insistence on purely proletarian themes of immediate agitational import. The stringent demand for a literature which would concentrate on the revolutionary activities of American workers was somewhat relaxed, and a less puristic attitude toward the writer's choice of topics and methods of treating them appeared. From 1935, when the IURW was dissolved and replaced by the International Association for the Defense of Culture, until the end of the Popular Front period in 1939, this more liberal trend continued. Throughout the entire decade, however, certain fundamental demands remained constant. The need for a militant and timely treatment of current political, economic, and social issues was always stressed, and writers were enjoined to direct their attention to the immediately contemporary scene. And despite a growing tendency in the middle and late thirties to tolerate works which were only implicitly critical of the capitalist system, literature which pointed directly to the inevitable necessity of revolution was still favored. While there was a greater tolerance of works devoted to the middle and upper classes, concentration on the proletariat—their lives, their problems, and their psychology—continued to be most highly prized. The basic literary principles of the Third International remained unchanged; variations were a matter of emphasis, not of substance.

When the drive for a proletarian literature began, Soviet critics, accustomed to meticulously examining Russian writing for deviations and heresies, were already keeping a close watch on American books, literary reviews, and popular magazines, and were commenting regularly on them in their journals. Among the intelligentsia of the left, most of them potential allies whom the Depression had only recently shocked into some degree of sympathy with Marxism, they found diverse intellectual tendencies. In the twenties a great deal of American radical thinking had been of a free-wheeling variety: any opinion which violated the standards of the bourgeoisie was acceptably revolutionary. Now it was time to come down from the clouds, but the ideological hazards in the descent were numerous. Many potential recruits, painfully anxious to believe, either were thoroughly confused by the movement or objected to certain of its implications. Some of the newly arrived "converts" attempted to gather all forms of protest against American mores under the rubric of the now fashionable radicalism. There sprang up in Hollywood a Bohemian magazine, claiming allegiance to the movement under the quaint name of *Pollen*. This, and similar fringe manifestations, the Russians quickly denounced.[2]

Numerous Americans wanted to become radicals on their own terms, and, in order to preserve as much freedom of action as possible, joined the movement with reservations. The Russians argued that such individuals, who desired the advantages and comforts of modish radicalism without under-

---

[2] A. Yelistratova, "Literatura sovremennoi Ameriki," *Internatsionalnaya literatura*, No. 5 (1933), p. 101.

taking sacrifices or submitting to discipline, were worse than useless,[3] and dubbed them "rotten liberals."[4]

Among heresies, the gravest was "vulgarization" of Marxism, such as equating it with sexual radicalism, or wrenching it away from Leninist doctrine as did the critic V. F. Calverton when he insisted that in the present crisis the essential choice was between "individualism" and "collectivism," ignoring that not only communism, but also fascism, claimed collectivist principles.[5] Vulgarizations of this sort, particularly painful to the Russians and frequently labeled "Trotskyist," were persistently hunted down.

Heresy could be boldly denounced, but deviations by those who sincerely considered themselves loyal to the movement required more delicate handling, and were therefore more difficult to cope with. The Russians found that many writers, and particularly those who had seldom rubbed elbows with the proletariat as a social class, were inclined to portray the workers' movement from a rigid, purely intellectual point of view. Others were too mild, and insufficiently militant in depicting the class struggle. In their ardor against imperialist war, still others emphasized the horrors of armed conflict to the point of absolute pacifism. Writers often failed to show with satisfactory prominence the role of the Communist Party as the "advance guard and organizer" of the struggle against capitalism. Failure to outlive "lost-generation disillusionment" and its attendant perplexities was another widespread cause of deviation. (Its cure, the Russians felt, was political activity, a particularly salutary form of which was a visit to the Soviet Union. Several American writers did this in the thirties, to "see for themselves," but the results did not always delight the Russians.) It is significant that the Russians complained that *The New Masses*, the organ of proletarian literature, lagged behind *The Daily Worker* in political acuteness.

While general Marxist orthodoxy and correct stands on

---

[3] Abel Startsev, "Vseobshchi krizis kapitalizma i novaya volna soyuznikov proletariata v literature Ameriki," *Marksistsko-Leninskoye iskusstvoznaniye*, Nos. 5-6 (1932), p. 56.

[4] Yelistratova, *"New Masses*, 1931," *op.cit.*, p. 108.

[5] Startsev, "Vseobshchi . . . ," *op.cit.*, p. 57.

specific political issues were always the first things the Russians looked for in current American proletarian literature, other characteristics were also thought to be indispensable. A quality especially prized, particularly in the early thirties, can be called folk militancy. In urging that works embody the popular traditions and psychology of the lower classes, Soviet critics did not ask for mere local color or a depiction of folkways alone. Specifically, they were seeking a demonstration of an elemental drive to revolution similar to that which, according to contemporary Soviet mythology, had moved the Russian people to the violence of October. The Bolshevik revolution had been an epoch of popular poetry, songs, and slogans, some of them representing the accumulation of generations of protest, some of them newly coined for the times, but all of them designed to inflame common people to action. The Russians wanted to see a comparable phenomenon in America's time of crisis.

Although the critics were always ready to welcome any writing that promised to inspire the masses to revolutionary ardor, at first they advocated immediately communicable genres, such as topical verse, the sketch, and the agitational drama. Genuine proletarian poetry, reasoned the critic Dinamov in 1930, had begun in the United States early in the twentieth century with the formation of the IWW. Initially it had been disseminated by hoboes, either by word of mouth or by chance manuscripts passed from hand to hand. In its early, most primitive period, the school had displayed a narrow, purely empirical grasp of social reality, since "an immature political class expresses itself in art in immature organic forms."[6] As the proletariat became more class-conscious, however, its poetry became more tendentious and gained in political acuteness. The tone of wistful contemplation and aimless complaining, of lyrical sentimentality, gave way to definite, pointed appeal. To date, the greatest proletarian poet of America had been Joe Hill, whose songs, conceived as a direct political weapon, had lacked the softness and "superfluous decoration" of poetry, were designed to

[6] S. Dinamov, "Amerikanskaya proletarskaya poeziya," *Literatura i iskusstvo*, No. 1 (1930), p. 94.

produce the maximum shock, and were "fierce, coarse, like the class struggle." However, Hill, as a politically naive "anarcho-syndicalist," had been content with agitating for the "one big union" of the IWW.[7] Hill's successor, according to Dinamov, was Michael Gold, who represented a higher stage in the development of proletarian poetry. A fully committed Communist of authentic working-class background, Gold had been known in the Soviet Union since 1925, when a volume of his stories was translated,[8] and was a delegate to the Kharkov conference in 1930. By the early thirties, his angry, stormy verse (together with his plays, stories, criticism, and editorial work) had given him the reputation in Russia not only as the "most powerful American proletarian writer,"[9] but also as the "only truly proletarian poet in America."[10] An almost equally strong poet of protest, according to Soviet critics of the time, was Langston Hughes, who imbued his verse with the folk spirit of the American Negro. Throughout the thirties, the Russians continued searching for an authentic contemporary bard of the working class—someone of the stature of Whitman. However, neither Hughes nor Gold, nor any of dozens of other left-wing versifiers whom they published in magazines and anthologies from time to time, fully satisfied the critics.

For the most part the literary sketch and the agitational drama, as written by Americans, likewise failed to impress the Russians. The sketches which they considered superior, with few exceptions, were all parts of larger works; the only one-act play that ever drew significant attention was Clifford Odets' *Waiting for Lefty*.[11] Soon it became apparent that

[7] *ibid.*, p. 106.

[8] A. Z. "Maikl Gold. *Proklyaty agitator i dr. rasskazy,*" *Oktyabr,* Nos. 3-4 (1925), pp. 241-42.

[9] "K plenumu MBRL," *Literatura i iskusstvo,* No. 2 (1930), p. 119.

[10] M. Zenkevich, "O novinkakh angliskoi i amerikanskoi literatury," *Novy mir,* No. 12 (1931), p. 170.

[11] P. Balashov, "Amerikanskaya dramaturgiya," *Inostrannaya kniga,* No. 4 (1934), pp. 36-40; P. Balashov, "Elmer Reis," *Internatsionalnaya literatura,* No. 5 (1936), pp. 205-9; Al. Abramov, "Amerikanskaya odno-aktnaya pyesa," *Internatsionalnaya literatura,* No. 2 (1940), pp. 181-84; A. Yelistratova, "Noviye yavleniya v literature Ameriki," *Kniga i prole-tarskaya revolyutsiya,* No. 11 (1933), p. 117.

while Americans were trying valiantly to cultivate brief, hard-hitting genres in tune with the times, the national talent lay elsewhere. And already in the early thirties, Soviet critics were forced to look to the American short story and, even more, to the novel, for the earthy, human qualities which they considered indispensable ingredients of politically correct art.

The problem of how to create works of art from the raw material of current events had plagued Soviet writers and literary theorists ever since the Revolution. Beginning in 1928, Party doctrine precluded the argument that it is not feasible to demand aesthetic perfection in a work that is designed primarily as a tract for the times. Inevitably the result was to lower aesthetic standards to accommodate writing that had the virtue of being politically timely and orthodox. But also, in an effort to preserve principles of taste and to avoid merely rationalizing bad art while insisting on the criterion of immediate utility, the critics sought new formulas. They began to advocate the sketch as a temporary, transitional mode of artistic expression for the proletariat. The critic Elistratova pointed out that the American working class had "only just started to achieve a certain self-assurance," and argued that "by means of reconstruction of his original observations, or of those facts that are socially important in his personal life, the revolutionary artist strives to reproduce the general class experience, and the general inheritance of his class."[12] Consequently the sketch (usually autobiographical), as the "most immediate and accessible method of fixing class experience,"[13] was a natural and legitimate step in the development of a proletarian literary talent. According to the critic Nemerovskaya, the first American to "raise the revolutionary sketch to artistic height" was John Reed, "in whom political activity was inseparable from literature."[14] Gold's *Jews Without Money*, which the Russians for a long time thought to be

[12] Anne Elistratova, "Jack Conroy: American Worker-Writer," *International Literature*, No. 1(7) (1934), p. 114.

[13] *ibid.*, p. 114.

[14] Olga Nemerovskaya, "Sudba amerikanskoi novelly," *Literaturnaya uchyoba*, No. 5 (1935), p. 106.

the brightest example of American proletarian writing, was a series of sketches held together by an autobiographical element.

Some critics also looked upon the sketch as a kind of training device for successful petty bourgeois writers who were turning toward the proletariat. Theodore Dreiser's use of the "portrait gallery" in *A Gallery of Women* was interpreted in this way by Nemerovskaya, who reasoned that "the process of ideological reconstruction, the construction of a new approach to reality, demands a different kind of veracious portrayal of reality."[15] When Dreiser led a group of prominent authors in investigating the strike in the coal mines of Harlan County, Kentucky, another critic commented that "if they turn to publicistics, become writers of sketches and newspaper reporters, that will be only a transitional step in their writing life."[16] Edmund Wilson was lauded for having turned from "literary-critical articles" to "passionate political invectives," and the change was explained as a "completely lawful and necessary stage for his rebuilding."[17]

Although it was endorsed as both a means of literary apprenticeship for working-class writers and a useful device in the political education of established petty bourgeois authors —and sanctioned as an aesthetically respectable proletarian genre in its own right—the sketch, in actual application, was seldom found satisfactory. Like the biographies in John Dos Passos' *U.S.A.*, nearly all the sketches the Russians considered superior were actually parts of larger works. And too often a sketch was merely political journalism. Typical were the complaint of Nemerovskaya that "the first attempts at a faithful, honorable, objective depiction of reality have led to the empirical clutching of facts, to a certain artistic primitivism," and her lament that "sharp social acuteness often brings agitationalism and publicism which lead to schematism and simplification."[18] Gold himself was a serious offender: the "convincing logical strength" of his art was often vitiated by

[15] *ibid.*, p. 105.   [16] Startsev, "Vseobshchi . . . ," *op.cit.*, p. 60.
[17] *ibid.*, p. 60.
[18] Nemerovskaya, "Sudba . . . ," *op.cit.*, p. 105.

"schematism, coldness, and rhetoric,"[19] so that "in him the publicist-agitator prevails over the artist."[20]

Thinly fictional accounts of actual events, in the form of short stories and novels usually based on eye-witness reporting, became prominent. More taxing to the inventive powers of the writer, these works occupied a middle ground between the sketch and pure fiction. Since they permitted a reshaping of actuality and the creation of imaginary characters within a framework of documentary fact, such works, in theory, had a potential both of aesthetic excellence and political usefulness. In portraying current revolutionary activities through the vivid images of fiction, they could humanize the political pamphlet. Upton Sinclair, the leading practitioner of this kind of writing, remained aloof from the proletarian movement, but it soon became evident that dozens of others were attempting to employ the documentary story as a revolutionary art form, or, as the critic Zenkevich put it, to "clothe dry newspaper reports in flesh and blood, to make them become a living reality."[21]

The labor strike, sharpest expression of the class struggle on the American scene, became the dramatic focus of much of this writing. In 1932, four novels were published about one strike alone—the bloody conflict in 1929 at the textile mills of Gastonia, North Carolina. Hailing their appearance, a Soviet critic wrote: "The fact that in 1932 four American writers almost simultaneously used the material of the Gastonia strike and the workers' movement in the South, is not wholly coincidental. From the romanticism of vagabondism and abstract, at times almost aimless, cosmic revolutionism, American revolutionary literature is approaching closely, at last, to an expression of the workers' movement in the USA in all its complexity and concreteness."[22] Heretofore there had been "many appeals to revolution, but no demonstration

---

[19] A. Startsev, "Maikl Gold," *Na literaturnom postu*, No. 12 (1931), p. 24.

[20] Al. Abramov, "Molodost veka," *Internatsionalnaya literatura*, No. 6 (1935), p. 142.

[21] Zenkevich, "O novinkakh . . . ," *op.cit.*, p. 174.

[22] Yelistratova, "Literatura sovremennoi Ameriki," *op.cit.*, p. 102.

of the concrete actuality of this revolution."[23] Now, at last, prose fiction was being employed both as a recorder and as a maker of history. The main value of these documentary novels, in Soviet eyes, was that they could put an immediately revolutionary interpretation on clashes that otherwise might appear as isolated symptoms of temporary economic and social maladjustment. Three novels of Gastonia were soon translated into Russian—Sherwood Anderson's *Beyond Desire*, Grace Lumpkin's *To Make My Bread*, and Mary Heaton Vorse's *Strike!* The latter was praised because it showed "living, developing, authentic events, artistically narrated by an eye-witness."[24] Miss Lumpkin's novel, together with another about Gastonia, Myra Page's *Gathering Storm*, were commended for showing the growth of class-consciousness among the working masses.[25] Committed to the belief that America was experiencing a fundamental, decisive revolutionary upsurge, Soviet critics demanded stories showing a confidently enthusiastic, militant, enterprising strike movement that would bear a qualitative resemblance to the Leninist revolution of Bolshevik legend.

Later in the thirties, as the flush of anticipation paled with the realization that America's proletarian upheaval might be postponed, the critics toned down their insistence on novels of the barricades, although such stories continued to be welcomed. Also, as the strike movement failed to assume classic Marxist proportions it became apparent that novels documenting actual strikes, if they were true to the facts, must perforce be lacking in political revolutionism. Accordingly, the documentary strike tale, which was at best a makeshift device for lending an aura of political veracity to American proletarian fiction, lost the appeal it had held for the Russians in the promising early days of the Depression. Finally, the documentary element in these works, considered aesthetically, was too often merely a crutch for writers who lacked

[23] "Dnevnik sekretariata MORPa," *Internatsionalnaya literatura*, No. 1 (1933), p. 158.

[24] Zenkevich, "O novinkakh . . . ," *op.cit.*, p. 174.

[25] A. Yelistratova, "Literatura S A S Sh," *Literaturnaya gazeta*, November 29, 1933, p. 2.

sufficient imagination to create pure fiction, and none of the American proletarian writing that borrowed its structure from authentic public events achieved success with either Soviet critics or readers.

With this in mind, it is possible to examine the attitude of Soviet critics toward the whole corpus of American proletarian literature without further differentiating between the documentary and the nondocumentary, or between that which was designed to be of immediate political use and that which was less urgently in the proletarian spirit.

At the center of this literature, the Russians steadily insisted, should be the living image of the individual man, in all his variety and complexity. Any depiction of institutions and forces, of social groupings and trends, would not be artistically successful if it did not contain emotionally rich and verisimilar characters. But, they further insisted, such characters must embody attitudes and responses that were typical of their time and place, and to be truly representative, the most important of them should be persons psychologically oriented toward the working class, or, better yet, ordinary workers. The Gastonia novels of Myra Page and Grace Lumpkin were praised specifically because they portrayed "rank-and-file working men," instead of isolated leaders and agitators.[26] And one of the most attractive features of Jack Conroy's The Disinherited was that its hero, Larry Donovan, is a typical "unheroic" proletarian.[27] Conroy's novel, in the opinion of the critics, had another major virtue: its intimate account of the private lives of its characters. Whereas even Michael Gold did not succeed in giving a "full-blooded image of a worker,"[28] Conroy dealt not in "abstract discussions but in very live, human characterizations."[29] Albert Halper's The Foundry was praised for its "artistic representation of the life and mores of an American type-foundry,"[30] and Leane

[26] ibid., p. 21.
[27] O. Nemerovskaya, "Dzhek Konroi, 'Obezdolenny,'" Zvezda, No. 3 (1936), pp. 203-4.
[28] Abramov, op.cit., p. 142.
[29] Elistratova, "Jack Conroy . . . ," op.cit., p. 116.
[30] S. Dinamov, "Pisatel i revolyutsiya," Izvestiya, June 8, 1935, p. 4.

Zugsmith's *A Time to Remember* was particularly interesting for its portrayal of the private lives of white-collar workers.[31] In the novel of Josephine Herbst, *A Rope of Gold*, a critic found it noteworthy that the author was able to show a close connection between "the personal and the social": "Along with a detailed depiction of the intimate world, along with lyrical portraits, Josephine Herbst can give a broad canvas of national life. Here Herbst shows the precise ability of a painter to see the man in the mass, in the crowd, and to discern in him the individuality which is peculiar to him."[32]

Even a brilliant characterization of a genuine proletarian was not sufficient, however, if it suggested the wrong ideological conclusions. Gold's sympathy for his characters was "not at all a tearful pity for the 'poor man,' idealizing and at the same time humiliating." Rather, it was the "valiant sympathy of a proletarian revolutionary. . . ."[33] Nevertheless, many of his stories bore the stamp of melancholy and pessimism, which vitiated their revolutionary message.[34] While Joseph Vogel's novel of unemployment, *Man's Courage*, was "permeated with a humanistic anxiety for a man who is refused that which is most dear—the right to work,"[35] it was criticized for presenting its hero's courage as something blind, purposeless, undirected, and hopeless.[36] Leane Zugsmith's portrayal of race injustice in *The Summer Soldier* terrified her readers and hindered them from "soberly evaluating" the class enemy.[37] Several of the plays of Odets were marked by "deep pessimism, a feeling of the tragicality of life, of spiritual desolation."[38] But in contrast to such bourgeois writers as Wil-

[31] Vl. Rubin, "Povest o 'lyudyakh v belykh vorotnichkakh,'" *Internatsionalnaya literatura*, No. 10 (1937), pp. 222-25.

[32] A. Mingulina, "Zolotaya tsep," *Internatsionalnaya literatura*, No. 9 (1939), p. 249.

[33] Startsev, "Maikl Gold," *op.cit.*, p. 24.   [34] *ibid.*, p. 23.

[35] P. Balashov, "'Muzhestvo' Dzhozefa Vogelya," *Literaturnaya gazeta*, August 15, 1939, p. 2.

[36] Ya. Frid, "Muzhestvo," *Literaturnoye obozreniye*, No. 19 (1940), p. 32.

[37] A. Lino, "Lin Zugsmit—'Soldat na leto,'" *Internatsionalnaya literatura*, Nos. 9-10 (1939), p. 254.

[38] R. Miller-Budnitskaya, "Mechta o chelovechnosti," *Iskusstvo i zhizn*, No. 10 (1940), p. 16.

liam Faulkner and Robinson Jeffers, who were "preoccupied with psychological sadism and the twitchings of a sick consciousness," a truly proletarian writer like Conroy was filled with "proletarian optimism," in which "a depressive helplessness finds no place."[39]

In Soviet doctrine, the chief source of hope and confidence for American working men should be a feeling of unity and solidarity centering on the organized labor movement, and the critics often complained that writers neglected it. Gold, in *A Damned Agitator*, depicted his strike-leader hero as a lonely figure, like the prophet Jeremiah.[40] In his story, translated into Russian under the title, "Faster, America, Faster," he displayed an "inability to show the organized workers' movement of revolutionary proletarians."[41] Whittaker Chambers, on the other hand, was singled out as the first to portray revolutionary stirrings among American farmers,[42] and was lauded specifically for placing the Communist Party at the core of the movement in his stories.[43] For the ultimate source of inspiration, the rallying force, and the collective hero of both the movement and the literature that belonged to it must be the Party itself.

Finally, American proletarian literature must be combative and dynamic, and must portray workers who are actively aware of the goals of their struggle. A defect of the novel of Mary Heaton Vorse was that its hero was more a martyr than a leader. And at times the novel "overly stressed" the "passivity and nonresistance" of the strikers.[44] While the plays of Elmer Rice contained much effective protest, they lacked militancy.[45] Of *We, the People*, a critic wrote: "After nineteen scenes of merciless unmasking of capitalism, in the final,

---

[39] Elistratova, "Jack Conroy . . . ," *op.cit.*, p. 113.
[40] N. Eishiskina, " 'Yevrei bez deneg' M. Golda," *Marksistsko-Leninskoye iskusstvoznaniye*, Nos. 5-6 (1932), p. 174.
[41] *ibid.*, p. 175.
[42] Yelistratova, "Literatura S A S Sh," *op.cit.*, p. 2.
[43] A. Matveyeva, " 'Noviye massy'—zhurnal amerikanskoi sektsii MORP," *Marksistsko-Leninskoye iskusstvoznaniye*, Nos. 5-6 (1932), p. 207.
[44] Zenkevich, "O novinkakh . . . ," *op.cit.*, p. 174.
[45] P. Balashov, "Elmer Reis," *op.cit.*, p. 207.

twentieth scene, Elmer Rice organizes a meeting at which the Declaration of Independence is read at length, a reformist appeal is proclaimed about a return to 'good old constitutional rights.' After a pointed criticism of capitalism, the author appeals to the good sense of sober Americans to make concessions voluntarily, lest they be imposed by force."[46] Proper revolutionary writers should make no concessions. They should be sanguine prophets, not content with merely relating what they have seen, but, rather, burning to write about "what they could see or might be able to see in the future."[47]

Toward the end of the Popular Front period, the critics became slightly less urgent in their insistence on supercharged revolutionary optimism, and displayed a somewhat greater willingness to accept works for their aesthetic merit alone. Although Elmer Rice's *Street Scene* was characterized as the work of a "confused liberal" when it was first published in Russian in 1935, new editions of the play appeared in 1937 and 1938. Albert Halper was not criticized for writing as a "detached onlooker" in *The Foundry*, or for failing to go beyond an indictment of capitalist working conditions. The mere revolutionary *implications* of the novel were enough to satisfy one critic.[48] Despite its "weary, autumnal" mood, Josephine Johnson's *Now in November* was adjudged superior to more militant agrarian novels of the time because of its "exceptional poetic quality, freshness, and acuteness of psychological observation."[49] Sidney Kingsley was praised simply for his "honest, lively, and talented" portrayal of the "screaming contradictions" of American life in *Dead End*, and was not blamed for failing to indicate a "way out."[50]

There were probably two reasons for this slight relaxation of standards. First, the policy of the Popular Front called for less ideological stringency. Second, the critics sounded con-

---

[46] P. Balashov, "Amerikanskaya dramaturgiya," *op.cit.*, p. 36.

[47] Elistratova, "Jack Conroy . . . ," *op.cit.*, pp. 114-15.

[48] P. Balashov, "Albert Halper—'Slovolitnya,'" *Internatsionalnaya literatura*, No. 5 (1937), p. 229.

[49] N. R., "Zhozefina Dzhonson, 'Teper v noyabre,'" *Internatsionalnaya literatura*, Nos. 2-3 (1938), p. 370.

[50] P. B. "Sidnei Kingsli—'Tupik,'" *Internatsionalnaya literatura*, No. 9 (1937), p. 222.

stant notes of aesthetic dissatisfaction throughout the thirties, and many of them may have come to the conclusion that the proletarian formulas they had devised were unworkable. Never, of course, could there be a frank admission that writing whose chief motivation is pressingly political has little chance of becoming art. But the instances of aesthetic disapproval of works that were politically acceptable were so numerous that, cumulatively, they suggest that the critics must have been at least partly aware that they were demanding the impossible.

From the very beginning Soviet critics observed a tacit distinction between art and political journalism, and even when their ideological purism and prescriptiveness were most intense, they continued to demand beauty, grace, and refinement in American proletarian literature. They seldom found them. Michael Gold, who was by and large the most respected American proletarian writer in the early thirties, was repeatedly criticized on aesthetic grounds. At first the critics attempted to excuse his awkward proclivity for parading his social messages by insisting that there was something so peculiarly fresh and original in his creative vices that they were actually virtues. In 1930 a critic argued that Gold's thin characterizations made his stories all the more "simplified and pointed": "In them there move not people, but algebraic symbols of social forces. They are telling allegories in which all of the typical is emphasized and all of the individual is blotted out. . . . Gold does not bother about objective truth: what is important to him is class truth."[51] Another critic, who seemed to be whistling in the dark, found a different way of dismissing his flaws: "In Gold there is a certain schematic quality, but in his creative method are all the necessary conditions for overcoming this schematism."[52] In 1931 Abel Startsev, who was Gold's most perceptive critic, complained of his "tendency toward schematic generalizations and allegorizing of images." The "rationalistic foundation," which "endowed his art with convincing logical strength," had its

[51] "K plenumu MBRL," *op.cit.*, p. 119.
[52] Dinamov, "Amerikanskaya proletarskaya poeziya," *op.cit.*, p. 111.

[71]

"reverse side of schematism, coldness, and rhetoric."[53] (Start-sev did not conclude, as he might well have done, that Gold's "coldness and rhetoric" were organically related to the "logical strength" of his politically motivated writing.) The critic Eishiskina made an exception of *Jews Without Money*, in which Gold had "conquered his rationalism, tendency to allegorize and . . . didactic, moralizing design."[54] But in 1935 still another critic repeated the general verdict that "with Gold the figures of workers suffer from dryness, a certain artistic inadequacy, schematism."[55]

Many other proletarians suffered the same criticism. A critic complained that Joseph Vogel, in *Man's Courage*, had shown only one aspect of his hero—his thirst for work.[56] In Leane Zugsmith's *A Time to Remember*, another critic noted "a certain schematism in the depiction of Communists."[57] The critic Mingulina observed the following relationship between structure and ideological purpose in the novels of Josephine Herbst: "In her striving to give an historically broad scope of events and types Josephine Herbst somewhat overpopulates her novels. To a certain degree this is determined by their structure, especially *Rope of Gold*, which is built on parallel narratives. The basic characters—besides the great number of episodic figures who arise—come together and then part again in various parts of the novel. But they are all necessary to Josephine Herbst so that in their comings together, in their quarrels, in their very fates, the various ideological-political tendencies in American life can be shown."[58]

Conroy's *The Disinherited*, because of its generally warm reception by the critics, probably provides the best illustration of the Soviet attitude toward the aesthetic shortcomings of the Americans. While Elistratova found in the novel "no hint of the placard, which often hinders young revolutionary writers,"[59] the critic Abramov complained of its "looseness of

[53] Startsev, "Maikl Gold," *op.cit.*, p. 24.
[54] Eishiskina, " 'Yevrei bez deneg' . . . ," *op.cit.*, p. 175.
[55] Abramov, *op.cit.*, p. 142.   [56] Frid, *op.cit.*, p. 31.
[57] Rubin, *op.cit.*, p. 225.   [58] Mingulina, *op.cit.*, p. 249
[59] Elistratova, "Jack Conroy . . . ," *op.cit.*, p. 117.

composition" and "sketch-like aridity, which constitute the disease of the majority of American revolutionary writers."[60] In a more detailed analysis of Conroy's work, Nemerovskaya pointed out:

"The novel does not have a single core. The characters appear, disappear, and appear again without any motivation, completely unexpectedly, and, perhaps, unjustifiedly. . . . But meeting each time anew, they come together anew, with that special firm closeness which unites more closely than physical nearness—class proximity.

"The facts of the novel are repeated. Misery, poverty, searching for work, glimmers of success, loss of work, again misery, again the search and so to the end. This makes for a certain monotony, which at times wearies the reader. But . . . each new corroboration of the same situation is connected with a certain psychological evolution of the heroes, with a new stage in the development of their social consciousness— and in this [evolution] is the internal, cementing dynamics of the whole story."[61] The essence of the critics' reaction to the work of their uncertain American allies is in this mixture of aesthetic disapproval and strained ideological justification.

"Schematism" is a fairly rare and innocuous term in American usage, but in the Soviet critical vocabulary it acquires a special force, denoting various kinds of artistic failure stemming from the subordination of form to content. Its persistent application to American proletarian writing suggests that Soviet critics were constantly disturbed over the contrived quality of the American efforts at superimposing ideological unity over diverse and unwieldy material. Too often American proletarian novels and short stories created a kind of political harmony at the expense of aesthetic persuasiveness, and Soviet critics seldom failed to notice this. Their strictures, however, were nearly always brief and general, and if they permitted themselves to brood over the ideological implications of these aesthetic faults, their meditations at least never made their way into print. Instead, the critics described

---

[60] Abramov, *op.cit.*, p. 143.
[61] Nemerovskaya, "Dzhek Konroi . . . ," *op.cit.*, p. 204.

these faults as the growing pains of a generation that was destined to create a brave new revolutionary art. Typical was the remark of the critic Abramov, who argued that "although there are mistakes . . . artistic crises, the line of development of American revolutionary literature goes steadfastly upward."[62] A more sober observation, and perhaps a more revealing one, was made by the critic Nemerovskaya, who wrote in 1935 that the craftsmanship of the contemporary petty bourgeois writers of America was so high that "not only their [proletarian] countrymen but even our Soviet short story writers can learn from them."[63]

Of all American works about the Depression, the story that made the strongest impact in Russia was John Steinbeck's *The Grapes of Wrath*. Parts of it were translated in periodicals in 1940, and in the same year the whole novel was issued in an edition of 25,000. The following year it was published in 300,000 copies—by far the largest single printing an American work had ever enjoyed in Russia. Its critical reception varied from sober, qualified endorsement to lavish enthusiasm, but the general tenor was warmly laudatory. Steinbeck's precise, unsentimental realism, the graphic simplicity with which he portrayed his dispossessed Oklahoma farmers, the novel's vitality and drama and its authentic closeness to the soil impressed the critics deeply. These elements, together with its humaneness and poetic treatment of nature, caused several of them to remark on its epic qualities. Nemerovskaya made the important point that the novel was fundamentally optimistic since "belief in the uniting and strengthening power of the collective . . . triumphs over the sadness and gloom of the events depicted."[64]

Ma Joad was compared to the heroine of Gorky's *Mother*, because she displayed "the same daily heroism in the face of a terrible life, the same growing understanding of reality, magnificent talent for enduring sorrow, and readiness to suf-

[62] Abramov, *op.cit.*, p. 143.

[63] Nemerovskaya, "Sudba . . . ," *op.cit.*, p. 108.

[64] O. Nemerovskaya, "Kniga o lyubvi i nenavisti," *Zvezda*, Nos. 8-9 (1940), p. 275.

fer."[65] Since Ma struggles merely to hold the Joad family together,[66] Gorky's heroine was "more progressive, more socially conscious,"[67] but the mere comparison to Gorky's novel, which was considered an eminent classic, was intended a high compliment. Ma's gradual assumption of greater and greater responsibility is restricted to her own family circle, but she increasingly identifies herself and her family with the masses of other unfortunates, and the critics liked her precisely because she demonstrated the development of proletarian understanding in an individual. Tom Joad, the critic Khmelnitskaya noted, was the kind of character folk legends are made of,[68] and the critic Chelovekov wrote that he was like "a younger brother of Pavel" in *Mother*. Although he is not as politically conscious as Gorky's hero, his fighting temperament and dawning proletarian awareness lead him to think like a revolutionary.[69] The critic Abramov found Casy, the ex-preacher, to be an implausible character, since he could not accept the proposition that a man with a recent background in organized religion could become a strike leader. Unimpressed by Steinbeck's attempt to emphasize the opposition between Christian and capitalist ethics, Abramov found Casy a vague, unresolved character, unworthy of his prominent position in the novel.[70] Khmelnitskaya disagreed: "Indeed, the boldness, originality and veracity of the picture of Casy consists just in the fact that, not tearing him out of his habitual mode of thought and expression, Steinbeck created a genuine revolutionary propagandist out of a preacher."[71] And Nemerovskaya thought that Casy was all the more effective specifically because "the former preacher changes into a revolutionary not on a basis of reasoning and study, but because

[65] F. Chelovekov, "Grozdya gneva," *Literaturnoye obozreniye*, No. 12 (1940), p. 38.

[66] Nemerovskaya, "Kniga o lyubvi . . . ," *op.cit.*, p. 273.

[67] Chelovekov, *op.cit.*, p. 38.

[68] Tamara Khmelnitskaya, "Grozdya gneva Steinbeka," *Literaturny sovremennik*, No. 12 (1940), p. 157.

[69] Chelovekov, *op.cit.*, p. 38.

[70] A. Abramov, "Dzhon Steinbek," *Internatsionalnaya literatura*, Nos. 3-4 (1940), p. 230.

[71] Khmelnitskaya, *op.cit.*, p. 159.

[75]

of the craving of his heart, filled with love for people and hatred for oppressors."[72]

All Soviet critics would have agreed, I think, that Balashov stated the cardinal virtue of Steinbeck's characterizations when he observed, "In these simple people . . . Steinbeck has found the fundamental human characteristics—the feeling of dignity and faith in humanity."[73] In questioning whether it is plausible for a preacher like Casy to become a militant labor leader without a fundamental transformation of character, and in judging Ma Joad not for what she is but in terms of the class-conscious proletarian heroine she should be, the critics were performing stern ideological duties. But they were tolerant and made allowances for the capitalistic environment in which these characters were conceived. Ma was measured on the scale of the ideal socialist heroine, but she was not condemned for not matching the ideal.

As an agrarian writer Steinbeck invited comparison with Erskine Caldwell, but the critics found striking contrasts between the two. Of *Tobacco Road*, Nemerovskaya wrote, "The social conclusion of the novel is deeply pessimistic—capitalism suffocates the human personality and reduces it to complete savagery."[74] But of *The Grapes of Wrath*: ". . . despite the downfall of the Joad family, despite the sad fate of the individual heroes, the final conclusion of the novel is optimistic: capitalism cannot destroy lofty human feelings in the working man. It hardens the spirit and will of a man and prepares him for an inevitable, decisive class conflict in the future."[75] Nemerovskaya was impressed by the way in which Steinbeck portrayed his Oklahomans' pride in their heritage of pioneering, self-reliance, and hard work in the plains, and pointed out, partially justifying Caldwell's characterizations, that *Tobacco Road* is set in an agriculturally sterile and culturally decadent area of Georgia, where an exhausted soil and changing economy have produced a dispirited people.[76] The inci-

[72] Nemerovskaya, "Kniga o lyubvi . . . ," *op.cit.*, p. 276.

[73] P. Balashov, "Pevets narodnovo gneva," *Novy mir*, No. 10 (1940), p. 214.

[74] Nemerovskaya, "Kniga o lyubvi . . . ," *op.cit.*, p. 273.

[75] *ibid.*, p. 273.   [76] *ibid.*, p. 273.

dents in *Tobacco Road*, however, thrust Caldwell's people deeper and deeper into stupefied acceptance of their lot, while in *The Grapes of Wrath* each succeeding misfortune increases the heroic stature of such people as Tom, Ma, and Casy and strengthens their determination to forge their own destiny. This growth of fighting spirit and heightened consciousness of common cause was the most positive ingredient in the book: "Steinbeck sees that changes are brewing, and he sees whom it is that they threaten, who it is that is terrified of these changes and revolutions. The awakening of class consciousness, the birth of new notions and thoughts, the transition from 'I' to 'we,' from the words 'my' land to the words 'our' land, the start of close comradeship among people who are caught up by one and the same misfortune—this is what now interests Steinbeck most of all and lends his novel its definite revolutionary direction, its power and its freshness."[77]

The critics were profoundly impressed by the expository chapters in which Steinbeck departs from his narrative of the Joad family in a sort of internal monologue to give a panoramic picture of the tragedy of the dust bowl, the mass migration to California, and the disillusionment and misery that awaited the refugees. Of these chapters, which convey social and economic interpretations, nature descriptions and poetic commentary, Balashov wrote: "They are written with extraordinary power and inspiration, they broaden the framework of the novel, but they do not demolish it; rather, they merge closely and indissolubly in the movement and sweep of his vast subject; they are not boring and rhetorical, as some critics have said . . . they are natural and vigorous and are simply indispensable to this monumental epos."[78] Nemerovskaya further defended these aesthetically controversial chapters: "These are not dry socio-economic tracts. They are a type of artistic journalism, tense, imbued with lyricism, and no less moving than the novel itself. An intense, lyrical in-

[77] Balashov, "Pevets . . . ," *op.cit.*, p. 213.
[78] *ibid.*, p. 210.

[77]

tonation rings from beginning to end, and never passes over into cold, rational analysis."[79]

None of Steinbeck's earlier works had been translated, but several critics soon turned to them. At first, they contended, he had pictured a world dominated by blind and malevolent fate. Convinced that humanity is ruled by "hidden and inscrutable laws of chance,"[80] in *The Pastures of Heaven* he had written about a "dark and destructive power of intangible and mysterious origin."[81] Such stories as "The Snake" and "The Vigilante" featured Faulknerian "psycho-pathological themes" and were tinged with "Freudism." Feeling "pity without anger, love without hatred," he wrote with a "fatalistic sneer."[82] Abramov believed that the novel *In Dubious Battle* had marked a "turning point" in Steinbeck's view of the world: "For the first time Steinbeck departs from his former theme of the personal happiness of little people, outside the real world, outside real historical and social actuality. For the first time he goes beyond the limits of the tiny world of intimate human feelings—love and friendship, it seemed, were the sole values for Steinbeck—and shows the world of social feelings, collective bravery, hatred, and volition."[83] Still, despite his sharp and intimate portrayal of class struggle complete with Communist heroes, Steinbeck had not yet absorbed the collective outlook and continued to vacillate between involvement and aloofness. He was unable to create an "epically persuasive" picture of a strike or to feel the "spirit, pathos, and dynamics of a mass movement."[84] Reviewing the American edition of *In Dubious Battle* in 1937, a Soviet critic had observed that Steinbeck's Communist strike leaders were merely "tendentious images" and his workers an "unreliable and even terrifying force."[85] Balashov reiterated this criticism

---

[79] Nemerovskaya, "Kniga o lyubvi . . . ," *op.cit.*, p. 274.

[80] Abramov, "Dzhon Steinbek," *op.cit.*, p. 223.

[81] Balashov, "Pevets . . . ," *op.cit.*, p. 206.

[82] *ibid.*, p. 205.

[83] Abramov, "Dzhon Steinbek . . . ," *op.cit.*, p. 223.

[84] *ibid.*, p. 225.

[85] N. M., "Dzhon Steinbek—'V somnitelnoi skhvatke,'" *Internatsionalnaya literatura*, No. 4 (1937), p. 222.

in 1940, arguing that the novel suffered from a muddled notion of the elemental and the conscious and from a false opposition between the hero and the crowd. He was annoyed by the author's frequent allusions to the biological world and his speculations on the notion that the masses are "blindly seething and uncontrollable elements."[86]

One critic found that in his next work, *Of Mice and Men*, the author had squandered his talent in describing a "clinical case,"[87] but another felt that a new warmth and tenderness had gone into the story: although Lennie was a throwback to such doomed, pathological figures as Tularecito of *The Pastures of Heaven*, there was more than inert fatalism in this book, since, after mercifully destroying his moronic partner, George starts a friendship with another worker. For Steinbeck now realized that "a man, even the most unfortunate outcast, homeless and miserable, must never and will never be alone."[88]

The Grapes of Wrath, in the Russians' opinion, was largely free of Steinbeck's earlier weaknesses. There were mild criticisms of the "accentuated naturalism of some of the episodes," his lingering "attraction for the description of the pathological in man," his "propensities for the unusual, romantic, or tragic ornamentation of situations" and "keen interest in freakish manifestations of human psychology." Nevertheless, he was "different, transformed." An extreme example of the critics' enthusiasm was Miller-Budnitskaya's comparison of the weird and demented character, Muley Graves, to Robin Hood: "Like this legendary hero of the Anglo-Saxon yeomen, banished from the land by the Norman barons, Muley is a rebel. In token of social protest he goes off into the forest and declares partisan war on the sheriff and the law."[89] Another critic objected to this extravagance, pointing out, incidentally, that Oklahoma is "steppe," not forest, and concluded: "To lavish praise on a trashy book is bad; but it is no better to

[86] Balashov, "Pevets . . . ," *op.cit.*, p. 207.
[87] *ibid.*, p. 205.
[88] Abramov, "Dzhon Steinbek . . . ," *op.cit.*, p. 225.
[89] R. Miller-Budnitskaya, "Kniga gneva," *Znamya*, No. 8 (1940), p. 195.

distort a good book. We must put an end to the tolerance of such manifestations in the literary sphere."[90] A more sober and telling appraisal of Muley was that of Abramov: "Had he been an inhabitant of *The Pastures of Heaven*, he would have been in the show-case of Steinbeck's monsters, suffering from the caprice of chance. But here it is not chance that determines the tragic fate of the farmer. Muley is a victim of the evil will of people, of cold-blooded capitalistic accounting, of soulless bank operations."[91]

But was *The Grapes of Wrath* a revolutionary novel? Not quite. It was true that instead of being opposed to the crowd, Steinbeck's heroes were now closely identified with it. Man was no longer a purely biological entity, governed by the same laws as are lower forms of life, but a noble creature, capable of transforming his environment. The critics could talk about Steinbeck's "revolutionary humanism"[92] and could feel, with Nemerovskaya, that his characters "compel one to believe that there will come a day when these people, hardened by poverty and sorrow, will rally and destroy the conditions that are ruining and mutilating their lives."[93] Or they could conclude, like Chelovekov, that although the author makes no specific call for revolution his meaning is unmistakable.[94] However, even the most sanguine of Steinbeck's critics, dreaming of a "new epos of the future revolutionary struggle" in America, called his novel "only its precursor."[95] The "new revolutionary epos" has not appeared to this day. Like so many American liberals who were temporarily stirred by the political and social enthusiasms of the thirties, Steinbeck took up other literary interests. The Russians have not forgotten, however, that of the hundreds of proletarian works to emerge from the Depression, his novel came closest to fulfilling their demands.

[90] "Roman Steinbeka i yevo kritiki," *Internatsionalnaya literatura*, Nos. 9-10 (1940), p. 222.

[91] Abramov, "Dzhon Steinbek," *op.cit.*, p. 230.

[92] *ibid.*, p. 232.

[93] Nemerovskaya, "Kniga o lyubvi . . . ," *op.cit.*, p. 272.

[94] Chelovekov, *op.cit.*, p. 40.

[95] Miller-Budnitskaya, "Kniga gneva," *op.cit.*, p. 203.

The proletarian movement is regarded today as a relatively minor and undistinguished episode in the literary history of the United States. By and large its writers were mediocre. Few of them were accorded any stature by American critics of the time, and even fewer are now remembered. Moreover none of them except Steinbeck achieved a genuine success in Russia. The reading public was unenthusiastic, and the critics found them to be not only artistically inadequate but also less interesting than their petty bourgeois compatriots. Yet the critics offered them warm and constant encouragement and proclaimed them the most important and promising force in contemporary American literature.

This situation was not as paradoxical as it seems. Special attention was given to these writers because they came closer than any other Americans to satisfying the political demands of Soviet criticism. Their choice of topics and situations—the unemployment, poverty, social dislocation, and industrial strife brought on by the Depression—involved the class struggle in its most urgent and dramatic American version. In featuring working-class characters as conscious and inspired agents of social change, these writers seemed to be responding to the Soviet call for increased ideological militancy. Their failure to create superior works of art while writing acceptable political tracts could be considered only temporary. Soviet criticism was operating under an imperative that insisted that artistic profundity and perfection, political timeliness, and ideological purity could be combined in one and the same work of fiction. All that was needed to bring this about was a more determined effort on the part of the writer himself.

Alfred Kazin has pointed out that the American writers of the thirties were too shocked and bewildered by the rapidly developing tensions of the Depression to write superior works of social fiction. They were inclined to turn to dramatic reportage and documentary journalism as the only way of grasping and interpreting the public events which affected them too intimately to permit of artistic detachment. Soviet critics understood this tendency and sympathized with it to some extent, but in their revolutionary impatience they could not accept it as a fact of artistic life. Consequently they continued to insist that American proletarians strive for a combination of political activism and creative perfection in their fiction. The writer who came closest to achieving this ideal combination was Steinbeck, but Steinbeck was not a true revolutionary. In the early thirties, however, another American novelist of the left had been found so attractive that he became a vehicle through whom the Russians could discuss their own urgent and indigenous literary problems. The writer who provoked this intensive Soviet self-examination was John Dos Passos.

CHAPTER IV

JOHN DOS PASSOS

☙☙☙ IN THE SPRING of 1932, two Soviet writers, Korneli Zelinski and Pyotr Pavlenko, addressed an open letter to John Dos Passos, which began as follows:

"Dear Comrade!

"The two Soviet writers who address this letter to you are in Moscow, on this side of the ocean, and are your attentive readers. A great part of what you have written, as you undoubtedly know, has been translated and published in Russian: from *Three Soldiers* to *Manhattan Transfer* and *The 42d Parallel. 1919* is being published. Your works have entered the circle of our artistic controversies. And this is understandable. The originality and boldness of certain of your artistic devices and the power of your descriptive means provoke the need to discover the principles and ideas which underlie them. Why? All of us here, in the land of the Soviets, feel ourselves to be the pioneers and prospectors of the new Communist culture. One problem has decisive significance for the art of the majority of us: what comprises the method of dialectical materialism in literature, which will enable us to present the richest and most profound picture of reality. All aspects of a literary work—theme, choice of heroes, method of rendering them, manner of contrast—we strive to examine from the point of view of their class significance. The struggle with the survivals of capitalism in our consciousness, in our artistic creations—this is what determines our writers' interests today, this is what mobilizes us."[1]

This letter was written on the eve of the largest and most fundamental literary dispute that has ever arisen over an American writer in the Soviet Union. The critics who participated were aware that the controversy over Dos Passos

[1] Korneli Zelinski and Pyotr Pavlenko, "Pismo Dzhonu Dos Passosu," *Literatura mirovoi revolyutsii*, No. 4 (1932), p. 77. The letter also appeared in *Literaturnaya gazeta*, March 23, 1932, and in *International Literature*, Nos. 2-3 (1932), p. 109.

would have important consequences in the Soviet artistic
world itself, and might affect the creative destinies of many
Soviet writers. This American became for them a cultural
symbol, indicating one of the chief courses along which Russian literature might travel in the future.

Dos Passos had been known only slightly in the Russia of
the 1920's. A small Russian edition of *Three Soldiers* came
out in 1924 and passed into Soviet bookshelves with little
notice. It was classified among the "antimilitaristic" works of
the postwar generation of Western writers, a document of the
"senseless character of the World War."[2] The influence of
Freud on the author was duly noted, and the book was found
to display the stamp of Tolstoy's *War and Peace*;[3] but in general it stimulated only a mild and fleeting critical interest.

The only other work of Dos Passos to be published in Russia in the decade was *Manhattan Transfer*, which came out
in 1927. This book made a much stronger impression. At
the outset it was proclaimed a "bitter criticism of capitalism."[4]
Stylistically, the novel was a revelation to the critics, who
praised its "originality" and its "cinematic" techniques for
exploring the life of a big city.[5] There were complaints, however, of its "overdone psychology"[6] and of the sacrifice of
"action" to "talk and discussion."[7] The critics also feared
that Dos Passos might prove too esoteric for the Soviet reader. Nevertheless, his innovations were defended:

"Certainly, *Manhattan Transfer* is not a work for the
broad masses. . . . This kaleidoscope of characters, episodes,
and city scenes might even irritate the mass reader.

"But indeed the significance of a fact for the evolution of

[2] P. S. Kogan, "Sovremennaya literatura za rubezhem," *Krasnaya nov*,
No. 2 (1923), p. 321.

[3] Yuri Poletika, "Dzh. Dos Passos. *Tri soldata*," *Russki sovremennik*,
No. 4 (1924), p. 270.

[4] A. Tsingovalov, "Dzhon Dos Passos. *Mankhetten*," *Molodaya gvardiya*, No. 12 (1927), p. 222.

[5] *ibid.*, pp. 221-22; R. Kulle, "O sovremennoi amerikanskoi proze,"
Oktyabr, No. 9 (1929), p. 155; O. Nemerovskaya, "Roman kino-lenta," *Na
literaturnom postu*, No. 2 (1928), p. 30.

[6] Tsingovalov, p. 222.

[7] *ibid.*

literature can by no means always be measured by success with the reading public or accessibility for the masses. The history of literature has shown us this repeatedly. *Manhattan Transfer* as a literary fact is too new for us to talk about its role in the evolutionary process of literature. But in the literary laboratories, where they collect, grind up, and combine the tiny elements of which an artistic entity is created—it is a fact of great and indubitable importance, which gives writers a key to new constructions."[8]

Still, as late as 1930 Dos Passos was a relatively unknown quantity in Russia. His political activity (especially his efforts on behalf of Sacco and Vanzetti) and his expressed admiration for the Soviet Union caused the critics to consider him, politically, a fellow traveler. But apart from some preliminary probing into his creative methods and the ideas about art which underlay them, Soviet criticism made no attempt to assess his achievement.

Beginning in 1930, however, Soviet critics and writers developed an intense interest in the author. This was encouraged by the publication of a second edition of *Manhattan Transfer* in that year, and by the quick translation of *The 42d Parallel* in 1931, within a year after its first American appearance. Dos Passos became recognized as the most significant among the postwar generation of American writers, and for a time many critics considered him the most important contemporary writer of the non-Soviet world. From 1930 to 1936 there were three Russian editions of *The 42d Parallel*, two editions of *Manhattan Transfer*, two editions of *1919*, and one collection of Dos Passos' plays, one of which, *Fortune Heights*, was successfully produced on the Russian stage. He was repeatedly represented in Soviet periodicals, and parts of *The 42d Parallel* and *1919* were excerpted and circulated in book form. Altogether, over 117,000 copies of his various works were circulated during these years.

The years in which critical interest in the author was at its peak—1932, 1933, and 1934—were decisive in the history of Soviet literature. The Party envisaged the creation of a

[8] Nemerovskaya, p. 32.

single guiding literary theory which, after a period of exploration and development, would eventually be employed by all Soviet writers. The theory was called socialist realism.

As it was enunciated in this early period, however, socialist realism was a set of relatively broad principles. Furthermore, these principles were almost solely concerned with the ideological content of literature, and indicated very little of a specific nature about the manner in which this ideological substance could be made to take artistic shape. It remained for Soviet writers themselves—men of diverse artistic backgrounds and prejudices—to work out the creative techniques which would endow socialist realism with flesh and blood. A period of trial and error was inevitable.

The incentive for the study of Dos Passos was particularly strong for a number of reasons. First, there was a purely political justification for showing interest in this writer. The Russians must have felt that Dos Passos, both as a political figure and as a writer, could develop into a valuable ally. Second, his works had survived the passing of the NEP period in Soviet publication, and had continued to be issued in increasing numbers after 1929, at a time when those of other leading Americans were not. Third, Dos Passos, attempting to synthesize in his novels the leading concepts and techniques of American and European realism, embodied in his writing many of the best and most varied strains of twentieth-century literary thought. Through his books, Soviet writers could partake of a great variety of literary expression, representing trends in contemporary Western literature (Freudianism, for example) from which the Soviet literary world was to a great extent otherwise shut off. Finally, Dos Passos was a brilliant and original writer in his own right.

Sheer formal virtuosity, however, was never enough to arrest the attention of Soviet critics in the early 1930's. Accordingly, it is important that *U.S.A.* could be described as follows: "The trilogy of Dos Passos is the most powerful work of contemporary world revolutionary literature. The attempt to reveal the social motive forces of contemporary American capitalism; the relentless hatred toward the exploiting classes and the constant exposure of their hypocritical policies and practices, which acquire special significance now in the epoch of 'camouflage' tactics of world imperialism, the militant class purposefulness, which penetrates the pages devoted to the history of the revolutionary movement in America; and finally the aspiration to transmit the very pulse of a huge historical epoch, to catch and imprint the rhythm of social storms—all of this explains the tremendous revolutionary significance of the still unfinished trilogy."[9] Many critics gave the impression that here, for the first time, they had found an artist in American society who was capable of exposing its deepest contradictions. However, the question was always one of potentialities. Nearly every laudatory estimation of his accomplishment, such as the one just quoted, was accompanied by a reservation such as the following, which is quoted from the same context: "Therefore all of the vacillations, all of the internal contradictions of the art of Dos Passos must be disclosed with great attentiveness, and his artistic devices must be subjected to minute analysis from the point of view of their class significance."[10] In the course of examining these "vacillations" and "internal contradictions" Soviet critics employed their concept of the unity of form and content, and indicated their views of the relationship between style and ideology.

At the outset the critics had become convinced that Dos Passos' inventiveness in literary craftsmanship was closely linked with the subjective sources of his creative urge. The basis of this urge, they felt, was a strong sensitivity to injustice and a powerful idealism, and a consequent rebellion against the evils that confronted him in the real world. But more important, they believed, was the inner struggle to resolve for himself the glaring contradictions between his revolutionary aspirations and his bourgeois tastes. One critic put it this way in 1933: "At the basis of the creative genius of Dos Passos lies a huge thirst for petty happiness, a peaceful,

---

[9] R. Miller-Budnitskaya, "Kniga o velikoi nenavisti," *Zalp*, No. 5 (1933), p. 68.
[10] *ibid.*

comfortable Philistine happiness, which in the age of imperialism and proletarian revolution becomes especially unfeasible. The deep organic soil of his revolutionism is resentment toward the capitalist world because it impedes this happiness."[11]

Tracing his ideological development, the critics found that Dos Passos' rebellion had first been impelled by a horror of war. In *One Man's Initiation* and *Three Soldiers* his protest against the "senselessness" of the World War had taken the form of a "yearning to flee from reality, to find a subjective, unreal, imaginary solution to its objective disharmony."[12] His early pacifism was colored by a hatred of all forms of organization, especially the military, which, he felt, repressed the individual.[13] While he perceived the connection between imperialism and war, the critics argued, he could not bring himself to accept a solution—revolution—which involved organized and disciplined struggle. All through his works, they contended, there ran a thread of anarchistic individualism, of fear lest the private personality become engulfed in the mass effort. While he hated capitalism because it stultified the soul, he feared that socialism, which involved strong obligations to the collective, might prove equally oppressive.

Still, he had made great progress in overcoming these petty bourgeois attitudes.[14] Both his political activities and writings, the critics felt, showed that he was losing his subjective distaste for collective action and had ceased to shrink from social necessity in an industrial age. As one critic described his development: "That anticapitalist spirit which permeated the

[11] D. Mirski, "Dos Passos, sovetskaya literatura i zapad," *Literaturny kritik*, No. 1 (1933), p. 121.

[12] A. Yelistratova, "Pervaya kniga Dzhona Dos Passosa," *Literatura mirovoi revolyutsii*, Nos. 9-10 (1932), p. 123.

[13] Miller-Budnitskaya, *op.cit.*, p. 65.

[14] Comparing him with Ernest Hemingway in 1934, a critic wrote: "From the crossroads where Hemingway and Dos Passos parted, two roads lead—that of Dos Passos . . . is the road of hunger marches, the road on which cyclones of social shock and whirlwinds of revolution rage. And the other path, that of Hemingway, leads to the closed arena of bull fights, to the stifling confession-chair, where they atone by prayer for the sinful thirst of life." Ivan Kashkin, "Smert posle poludnya," *Literaturny kritik*, No. 9 (1934), p. 147.

first works of Dos Passos—that powerful and at the same time passive protest against bourgeois conditions with which these books are impregnated—permits one to describe Dos Passos' manner of writing in his first period as critical realism. But Dos Passos has gone further in his criticism: he has understood that the future belongs to the proletariat, and has presented in his epic a series of extremely powerful examples of revolutionary fighters. The critical realism of Dos Passos is pervaded with revolutionary tendencies. . . ."[15]

At the same time, neither his ideology nor his writing was genuinely revolutionary as yet. He was still too greatly overwhelmed by the irony inherent in the contradictions of capitalism, and was consequently too preoccupied with showing decay. One critic commented: "Dos Passos . . . still knows only the negative work of sociology, and not the positive. He knows how to hate better than to love."[16]

The theory of socialist realism insists that there is an organic relationship between the ideological content of a work and the style in which it is written. In the case of Dos Passos, the problem of the relationship between form and content was a particularly nagging one and, as it developed, exceedingly complex. (The transcript of a three-day symposium on the author in 1933 alone runs to sixty pages of searching polemic.) In discussing Dos Passos, Russian writers and critics were actually, to a great extent, discussing themselves. Dozens of pages of criticism which were nominally devoted to Dos Passos were actually concerned with an interpretation of the ideas of Marx, Engels, and Lenin, with the theoretical relationship between radical bourgeois and revolutionary proletarian literature, with a criticism of Freudian psychology, and with the evaluation of such Western literary influences as James Joyce and Gertrude Stein. All of these topics were made to bear directly on the question of the relationship between form and content in Dos Passos' art and, ultimately, on the question whether Russian literature could follow the

[15] A. Mingulina, "K sporam o Dos Passose," *Znamya*, No. 11 (1934), p. 255.
[16] T. Levit, "Dos Passos," *Literatura i iskusstvo*, Nos. 3-4 (1930), p. 213.

path of Dos Passos and still remain true to Soviet ideology.

Although most of the Soviet discussion of the author applied to everything he had written, the critics concentrated on the first two books in the *U.S.A.* trilogy. More specifically, they studied the Newsreel and the Camera Eye, two of the four devices used in the novels. The Newsreel received the most favorable appraisal, although there was, characteristically, a difference of opinion regarding it. The Newsreel consists chiefly of bits of news stories, newspaper headlines, slogans, and snatches of popular songs, which are interspersed between the narrative sections of the book to suggest the general or collective atmosphere of a given period. Here is one Soviet opinion of the device, addressed to the author himself: ". . . in the attempt to arrive at maximum objectivity, you tend to become mentally divorced from life. . . . The stenographs of newspapers and everyday life in *The 42d Parallel* involuntarily recall the empirical method of Joyce, who wants to produce an inventory of the world, like a sheriff or agent of justice in the pursuit of his legal duties. This is not ours, this is the bourgeois approach to things. Our problem is not to see the world like an ant, crawling from particle to particle, but to comprehend the real makeup of the world, in order to change it."[17]

But a Soviet defender of the Newsreel challenged this criticism in the following terms: "How can one speak of the author's 'mental divorcement from life' when every line of the Newsreel bears witness to the active involvement of the author, to the fact that the author takes from the archives of history precisely those facts, those documents which all, to a greater or less degree, present a clot of the contradictions of a given historical moment."[18] This critic cited passages from a typical Newsreel and asked, rhetorically: "Can this be 'accidental' selection of the first facts that came into his hands? An objective, indifferent, indiscriminate inventory of living phenomena, without a demonstration of their interconnections, their contradictions? Is it indeed possible that the ab-

[17] Zelinski and Pavlenko, *op.cit.*, p. 77.
[18] Yelistratova, *op.cit.*, p. 123.

sence of any sort of integrating commentary on the part of the author lessens the ideological-political significance of these images which help to tear the mask from reality and to show the quivering, living tissue, muscles, and nerves of its social contradictions?"[19] The critic concluded that the Newsreel was "... not only not an alien echo of Joycean empiricism, but, on the contrary, the most progressive, most revolutionary link of his creative method as a whole, permitting him to approach ... a genuine example of revolutionary realism in literature."[20] The opposition between these two interpretations of the Newsreel is fundamental. One of them suggests that the author acts merely as an unselective reporter, recording scenes and events chaotically, without attempting their synthesis. The other contends that there is in fact a principle governing the apparent chaos, and that the author's juxtaposition of superficially unrelated materials is calculated and tendentious.[21]

There was yet a third interpretation of the Newsreel, which partook of each of the other two. In this view, the Newsreel is the work of an artist who is indeed opinionated, but whose powers of discrimination, clouded by an immature ideology, are not sufficiently sharp to enable him to distinguish between the historically important and the unimportant:

"Some of our writers have read Dos Passos and said: 'How interesting! At the beginning there are some newspaper cuttings and then in the middle there are biographies of people.'

"Dos Passos' form is his weakness—a weakness not only of a formal character. What is the source of this weakness? The young American intellectual went to the war. He saw the spectacle of ruin, but he lacked an integral view of life. For this reason he writes the biographies of his heroes one after the other, so that these biographies may compose a general picture. But he feels that these biographies are taking

[19] *ibid.*
[20] *ibid.*
[21] Zelinski was the only critic to contend that this underlying principle was bourgeois in nature. "Dnevnik proisshestvii," *Literaturny kritik*, No. 3 (1933), p. 92.

place against the background of history; and he cannot generalize. He therefore puts in insertions and excerpts from newspapers in order to glue together that background which his inability to generalize prevents him from portraying."[22] Nevertheless, not all of those who put forth this interpretation found the Newsreel to be devoid of value: "The inventiveness of Dos Passos is a result of his inability to show an epoch rationally, to unfold it completely. But the merit of the writer is nevertheless in the fact that he has succeeded in transforming his shortcoming into a positive quality, and although the newspaper headlines are no substitute for the extremely complex contour-maps of the epoch, nevertheless they do constitute a certain background, and the acuteness of the device compensates somewhat for its lack of depth."[23]

The Camera Eye is a subjective, impressionistic, stream-of-consciousness kind of passage which the author regularly inserts among the main narrative passages, Newsreels, and biographical essays. Largely autobiographical in nature, it is designed to convey the author's pristine impressions of his surroundings and growth from time to time. This device in Dos Passos' writing was the one most severely criticized; while many Soviet critics undertook to explain its use in terms of the problems which the author set for himself, few of them attempted to defend it. There were a number of aspects to the attack. First of all, with its emphasis on subconscious motivation the Camera Eye, it was contended, suffered severely from "Freudianism."[24] Second, the method bespoke, in the opinion of some critics, a passive attitude toward the complexities of the human situation: ". . . the Camera Eye is a clear expression of a passive, fatalistic world perception. The author wants to be merely a sensitive plate, an objective camera, photographing reality as a chaos of broken sensations."[25]

[22] Karl Radek, "Contemporary World Literature and the Tasks of Proletarian Art," *Problems of Soviet Literature* (New York, 1934), pp. 180-81.

[23] Ilya Selvinski, "Novatorstvo ili 'nyumenstvo,'" in "Sovetskaya literatura i Dos Passos," *Znamya*, No. 6 (1933), pp. 155-56.

[24] Miller-Budnitskaya, *op.cit.*, p. 70; Levit, *op.cit.*, p. 214.

[25] Miller-Budnitskaya, p. 70.

Furthermore, it was hostile to the materialist world view: "The very form of the Camera Eye—the internal monologue —is borrowed from Joyce and has deep roots in reactionary idealistic philosophy, hostile to the intellect and glorifying the cult of the irrational. The philosophical basis of this form is the representation of the subconscious as the fundamental core, the omnivorous element of the human psyche, which is at the same time the primary substance of the universe."[26] Finally: "The Camera Eye of Dos Passos is absolutely unconnected either in plot or association, or tactically, with the general text of the novel. . . . This is not a poetic trick, nor the marginal drawings of a poem—this is something from the spinal cord, pretentious and sick."[27] The Camera Eye was thus associated with cultural decadence, with philosophical theories and psychological attitudes inimical to the dialectical-materialist conception of the universe.

The Newsreel was not universally condemned in Soviet criticism, whereas the Camera Eye was rather consistently disparaged. Nevertheless, in most instances the critics tended to lump the two devices together, since each was an innovation and both were attempts to present ideas and images in what was considered a bizarre manner of association. Furthermore, although the two were discussed separately and together, the critics were ultimately concerned with their relationship to the novels as a whole, since it was universally agreed that the total impact of a work is far more important than the brilliance of its parts. And in this respect, they decided, the novels of *U.S.A.*, while extremely powerful in sum, did lack unity and integration. As one critic expressed it: "He has been compelled to combine mechanically several methods of creative work, various modes and genres. I repeat, combine mechanically, not dialectically, not organically. One can regard the Camera Eye, the Newsreel, and the biographical interludes with which he breaks up the trend of his novels, variously, but one thing is incontestable: the effectiveness of

[26] *ibid.*
[27] Selvinski, *op.cit.*, p. 155.

the novels is weakened by the mechanical coexistence of these
various genres."[28]

There were conflicting explanations of this annoying dif-
fuseness in Dos Passos' work. One of the most frequent was
that he was simply trying to match his revolutionary political
and social ideas with a comparably revolutionary art form,
which resulted in a sincere, if mistaken, avant-garde pose.[29]
Unsure of himself and lacking firmness in his revolutionary
convictions, the author sought to buttress his ideological position by becoming an artistic iconoclast.

A second explanation held that the coexistence of conflicting methods in Dos Passos' novels was simply a product of
poverty of understanding. As one critic put it, ". . . it seems
to me that his complicated structure is explained precisely by
his inability to see all of the diversity of the world as a unity,
the inability to find the fundamental, to find the pivot around
which one must place that which is necessary, and to discard
that which can be dispensed with."[30] According to this view,
Dos Passos' method beclouded his thinking and rendered
complex many phenomena that were intrinsically simple. By
being so all-inclusive and trying to combine several different
approaches in one novel, Dos Passos failed to give pattern
and direction to his picture of bourgeois society.

Another explanation of his puzzling mixture of genres,
however, held that this was actually an artistically legitimate
and indeed politically progressive means for exploring the life
of bourgeois society. Some thought that his picture of complexity reflected most accurately the contradictions and chaos
of the bourgeois world. These critics said in effect: Dos Passos is confused and he has deep bourgeois roots. But he is
aware of his confusion, and he is honest. Under the circumstances it is sufficient that he give us an honest picture of the

[28] A. Leites, in "Soviet Literature and Dos Passos," *International Literature*, No. 5 (1933-34), p. 104.

[29] V. Stenich, "Kak rabotayet Dos Passos," in "Sovetskaya literatura i Dos Passos," *Znamya*, No. 6 (1933), p. 153.

[30] I. Makaryev, "Za literaturu 'tipichnykh kharakterov' i 'tipichnykh obstoyatelstv,'" in "Sovetskaya literatura i Dos Passos," *Znamya*, No. 6 (1933), p. 148.

complexities of his world. The authority of Engels was cited: "The words of Engels about the socialistically tendentious novel—that this novel shatters the 'optimism of the bourgeois world'—are well known. Dos Passos is a revolutionary pessimist in relation to capitalism. In this he is near to us. Dos Passos feels sharply the crash of the old world, and all of his artistic system is adapted to showing this feeling of crash."[31]

There were also those who contended that underneath the apparent confusion of four separate genres in one novel there existed a thematic unity that transcended all the superficial discord, and that "the compositional structure of Dos Passos' novels is subordinated to an extremely specific objective. . . ."[32] This objective was to "disclose the shocking inhumanity" of capitalism:[33] "He has directed himself from the pulverization and dismemberment of the world into the separate details and aspects of life—to an understanding of the laws of the whole. By this means he reconstructs the genuine wholeness of the world, and for art its fabric of imagery. . . . He presents not the simple empirics of a newsreel's scattered mass of separate details, he gives his own reasoned and, for his level of understanding, precise expression of this world . . . he proceeds from details to generalization, and by this very means he saves and restores the integrality of the image. . . ."[34] These critics did not argue, however, that Dos Passos had attained a complete unity of theme. In the opinion of one of them, this "is not yet socialist realism, but it is already anti-capitalist revolutionary realism."[35]

But there was yet a fifth interpretation of Dos Passos' stylistic complexities, offered by the sophisticated critic Mirsky, who had recently returned to Russia after years of self-exile in Western Europe and had the advantages of an in-

---

[31] V. Pertsov, "Litsom k deistvitelnosti," in "Sovetskaya literatura i Dos Passos," *Znamya*, No. 6 (1933), p. 158.

[32] Mingulina, *op.cit.*, p. 252.

[33] V. Kirpotin, "O sotsialisticheskom realizme," *Literaturny kritik*, No. 1 (1933), p. 40.

[34] Kirpotin, as quoted in Mingulina, *op.cit.*, p. 252.

[35] Kirpotin, *op.cit.*, p. 40.

timate acquaintance with modern Western literature. Mirsky pointed out that Dos Passos' association with the circle of Gertrude Stein in Paris had provided the author with strong incentives to experimentation in technique and had encouraged him to seek new prisms through which to study the world about him. This led Mirsky to suggest that there was a more profound reason for Dos Passos' formalistic tendencies. In commenting on what he considered the essentially selfish source of the writer's rebellion, Mirsky wrote that "Dos Passos is so intelligent, such a powerful artist, that he is able to approach his own bourgeois infantilism ironically."[36] What is important here is that, in addition to being a source of his irony, Dos Passos' understanding of himself was also the wellspring of his formal method. Realizing that his bourgeois background distorted his vision of reality, so this argument goes, he often affected a kind of artificial naivete, as exemplified in the Camera Eye. This characteristic he had in common with Gertrude Stein. But Miss Stein's infantilism, Mirsky contended, was an escapist device. In contrast: "Dos Passos 'makes himself little' in order to become like that boy who alone of all the people in the hall divined that the king was naked. The naivete of Dos Passos is first of all an act of freeing himself from various and sundry false conceptions imposed on reality by bourgeois ideology. He disowns any explanation of reality because all of the old has turned out false and to the new he has not come, organically, as an artist. His naivete is legitimate and indispensable; it is a necessary stage for him on the path to revolution."[37] Dos Passos' affected "naivete" was thus a defensive weapon in his battle to master the complexities of the capitalist world about him. It protected him from the necessity of pronouncing judgments which he lacked the ideological maturity to make. Hence his "infantilism" and the stylistic innovations which it bred were necessary to his creative process during his period of transition from rebel to revolutionary.

From the opinions I have quoted thus far it is evident that the question of Dos Passos' style was viewed not simply as

[36] Mirski, *op.cit.*, p. 121.   [37] *ibid.*

a matter of compositional technique, but, much more fundamentally, as a problem in the cognition of reality. By the
early 1930's there was a distinct Dos Passos vogue in Russia;
young Soviet writers were imitating this American, and Russian books were being published which, to Soviet critics, displayed an unmistakable Dos Passos influence.[38] It was clear
that, if Russians were writing like Dos Passos, they must also
be inclined to think like him. And if, as many Soviet critics
contended, his methods were ideologically unsound, then anyone who attempted to follow them would be bound to arrive
at distorted conclusions. As a consequence, much of the discussion of Dos Passos centered around the theory of realism
in art and its application to the specific problems of literature
in a socialist society.

The main point at issue was the question of selectivity.
Some critics felt that "Marxism-Leninism" had given Soviet
literature a mandate to "capture phenomena in all their many-
sidedness and complexity." They were inclined to defend
Dos Passos' methods, and to suggest that Soviet literature
would profit by emulating him. If the problem of realistic
literature was to expose life as fully as possible, these critics
argued, then why not employ any and every device that comes
to hand, if it is practicable and intelligible? Further, they
contended, psychological and sociological truth is composed
of an infinity of details, each of which can be made to shed
light on the whole. To neglect these details would be to neglect integral parts of the larger truth, for truth is complex
and can be comprehended only through painstaking attention
to its smallest parts. The artist must be selective, they agreed,
but he cannot afford to ignore the most subtle facets of reality;
and, if he can display these facets only through a multiplicity
of means, then he is obligated to do so.

[38] Stenich, "Kak rabotayet . . . ," *op.cit.*, p. 153; Pertsov, *op.cit.*, p.
157; Kirpotin, *op.cit.*, p. 37; Zelinski, "Dnevnik . . . ," *op.cit.*, p. 88.
Zelinski mentioned two current Soviet works with a Dos Passos influence: S. Gekht, *Moi posledniye vstrechi*, and A. Kucherov, *Dvenadtsat let*,
"whole pages of which simply imitate Dos Passos." Other strongly negative comments on the Dos Passos influence are in Ye. Tager, "Dos Passos
v 'perevode' Gekhta," *Khudozhestvennaya literatura*, No. 1 (1933), pp.
11-12.

The opponents of these critics contended that, while the artist must not neglect the nuances of objective truth, he must concentrate his attention on the essentials of life, which is an historical and social process whose tendency is measurable and predictable. The material with which the realistic writer must work, they agreed, is complex, but it must be repeatedly winnowed and sifted, because truth is dynamic and selective in itself. There is a hierarchy among observable phenomena, so this argument goes, since many phenomena are dying and passing from the human scene. The problem of the artist is to discriminate among this infinity of details, and to keep himself from becoming involved in minutiae which are remote from, or unessential to, the pattern of human progress. These critics held that there is always a pattern in the most diverse manifestations of life, and that this pattern is capable of being captured in literature. Therefore, they maintained, the writer need not draw a picture of chaos, and, further, a true picture of life will not be chaotic. As one critic stated it: ". . . to see the many-sidedness of the world does not mean to see its fundamentals. . . . The world is complex and varied, one must study it in all its variety, in the movement of its multiformity, but one must always know how to select the fundamental link."[39] This fundamental link, of course, was dialectical materialism. Equipped with this, the critics argued, a writer can distinguish between the significant and the insignificant, can find the typical in the midst of diversity, and can consequently reject the multitudes of irrelevant details— such as the nuances of subconscious psychology and the transitory minutiae of daily existence—that distract him from the pursuit of central truth about life.

These, in their bare essentials, are the opposing points of view that underlay the disagreements over whether the methods of Dos Passos should be allowed to influence Soviet writers. While some of the critics who participated were content to present largely theoretical and doctrinal arguments, the best of them (always risking the accusation of "formalism" themselves) engaged in close and detailed formal analysis

[39] Makaryev, *op.cit.*, pp. 147-48.

of Dos Passos' works in an attempt to show concretely the relationship between the author's aims and his devices in the light of his ideology and the literary influences which shaped his art.

Some critics felt that Dos Passos was actually working his way out of complexity of style and into simplicity. They noted that, in some respects, the first two novels of *U.S.A.* were more unified than *Manhattan Transfer,* and even predicted that, once he had completed the final novel in the trilogy, Dos Passos would adopt a less complex technique.[40] This would be an artistic consequence of ideological "maturity."[41] Were he to eliminate the last vestiges of his dying "bourgeois" ideology and commit himself fully to communism, his doubts and vacillations about the way in which he should look at the world, about which prism to choose in studying reality, would disappear. A firm social and political philosophy would unify his thoughts about his characters. His writing would show the rise of the new as well as the decay of the old. It would show optimism, not pessimism, would be harmonious, not discordant. None of these critics, however, could point to a single example of a contemporary author of similar stature who had been able to accomplish more than Dos Passos along these lines. Herein was the crux of the problem which Dos Passos posed for Soviet literature.

Soviet criticism was committed at the time to a theoretical proposition concerning literary style which had not been demonstrated in practice. Ironically enough, it might turn out that this writer from the "decadent" world of capitalism would show them the way. And in fact much of the argument, both in favor of and against accepting a Dos Passos influence, was presented in terms of the larger question of the degree to which contemporary Russian literature should borrow from the bourgeois West. The implications of this question were as much political as they were aesthetic; for, while it was possible at that time to argue that Soviet literature might

[40] V. Stenich, "Rech o Dos Passose," *Zvezda*, No. 8 (1933), p. 164; Leites, *op.cit.*, p. 168.

[41] Stenich, "Kak rabotayet . . . ," *op.cit.*, p. 153.

profit from a study of Western creative techniques, it was impossible to argue that these techniques denoted fundamental cultural superiority of the capitalist West over the Soviet Union. This was a paradoxical situation, and it involved much intellectual tightrope walking, particularly on the part of those who argued in favor of studying contemporary Western literature.

I have indicated that a particularly strong Western aspect of Dos Passos' writing which gave the critics pause was the reputed influence of James Joyce on the author. The critics generally agreed (although the agreement was extremely reluctant in some quarters) [42] that Joyce was a bourgeois intellectual whose methods were reactionary. Describing these methods and their influence on Dos Passos, one critic wrote: "This style as a method of imaged cognition of the world served the following aim: the proclamation of the preeminence of the subconscious; the destruction of the causal and temporal connections of phenomena; the recognition that the only reality of the world is splintered into the simplest fractured elements of sensation; the depiction of reality as chaos, a hellish dance of sensation. The influence of the style of Joyce on Dos Passos, this artist of the most profound rotting of the imperialist epoch, had a deeply onerous, destructive character, leading the author of the trilogy into the dead end of unresolvable contradictions." [43] Here it should be noted that some critics who ostensibly agreed that Joyce was reactionary in method nevertheless argued he should be studied: "When, in the course of seven years, Joyce created *Ulysses*, he broke new ground and entered areas where no one had been before. The fellow worked gropingly, and, as Copernicus discovered the rotation of the earth around the sun, he also found his own system. We ought not to imitate Joyce entirely. I repeat, this is a pattern of literature, but it is necessary to study the separate devices of Joyce. Not to study, to ignore Joyce, is laughable, just as it would be laughable for a physi-

[42] Vishnevski even interrupted the speech of an opponent to insist: "Joyce is not bourgeois." This is in the context of Makaryev, p. 144.
[43] Miller-Budnitskaya, *op.cit.*, p. 69.

cist to say that he wants to work without considering Einstein's theory of relativity, or without considering the system of Copernicus—but instead the system of Ptolemy."[44]

Some contended that it was in the spirit of this inquiring physicist that Dos Passos had studied Joyce. The critic Levit argued, for example, that Dos Passos had employed Joyce's methods of perceiving reality in an attempt to develop a revolutionary understanding, and that he was "growing up out of naturalism, proceeding through Joyceism on the path to realism."[45] Still others, in a related argument, contended that some of Dos Passos' borrowing from Joyce had been for the very purpose of undermining the ideology which Joyce was purported to represent:

"Dos Passos availed himself of the method of Joyce for the creation of a huge foundation, a tremendous roadbed for the social life of the USA in the beginning of the twentieth century. But with Dos Passos this method serves for the unmasking of the 'average man,' that is, an aim diametrically opposed to that of Joyce."[46] To this degree, they argued, Dos Passos' writing was a triumph of ideology over method.

Others insisted that the resemblance between Dos Passos and Joyce was superficial, and that a much more decisive influence on the author had been that of Gertrude Stein. Mirsky contended that the Steinesque "naivete" was actually an aid to Dos Passos in developing a revolutionary perception of reality. Here again the theory developed that, in borrowing from a purely bourgeois influence, Dos Passos had actually worked toward undermining that influence. One critic remarked that his "primitivism" and "childish syntax" had become his "satirical armor," and concluded: "Yes, the 'studies' of Dos Passos with Stein became . . . armament directed against the very kernel of her art."[47] Nevertheless, these critics agreed that it would be dangerous for Soviet writers to experiment with such a method. Mirsky outlined this peril as

[44] Stenich, "Kak rabotayet . . . ," *op.cit.*, p. 151.
[45] Levit, *op.cit.*, p. 210.
[46] Miller-Budnitskaya, *op.cit.*, p. 71.
[47] N. Eishiskina, "Primitivism i prostota," *Literaturny kritik*, No. 1 (1936), p. 180.

follows: "I have already shown how external and superficial is the resemblance between Dos Passos and Joyce. But it is precisely this lack of resemblance that makes Dos Passos an especially plausible escort into the lost paradise of formalism. The path to Joyce through Dos Passos is opposite from the path of Dos Passos himself. Having received (not as much from Joyce as from other formalist writers) a series of formalist devices, Dos Passos weakened them and deprived them of their specifically formalistic character, so that formalism is confined to the purpose of moving from a less sharp and penetrating form to a more pointed and protruding one. Our 'innovators' want to turn back the stream of history, and to proceed from the latter to the former."[48]

All of this led up to the final question of whether or not Dos Passos should be allowed to influence Soviet writers. The answer was, in the aggregate, that he must not. Most critics insisted that he was worthy of study, and no one suggested, at least at that time, that he should not be read. But they decided (although not unanimously) that, in the first place, many of his methods were intrinsically reactionary in an ideological sense. Second, they agreed (although again not unanimously) that the artistic problems which confronted Dos Passos were those of the bourgeois world, and that his solutions, by and large, could not be applied to the problems of Soviet artists.[49]

The notion that the problems of literary technique under socialism should be fundamentally different from those under capitalism has produced an attitude of exclusiveness that has done great harm to Soviet literature since the early thirties. It is one of a series of prejudices that come from the assumption that since the Soviet way of life is qualitatively superior, the Soviet manner of doing things in all spheres must also be distinct from and superior to the capitalist way. As a consequence of this ideologically dictated narrowing of horizons,

[48] Mirski, *op.cit.*, p. 123.
[49] Vishnevski's was the loudest minority voice in this respect. For his dispute with Mirsky on the subject, see Mirski, *op.cit.*, and Vishnevski, "Znat zapad!" *Literaturny kritik*, No. 7 (1933), pp. 79-95.

the Soviet arts in general have been deprived of a great many ideas and influences that could have freshened and enriched them. The imperative of finding new laws of creativity to suit a brave new socialist art has led to the distortion, and even the corruption, of many of the principles that have inspired the great literature of the world. The concept of tragedy, for example, has become pallid and shallow in the hands of Soviet theorists. Only by adhering rigidly to a fixed aesthetic code and by refusing to experiment with devices that are current in the literature of capitalist nations can the Soviet writer protect himself from the danger of falling into heresy. Formal experimentation that can lend depth, vitality, and interest to a work of literature can also lead to misinterpretation by Party critics that can be fatal to the career of the writer.

It is of course questionable whether *any* literary device, in and of itself, can rightly be called reactionary in a political or ideological sense. The very attempt to arrive at such a finding is totalitarian in its essence. And it is important to note that some critics objected to having the discussion of Dos Passos formulated in these terms. But their objections were overruled. Not only did the doctrinal intolerance that stifled their arguments rob Soviet literature of valuable Western sources of fertilization; it also instilled an attitude of condescension and a tone of hidebound self-righteousness in Soviet pronouncements on Western literature. For the next two decades the majority of Soviet critics complacently dismissed the formal experiments of contemporary American writers by disparaging them with an arsenal of clichés that were as obtuse as they were monotonous.

Having decided that Dos Passos must not be allowed to influence Soviet writers, several critics asserted that, in the last analysis, Dos Passos himself should do the borrowing. Only by adopting the Communist approach could he find complete artistic fulfillment. Many gave the impression that they felt that Dos Passos was eagerly awaiting such comradely advice as they could give him, and that one of the main purposes of the dispute was to determine just how they could guide their American ally. The artist himself had not asked for Soviet technical assistance. But the sense of leading a global cultural revolution had lent a tone of paternal solicitude to Soviet criticism. Smug in the certainty of ultimate cultural victory, the critics were also naive in their belief that the discontented writers of America needed their aesthetic advice.

The discussion of the relationship of Soviet literature to Dos Passos extended from 1930 to 1936. There are two notable facts, however, which indicate that a policy decision was arrived at shortly after the symposium in 1933, perhaps as a direct consequence of that symposium. For the last year in which it was mentioned that Dos Passos was actually influencing, or threatened to influence, Soviet writers was 1933. Likewise, the last open plea for accepting a Dos Passos influence was published in that year.[50] If it can be presumed that this American was as interesting to practicing Soviet artists as the critics and writers whom I have cited thought he was, then, in the absence of authoritative pressure to discourage it, a "Dos Passos school" in Soviet literature would have continued to develop. The fact that this did not happen shows that the critic Pertsov was right when he predicted in 1933 that Dos Passos would prove to be "the vogue of a single literary season."[51] It is obvious, however, that the apparently unanimous eschewal of Dos Passos by practicing writers after 1933 must have been achieved at the cost of some individual frustration.[52]

The decision not to endorse Dos Passos' methods by no means indicated a loss of publishing interest in the writer. In fact, 1936 was the peak year of his publication in Russia. Despite his reputed deficiencies, he was still considered the leading and the most promising anticapitalist writer in America. It is true that the optimism with which Soviet critics viewed his development was tinged with anxiety and caution, as indicated in the following remarks, both made in 1935:

[50] Vishnevski, "Znat zapad!" op.cit.   [51] Pertsov, op.cit., p. 157.
[52] Zelinski, for example, used the argument that Dos Passos had influenced two Soviet writers because they themselves were "petty bourgeois." Zelinski, "Dnevnik . . . ," op.cit., p. 88.

"We do not yet know where Dos Passos is going, just as we do not know the destiny of all those who, together with him, have torn themselves away from the world of desolation and death."[53]

"Dos Passos is subjectively with us, with the proletarian revolution. But his creative method is bound to a position of neutrality, to a passive attitude to life."[54]

As late as 1936, however, several critics contended that he was on the way to conquering his bourgeois inheritance. One of them asserted that in *1919*, which was his most "realistic" novel to date, he had at last found a "positive hero" in his character, the labor organizer Ben Compton. His art had progressed "at first uncertainly, and then more and more persistently, gradually overcoming the formalistic inventions of his complex composition."[55] And in this year it was still possible to express admiration for his devices, as one critic did when he asserted that Dos Passos had "reconstructed the very rhythm of prose narration," and had "increased the scale of activity of the writer,"[56] although there was the usual reservation that "not every reader is prepared for this influence," and that for even sophisticated readers Dos Passos' style was, unfortunately, calculated to appeal more to emotion than to intellect.[57]

Then, at the end of 1936, Soviet publication of Dos Passos abruptly ceased. Likewise, he nearly vanished from the pages of Soviet criticism. The contrast between the period through 1936 and the years following is profound. It was almost as if this man, the "outstanding American revolutionary writer,"[58] had never existed. Dozens of American writers were listed time after time in articles, bibliographies, chronicles, open letters, "comradely greetings," and reviews in Soviet periodicals, but Dos Passos' name was always absent.

[53] Al. Abramov, "Molodost veka," *Internatsionalnaya literatura*, No. 6 (1935), p. 141.
[54] Korneli Zelinski, "Dzhon Dos Passos," *Pravda*, September 10, 1935.
[55] Olga Nemerovskaya, "Sovremennaya amerikanskaya literatura," *Sovetskoye studenchestvo*, No. 6 (1936), p. 85.
[56] Nik. Aseyev, "Dos Passos," *Literaturnaya gazeta*, January 15, 1936.
[57] *ibid.*   [58] Radek, *op.cit.*, p. 79.

This development roughly coincides with Dos Passos' own departure from American left-wing literary activity. There appears to have been no formal denunciation of him in Russian journals, and there is no documentation of the correlation between the change in his politics and the curtailment of critical literature about him in the Soviet Union. It is probable, however, that this boycott of the author was an act of political reprisal. His opinions had ceased to suit the Communist Party, and so the publication of his works, and critical consideration of them as well, were officially terminated.

It will also be remembered that his Russian popularity was based, in the main, on the novels *The 42d Parallel* and *1919*, and that Soviet critics eagerly awaited the final novel in the trilogy which, they hoped, would show ideological "progress" over its predecessors. This novel, *The Big Money*, was published in the United States in 1936. It was not only more pessimistic and defeatist than the first two, but could also be interpreted as a denunciation of American Communists. Contrary to the hopes and even the predictions of Soviet critics, Dos Passos' outlook on the world had become increasingly desolate and, from the Soviet standpoint, passive. This book may have convinced Soviet critics that there was no more to expect from him. *The Big Money* was never published in Russia. Further, "the simpler style" which some critics had looked forward to did materialize in *The Adventures of a Young Man* (1939), but this was certainly not the result of the kind of ideological development they had hoped for.

The repudiation of Dos Passos that took place in 1936 has remained in effect to the present. Soviet critics have since referred to him, but only for the purpose of illustrating the reputed deterioration of current American literature. In 1949 a critic wrote that "the books of Dos Passos have for many years been viciously advocating the cause of war against all progressive ideas," and accused him of "trying to direct the decadent literature of the USA along the road of deliberately catering to the interests of American imperialism."[59] This,

[59] M. Mendelson, "Decadents in American Literature," *Soviet Literature*, No. 2 (1949), p. 146.

of course, was a purely political judgment. Since his later works have been proscribed, there is no incentive for Soviet critics to judge them aesthetically. It is interesting, however, that in referring to the works which once caused so much ferment in Soviet literary circles, present-day Soviet criticism merely echoes the most negative of the aesthetic judgments of the early 1930's: "Even in the past, when he called himself a radical, it was a characteristic decadent tendency of Dos Passos to portray even the men carrying on revolutionary activity as spiritually poor creatures. The moral and intellectual degradation of his characters, their dehumanization, is reflected in the disintegration of form as expressed in the chaotic, deliberately involved structure of his novels."[60]

Remarks such as these indicate that the question of Dos Passos has long been settled in Russia. The mandate of socialist realism, as Party ideologists interpret it, has precluded the kind of stylistic experimentation which the Newsreel and the Camera Eye represent. Yet Dos Passos' devices, and the aesthetic attitudes implicit in them, did appeal strongly to significant numbers of writers and critics in Soviet literature's most decisive years. Only a close ideological analysis prevented *U.S.A.* from becoming an important influence on Russian writers.

The significant fact is that an ideological analysis had to be made. Of all the Americans who expressed strong "proletarian" sympathies in the thirties, Dos Passos had achieved the greatest artistic breadth and profundity. His attempt to give a feeling of the contemporary mass historic trend and to chart the main directions of an intricate society in flux suggested a possible methodological model for Soviet writers. The spirit of the Five Year Plans called for Russian works that would convey a sense of the movement of the national collective in a time of complex and continuing social revolution. In a sense Dos Passos had already done for his society the same thing that Soviet writers now felt themselves obligated to do for theirs. What gave the critics pause was the very fullness and complexity of Dos Passos' vision of men

[60] *ibid.*

and events. For in their search for doctrinal purity the official advocates of socialist realism had imposed crippling limitations on the practice of literature.

One of the severest of these limitations was the insistence on the didactic function of literature. The writer was to serve as an educator, instructing his readers in the truths of a single ideology. To do this he must express a feeling of certainty about the laws of social development, and specifically about the direction which civilization should take in the twentieth century. A confident sense of the purposefulness of history, and belief in the inevitable progress of the world toward communism, would provide unity and a convincing clarity to works of literature. Dos Passos, however, wrote not as a teacher but as a seeker, confused and unsure of himself. His position was one of artistic humility, of groping for the truth by examining reality in all possible ways. In the last analysis, *U.S.A.* could scarcely appeal to critics who demanded in literature the single-minded, authoritarian simplicity of the social pedagogue.

We have seen, however, that many Soviet critics in the early thirties spoke in favor of Dos Passos' creative methods, undismayed by the multiplicity of his devices. They saw that the richness, precision, and irony in his writing were products of his unwillingness to make large, confident generalizations about complex individuals in a complex society. In defending Dos Passos, these critics were fighting, indirectly, for the freedom of the *Soviet* artist to speak in a variety of voices, to express ambivalence, and to present his unique subjective vision of things. In insisting on the right of Russian writers to imitate Dos Passos, these critics were implicitly objecting to the increasingly fixed and dogmatic set of values that were currently narrowing the creative scope of Soviet literature in the name of socialist realism. The decision to eschew Dos Passos marked a serious defeat for the forces of liberalism and tolerance in the Soviet literary world.

CHAPTER V

OTHER OPINIONS OF THE

NINETEEN THIRTIES

꘡꘡꘡ LIKE ALL of Soviet ideology, the literary doctrine that jelled in the thirties aspired to be all-encompassing. Not only did it prescribe the goals for writers who ardently desired to achieve the political correctness of socialist realism; it also established criteria for appraising authors to whom the Soviet system of values was alien. Judged by these criteria, a great many prominent American authors were quickly damned and banned. A good many others, however, attracted the Russians' attention, despite their deficiencies, because their works combined narrative interest with a sense of serious social involvement.

The two preceding chapters have been concerned with writers of the thirties who were sufficiently involved in the trend toward an American "proletarian" literature, and sufficiently (though temporarily) close to the Soviet view of things, to command solicitude and encouragement from Russian critics. Most of these writers—Steinbeck and Dos Passos are notable exceptions—were inferior artists who merited serious concern only because of their ideological proximity and potential usefulness to the Soviet political program. The amount of attention the Russians devoted to them was far out of proportion to their talent.

Soviet critics were also interested, however, in other Americans whose literary quality was higher but who were ideologically less congenial. Some of them, such as Sherwood Anderson and Waldo Frank, had already been translated and discussed in the twenties and had already established literary reputations in Russia. Others, such as Erskine Caldwell and Richard Wright, became known only in the thirties. They were a varied group, but they had in common a sensitivity and deep concern over American social problems that made them turn to the burning themes of the Depression period. At the same time, they remained committed to aesthetic modes and principles which the Russians often deplored, and emphasized themes which the Russians found irrelevant, ideologically harmful, or simply distasteful.

Sherwood Anderson had first become known in Russia when Soviet criticism was still relatively eclectic. In 1924, the first translation of *Winesburg, Ohio* startled a reviewer with its "surprise emotions," and prompted him to remark that "in the long run, it might turn out that we have not yet discovered America."[1] A year later *The Triumph of the Egg* reinforced this "unusual impression": "The author shows that under the external glitter and dynamism of life in America there is hidden a complete inertia and emptiness. Unhappy little people stir about in it, caught in the capitalist vise. . . ."[2] Anderson's presentation of America as a place of sad and empty souls—a society of groping, maladjusted individuals for whom life has no positive meaning and who despair of knowing why they must suffer loneliness, frustration, ugliness, and want—affirmed Soviet assumptions about the spiritual poverty of life under capitalism. On the other hand, the stories and poems in *The Triumph of the Egg* were thought to be rather monotonous psychological abstractions, "weakly executed and prolix." ". . . however good the tendencies of the artist may be in a social sense, if the material for their exposure is borrowed from psychological theory, and not from any organic approach of the artist to man, then the work that results will not have artistic, and, consequently, social significance."[3]

In spite of misunderstanding and disapproval, six editions of Anderson's various works (including three of *Winesburg, Ohio*) had come out by the end of 1926. He was respected as a craftsman,[4] although one critic found him obscure and was

[1] Yuri Poletika, "Shervud Anderson. *Vainsburg, Ogaio*," *Russki sovremennik*, No. 3 (1924), p. 283.

[2] E. Ramm, "Shervud Anderson. Torzhestvo yaitsa," *Novy mir*, No. 8 (1925), pp. 155-56.

[3] *ibid.*, p. 156.

[4] L. Rozental, "Shervud Anderson. *Vainsburg, Ogaio*," *Pechat i revolyutsiya*, No. 1 (1926), p. 243; "Shervud Anderson," *Bolshaya sovetskaya entsiklopediya*, Moscow, 1926, II, 729.

irritated by his narrative pose of naivete.[5] While he represented "the literature of protest against the [American] illusion of optimism with all its childlike inclination to run away from the hard facts of life,"[6] he was socially passive and wrote "without a feeling of sharp protest," opposing to bourgeois ideals "merely the subjective ramblings of vagabonds and dreamers. . . ."[7] Nevertheless, in 1927 a critic praised his "rich, brilliant style, broad scope, and deep psychological motivation,"[8] and another found him to be the herald of a dawning American sobriety: ". . . in the provinces . . . a new man has stirred, who has suddenly tried to open his eyes and to meditate on the question of what, in essence, this headlong tempo of accumulation of material value is leading to."[9]

In 1929, making the first attempt at a full Marxist analysis of Anderson, Sergei Dinamov called him "an artist of the decadent layers of the petty bourgeoisie," and added: "The majority of Anderson's heroes are pathological . . . they have no real ties with life, cannot approach other people; disillusioned and despondent, broken by internal contradictions, without support in surrounding reality, they present a gloomy picture of the hopeless decay of the middle class."[10] Such early works as *Windy McPherson's Son, Marching Men,* and *Poor White* had shown concern for social movements and the aspirations of the lower classes. But Dinamov argued that in *Dark Laughter,* written in 1925, he had begun to "reconcile himself with reality," and that "his negation grew into the declaration that love and sex are the only path of freedom from social disorder."[11] During the early thirties Anderson was consistently categorized as an aesthetically gifted and

[5] Rozental, "Shervud Anderson. Vainsburg, Ogaio," *op.cit.,* p. 243.

[6] *ibid.,* p. 243.

[7] "Shervud Anderson," *Bolshaya sovetskaya entsiklopediya, op.cit.,* p. 729.

[8] R. Kulle, "Khudozhestvennaya proza sovremennovo zapada," *Sibirskiye ogni,* No. 1 (1927), p. 128.

[9] Yevgeni Lann, "Standartni yanki," *Krasnaya nov,* No. 1 (1927), p. 252.

[10] S. Dinamov, "Shervud Anderson," *Literaturnaya entsiklopediya,* Moscow, 1929, I, 152-53.

[11] *ibid.,* p. 153.

perceptive, but morally defeatist, petty bourgeois writer who displayed an affinity for pessimistic theories of human behavior. His aversion to capitalism was largely emotional, based on distaste for its spiritual values rather than on careful social, political, and economic analysis. He was concerned over the class struggle, but persistently refused to draw revolutionary conclusions; terrified and perplexed, he was helpless before the challenge of social evil. Ultimately, the critics felt, Anderson saw man as a prisoner of his own irrationality, doomed to frustration by the tension between his instincts and the opposing demands of society. Compassionate and devoid of cynicism, his attitude was nevertheless considered destructive, since it denied the validity of attempts to create social harmony through acts dictated by the intellect. His heroes were slaves of biological impulses which prevented them from realizing their lofty aspirations. Endowed with a sense of justice and decency, longing for meaningful activity, Anderson's characters were unable to break out of the vicious circle of personality problems by engaging in social action.

Then in 1932 Anderson was stimulated by the Depression to write *Beyond Desire*, a novel about an industrial strike. It was translated into Russian in 1933. *Beyond Desire* is certainly one of Anderson's weakest books. It is diffuse and sentimental, and develops the Andersonian strain of sultry morbidity close to the point of self-parody. Soviet critics were quick to recognize its faults, but they also hailed its proletarian theme as a sign of his "creative transformation."[12] He had become an "ally of the working class."[13] Depicting the lives of Southern textile workers and a Communist-led strike, Anderson had carefully disclosed the economic and social effects of the capitalist rationalization of industry—the conditions of production, the workers' enslavement to the factory —and the intimate human consequences of the clear-cut opposition between capital and labor.[14] And it featured a hero

[12] Sergei Dinamov, "Sherwood Anderson: American writer," *International Literature*, No. 4 (1933), p. 91.

[13] O. Nemerovskaya, "Novy roman Shervuda Andersona," *Literaturny kritik*, No. 4 (1934), p. 199.

[14] *ibid.*, p. 201.

who finally seeks a solution to his personal problems through social involvement.[15]

But the reservations of the critics were so numerous that their guarded enthusiasm seemed like a gesture of charity. Anderson's Communists were hazy figures, done in hasty strokes,[16] and the strike movement he depicted was chaotic, ending in total defeat, since the author himself was frightened of the inevitable bloodshed and sacrifice involved in the making of a revolution.[17] The final heroism of his central figure was irrational and his death was futile and accidental.[18] Anderson had always vacillated between rapturous worship of the machine and hatred of it as a destroyer of a simple way of life. This continued in *Beyond Desire*, where "sickly, half-hysterical notes" crept into his description of a textile factory.[19] More fundamentally, Anderson was still excessively psychological, subjective, and pessimistic. He still "wanders in a mist of subconscious activity and inclinations. . . ."[20] "The novel is static, devoid of action, the heroes perpetually relive their own personal sensations and peer into themselves and into their pasts. . . . The probing and refined psychoanalysis of the author smashes the psyche of the hero to atoms, and as a result there is created a sort of cosmic chaos, unordered by any kind of objective principle."[21] While Anderson recognized the class struggle, "an even greater role in his art is played by the struggle of the sexes."[22]

Under the influence of the Depression and, one critic contended, "impressed by the success of socialist construction in the Soviet Union,"[23] Anderson had partially purged himself

[15] A. Yelistratova, "Literatura S A S Sh," *Literaturnaya gazeta*, November 29, 1933.

[16] S. Dinamov, "O tvorchestve Shervuda Andersona," *Literaturnaya gazeta*, September 29, 1933.

[17] Nemerovskaya, "Novy roman . . . ," *op.cit.*, p. 200.

[18] *ibid.*, p. 200.

[19] A. Startsev, "Po etu storonu barikad," *Khudozhestvennaya literatura*, No. 1 (1934), p. 36.

[20] "Shervud Anderson," *Literaturnaya gazeta*, September 26, 1936.

[21] Nemerovskaya, "Novy roman . . . ," *op.cit.*, p. 203.

[22] *ibid.*, p. 201.

[23] Dinamov, "O tvorchestve . . . ," *op.cit.*

of ideological inertia. *Beyond Desire* indicated a "way out of
the labyrinth in which the artist has been wandering, creating
endless refrains and variations on the same melancholy themes
and hopeless situations."[24] But he had come only part of the
way: "Anderson's very approach to revolution has been for
him to a significant degree a matter of feeling, an act of elemental emotional sympathy for the tasks of the working class
in America. This approach is part of Anderson's strength in-
asmuch as it determines the unquestionable sincerity of his
political pronouncements and the spontaneity of his creative
reaction to reality. But in it is also his weakness: revolutionary sympathies, based only on spontaneous 'feeling,' inevitably prove to be shaky and unstable."[25] This apprehen-
sion was fully justified. *Death in the Woods*, which appeared
in Soviet periodicals in 1934, was a return to his "pessimism,
helplessness, and departure from social themes," and Anderson never again wrote anything approaching Soviet political
standards. In 1935, a critic complained that he had become
"respectable," had "departed to the right," and had begun
"cynically to ridicule himself."[26] He continued to be tolerated,
even respected;[27] *A Story Teller's Story* came out in translation in 1936. But this American liberal, who had tried un-
successfully to write a proletarian novel, had clearly disappointed the sanguine hopes of his Soviet critics. Anderson
himself put it this way: "It seems to me that the story-teller
is one thing, and the thinker, the political economist, the
reformer another. The business of the story-teller is with life,
in his own time, life as he feels it, tastes it. Not for him surely
the making of the revolution."[28]

American critics have often found fault with many of the

[24] Startsev, "Po etu storonu . . . ," *op.cit.*, p. 35.

[25] Yelistratova, *op.cit.*

[26] S. Dinamov, "Tvorcheskiye priznaniya Shervuda Andersona," *Internatsionalnaya literatura*, No. 10 (1935), pp. 135-36.

[27] N. Eishiskina, "Stranstvovaniye v mire fantazii i faktov," *Literaturnaya gazeta*, May 10, 1936; Olga Nemerovskaya, "Sudba amerikanskoi
novelly," *Literaturnaya uchyoba*, No. 5 (1935), p. 98; Al. A-v, "Smert
Shervuda Andersona," *Internatsionalnaya literatura*, No. 3 (1941), p. 186.

[28] As quoted in Fred B. Millet, *Contemporary American Authors*, New
York, 1944, p. 222.

same traits in Anderson to which the Russians objected. His brooding pessimism, mystical preoccupation with sex, and heavy emphasis on subconscious behavior and the forces of instinct have all been repeatedly criticized by his compatriots. Too often his writing is distinguished by a rambling uncertainty, a lack of form and discipline. What Americans regarded as aesthetic faults and annoying excesses, however, the Russians regarded as ideological heresy. For Soviet critics, Anderson's fascination with sex and the unconscious was not merely an error of proportion and a source of irritating vagueness. Rather, it was a grave ideological flaw, leading to fundamental misinterpretations of man as a social being. Anderson's wistful protest against the machine as a destroyer of freedom seemed to many of his countrymen to be quaint, and perhaps anachronistic, but nevertheless intelligent and legitimate. For the Russians, however, it indicated a reactionary, antihistorical article of belief and therefore a pernicious ideological evil. They argued that literature must portray man as the conscious, rational builder of his own destiny and the machine as his obedient ally. Concern over the individual psyche and its unknown recesses, speculation on the instinctive motives of human action, or fear that such products of the human intelligence as the machine might destroy their creators—all distracted attention from the cardinal social issues that were the proper province of literature.

Like a great many socially conscious writers of the thirties, Sherwood Anderson used the material of the Depression but gave it a heavily personal coloration to suit his individual needs as an artist. One must agree with the Russians that the result was an inferior novel—a weak amalgam of class militancy and social mysticism, of vague sexual searching and undefined, poorly articulated desire. The implication of Soviet criticism, however, was that Anderson's novel would have been successful had he not permitted ideologically improper elements to compete with its civic message. With this one cannot agree, for Anderson's failure was an artistic one. At the moment he was simply writing badly, and no amount of ideological tinkering, no increase in revolutionary purpose, could have prevented this failure. But by the mid-thirties the distinction between ideology and artistry had been nearly obliterated from Soviet criticism. Aesthetic phenomena were treated in terms of rigid, and usually irrelevant, ideological categories.

Waldo Frank was another American whose leftward development, betokened by a proletarian novel, encouraged the Russians in the thirties. Like Anderson, Frank had been published in the Soviet Union in the twenties. (*City Block* and *Holiday* were translated in 1926.) An essay in 1928 praised him as a stylist and as a pioneer of twentieth-century American cultural introspection, but criticized his novels for prolixity of psychological detail and excessive "Freudianism."[29] In 1930 the author of the same essay (and the only critic who heretofore seemed to have paid him close attention) called him the "most powerful phenomenon of contemporary American literature," and stressed his contribution to the "reappraisal of the spiritual values" of the American bourgeoisie by the "radical intelligentsia."[30]

Frank made a trip to the USSR in 1931, and the next year published an account of his travels, *Dawn in Russia*. Despite a "certain touristic naivete" and an "excessive inclination toward half-mystical philosophizing about the 'Eastern soul' of the Soviet land," a Soviet critic called it a "new step forward on the path of ideo-political development" of the author, and noted that Frank had "recently been coming closer and closer to the revolutionary movement in the USA."[31]

Frank's participation in various left-wing causes and his activity in the League of American Writers, of which he became chairman, further heartened Soviet observers, so that when his novel *The Death and Birth of David Markand* appeared in 1934 it was soon translated and reviewed with great

[29] Yevgeni Lann, "Literatura sovremennoi Ameriki. Valdo Frenk," *Novy mir*, No. 2 (1928), pp. 237-49.

[30] Yevg. Lann, "Probeg po sovremennoi amerikanskoi literature," *Novy mir*, No. 10 (1930), p. 201.

[31] A. Yelistratova, "Noviye yavleniya v literature Ameriki," *Kniga i proletarskaya revolyutsiya*, No. 11 (1933), p. 122.

interest. Concerned with a successful businessman who repudiates his comfortable life to wander incognito about his country in search of fresh purpose, the novel in part explores economic and social miseries of America in the second decade of the twentieth century and comes up with a fairly strong indictment of the capitalist order. The critics unanimously lauded Frank for bringing about the "death" of his hero's bourgeois world-view and for showing the "birth" of his new proletarian sympathies. One of them wrote that "as you turn the pages you feel not only the movement of the hero but also of the author himself,"[32] and all of them similarly viewed the book as figurative spiritual autobiography. Heretofore he had revolted against bourgeois reality as a "confused idealist" and had sought a solution "in the world of the individual psyche," but now, through political activity, he had found a positive ideology.[33] His narrative method was still burdened with "refined compositional devices,"[34] "cloudy psychologism,"[35] "biologism,"[36] and "hypertrophied Freudist-sexual motifs,"[37] and the book contained "many elements of naive mysticism and other confusions, which have remained as a heritage from his former idealism."[38] Nevertheless, in his "striving to find in every cell of a human being a particle of the great process of quest and revaluation," Frank was a "great psychologist and artist."[39]

A curious, and perhaps the most significant, aspect of the criticism of this novel, however, was the Russians' insistence on comparing the author to his hero. At the end of his wanderings, David Markand returns home to his family and

[32] N. Eishiskina, *"Smert i rozhdeniye Davida Markenda,"* *Literaturnaya gazeta,* February 29, 1936.

[33] A. Startsev, "Uoldo Frenk," *Izvestiya,* August 15, 1935, p. 3.

[34] Eishiskina, "Smert i rozhdeniye . . . ," *op.cit.*

[35] Al. Abramov, "Smert i rozhdeniye Devida Markenda," *Internatsionalnaya literatura,* No. 12 (1936), p. 207.

[36] Evgenyi Lann, "Waldo Frank: American Writer," *International Literature,* No. 1 (1936), p. 82.

[37] Eishiskina, "Smert i rozhdeniye . . . ," *op.cit.*

[38] Vl. Dmitrevski, "Rozhdeniye revolyutsionnovo pisatelya," *Internatsionalnaya literatura,* No. 10 (1935), p. 141.

[39] Eishiskina, "Smert i rozhdeniye . . . ," *op.cit.*

bourgeois surroundings, wiser, but not yet a fully committed revolutionary. From the Soviet point of view, this outcome could have been considered ideologically unsatisfactory. Other American works of the time were criticized for this reason. But Soviet critics were tactfully generous with Frank. The reviewer Abramov found it sufficient that David Markand was destined to begin a new, if unspecified, kind of life.[40] Abel Startsev defended the novel's conclusion by pointing out that Markand was a character out of the writer's "artistic past," and argued that since the hero was not a revolutionary type, Frank had made a correct aesthetic judgment in not thrusting him onto the barricades. Startsev added, however, and rather severely, "Reality demands of Frank new heroes—revolutionaries, fighters; to create them, Frank must decisively take his leave of mystical idealism."[41]

Two other commentators achieved singular feats of criticism by justifying the ending of the novel, not as a part of either an aesthetic or an ideological entity, but as a piece of the author's political biography. Eishiskina wrote: "Did Frank conclude the journey of Markand with his internal rebirth? Of course not. We meet the Frank of recent years among our active friends. We hear his speech at the Paris congress,[42] in which he announces his decision to support 'the party that created the Soviet Union'. . . . The end of the book is the beginning of a new life, about which Frank has not yet told us."[43]

Yevgeni Lann put it another way: "There are writers of two categories. The first compel their heroes to out-strip them, and then they live on the rent brought in by the hero. The hero earns them a reputation. The others detain their heroes halfway, and continue the journey beyond that point. . . . Frank belongs to this second category. . . . Markand's return home . . . is before everything a testimonial to Frank's faultless artistic touch. At the stage at which the novel

[40] Abramov, *op.cit.*, p. 206.
[41] Startsev, "Uoldo Frenk," *op.cit.*
[42] Cf. Chapter II, p. 51.
[43] Eishiskina, "Smert i rozhdeniye . . . ," *op.cit.*

breaks off, Markand is still not ready to follow the author who created him. . . . Frank broke off the book where he had to break it off."[44]

One is tempted to interpret these indulgent ideological rationalizations as gestures of political courtesy, directed at a potentially valuable ally. For the Russians clearly hoped that Frank's next book would be a genuinely militant effort, free of the taint of "sexual mysticism" and fully supporting the revolutionary cause. As head of the League of American Writers, moreover, Frank occupied a strategic position in the world of American letters; such a prominent fellow traveler required delicate handling. Hence the extraordinary tactfulness in Soviet criticism of the close of his novel on the one hand, and the critics' gratuitous concern over its autobiographical relevance on the other. Like numerous other American liberal intellectuals, however, Frank soon ceased enjoying the role of fellow traveler.[45] The expected novel did not appear, the Russians lost interest in his writings, and he was never again published in the Soviet Union.

The refrain of displeasure over Frank's stress on the "individual psyche," his mystical idealism, and his "biologism" had often been sounded in the criticism of other American authors and was to be heard repeatedly in the decades to come. Soviet intellectual horizons had begun to narrow in the twenties. The writings of Sigmund Freud, for example, ceased appearing in Russian translation in 1924. By the early thirties, the wholesale Soviet commitment to a dialectical materialist view of human nature and society had outlawed many strains of thought that were prominent in the non-Communist world. These prohibitions restricted the operation of the literary imagination to that which was cognizable, rationally measurable, and ultimately optimistic with respect to the fate of the human race. Any writing that stressed the individual at the expense of the collective, the subjective at the expense

---

[44] Lann, "Waldo Frank: American Writer," *op.cit.*, pp. 81-82.

[45] In 1937, Frank publicly questioned the validity of the Moscow Trials, and from then on remained openly skeptical of Stalinism. See Waldo Frank, "The Moscow Trials," *New Republic*, May 12, 1937, pp. 19-20.

of the social, was proscribed. Concern over the political implications of literary activity had become so intense that, as in the case of Frank, a novel could be criticized not in terms of what it was, but in terms of the political action in which the critics hoped its author might engage in the future.

Erskine Caldwell drew the attention of Soviet critics in 1933, when Anna Elistratova, after having read him in English, suggested that his first book of stories, *American Earth*, in its portrayal of the "stupefying emptiness of provincial bourgeois existence," and its mystical treatment of sexual longing and death, might well serve as a sequel to Anderson's *Winesburg, Ohio*. Elistratova went on to say that while sexual motifs had played a "significant role" in Anderson's *Beyond Desire*, they had acquired a "decisive significance" in Caldwell's *God's Little Acre*. This novel, embracing "the life of a southern farmer's family, the workers' movement, [and] a textile strike smashed by the police," might have provided a "revolutionary disclosure," but all of these themes were "drowned in a sea of sexual mysticism."[46]

In 1934 Caldwell began to be translated in Soviet periodicals. Two years later, when the first Russian collection of his stories appeared, he had already gained a large Soviet following, and Ivan Kashkin surveyed his evolution as a writer. Describing him as a warm, sensitive artist with a strong love of simple people and a deep appreciation of folkways, Kashkin pointed out that Caldwell's characters vary from ordinary, recognizable figures subject to natural sorrows and joys, to frightful grotesques. His humor ranged from light, good-natured chuckling to wild, mocking, terrible laughter. Kashkin attributed this variety to Caldwell's awakening social consciousness. He had begun his career by experimenting with "abstract psychological etudes," marked by "superficial impressionism." The *"intime* psychological novellas" of *American Earth*, with their "imitative internal monologues," use of stream-of-consciousness, Andersonian treatment of sex, and "tragic-sentimental" love themes, differed greatly from Cald-

[46] A. Yelistratova, "Literatura sovremennoi Ameriki," *Internatsionalnaya literatura*, No. 5 (1933), p. 105.

well's more mature works. After this early experimentation, Kashkin felt, Caldwell had turned to satirizing universal human failings and poking fun at mundane conventions, but as he looked more narrowly at the scenes he found amusing, he recognized bestial qualities and his laughter became constrained. Mild humor gave way to terrifying grotesqueness, and his anecdotes developed into grim farces. Darker facets of human relations were introduced into his stories, and laughter was gradually replaced by horror. New motifs—poverty, hunger, brutalization, the oppression of poor whites, and the lynching of Negroes—had appeared in his most recent book of stories, *Kneel to the Rising Sun*, where horror was occasionally accompanied by anger and fierce protest. While his characters remained numb and spiritless in the face of social injustice there were notable exceptions, such as the hero of "Candy-Man Beechum," whose protests, though unavailing, were clear and powerful. In one story the author went even farther, for in "Slow Death," "here for the first time in Caldwell a man intercedes in behalf of his comrade."[47] Caldwell was progressing from a state of shock, in which he could only laugh bitterly at social injustice, to a state of understanding, in which sustained seriousness was tempered by a sense of purpose and direction.

The critic Silman in 1937 found formal similarities between Caldwell's stories and those of Ernest Hemingway. For Hemingway, however, the short story was a medium for the expression of mood—a subtle, refined, impressionistic, even "aristocratic" form—while Caldwell was a "writer with another world-feeling, less indifferent, more straightforward." Since Caldwell was more interested in dynamics than in mood and wanted to criticize the world instead of merely contemplating it, "the forms of the Hemingwayesque writer are alien to him and remain only forms." The struggle to find a form appropriate to his materials was causing him "growing pains." A case in point was the story "Saturday Afternoon": "The depiction of loathsome ugliness with the methods of 'subtle'

[47] Ivan Kashkin, "Ne ta Amerika," *Internatsionalnaya literatura*, No. 4 (1936), p. 141.

impressionism cannot help but produce contradictory impressions. The description of the lynching of a persecuted Negro hardly calls for a musical symphony. . . . A form created for narcissism and elegiac sadness cannot serve for the expression of terror and indignation. . . . The subtle method of disclosing a symbolic external world, as a reflection of the experiences of a 'tender soul,' which is employed by all impressionists, seems out of place when rough, cruel conditions, which cry out for intervention, are being talked about."[48] Caldwell's ideology, Silman argued, had outgrown his stylistic medium; he was employing decadent means for constructive ends. (The critic's aesthetic perceptions were sadly amiss. "Saturday Afternoon," and many of Caldwell's stories in the same vein, rely on irony and understatement. These devices in no way obscure the social message; in fact, they increase its impact, and other Soviet critics had no difficulty in grasping the effect.) Although Silman agreed that "Slow Death" introduces a fighter, a man who is beginning to see the necessity for common action among proletarians, she felt that Caldwell's art was not maturing as rapidly as his political understanding. Generally his heroes still expressed only a weak and timid dissatisfaction. Noting that recently Caldwell had begun writing essays, the critic concluded: "Caldwell is now occupied in a purely literary search. But the fact is that Caldwell must seek in the first place not new forms, but new heroes (not in literature, but in life). And not as much to seek as to recognize them. And then the novella form which he has now deserted will turn out to be full of new content."[49]

The author's proclivity for exploring the depths of degeneracy continued to disturb the critics. Silman asked, "Is it possible that such monsters exist in the world?" Of *Tobacco Road*, translated in 1938, the critic Balashov wrote: "We understand that Caldwell was paying tribute to the fashionable theme of sex, but we cannot tolerate the one-sided, almost caricatured description of the desolate and impoverished fam-

[48] T. Silman, "Erskin Kolduell. *Amerikanskiye rasskazy*," *Zvezda*, No. 2 (1937), p. 294.
[49] *ibid.*, p. 297.

ily of Jeeter Lester. Indeed, Erskine Caldwell in his *Tobacco Road* presented not humans, but brutes, and depicted a grotesque, primitive Bacchanale of crude lusts."[50] The novel did contain compassion and social protest, but it was dominated by "mockery over a man whom capitalism has destroyed." Nemerovskaya assessed the writer's progress in these terms: "Caldwell has learned to hate. More than this—he knows *what* he hates: the rapacious capitalistic system. . . . But in his works there still is not heard an appeal for the revolutionary overthrow of this order. He speaks about a 'change in the system,' but he does not say that this change can come about only as a result of the solidarity of all working people in a single front of organized struggle."[51]

When *Trouble in July*, a novel of a lynching, appeared in Russian in 1940, Balashov concluded that "here is not the indifferent narration of passive contemplation, but vigorous and warm sympathy, indignation, and an almost complete absence of senseless, farcical passages, such as horrified and angered us in *Tobacco Road*."[52] Formerly Caldwell had been interested mainly in "the ugly manifestations of a rude and blind force," "brutality and inhumanity" and "primitive passions," but recently, in the stories of *Kneel to the Rising Sun* and *Southways* he had begun exploring the "feeling of love and human nobility" and "comradeship and friendship among the unemployed." Impelled by a deeper hatred for the "oppressor-landlords," he had begun finding characters "who want to take care of themselves," are not afraid to fight against exploitation and misery, and are determined to stand up for their rights. While *Trouble in July* lacked such positive characters, it was nevertheless the "precursor of powerful and still more significant successes," since "close acquaintance with the world of 'people consumed by hatred' has left its traces on the artist."[53] In 1941 Kashkin remarked

[50] P. Balashov, "Udacha Erskina Kolduella." *Literaturnaya gazeta*, April 18, 1940.

[51] Olga Nemerovskaya, "Tabachnaya doroga," *Literaturny sovremennik*, No. 9 (1938), p. 219.

[52] Balashov, *op.cit.*   [53] *ibid.*

that "formerly Caldwell liked best of all to show various deviations from the norm—all sorts of freaks and monsters," but added that "more and more often we see genuine people with their large sorrow and hunger and little joys," and concluded that "this new attitude to humanity is more and more rooted in Caldwell's works."[54]

Caldwell's subsequent reception in Russia will be discussed in later chapters. But in the thirties the main critical themes had already been established. He was a writer of conflicting tendencies, whose sympathies lay with his destitute sharecroppers and proletarians but who, fascinated by the loathsome human phenomena that sprang up in a social and economic system that was repulsive to him, indulged in pictures of extreme degradation and degeneracy beyond the point of social or artistic utility. His frequent preoccupation with the pathological aspects of humanity, and with the warped individuals produced by unnatural social relationships, held the danger of an obsession with the biological sources of human conduct and, even worse, of ideological stagnation and neutrality. His art, the critics felt, did not measure up to his progressive social views.

It is interesting that American critics have always shared the Russians' aversion to certain traits in Caldwell: pathological characters that border on the ridiculous, bizarre social situations that give way to burlesque, and an extravagance in treating sexual themes that violates the canons of plausibility and good taste. But the Russians' criticisms were more explicitly ideological. To them, Jeeter Lester was an implausible emblem of the American proletariat because he was *organically* incapable of positive social action. Since Jeeter ran counter to the Soviet conception of the laws of human development, he did not belong in literature.

Literature about the American Negro has long been of special interest to the Russians. Several decades before the Revolution *Uncle Tom's Cabin* had been established as a classic in Russia, and in the twenties numerous contemporary

[54] Ivan Kashkin, "Kolduell—novellist," *Internatsionalnaya literatura*, No. 5 (1941), p. 175.

works on Negro themes were translated. While the lure of the culturally exotic[55] and a natural sympathy for the social underdog account to some extent for the Russian readers' interest, there was also a strong political incentive, for Soviet theorists have always considered the American Negro community a latent force for revolution. For the purposes of Soviet domestic propaganda, it has made little difference whether American works on racial topics were authored by Negroes or whites: any writing that correctly emphasized racial injustice in the United States was acceptable. But Soviet critics, especially in the restless thirties, were particularly anxious to see the development of a school of revolutionary writing *by Negroes*, to serve as a point of ideological orientation for an increasingly discontented American colored population. At the same time, the critics preferred not to regard the Negro literary effort as something separate from the main revolutionary stream. Rather, they felt, it should follow the general principles of the movement, while contributing its own unique social and cultural ingredient.

American Negro literature should be "proletarian" first of all. It should show that the social discrimination and economic inequities suffered by colored people are products of the capitalist class structure and should indicate, further, that class antagonisms operate within the Negro community itself. The writer's concern with racial inequality should not permit him to obscure the roots of the race problem—the economic class struggle. One of his functions is to break down the wall of artificial prejudice that separates the working people of one race from the working people of another. For proletarians of all races have a common bond that transcends other hostilities—their hatred of capitalist exploitation.

Among the ideological pitfalls which the Negro writer must be wary of was the temptation simply to avoid the race problem and assert his intellectual equality by emulating his white bourgeois contemporaries in the realm of "pure art." Con-

[55] Translation of the stories of Octavus Roy Cohen and van Vechten's novel *Nigger Heaven*, which were greatly at variance with Soviet ideology, can only be explained in this way. Significantly, such works were published only in the twenties.

versely, he must also beware of overly accentuating the distinguishing features of Negro culture by indulging in "race psychology," to suggest that Negroes properly and organically form an alien community. He must avoid accepting things as they are by glorifying the Harlem "jazz-band tradition"—the niche into which the American bourgeoisie has thrust the Negro for his "cultural disarmament." Above all, he must not be seduced by the strain of religious stoicism in his people, or in any way advocate passive acceptance by the Negro of his lot.

Langston Hughes has been the most popular American Negro writer in Russia since the early thirties. (Claude McKay, who had been a Communist in the twenties, had been widely translated, but was soon considered merely a "pseudo-radical.")[56] Four volumes of Hughes's stories, poems, and plays were translated in the thirties and his works appeared regularly in Soviet periodicals. The critics liked his verse for its graceful simplicity and directness, its varied and original rhythms, reminiscent of folklore,[57] and for its agitational quality of social protest.[58] His eloquent and colorful prose was thought to be as "fresh, lyrical, and direct as his poetry."[59]

His development had been complicated. In his earliest collection of poems, *The Weary Blues*, the critic Filatova pointed out, he had dreamed of somehow solving the "Negro problem" within the framework of capitalism. Naively believing that "the whites, recognizing the beauty of the Negroes, will extend the hand of fellowship and all questions of race inequality will disappear," he had indulged in "exotics which in no way reflect the life of the toiling Negro masses." Nevertheless, his African motifs served to "contrast the conventionality and inward emptiness of capitalist America with the

---

[56] Al. Abramov, "Molodost veka," *Internatsionalnaya literatura*, No. 6 (1935), p. 141.

[57] Lydia Filatova, "Langston Hughes: American Writer," *International Literature*, No. 1 (1933), p. 103.

[58] Yulian Anisimov, "Negro-amerikanski folklor," *Internatsionalnaya literatura*, No. 1 (1935), pp. 111-13.

[59] M. Zenkevich, "O novinkakh angliskoi i amerikanskoi literatury," *Novy mir*, No. 12 (1931), p. 176.

spiritual richness of the race that had not been spoiled by civilization," and his "strong notes of death, suicide, and hopelessness" indicated that "the poet is lonesome in the cold prison of capitalist culture." On the whole, however, his protest resolved itself into a "vague striving toward sunshine."

With the novel *Not Without Laughter* he had overcome his theme of "passive obedience and piety." However, he was "still swayed by the theory that the Negro can attain social equality only through education, through demonstrating the creative abilities of the Negro people," and did not realize that "culture and talent will not solve the problem." A turning point had come in the early thirties, when his art became social and he entered his "revolutionary period." Discarding the pursuit of pure beauty, Filatova argued, he became an "agitator-poet," whose militant verse sang of the "struggle and the solidarity of the world proletariat."[60] Although he was still only "emotionally repelled by capitalism" and felt, rather than understood, its evils, he now portrayed the Negro "not only as a Negro, but also as a proletarian."[61] Nevertheless, Hughes continued to disappoint the critics. The stories in *The Ways of White Folks* showed Negroes taking moral and psychological revenge on their white exploiters, but lacked images of "brave and daring fighters on the proletarian front."[62] It was true that in stories like "Home," in which a colored musician, after triumphant successes in Europe, returns to America only to be destroyed by insanely prejudiced whites, he had spoken out against the illusion that art is exempt from discrimination.[63] But he still stressed race antagonism at the expense of class-consciousness.[64] While his poems showed that "a man overcomes weaknesses, humiliation, and all the blows of a cruel life if his spirit is kindled

[60] Filatova, *op.cit.*, p. 105.
[61] Abramov, "Molodost . . . ," *op.cit.*, p. 141.
[62] A. Mingulina, "*Nravy belykh*," *Literaturnaya gazeta*, March 5, 1936.
[63] "Lengston Khyuz," *Internatsionalnaya literatura*, No. 11 (1937), p. 213.
[64] Mingulina, *op.cit.*

with the flame of free thought,"[65] his lyric gift was greater than his social understanding.

The Russians found a fresh and vigorous approach in the works of Richard Wright, which began to be translated in 1938. The critic Barsov remarked that Wright's collection of stories, *Uncle Tom's Children*, was the first book about Negroes that was directed neither to Negroes nor to whites, but to the proletariat, and praised the author's attempt to dispel the notion of the "Uncle Toms" that all whites hate Negroes or, at best, are incapable of understanding them.[66] And Elistratova noted warmly that unlike "superficial bourgeois writers" who had "penned works influenced with sincere but futile sympathy and compassion for the Negroes," Wright "does not complain, he accuses."[67]

In the Russian edition of *Uncle Tom's Children*, the stories were rearranged in a sequence that, the critic Nevelski pointed out, underlined their revolutionary character:

"In the first story a man defends himself alone. In the second story a man fights for his family. In the third story a man struggles for the Negro people. In the fourth story a man fights for the oppressed people, whether this people be white or black."[68]

"And so, step by step with each story, man's understanding grows, step by step man raises himself, spurred on by the blows of fate, to an understanding of objective truth—the inevitable struggle among the opposed classes, justice, and the final triumph of the oppressed."[69] Once again the heroine of Gorky's *Mother* was brought forth. Sue, of "Bright and Morning Star" strongly resembled Gorky's heroine in her understanding of the class nature of the fight in which she was

[65] Anna Karavayeva, "Ob Eptone Sinklere i Lengstone Khyuze," *Internatsionalnaya literatura*, Nos. 7-8 (1939), p. 368.

[66] V. Barsov, *"Deti dyadi Toma,"* *Literaturny kritik*, No. 11 (1938), p. 197.

[67] A. Yelistratova, *"Deti dyadi Toma,"* *Pravda*, October 21, 1938.

[68] The sequence of stories in the Russian edition was: (1) "Big Boy Leaves Home," (2) "Down by the Riverside," (3) "Fire and Cloud," (4) "Bright and Morning Star."

[69] V. Nevelski, *"Deti dyadi Toma,"* *Oktyabr*, Nos. 10-11 (1939), p. 326.

engaged.[70] Moreover, Wright, then a Communist, had creditably designed prominent and sympathetic roles for Party members.

When *Native Son* was translated in the magazine *Internatsionalnaya Literatura* in 1941, the American edition had already been reviewed at length in Soviet periodicals. It was evident from these reviews, which consisted chiefly of long and impassioned synopses, that, in the opinion of the critics, Wright had written a profound and dramatic report on American social tensions. Aesthetic judgments were sparse, however, and their paucity suggested that the critics had become nervous over Wright's art, or perhaps had been overpowered by it. The critic Rokotov did note that while the "adventure line" had in places been "developed to the detriment of the ideological ring of the novel as a whole," Wright had cleverly employed the suspense devices of the traditional "bourgeois" crime story "to bring leading progressive ideas to the consciousness of the reader" and had thus "masterfully used the armament of the enemy in order to inflict a blow upon him."[71] And Abramov hinted at criticisms which, later in the forties, were to be the basis of severe Soviet denunciations of Wright, by suggesting that "perhaps the naturalism of certain episodes is superfluous" and mentioning the influence of Dostoevski.[72] But for the most part the virtues and shortcomings of the book as a work of fiction were seldom discussed.

Generally the most controversial aspect of Wright's novel, among critics everywhere, had been his choice of a "bad Negro" for a hero. Both of the Russians who commented on this question defended the author's right to make Bigger Thomas his protagonist—Rokotov on the ground that Bigger is typical of the resentful, though misguidedly individualistic, new generation of Negroes who will not stand being oppressed,[73]

[70] *ibid.*, p. 328.
[71] T. Rokotov, "Tvorcheski rost Richarda Raita," *Internatsionalnaya literatura*, No. 2 (1941), p. 154.
[72] Al. Abramov, "Syn dyadi Toma," *Literaturnaya gazeta*, September 8, 1940.
[73] Rokotov, *op.cit.*, p. 155.

and Startsev on the ground that Bigger is a memorable image of an unfortunate, maimed victim of American racial injustice.[74] But both critics also noted the absence of a positive antidotal Negro character in the novel. Startsev was not dismayed by this lack, arguing that the presence of American Communists in the novel was in itself a sufficiently eloquent symbol of its positive trend.[75] Rokotov, on the other hand, felt that the Dostoevskian "zoological individualism" of Bigger, for whom "personal interests stand in the center of the universe," required a counterirritant in the form of a more constructive character.[76]

The Russians, eminently aware that Wright was himself a Communist, were generous and hopeful in treating the ideological deficiencies in *Native Son*, and their good will came more easily because they knew that he had written a strikingly good novel. By the time his next book came out, however, his vision of politics had changed, and he was no longer a Communist. Only then, as a later chapter will show, did the critics discover elements in *Native Son* that should have given them pause at the time they were praising it.

Although Anderson, Caldwell, Frank, Hughes, and Wright were discussed by Soviet critics in other decades, it has been appropriate to consider them at this point because the Russians' attitude toward these representative Americans became fixed in the thirties. The basic set of prejudices which Soviet criticism adopted in those years has governed its outlook ever since. There have been variations in thematic emphasis and in degree of militancy and ideological purism, but the fundamental assumptions about the literary tendencies which these five writers represent have remained the same.

The critics often warmly appreciated the best qualities of these Americans—psychological profundity, narrative finesse, the sense of local color, social breadth, and individuality of style. And the critics were willing to recognize that their writing was generally better than that of their less talented

[74] A. Startsev, "Amerikanskaya tragediya," *Internatsionalnaya literatura*, Nos. 9-10 (1940), p. 212.
[75] *ibid.*, pp. 211-12.   [76] Rokotov, *op.cit.*, pp. 155-56.

but more orthodox American "proletarian" compatriots. On the other hand, their very virtues, in Soviet opinion, had their reverse side, since these virtues were often associated with serious ideological corruptions. The collection of sins which Soviet critics found in these writers was thought to be broadly representative of the ideological defects of contemporary American literature.

Preoccupation with instinctive behavior, which lent psychological depth to the works of Anderson and Frank, also led them to embrace mystical philosophies of unconscious motivation that were totally incompatible with the Soviet concept of human nature. Frank, Anderson, and Caldwell (and the others to some degree) overemphasized sex. By the mid-thirties the private mysteries of the human personality were no longer a legitimate concern of literature. Marxism-Leninism, with its exclusive emphasis on the rational and social aspects of behavior, was purported to provide all that needed to be known about the psyche. Any approach to character that was not socially oriented or failed to use the measuring rod of civic utility was considered false and superfluous. The critics insisted that writers portray the whole man, but at the same time imposed limitations that made such a depiction impossible. One reason for this paradoxical stance was the ideological passion for order—often a contrived, artificial order—that permeates all Soviet pronouncements about man and society. Whereas these American writers knew that the human psyche is compounded of contradictory and often chaotic elements, their Soviet critics demanded characters whose motivation was clear-cut, simple, and logical. In addition, the critics' desire for political militancy made them suspicious of writing that lingered on the psychology of the individual. Close and detailed psychological analysis, in their view, created side issues and gave to fiction a static quality that diminished its effectiveness as a call to political action. Related to this view was the conception that the writer must concentrate on socially oriented characters who are "typical" of the revolutionary trend of humanity and therefore worthy of emulation. Psychological probing by a writer too often dis-

closed disturbing flaws in even the most positive characters.
To inspire the reader's compassion and tolerance of such flaws
was to risk a loss of didactic effectiveness. For this reason
it was best to avoid the exploration of recondite emotions and
to eschew the realm of subconscious desires.

An element of pre-Revolutionary Russian puritanism is
recognizable in Soviet objections to the employment of sex in
literature. Russian writers and critics have usually been Vic-
torian in this respect. Traditional standards of taste, however,
are not mainly responsible for this attitude in Soviet times.
The cause, rather, is an ideology which considers intimate
and personal emotions unfit subjects for literature. The attention these American writers paid to sex, loneliness, and individual frustration may well have been repugnant to some
critics, but the critics' objections were rooted in their ideological refusal to recognize the validity of such investigations
in literature. Whereas American writers claimed an interest
in everything that happens to mankind, the Soviet conception
of human nature had become narrow, and, to the extent that
it ignored basic emotional concerns, inhumane.

But it was in the name of "humanity" that the critics objected to the American literary practice of "biologism"—the
drawing of implicit or explicit analogies between man and
lower forms of life. To stress the irrational motives of behavior, the critics argued, is to deprive man of dignity. The
"pathological" characters of Caldwell and Anderson, and
Wright's elemental Bigger Thomas, all suggested that society
is composed of biological accidents over which human reason
ultimately has no control. In Anderson the critics perceived
an extension of this attitude to the point of an aesthetically
systematized and hopeless fatalism. The portrayal of a blind,
pathetic human race victimized by nature ran counter to the
Soviet image of man as a noble creature in charge of his own
destiny. By questioning the power of human volition to shape
social development, such a portrayal weakened the effectiveness of literature as an instrument of social change. To Soviet
critics, it did not matter that an examination of the limitations
of human endowment or the depiction of man in humiliating

circumstances produced understanding and compassion. These luxuries could be dispensed with in the optimistic literature of a rapidly changing world.

In denying the validity of these aspects of American writing, Soviet critics were attacking a fundamental source of narrative interest as it is conceived in twentieth-century Western literature. Immediate politics aside, conformity to Soviet demands by these American writers would indeed have involved their total transformation as artists. It would have imposed on them a uniformity both of theme and of approach, based on a shallow, monotonous conception of human nature and a false and superficially optimistic analysis of social forces. There would have been no room for irony in their writing, or for the profundity that comes from uncertainty and ambivalence. We have seen that such a creative transformation was impossible. But why, with ample evidence of these Americans' ideologically uncongenial and individualistic tastes and aspirations, did Soviet publishers and critics display such interest in them?

The answer is elusive and complex, but it should include the following considerations. First of all, Russian literary taste was probably more catholic and imaginative than Soviet criticism, constricted by its ideological obligations, would indicate. Russians like good literature. Even if this were not so, however, interest in these writers was justified solely for their critical portrayal of the American scene, since a Russian reading their works could only conclude that life in the capitalist United States was painful, grim, and brutal. The interests of the international proletarian literary movement also demanded that the friendship of liberal and radical writers such as these be cultivated. Translation of the proletarian endeavors of Anderson and Frank, which rank aesthetically near the bottom among their writings, was probably in part an act of political courtship.

In this decade the critics wrote as if they were entirely confident of the mounting success of the Soviet attempt to win allies among politically uncommitted American writers of left-wing sympathies. While they did not ignore organic elements in the aesthetic philosophies of the Americans that should have given them pause, their tone conveyed assurance that the relentless logic of political necessity would overcome all of these writers' ideological, and therefore aesthetic, misgivings. The Russians' obvious miscalculation came partly from ignorance. With only limited, crude, secondhand information at their disposal, based largely on the reports of ideologically intoxicated American Communists, they were inevitably prone to overenthusiastic conclusions.

But their error was also a product of the peculiar unrealistic *élan* that dominates a great many Soviet cultural pronouncements. Soviet ideology is oriented toward the future. Operating with a Marxist dialectic that presupposes the predictability of history, Soviet thinkers often set up goals and then proceed to persuade themselves that, since the historical process is a dynamic one, those goals are already being attained. They get to thinking that because a thing *should* exist and *will* exist, it already exists. This habit of mind accounts for the practice we have observed in the present chapter of judging works of American literature not for what they are, but in terms of what their authors might write in the future.

As it turned out, the loose involvement of these five writers in the proletarian movement of the thirties was only a phase in their varied and colorful careers. For all of them, in fact, proximity to revolutionary literature was tentative and transitory and all, sooner or later, developed other literary interests. The passing of the Depression, the onset of World War II, and the natural evolution of their individual talents account in large measure for their estrangement from proletarian literature. A more organic reason, however, has been suggested by Langston Hughes, recalling his year's stay in the Soviet Union in the early thirties: "Arthur Koestler asked me one day why in Moscow I did not join the Communist Party. I told him that what I had heard concerning the Party indicated that it was based on strict discipline and the acceptance of directives that I, as a writer, did not wish to accept. I did not believe political directives could be successfully applied to creative writing. They might well apply to the preparation of tracts and pamphlets, yes, but not to poetry or fiction, which to be valid, I felt, had to express as truthfully as possible the *individual* emotions and reactions of the writer, rather than mass directives issued to achieve practical and often temporary political objectives."[77] Individual shock, projected into a social emotion, had caused these men to write on proletarian themes in the first place. Swept up temporarily by the collective enthusiasm for radical change, they remained individualists at heart. The only one of them who ever joined the Communist Party, Wright, left it, bitter and disillusioned.[78] After all, they were—to use the Soviet term which the critics carefully avoided in their most sanguine and hopeful moments—"petty bourgeois radicals."

The Soviet proclivity for evaluating a book in terms of the current state of its author's personal politics became well established in the thirties and has continued to the present. Although they maintained close ideological scrutiny over literature, the critics' judgment of a given work was often decisively influenced by the current position of its author in public life. Their comments on Waldo Frank and Richard Wright, for example, indicate that they were more interested in the authors than in the books they wrote. At the heart of the criticism of these Americans, and of dozens of others in whom the Russians were interested, was the desire that they become disciplined Communists. Ideology was prominent in Soviet criticism, but even more decisive were the demands of practical politics.

The writing of Langston Hughes was judged not in terms of its own verisimilitude, but rather in terms of the proper strategy for arousing Negro Americans to revolutionary action during the Depression. All the negative criticism of Hughes reduces to the complaint that he did not constantly rivet his attention on the urgent necessity for revolution. For Soviet critics, at their worst, were not content with trimming from literature everything but the rigid steel framework of

[77] Langston Hughes, *I Wonder as I Wander*, New York and Toronto, 1956, pp. 121-22.
[78] Richard Wright in Richard Crossman, ed., *The God that Failed*, New York, 1949, pp. 115-62.

a single, simple ideology. Going still farther, they were willing to ignore even that ideology when the political situation demanded it. The extraordinary attention to the day-to-day political complexions of individual writers was more than just an indication of Soviet willingness to subordinate literature to the class struggle. It bespoke a need to supplement broad ideological propositions about literature with tactical guidance of immediate political import.

CHAPTER VI

FROM WORLD WAR II TO 1955

༄༄༄ FOR THE July-August issue of *International Literature* in 1939, scarcely a month before the signing of the Soviet–Nazi nonaggression pact and the start of the war between Germany and the European allies, Abel Startsev wrote an article entitled "America and Russian Society," in which he traced in scholarly detail the historic bases of American-Russian friendship since the eighteenth century. While Startsev was careful to point out that for the past half-century the United States had been a typical "leading capitalist power" in her cynical exploitation of workers and asserted that "the forms of the democratic order scarcely hid the dictatorship of industrial and finance capital," he nevertheless argued that the two peoples could work together as a powerful deterrent to "Fascist aggression."[1]

A few weeks later the Soviet army marched into Poland in benevolent collaboration with "Fascist aggression," and Startsev's article was woefully outdated. But its usefulness was not over. In June 1941, Hitler turned against the Soviet Union, and in the September-October issue of *International Literature* for that year Startsev's article appeared once more, with revisions. The main body of the piece was the same—both versions either ignored or glossed over historic frictions between the two countries—but now the American class struggle was virtually eliminated from consideration and in its place the chronicle of friendly cultural relations between the two countries was expanded.[2] The Soviet Union was eagerly awaiting a new ally, and Pearl Harbor soon brought that ally.

In the tense two years that elapsed between the first and second versions of Startsev's article, Russia had begun to

[1] Abel Startsev, "Amerika i russkoye obshchestvo," *Internatsionalnaya literatura*, Nos. 7-8 (1939), pp. 289-309.

[2] Abel Startsev, "Amerika i russkoye obshchestvo," *Internatsionalnaya literatura*, Nos. 9-10 (1941), pp. 208-26.

close the door on American culture. The only literary event of any importance was the publication of *The Grapes of Wrath*. The Popular Front had been shattered, a humiliating war with Finland was in progress for part of this period, and Russia was preoccupied with a menacing and uncertain ally in Hitler. When the German armies attacked, the trend of indifference toward America halted immediately. Testimonials of affection for American literature were elicited from numerous prominent Soviet writers, and the critics began an optimistic assessment of America's potential for cultural defense.[3] There could be no increase in the printing of American works, because the Soviet publishing industry, mobilized for war like everything else, had to turn away from nonessentials. The pattern of publication of American books, in fact, became quite similar to that which had prevailed under War Communism twenty years before. Printing of belles-lettres was sharply curtailed, and the selection of titles became conservative. Of the fifteen writers whose books were published at this time, nine—Twain, Sinclair, O. Henry, Poe, London, Whitman, Bret Harte, Cooper, and Dreiser—were favorites of long standing. Three others—Caldwell, Steinbeck, and Albert Maltz—had established Russian reputations in the thirties. Only three—Stuart Engstrand, Edgcum Pinchon, and Lillian Hellman—were new. Periodicals also followed this pattern, and confined their new translations, for the most part, to the political and military reportage of such persons as William L. Shirer and Quentin Reynolds. Most of the writers who continued to be printed were the same ones who had been singled out in previous times of crisis. Writers such as Twain, Sinclair, London, Whitman, and Cooper had come to be regarded as sources of cultural stability. Russians could rely on them in a period of grave national danger.

Like every other branch of cultural activity, Soviet criticism pursued the single aim of defending the country and

[3] "Sovetskiye pisateli ob angliskoi i amerikanskoi literature," *Internatsionalnaya literatura*, Nos. 9-10 (1941), pp. 230-42; Al. Abramov, "Amerikanskiye mastera kultury v borbe s fashizmom," *Internatsionalnáya literatura*, Nos. 9-10 (1941), pp. 223-26.

winning the war. The ranks of critics were greatly thinned by military and home service, and those who remained at their desks seldom enjoyed the luxury of browsing in current foreign literature. Nevertheless, they did display a concern for what was being written in America. In an article probably completed at about the time of Pearl Harbor, the critic Roko-tov wrote: "The leading writers of England and America are obligated to do much more than they have done so far to create vivid, picturesque, strong works capable of instilling in readers a feeling of implacable hatred for fascism and of strengthening their moral firmness and resolution to fight to the end, to the complete destruction of the Huns of the 20th century."[4] All subsequent remarks on our wartime writing were in this same spirit of urgency. The sole criterion of literary value was practical effectiveness in building a fighting morale among Russia's allies.

The contemporary work best known in Russia during the war was Steinbeck's *The Moon is Down*, which was translated in two magazines in 1943. Although this work was a commercial success in the United States as a novella, a play, and a film, American critics have generally considered it one of Steinbeck's weakest efforts. Appearing at a time when the Soviet cause was still in grave danger, the story proved too pallid in its treatment of fascism to satisfy Russian critics.[5] Most of them felt that the author was too compassionate in his treatment of Fascist officers and showed a foggy understanding of Fascist mentality.[6] The enemy was too "humanized": the Fascist commandant was presented as a philosopher instead of as an inflexible, mechanical, unreasoning brute. And the resistance of the natives of Steinbeck's mythical town against the Nazi occupiers was vaguely portrayed:[7] the mayor, who heroically gives his life for his people, was

[4] T. Rokotov, "Anglo-amerikanskaya voyennaya novella," *Internatsional-naya literatura*, Nos. 11-12 (1941), p. 117.

[5] Only one critic endorsed the book strongly. N. Sergeyeva, "Novaya kniga Dzhona Steinbeka," *Pravda*, December 21, 1942.

[6] E. Knipovich, "Novaya kniga Dzhona Steinbeka," *Znamya*, Nos. 5-6 (1943), p. 241.

[7] T. Motyleva, "Angliskiye i amerikanskiye romany o voine," *Oktyabr*, Nos. 1-2 (1944), p. 162.

motivated by "rosy dreams of bourgeois democracy."[8] This latter defect was symptomatic of a general weakness in the current literature of Russia's allies: "In all the works of contemporary Western literature devoted to the struggle of freedom-loving peoples against fascism, the life of prewar Europe is described as a patriarchal idyll, like a rosy Utopian kingdom, where there were neither social contradictions nor social distress nor conflicts."[9] Even in the midst of a war for survival, it seemed, the free world should keep in mind that it was fighting, not to preserve the past, but to clear the way for a collectivist future!

As late as 1944, Soviet critics saw little evidence that American writers were giving the war adequate treatment. The critic Rubin noted that while Steinbeck and Caldwell (the latter did firsthand reporting in Russia) were at least writing war journalism, very few established writers were attempting to create works of art from the material of the war, and observed sadly that many of them, such as Lewis and Dreiser, seemed to be ignoring it altogether. An exception was Edna St. Vincent Millay, whose ballad "Murder of Lidice" impressed the critics deeply.[10] And three plays— Maxwell Anderson's *The Eve of St. Mark*, Moss Hart's *Winged Victory*, and Sidney Kingsley's historical drama *The Patriots* waged satisfactory "war on the ideological front."[11] But while Soviet writers, almost to a man, were deeply involved in the conflict, too many Americans were merely doing "business as usual."[12] Even in 1945, when the Allies were on the threshold of victory, the complaint continued that the war had "not yet been given a wide illumination" in either English or American literature.[13] A full Soviet assessment of American war writing would only emerge in

[8] Knipovich, *op.cit.*, p. 241.   [9] *ibid.*, p. 241.

[10] Vl. Rubin, "Voyennaya tema v amerikanskoi literature," *Znamya*, No. 4 (1944), p. 156.

[11] V. Rubin and I. Karintsev, "Obzor sovremennoi amerikanskoi i angliskoi dramaturgii," *Novy mir*, No. 7 (1945), p. 114.

[12] Rubin, "Voyennaya tema . . . ," *op.cit.*, p. 157.

[13] "Vtoraya mirovaya voina v angliskoi i amerikanskoi literature," *Sovremenniye angliskiye i amerikanskiye pisateli*, Moscow, 1945, p. 6.

the next decade, but already the critics were proclaiming that America's cultural strength lagged far behind her military might.

As Frederick C. Barghoorn has demonstrated in his comprehensive study of the Soviet image of the United States, all during the war the Kremlin maintained a guarded attitude toward America, and underneath the enthusiasm for a badly needed ally the traditional doctrinaire suspicion against the stronghold of capitalism continued to mark official Soviet propaganda and behavior.[14] The critics' complaints about the inadequacies of current American war writing were symptomatic of this ingrained ideological suspicion. To the prevailing Soviet opinion that the Americans, either through sinister calculation or lack of sufficient effort, had excessively delayed the opening of a Second Front in Western Europe and, in their geographical isolation, were having an easy time of it while Russians bore the brunt of the struggle against fascism, there was added the notion that American capitalist culture might be too effete to produce a really profound literary work about the war.

What Soviet critics demanded of American writers was a recognition of the principle that total war included the total mobilization of literature. Accustomed to a disciplined response to social command in times of national crisis, Soviet writers had turned to war literature with a will. Their own artistic success was not great. But it is also true that the American literature written during the war was seldom distinguished by profundity or patriotic persuasiveness. The war was too large, too complex, and very often too remote to be comprehended quickly and written about with both moral certainty and artistic fullness. It was natural for the writers of the United States, who were not used to employing fiction, poetry, or drama as a means of interpreting rapid public developments, to turn to reportage for their treatment of the war. Just as Americans, by and large, had failed to create a great literature from the events of the Depression, so now

[14] Frederick C. Barghoorn, *The Soviet Image of the United States: a Study in Distortion*, New York, 1950, Chapters II-VI.

their treatment of the swiftly moving events of the war seldom rose above the level of journalism. The ability to produce quickly a hortatory literature, however, is a dubious measure of the strength of a national culture. America contained other moral resources in abundance, and these saw her through the war.

Although vast quantities of good will and admiration for America were engendered by the wartime coalition, and although Soviet propaganda recognized that capitalist democracy was indeed qualitatively different from fascism, there were really no fundamental innovations in the Soviet evaluation of American culture. The refrain of capitalist decadence could be heard much less clearly in Soviet utterances than it had been before the war, but only because other, more urgent strains temporarily dominated it. As the coalition broke up and the period of cold war set in, Soviet doctrine, undisturbed by the minor revisions that had been made to accommodate the anti-Fascist alliance, was capable of supporting the most virulent attacks on the culture, and specifically the literature, of the United States.

For a short while after the war, however, it appeared that Soviet critics might be able to continue to discuss American literature with some respect and good sense. In 1945, for example, the magazine *Znamya* printed an article by Stanley Edgar Hyman, in which the American critic speculated on the need for an epic novel of World War II, on the order of *War and Peace*. In early 1946 the same magazine printed a reply to Hyman that restricted itself to dispassionate literary argument and did not specifically disparage American culture.[15] But all possibility of reasonable Soviet discussion of literary problems vanished in the late summer and fall of 1946, when the Communist Party launched an unprecedentedly bitter and thoroughgoing attack on Western culture that was to last for nearly a decade. Spearheaded by a series of resolutions of the Central Committee against "ideological

---

[15] Stenli Edgar Khaimen, "Novaya *Voina i Mir*," *Znamya*, No. 9 (1945), pp. 137-50; Viktor Fink, "Otkrytoye pismo Stenli Edgaru Khaimenu," *Znamya*, Nos. 2-3 (1946), pp. 143-52.

neutrality" in the arts, and by Andrei Zhdanov's denunciation of the journals *Leningrad* and *Zvezda* and of the scapegoat writers Mikhail Zoshchenko and Anna Akhmatova, the Party assiduously undertook to stamp out all vestiges of "servility before the capitalist West" on the part of both writers and critics. While by far the saddest effect of the ensuing series of political probings, directives, and denunciations was its sterilizing influence on Soviet creative writing, criticism too, and particularly that devoted to American literature, became a severe casualty. In 1944 and 1945, Vladimir Rubin had complained that British and American writers were neglecting the war, but he had done so with restraint. By the end of 1946 the same critic was proclaiming, in the new abusive spirit, that British and American poetry of the war years was simply "bankrupt."[16]

From the beginning of the "Zhdanov era" in 1946 to the summer of 1955, when the "Geneva spirit" introduced a period of relative friendliness toward Western culture, Soviet criticism of American literature was so homogeneous in its essentials that the whole must be considered as a single epoch. The cold war had set in and literary criticism, more than ever before, was subordinated to the purely political task of denigrating the capitalist West. By 1947 the theory of "two worlds"—the nascent Soviet world of peace, democracy, and socialism and the decadent Western world of militaristic, imperialistic, capitalist reaction—had come to govern all Soviet writing about America. To this implacable attitude there was added a new ingredient of Great Russian chauvinism, in terms of which it became impossible to recognize Western preeminence in any field of human endeavor, past or present. At the same time, however, the quantity of Soviet writing about the West, and America in particular, grew much larger than it had been either before or during the war. Millions and millions of words, most of them hotly vituperative, on every conceivable aspect of America were turned out in the form of pamphlets, editorials, news stories, plays, poems,

---

[16] Vl. Rubin, "Nishcheta ideinaya i khudozhestvennaya," *Literaturnaya gazeta*, December 21, 1946, p. 4.

novels, and—by no means the least prominent—literary criticism.

All Soviet criticism in this period started from the premise that the postwar United States was undergoing a fundamental and perhaps fatal crisis of capitalist development. Reconversion of her colossal war industry to peacetime production, Soviet doctrine argued, must strain America's economy to an extreme. Unemployment, strikes, and inflation would increase economic inequality, intensify the class struggle, and put an end to the comparative social harmony that had marked the war years. Simultaneously, monopoly capital, straining for markets, would force the nation to undertake imperialist adventures in a new era of atomic jingoism. The arts, degenerating under the pressure of this black reaction, were becoming the misanthropic tool of capitalist exploitation at home and imperialistic expansion abroad. Only those alert and ideologically advanced Americans who were fortunate enough to see the wisdom and virtue of Soviet policies could combat effectively this trend toward war and cultural effacement. For, as Startsev put it with simple black-and-white fidelity to the Party line, the world was now divided into two camps, the one "imperialist and antidemocratic" and the other "anti-imperialist and democratic."[17]

Nearly all American literature about World War II, the critics decided, testified to the cultural sterility of the country and served, either directly or indirectly, the interests of the bankers and industrialists who were promoting the new imperialism. The war did not produce a single outstanding work. Many writers who in the thirties had "joined the cause of progressive literature," such as Dos Passos, Waldo Frank, and Richard Wright, had "gone over to positions of reaction," while established talents like Steinbeck, Faulkner, Hemingway, and Caldwell had all failed to write significant things.[18] The poets had boycotted the conflict, preferring to

[17] A. Startsev, "Imperialisticheskaya agressiya i sovremennaya ameri-kanskaya literatura," *Znamya*, No. 11 (1948), p. 124.
[18] R. Orlova, "Vospitaniye landsknekhtov," *Novy mir*, No. 3 (1948), pp. 202-3.

cling to "pure art" for the duration.[19] One reason for the general barrenness was that the "predominant mass of Americans took the war with Hitlerism as something very remote from their life, almost unconnected with it," since they were free from bombardment and the threat of invasion.[20] A more deep-seated cause was the organic failure of American ideology to grasp the political nature and purpose of the war. The critic Orlova reasoned that "in the literature about the Second World War only those works which showed patriotism, antifascism as the source of great deeds, could be genuinely artistic."[21] American literature, however, did not notice the war's "great liberating meaning, which brings forth and nourishes great ideas and creates significant works of art." The source of the trouble was obvious:

"The ideologists of American reaction did not want the working masses of America to understand the unbreakable tie existing between the basic goals of the war against fascism and the interests of the people, their future. A recognition of the just character of the anti-Fascist war would lead inevitably to an understanding of the necessity of fundamental social changes in America itself. Therefore American literature was ordered to stifle the truth about the character of the war, to present the war as some kind of 'biological' inevitability, to show that war is a manifestation of ungovernable forces standing above men, and finally to smear over the difference between just and unjust wars. Literature must show at the same time that ordinary Americans are indifferent to the events which have taken place, are not inspired by anti-Fascist ideas."[22]

When a nation does not know precisely what it is fighting for, the Soviet argument went, its art also lacks focus. In the early stages of the war, Rubin pointed out, Americans confined themselves largely to reportage and sketches, and when war themes did enter into novels and stories, their au-

[19] Rubin, "Nishcheta . . . ," op.cit.
[20] Vl. Rubin, "Krizis sovremennoi amerikanskoi literatury," Zvezda, No. 8 (1948), p. 190.
[21] Orlova, "Vospitaniye . . . ," op.cit., p. 204.   [22] ibid., p. 201.

thors "could not rise up to large generalizations and conclusions." The war served merely as an "exotic background," and its purpose was treated "timidly and indecisively." Feeling that readers wanted most of all distraction from the war's burdens, writers concentrated on "light" literature. Military action was largely confined to adventure thrillers.[23] When, in the later stages of the conflict, some writers began treating war themes more seriously, the ideological poverty of the times became even more clearly evident. Harry Brown's *A Walk in the Sun*, a fictional account of an infantry patrol action in the Mediterranean theatre, gave "lifelike and individualized" portraits of American soldiers,[24] but its narrative was too laconic for psychological profundity.[25] The book was "merely photographic," since the author only "slithers on the surface" of his material.[26] In the opinion of Soviet critics, its main defect, typical of most American war writing, was that it sealed off military action from the political issues behind it. Brown's infantrymen were "inwardly empty."[27] Profoundly indifferent to the aims of the war, "these American soldiers have no curiosity, they think about almost nothing," since the author "takes great pains to remove from the consciousness of his heroes anything that might have even a remote connection with the actual problems of war and contemporary life."[28] In this ideological and moral vacuum, the critics complained, there were no "examples of exceptional heroism,"[29] and in fact the book was devoid of a hero "in the literary sense of the word."[30] Without an exemplary hero, or of any thought that could "unite these people,"[31] the story lacked the inspirational quality that Soviet critics have always prized above all else. Mendelson partially defended the author on the grounds of realism: "One cannot

[23] Rubin, "Krizis . . . ," *op.cit.*, p. 190.
[24] Orlova, "Vospitaniye . . . ," *op.cit.*, p. 205.
[25] Rubin, "Krizis . . . ," *op.cit.*, p. 191.
[26] M. Mendelson, *Soviet Interpretation of Contemporary American Literature*, translated by Deming B. Brown and Rufus W. Mathewson, Washington, D.C., 1948, p. 7.
[27] *ibid.*, p. 6.   [28] *ibid.*, p. 6.
[29] *ibid.*, p. 6.   [30] Orlova, "Vospitaniye . . . ," *op.cit.*, p. 205.
[31] *ibid.*, p. 205.

deny the right of an author to construct his tale around such 'heroes,' particularly since a great many Americans did actually enter the war without comprehending, and emerged from it without learning, its meaning." Brown's dispassionate attitude, on the other hand, was inexcusable: "But the most singular trait of Brown as a writer consists in the fact that he looks upon all this with complete indifference. He is not disturbed by the astonishingly narrow interests of the characters whom he chooses to portray. The spiritual blindness of the American soldiers he describes—partners in a fight against the Fascist armies—does not move him. Ultimately, Brown does not rise above the level of his unintelligent heroes.[32]

For all its concentration on the ordinary soldier and the "little man" in general, Soviet critics argued, American war writing was only superficially democratic. In the absence of an elevating ideology, close attention to the rank and file only served to degrade the image of the individual and to make war a meaningless and humiliating experience. The cartoonist Bill Mauldin showed the G. I. as a "drunken barbarian with his helmet set at a rakish angle and an idiotic leer on his un-shaven face," and represented this monster as "the active principle, the only constructive element amid the ruin and chaos."[33] While he sympathized with the "plain soldier, the toiler of the war" and ridiculed the "boastful self-satisfied American officer," his caricatures of officers were "entirely too mild—mere friendly quips, no more."[34] Correspondent Ernie Pyle not only featured the soldiers' lack of political awareness, but even "elevated it to a virtue."[35] In *The Naked and the Dead*, Norman Mailer "clearly demonstrates how the American militarists, aping the Fascists, are stultifying the average American dressed in military uniform, how they are deliberately perverting the minds of the soldier masses and playing on their basest instincts." But the characters with

[32] Mendelson, *Soviet Interpretation* . . . , *op.cit.*, pp. 6-7.

[33] R. Samarin, "Miles Americanus," *Soviet Literature*, No. 3 (1949), pp. 180-81.

[34] M. Romanov, "Problems of Progressive Literature in the U.S.A.," *Soviet Literature*, No. 11 (1949), pp. 172-73.

[35] Orlova, "Vospitaniye . . . ," *op.cit.*, p. 205.

whom he opposes his Fascist-minded general are weak, since Mailer wrote under the influence of "decadent literature," with its "disbelief in the spiritual strength of the people, its distorted, falsified depiction of man as a completely unstrung, debilitated hysterical creature."[36] Posing as the champion of the enlisted man in *From Here to Eternity*,[37] James Jones limited the soldier to "the most primitive impulses," so that "the whole meaning of the existence of these heroes is in the fact that they stupefy themselves with alcohol and seek distraction in brothels."[38] The same lack of genuine democracy was in John Hersey's *A Bell for Adano*. Although Hersey criticized the military bureaucracy, and his earthy hero Major Joppolo opposes the "wild, hysterical general" who represents the worst of the occupation policies in Italy,[39] the hero "does not struggle with fascism and does not even think of supporting the democratic elements in their fight with reaction."[40] Furthermore, Hersey's Italians are "completely unnatural, sentimentalized, and childlike natives," and their main function is to be "moved by the generous actions of the good American,"[41] whose "complacent attitude . . . betrays the lordly patronizing and bantering tone of the conqueror who may at any moment raise his voice and bawl commands."[42]

The elements of crude polemics and cold-war propaganda in this criticism are obvious. It was baldly unjust to argue that American writing about World War II was inspired by social malevolence and imperialistic arrogance, and that American authors were following a Fascist mandate to obscure the political character and goals of the conflict. The accusation of ideological poverty, however, constituted a more interesting and much deeper indictment and it requires close

---

[36] Romanov, "Problems . . . ," *op.cit.*, pp. 170-71.

[37] I. Maslova and V. Glunin, "Reaktsionnaya literaturnaya kritika na sluzhbe podzhigatelei voiny," *Znamya*, No. 10 (1952), p. 189.

[38] Ye. Romanova and V. Rubin, "Protiv marshallizatsii kultury," *Novy mir*, No. 1 (1953), p. 214.

[39] Mendelson, *Soviet Interpretation . . .* , *op.cit.*, p. 8.

[40] Startsev, "Imperialisticheskaya agressiya . . . ," *op.cit.*, p. 136.

[41] Mendelson, *Soviet Interpretation . . .* , *op.cit.*, p. 8.

[42] Samarin, "Miles Americanus," *op.cit.*, p. 178.

attention. Certainly American writing did not help to win the war, and it has not tried to convince the world, in retrospect, that American troops were consistently the bearers of light and justice. (Soviet literature, on the other hand, has uniformly insisted on the absolute political and moral rectitude of the Soviet armed forces.) In this century American literature has been traditionally antimilitary. It became conventional in the twenties for the writer to look upon war as futile and aimlessly destructive, and the generation of the forties, under the powerful influence of their literary masters of the twenties, found it impossible to break tradition by viewing war as constructive and purposeful. Even though they were convinced of the political justice of the Allied cause, they could not switch suddenly to the affirmative and glorify war as a school of heroism and patriotism. Likewise, the American literary habit of social criticism encouraged the writers of the forties to disparage many aspects of the military and to emphasize the frequent contradictions between our national goals and our national behavior. The military organization with its repression and confinement of the individual, its inevitable antidemocratic character, and its waste of time and talent, was a natural target for a writing generation bred in the spirit of skepticism and objection.

The Americans who wrote about World War II were preoccupied with the question of what war did to the individual who was experiencing it and of how it affected his values. To the extent that these writers largely avoided the explicit political context and did not constantly proclaim its meaning in ringing political phrases it might be said that American literature failed to grasp the political purpose of the war. The accusation of ideological poverty, however, does not stand up, for Americans did know, and cared deeply about, the political issues. It is true that the writers of the forties did not arrive at a consistent point of view from which to interpret the anguish, violence, and dislocation about which they wrote. Unlike Soviet writers, they were not equipped with a prescribed, monolithic set of answers to the questions of the war. Rather, the Americans were faced with the much more complicated task of affirming and at the same time critically examining the operation of a subtle and fragile democracy under the impact of a massive armed conflict.

Had Soviet critics at this time really been concerned with literary values, they would have concluded, correctly, that American writing about World War II was not as original, as arresting, or as enduring as that of the first war. The accomplishment of Mailer, Jones, Irwin Shaw, and the other prominent writers of the forties does not measure up to that of the war generation of Dos Passos and Hemingway. But Soviet critics during the cold war were simply not interested in genuine aesthetic comparisons.

Many of the attitudes that Soviet critics claimed to find in this literature can be explained in terms of their assumption that even during the war against the Axis, the United States was planning imperialist aggression. Of the ideological passivity of the characters in *A Walk in the Sun*, Orlova remarked that "the education of this type of soldier is one of the most important political problems of American imperialism, which was by no means forgotten during the Second World War."[43] Ernie Pyle disclosed the same sinister aim in describing the war with Germany "as a sport, as a game." Since "the goal of war is a matter of deep indifference to them," Orlova contended that "it would not be difficult to imagine the soldiers described by Ernie Pyle as fighting against the freedom of any people."[44] The critic Samarin cited a passage in Mauldin's *Up Front* in which a gullible American sergeant distributes cigarettes among malingering German prisoners, and Mauldin's wry comment, "I wouldn't be surprised if a German corporal named Schicklgruber received an American cigarette under similar conditions twenty-six years ago." Crudely ignoring the author's irony, Samarin concluded: "Mauldin's blether thus reveals as far back as 1944 the outline of that plan of American-Nazi cooperation which has now in many cases, and despite the protests of progressive circles in the USA, become an established fact.[45]

[43] Orlova, "Vospitaniye . . . ," *op.cit.*, p. 205.   [44] *ibid.*, pp. 205-6.
[45] Samarin, "Miles Americanus," *op.cit.*, p. 182.

A Bell for Adano was "a form of propaganda, objectively serving the interests of those in America who aspire to dominate the world." An attempt to "gloss over and to justify the work of the American military authorities in occupied territory,"[46] the novel was "one of the first forebears of the postwar works that propagandize the 'superiority' of the American way of life,"[47] through a "stylized-idyllic depiction of bourgeois democracy."[48] Hersey's *Hiroshima* was useful to American reactionaries in "their attempt to frighten whole peoples and nations."[49] By likening the atomic bomb to an "elemental catastrophe—a flood or an earthquake" and implying that the new horror is beyond the control of mankind, the book served to terrify readers instead of enlightening them.[50] It thus contributed to the "atomic fever" that was being intensified in an attempt to promote a "preventive war" by such writers as Philip Wylie[51] and Upton Sinclair,[52] whom the critics called irresponsible alarmists. The most flagrantly imperialistic book of all, however, was *From Here to Eternity* —"the work of an enemy of the American people who sold his pen to Wall Street and the Pentagon, and whose ignoble aim is to glorify the mercenaries of the Dollar Empire's plundering army."[53] (The critics, incidentally, unanimously deplored its "wallowings in cynicism and pornography.")[54] In his Kiplingesque scorn of the natives of the "Pacific colonies of the USA."[55] Jones was a "flagrant racist, trying to 'prove'

[46] Mendelson, *Soviet Interpretation . . .* , *op.cit.*, pp. 7-8.

[47] Rubin, "Krizis . . . ," *op.cit.*, p. 191.

[48] Startsev, "Imperialisticheskaya agressiya . . . ," *op.cit.*, p. 136.

[49] Romanov, "Problems . . . ," *op.cit.*, p. 173.

[50] Orlova, "Vospitaniye . . . ," *op.cit.*, p. 207.

[51] B. Izakov, "Zapad nervnichayet," *Oktyabr*, Nos. 7-8 (1946), pp. 177-79; "Atomny bred Filippa Uaili," *Literaturnaya gazeta*, February 6, 1954, p. 4.

[52] Ye. Romanova, "Teoriya i praktika literaturnykh biznesmenov," *Novy mir*, No. 11 (1951), p. 271.

[53] D. Zhantiyeva, "Soldiers of the Dollar Empire," *Soviet Literature*, No. 9 (1952), p. 160.

[54] I. Levidova, "Slander and Falsification Pillorized," *Soviet Literature*, No. 2 (1952), p. 177.

[55] Zhantiyeva, "Soldiers . . . ," *op.cit.*, p. 159.

the supremacy of the Anglo-Saxon race."[56] His sentimental attachment to the "common American soldier, who has to do all the dirty work, conquer and 'pacify' foreign lands, loot, and shed blood"[57] was a "demagogic device which camouflages a sermon of reactionary ideas."[58] Jones was a "hired agent of reaction": "Nearly all the action in Jones's novel takes place several months before Pearl Harbor. But *From Here to Eternity* was published in 1951, and the influences which operate in the U.S.A. today are clearly felt in the book. So, when its heroes speak of the 'coming war' there is no doubt that they mean a third world war which the rulers of America are trying to start."[59]

Much of this Soviet commentary on American writing about the war is absurd. It is clear that the critics combed American war literature for every possible indication of moral weakness and political malevolence, and that they were capable of the wildest invention in their search for specters and ogres. Even the valid criticisms that can be traced through this tangled mass of contradictions, quarter-truths, misinterpretations, and lies somehow seem poisoned in their abusive, polemical context. Most American critics would agree, for example, that the American soldier, as reflected in our war literature, was indeed politically naive and seemed to be acting in an ideological void. But they would also insist that a writer, if he was faithful to his material, could only portray the G.I. of World War II in this way. The Russians reasoned differently. They were quite anxious, as we have seen, to cite this literature as proof that American soldiers were spiritually empty. But they also blamed the writer for not prettifying the soldier by improving upon the prevailing ideology, and thus they proved to their own satisfaction that American literature itself was devoid of moral strength. This you-are-damned-if-you-do-and-damned-if-you-don't approach, of course, is dialectically justified in the Soviet way of think-

[56] Maslova and Glunin, "Reaktsionnaya . . . ," *op.cit.*, p. 189.
[57] Zhantiyeva, "Soldiers . . . ," *op.cit.*, p. 157.
[58] Maslova and Glunin, "Reaktsionnaya . . . ," *op.cit.*, p. 189.
[59] Zhantiyeva, "Soldiers . . . ," *op.cit.*, p. 160.

ing. Any device for deprecating the capitalist United States was legitimate. While they never admitted it explicitly, Soviet critics knew that the Russian soldier was just as apolitical as the American, if not more so. In Soviet literary theory, however, it was not the part of realism to admit the average or to celebrate the mean. Orlova, for instance, contended that the American practice of featuring "the 'little man' with all his defects" was democratic only on the surface. She argued, ". . . the experience of Soviet literature shows that one can write also about generals and that will be genuinely democratic, if the generals represent the people. . . . The typical images of Soviet literature are images of heroes. They are not 'average people' in the American sense of the word. These are typical examples in the Soviet, in the dialectical sense, these are the new, the rising, the invincible, perceived and reflected by the writer. The typical in the Marxist sense is the leader, the chief, even though this leader is just coming into being."[60]

To any reasonably reflective individual who is acquainted with the American scene, the various devices in the Soviet arsenal of vilification on display here—obtuse impugnation of authors' motives, groundless name-calling (Hersey was "an intelligence agent of American expansion in the Far East"),[61] strained parallels between postwar America and Nazi Germany, and semantic shortcuts such as the indiscriminate use of the symbols Wall Street and Pentagon—are beneath contempt and simply ridiculous. The image of the American writer, and of the whole literary process in the United States, that emerges from these comments is, however, morbidly interesting and sadly revealing. In employing American war literature as political documentation for their own preconceived conclusions, the critics irresponsibly, and perhaps purposefully at times, confused writers' intentions. The American writer was either an honest realist (since, the Russians insisted, the G. I. *was* shallow and brutish), a spineless prisoner of capitalist decadence, or a hireling of Wall

---

[60] Orlova, "Vospitaniye . . . ," *op.cit.*, p. 208.
[61] Samarin, "Miles Americanus," *op.cit.*, p. 178.

Street. Often, in the hands of a particularly ingenious critic, he was all three of these at one and the same time. Underlying all this criticism, however, was the premise that the American writer does not express his individualized vision of things, that he speaks not for himself but for an efficient, well-integrated propaganda center that buys masses of writers and issues unbreakable directives with machine-like precision. Here the critics were not talking of some subtle social process through which "Wall Street" and "The Pentagon" infiltrate reactionary concepts into the books of unwitting authors. In contending that writers obscured the meaning of World War II and used it as an opportunity for instilling imperialist ambitions in the American people, Soviet critics were in fact projecting to the United States the image of a controlled literature whose mode of operation was remarkably similar to their own.

The chain of command through which the sinister conspiracy of Wall Street and the Pentagon was purportedly activated in literature was never detailed by the critics. Any Soviet reader who attempted to construct a logically coherent picture of the situation in American writing from their comments was liable, in fact, to get lost in a jungle of contemptuous epithets. For the critics' remarks, taken as a whole, seemed designed to create an emotional impression rather than to provide a rational interpretation of a living cultural phenomenon. The scattergun technique of denouncing, in extravagant, imprecise terms, nearly every aspect of contemporary American writing offered such a confusing variety of dire explanations for its low state that only the most unimaginative and unquestioning reader could accept them without puzzlement. Through the thick haze of abuse, however, the more gullible Russian readers probably concluded that American literature was in decay because of (1) the natural, organic rottenness of capitalist culture and (2) intensified (although loosely defined) pressure from financiers and militarists.

From the end of World War II to the autumn of 1955, Soviet publishers were chary of printing any contemporary American work that did not closely document the Party line.

(With the exception of *The Moon is Down*, none of the American war literature just mentioned has ever been translated in the Soviet Union.) In the absence of translations, the Russian public was almost entirely at the mercy of the critics for its knowledge of what was currently being written in the United States. The general tenor and flavor of the critics' claims is suggested in the lead paragraphs of an essay by Mendelson that appeared in December 1948:

"A suffocating stench of putrescence blows from contemporary American decadent literature, which has captured the book markets of New York and San Francisco, Chicago and New Orleans. This literature talks endlessly of violence and death. It is soaked through and through with cynicism, it is drunk with nightmares and filth, it scorns mankind. Springing from the womb of rotting capitalist society, it is infected with its sins, and, like capitalism, is doomed to destruction.

"The brigands of American monopoly capital widely use the bourgeois-decadent literature of our day for their avaricious, antipopular aims. Corrupting the human soul, the newest works of the decadent authors of the USA serve reaction, serve American imperialism. In essence the contemporary reactionary-decadent literature of America helps the American imperialists to disarm the people spiritually, to sap its will to resist fascism, to clear the road to openly Fascist ideas and moods."[62]

The "general crisis" of American capitalism, in the words of the critic Anisimov, had brought literature to a state of "marasmus," so that "scorn of man, obscurantism, amorality, stupidity, misanthropy, bestial cruelty—this is what one meets up with at every step."[63] Wall Street had established a near monopoly of American publication[64] and used books "by the kilogram and by the metre"[65] in a "systematic endeavor

[62] M. Mendelson, "Amerikanskiye smertyashkiny," *Novy mir*, No. 12 (1948), p. 205.

[63] I. Anisimov, "Sovremenny literaturny raspad," *Oktyabr*, No. 11 (1947), p. 140.

[64] I. Anisimov, "Literature in the Service of Reaction," *Soviet Literature* No. 10 (1948), pp. 147-48.

[65] Anisimov, "Sovremenny literaturny raspad," *op.cit.*, p. 147.

to corrupt and pervert the mind."[66] "Best seller" was a term which had been "propagated by the advertising machine of the USA" to "impose on readers precisely those works which in spirit do the bidding of the American war mongers."[67] Another weapon in this huge conspiracy were the book clubs, through which "every member is obligated to acquire all books selected by the jury, without exception [sic]."[68] "Why," the critic Romanova asked, "do American publishers pander to the lowest and crudest tastes?" Here is her considered answer: "Commercial considerations are not the sole explanation here. The situation on the book market is determined primarily by the deliberate desire of the country's ruling circles to divert the mind of the reader from the momentous social and political problems that urgently require solution, and this is to be achieved by disseminating bunk that will appeal to the lowest instincts in man. Books are used by the minions of Wall Street to create a mass war psychosis that will help the warmongers in their dirty plans."[69]

The mass literature of America consisted of cheap magazine fiction, comic books featuring crime and violence,[70] gangster novels, and the brutal trash of Mickey Spillane.[71] Occasionally a bit of fluff like *The Egg and I* would distract the mass reader from his visceral preoccupations, but dramatizations of hopeless alcoholism on the order of *The Lost Weekend* would soon return him to a world of bestial fantasy.[72] The same dark qualities, the critics insisted, carried over into literature of more aristocratic pretensions. Thornton Wilder, who had long been a favorite whipping boy of

[66] Levidova, "Slander and Falsification Pillorized," *op.cit.*, p. 177.

[67] Yel. Romanova, "Cho takoye 'best-seller,'" *Literaturnaya gazeta*, December 7, 1951, p. 4.

[68] *ibid.*

[69] E. Romanova, "Masses and Mainstream," *Soviet Literature*, No. 1 (1950), p. 189.

[70] Kornei Chukovski, "Rastleniye amerikanskikh detei," *Literaturnaya gazeta*, October 15, 1949, p. 4; N. Novoselski, "Vospitateli ubits," *Literaturnaya gazeta*, June 1, 1954, p. 4.

[71] Romanova and Rubin, "Protiv marshallizatsii kultury," *op.cit.*, p. 215.

[72] Rubin, "Krizis . . . ," *op.cit.*, p. 192.

American Communist critics and whom the Russians even in the early thirties had dubbed a decadent reactionary,[73] was singled out once more for having written *The Skin of Our Teeth*—a play loaded with "gloomy, hopeless pessimism."[74] Preaching that history operates in a closed circle that excludes human volition and the progress of civilization,[75] Wilder depicted man as a "pitiful grain of sand," and his message was one of "sober misanthropy."[76] Similarly depressing was the work of William Faulkner, in which "the aimless cultivation of horror, the absorption in life as a nightmare, the celebration of monstrosity and sexual perversion are ubiquitous."[77] The critic Rubin found that "from time to time Faulkner succeeds in drawing an image that reflects reality to some degree." On the whole, however, his art was "permeated with motifs of madness and death": "This is a world of rot and carrion. It oppresses the reader, paralyzes his will. The novels of Faulkner are the brood of rotting capitalist society with its noxious, putrid morals. The moods and motifs cultivated by him serve the aim of the demoralization, the perversion of the reader. They inoculate him with a feeling of the most complete indifference to surrounding reality. Human passions, joy, love, strong characters are alien to Faulkner, as are images of fighters for the right and dignity of man. His world is a world of dying and dissolution."[78] Rubin added that all of Faulkner's characters, "the positive as well as the negative" are equally devoid of will in their spineless submission to fate. Although he was repelled by capitalist society, the author was incapable of criticizing it intelligently, since his alternative was an idealized "slave-holding South" and he merely longed to "suspend the movement of time" and

[73] A. Startsev, "Vseobshchi krizis kapitalizma i novaya volna soyuznikov proletariata v literature Ameriki," *Marksistsko-Leninskoye iskusstvoznaniye*, Nos. 5-6 (1932), p. 45; Al. Abramov, "Molodost veka," *Internatsionalnaya literatura* No. 6 (1935), p. 141.

[74] Rubin, "Krizis . . . ," *op.cit.*, p. 199.

[75] Orlova, "Vospitaniye . . . ," *op.cit.*, p. 209.

[76] Anisimov, "Sovremenny literaturny raspad," *op.cit.*, p. 148.

[77] Mendelson, *Soviet Interpretation* . . . , p. 18.

[78] Rubin, "Krizis . . . ," *op.cit.*, p. 197.

prolong the life of his "putrid, dying world."[79] Noting that "in almost all of Faulkner's books there are represented decomposed corpses, lunatics, triumphant prostitutes, sadists, idiots," Mendelson observed that "not without cause" had this Southerner in recent times been proclaimed a writer of "all-American proportions." In spirit his works were "especially close to American monopoly capital."[80]

Poetry, in the hands of such "representatives of militant reaction" as e. e. cummings, Robinson Jeffers, and T. S. Eliot,[81] had become a kind of "fifth column in literature," whose aim was to "disarm the people in the struggle with fascism, to sow cynicism, defeatism, to instill Fascist ideas."[82] It was "no accident" that the traitor Ezra Pound found numerous American defenders who proclaimed that "every artist has a motherland that knows no borders" and protected him as art's "holy idiot."[83] Only a few poets, Langston Hughes and Stephen Vincent Bénet among them, dared to "go against the stream of reactionary and 'apolitical' works."[84] For, supported by the "antihumanist philosophy" of John Dewey, Bertrand Russell, Santayana and others, American poetry had come to advocate withdrawal from life and haughty indifference to the needs and aspirations of the people.[85]

Such "ivory-towerism," to the Soviet way of thinking, was also reflected in the universal obsession with sex under the spell of the high priest, Henry Miller. Exaggerating Miller's popularity and influence out of all proportion, the critics repeatedly referred to him as the leader of a movement to divert American literature away from social responsibility by exploiting sex at every turn.[86] Miller's writing, the critic Ya-

[79] Mendelson, "Amerikanskiye smertyashkiny," *op.cit.*, p. 211.

[80] *ibid.*, p. 211.

[81] Irina Golovnya, "Poeziya opustoshennykh lyudei," *Literaturnaya gazeta*, April 28, 1948, p. 4; A. Startsev, "Mednoloby Eliot," *Literaturnaya gazeta*, October 22, 1949, p. 4.

[82] Rubin, "Krizis . . . ," *op.cit.*, p. 198.

[83] Aleksandr Isbakh, "O 'zhretsakh chelovecheskovo dukha' i predatelyakh roda chelovecheskovo," *Novy mir*, No. 2 (1948), p. 215.

[84] Rubin, "Krizis . . . ," *op.cit.*, p. 199.

[85] Isbakh, *op.cit.*, pp. 213-18.

[86] L. Yakovlev, "Literature of Decay," *Soviet Literature*, No. 6 (1950),

kovlev asserted, "cannot really be called simple pornography." Rather, it was a "moral plague, a leprosy of the mind," which "leads his reader into a world of perversion and sexual licentiousness and moral degradation with the object of inculcating upon him slavish obedience to the ruling classes." Thus Miller performed "the job assigned to him by his imperialist masters." (Another aspect of Miller's work was far from the ivory tower. For the author "eulogizes death and bloodshed" and thus "reechoes Hitler," since his "creed of universal negation acts like a narcotic, enervating people's will and building up the gangs of thugs which the exploiting classes need to defend their own existence in the face of approaching, inevitable doom.")[87] Most American writers, of course, were less frankly depraved than Miller. Nevertheless, the critic Anisimov insisted, the general climate was so poisonous that "normal people have almost disappeared from literature because they have become completely uninteresting" to a jaded public.[88]

Eugene O'Neill's *The Iceman Cometh* was likewise "shockingly decadent," not only for its argument that "all man's dreams about a better future are quite baseless,"[89] but also because the author, who had formerly included "critical notes" in his plays, had now gone to preaching the "general baseness" of humanity.[90] In the twenties the Russians had regarded him as a kind of latter-day Ibsen,[91] and several of his plays had enjoyed long and repeated runs on the Soviet stage.[92] Despite his "anarcho-Bohemian" overtones[93] he had handled social problems with "realism," stemming from his

---

pp. 172-78; Mendelson, *Soviet Interpretation . . . , op.cit.*, p. 18; Anisimov, "Sovremenny literaturny raspad," *op.cit.*, p. 148; Isbakh, *op.cit.*, p. 215.

[87] Yakovlev, *op.cit.*, pp. 173-77.

[88] Anisimov, "Sovremenny literaturny raspad," *op.cit.*, p. 147.

[89] Mendelson, *Soviet Interpretation . . . , op.cit.*, p. 20.

[90] Mendelson, "Amerikanskiye smertyashkiny," *op.cit.*, p. 215.

[91] Mikh. Zabludovski, "Ot realizma k mistitsizmu," *Literaturny kritik*, Nos. 7-8 (1934), pp. 211-13.

[92] Horst Frenz, "Eugene O'Neill in Russia," *Poet Lore* (1943) XLIX, 242-47.

[93] Al. Abramov, "Konets buntarstva Yudzhina O'Neilya," *Internatsionalnaya literatura*, No. 2 (1936), p. 146.

healthy concern for the plight of the individual in capitalist society.[94] In his work of the late twenties and early thirties, and especially with the appearance of *Strange Interlude* and *Mourning Becomes Electra,* Soviet criticism began to perceive a repudiation of "positive social values" and a turning to the deepest pessimism, disillusionment with humanity, and fatalism.[95] When *Days Without End* was published in 1934, a critic lamented that O'Neill had finally passed from "revolt against surrounding reality in the early stages of his work, through psychoanalysis, eroticism, and mysticism . . . into the bosom of the Catholic Church."[96] Although his plays never recovered their high prestige of the twenties and he was almost a dead letter in Russia in the following two decades, a belated production of *Ah, Wilderness!* enjoyed considerable success on the Moscow stage during the war.[97] In view of this triumph, and of the memories of his earlier successes in the Russian theater, the harsh indictment of *The Iceman Cometh* may have had special force for Soviet readers. With its collection of tramps, drunks, and harlots, the play invited comparison with Gorky's familiar *The Lower Depths.* However, Gorky's down-and-outers retained some human dignity,[98] whereas O'Neill's characters were "completely lost" and his only plea was for the "need to permit people to lull themselves with hopes."[99] *The Iceman Cometh* testified to the "decomposition . . . of a once greatly promising talent"[100] and to the depressed state of the contemporary American drama.

The critics professed to be particularly distressed over Caldwell and Steinbeck, who, they felt, had not lived up to their prewar expectations. During the war Caldwell's collec-

[94] Zabludovski, *op.cit.,* pp. 211-12.

[95] A. Yelistratova, "Literatura sovremennoi Ameriki," *Internatsionalnaya literatura,* No. 5 (1933), p. 107; Abramov, "Konets buntarstva . . . ," *op.cit.,* p. 147.

[96] Zabludovski, *op.cit.,* p. 217.

[97] Rubin and Karintsev, "Obzor . . . ," *op.cit.,* p. 117.

[98] Anisimov, "Sovremenny literaturny raspad," *op.cit.,* p. 148.

[99] Mendelson, *Soviet Interpretation . . . ,* *op.cit.,* p. 20.

[100] Anisimov, "Sovremenny literaturny raspad," *op.cit.,* p. 148.

tion of stories, *Georgia Boy*, had been translated and favorably reviewed.[101] *Tragic Ground*, his novel of 1944 about Southern poor whites in a wartime industrial boom town, was never translated, and was not mentioned by the critics until 1947. Within the next year, however, the novel was discussed extensively, since it provided a choice opportunity to elaborate on two themes of propaganda: America's imminent economic crisis and the moral decay of her literature.[102] On the one hand, in depicting the squalor and confusion resulting from mass layoffs at a war plant, Caldwell showed that full employment was merely an illusion, fostered by the temporary need for war production.[103] Mass unemployment and poverty must soon return to the United States with unprecedented virulence, for Caldwell "mercilessly shows the authentic, wretched America, shows how reality has been hidden behind the war 'boom' and the thirty-eight billions of profits which have fallen into the pockets of the American monopolists."[104] On the other hand, the reader had the right to expect answers to the "fundamental problems of the times" from Caldwell, but the author offered no "ray of light in the kingdom of darkness."[105] Dwelling on the misery and hopelessness of the brutalized lives of the unemployed, he showed them as "completely powerless in the face of a blind, elemental, cruel force which directs their fates," for to him man was a "slave, a plaything of circumstances."[106] Caldwell's sympathy was heavily mixed with sheer ridicule, since he turned his suffering humans into comic "monsters" of "biologically motivated enormity."[107] His "endless enlargement of erotic motifs," his description of filth (which became "an end in itself")[108] and his scorn for human dignity were all typical

[101] "A Selection from Caldwell," *Soviet Literature*, No. 6 (1946), p. 65.
[102] A. Elistratova, *"Tragic Ground," Soviet Literature*, No. 9 (1948), pp. 119-23; R. Orlova, *"Tragicheskaya Zemlya," Znamya*, No. 2 (1948), pp. 168-71; Mendelson, *Soviet Interpretation . . . , op.cit.*, pp. 12-15.
[103] Orlova, *"Tragicheskaya Zemlya," op.cit.*, p. 169; Mendelson, *Soviet Interpretation . . . , op.cit.*, p. 13.
[104] Orlova, *"Tragicheskaya Zemlya," op.cit.*, p. 168.
[105] *ibid.*, pp. 170-71.   [106] *ibid.*, p. 170.
[107] Mendelson, *Soviet Interpretation . . . , op.cit.*, p. 14.
[108] Orlova, *"Tragicheskaya Zemlya," op.cit.*, p. 170.

of the moral level of current American writing. Finally, the war with Hitlerism served mainly as a dim background for the story, and its meaning completely escaped the author.[109] *Tragic Ground* was indeed one of Caldwell's worst books, and the author deserved the reproach he received from Soviet critics. But this novel was considerably beneath the prevailing level of American writing, and the critics were unfair in generalizing about the literature of the United States on the basis of Caldwell's decline.

In 1945 a Soviet critic stated that the task of contemporary world literature was "to absorb the colossal experiences of the war years, to summon to the reconstruction of peace, excluding the very possibility of such threats to the freedom of peoples as grew up in Germany. . . ."[110] In view of this injunction, the Russians' discovery that during the war John Steinbeck had spent part of his time writing *Cannery Row*, a novel centering on an "imagined idyllic fraternity of tramps, prostitutes, and eccentrics" who live in a "rigidly limited and artificial little world,"[111] was more than mildly exasperating. There was a kind of protest against "American bourgeois reality with its pursuit of material goods, its universal greed, and its egotism" in Steinbeck's whimsical society of contentedly unemployed and indigent Monterey bums.[112] But the novel preached "flight from the real contradictions of life"[113] and suggested that "life is loathsome, that it does not give way to change."[114] The writer was "disconcerted by the fact of a complex, inconstant American reality," and had tried to "hide in his own shell."[115] This from the author of *The Grapes of Wrath!* The same urge toward the "anarchistic liberation of the personality from obligations to society" poisoned his next novel, *The Wayward Bus*.[116] Steinbeck "stressed sexual dissatisfaction"[117] to suggest that "man is powerless before

---

[109] *ibid.*, p. 170.   [110] "Ot redaktsii, *Znamya*, No. 9 (1945), p. 137.
[111] Mendelson, *Soviet Interpretation* . . . , *op.cit.*, pp. 16-17.
[112] *ibid.*, p. 116.   [113] Orlova, "Vospitaniye . . . ," *op.cit.*, p. 203.
[114] M. Mendelson, "Amerikanskaya literatura v poiskakh obraza nastoy-ashchevo cheloveka," *Znamya*, No. 3 (1947), p. 172.
[115] Mendelson, *Soviet Interpretation* . . . , *op.cit.*, p. 17.
[116] Orlova, "Vospitaniye . . . ," *op.cit.*, p. 204.
[117] *ibid.*, p. 203.

instinct."[118] The novel was devoid of truly emblematic Americans—workers or farmers—and figuratively "came out against the Joads."[119] By implying that the aim of life is the satisfaction of the most primordial impulses,[120] Steinbeck had "rushed into a blind alley of the blackest decadence."[121]

In 1954 the critic Romanova wrote: "The most recent works of Steinbeck, such as *The Wayward Bus* and the play *Burning Bright,* have often brought forth a feeling of justifiable perplexity, vexation, and bitterness over how low can fall a writer who in his time could reproduce that which he has seen in life with such great power. The novel *East of Eden* continues and completes this fall."[122] *East of Eden* was clearly designed for readers who had been "reared on the 'comics' and detective novels," since "only they can accept, as mandatory, [its] loathsome scenes of violence and lechery." Pointing out that the novel included "arson, suicide, two poisonings, two murders, two more unsuccessful attempted murders, and, in addition, a series of scenes from the 'life' of a brothel," Romanova argued that its subtle purpose was to "convince readers that the fate of man is preordained and the evil existing in the world is insurmountable." Its aim was to "sow seeds of dejection, unbelief, submissiveness, to hand man over to the power of a slave's psychology," and accordingly it had been applauded by reactionary American criticism.[123] Few American critics would argue against the contention that the power and significance of Steinbeck's writing have decreased since *The Grapes of Wrath.* However, Steinbeck had not become the cynical, sinister servant of reaction whom Soviet critics portrayed. Soviet critics made a generally accurate aesthetic judgment, but they poisoned it with irrelevant political speculations.

Although these reactions to Caldwell and Steinbeck were

[118] Rubin, "Krizis . . . ," *op.cit.,* p. 196.
[119] Orlova, "Vospitaniye . . . ," *op.cit.,* p. 203.
[120] Rubin, "Krizis . . . ," *op.cit.,* p. 196.
[121] Mendelson, "Amerikanskiye smertyashkiny," *op.cit.,* p. 213.
[122] Yel. Romanova, "'Filosofiya' mistera Steinbeka," *Literaturnaya gazeta,* July 10, 1954, p. 4.
[123] *ibid.,* p. 4.

in tune with Soviet criticism of other contemporary Americans, there was in them a note of genuine distress that set them off, somewhat, from routine propaganda. The change of emphasis in Steinbeck's writing and Caldwell's increasing tendency to convert social injustice into crude burlesque—developments that American critics also sorrowfully acknowledge—plainly shocked their former Russian admirers. In their excoriation of many writers such as Wilder, O'Neill, and Faulkner, Soviet critics often seemed to gloat over what they considered to be the moral failure of capitalist art. But in chronicling the decline of these two former favorites, they struck notes of sincere regret.

Actually the critics merely shed a tear or two over these writers, and easily passed on to sterner denunciations. The decline of individual authors, they argued, was only one aspect of the widespread trouble in American culture. Almost all literary criticism and scholarship, for example, was in the grip of reaction. According to Mendelson, "The propagandists of decadent literature at the present time direct the largest literary journals in the USA, head the [literary] departments in the universities, determine the policies of the most important publishing houses."[124] Literary scholars were waging concerted war against the "traditions of American critical realism, with its keen interest in social problems and social evils."[125] Vernon Louis Parrington (whom the Russians have generally favored among literary historians) was under heavy attack from his countrymen.[126] Erstwhile liberal critics such as Van Wyck Brooks[127] and Newton Arvin[128] had become reactionary. The "long dead and buried reactionary and idealistic theory of irrational and intuitive art"[129] was being resurrected, and there was a reemphasis of the

---

[124] Mendelson, "Amerikanskiye smertyashkiny," *op.cit.*, p. 217.

[125] Anna Elistratova, "Reactionary Tendencies in American Literary Science," *Soviet Literature*, No. 4 (1948), p. 56.

[126] *ibid.*, p. 57.

[127] *ibid.*, pp. 58-60; Startsev, "Imperialisticheskaya agressiya . . . ," *op.cit.*, pp. 130-31.

[128] Anisimov, "Literature in the Service of Reaction," *op.cit.*, p. 150.

[129] Elistratova, "Reactionary Tendencies . . . ," *op.cit.*, pp. 57-58.

notion that art is essentially apolitical. Just as the journey-men critics were encouraging the "fascizatsii and militariza-tion" of literature by praising to the skies such "frankly im-perialistic novels" as *From Here to Eternity* and *The Caine Mutiny*,[130] so also the scholars were becoming increasingly nationalistic.[131] *American Literature*, the most prominent learned journal in the field, had become smugly chauvinistic.[132] Among scholarly crimes, the most heinous was the pervasive distortion of critical themes in the writings of Mark Twain and the dastardly suppression of his anti-imperialistic and antireligious works.[133] Even his name had been seized in the sinister plot for American expansion. For many years the Mark Twain Society had been conducted "under the aegis of Truman, Churchill, and De Gaulle" and supported by such "ideologists of American imperialism as Dewey, Eliot, O'-Neill, and others," with the aim of falsifying the author's heritage. Now, the critic Romanova noted with alarm, an affiliate of the Mark Twain Society was being organized in Western Germany, with a contemplated membership of 50,000![134]

Foul exploitation of the name of Mark Twain, according to the critics, was only one of myriad devices for "ideological expansion"—an indispensable supplement to America's po-litical, economic, and military measures for conquering the world.[135] Culture had become a "smoke screen for disguising the genuine intentions of the American colonizers."[136] Litera-ture, movies, art, radio, music, and the theater were being employed to spread Henry Luce's concept of the American Century and thus to gain for Wall Street the slavish alle-giance of "Western Europe, Asia, and Latin America."[137] As early as 1947 a group of prominent Soviet literary figures

[130] Maslova and Glunin, "Reaktsionnaya . . . ," *op.cit.*, p. 185.
[131] Elistratova, "Reactionary Tendencies . . . ," *op.cit.*, p. 56.
[132] *ibid.*, p. 60.
[133] M. Mendelson, "Poslesloviye," *Znamya*, No. 4 (1948), pp. 150-55.
[134] Romanova, "Teoriya i praktika . . . ," *op.cit.*, p. 270.
[135] Startsev, "Imperialisticheskaya agressiya . . . ," *op.cit.*, pp. 124-25.
[136] Romanova and Rubin, "Protiv marshallizatsii kultury," *op.cit.*, p. 210.
[137] *ibid.*, p. 210.

addressed an open letter to American writers, protesting that any effort to proclaim the superiority of the American way of life was in fact a "reproduction of the shameful theory and practice of fascism."[138] In the next few years America's international cultural activities were constantly characterized as warlike. The Voice of America and the United States Information Service were designed for the "demoralization of the masses, the preparation of cannon fodder."[139] The State Department, by "regulating the book export of the USA," sent abroad "precisely that literature which accustoms the reader to murder and violence."[140] Crime comics, often loaded with racial prejudice, made up much of this export: "Propagandizing violence as the fundamental law of society and murder as the natural occupation of every man, the 'comics,' like the other types of book production for export, advocate that the highest good is power and personal wealth, to which one cuts a path with a revolver."[141] Such inelegant and obvious efforts, of course, could scarcely appeal to the foreign literati. In fact, the critics insisted, a great deal of American culture was being boycotted by intellectuals abroad. Therefore Americans were forced to make appeals on an ostensibly higher level, by organizing foreign performances of the plays of Wilder and Tennessee Williams,[142] and by distributing *Perspectives U.S.A.*,[143] the overseas organ of "that part of the American intelligentsia which has sold itself to the bourgeoisie."[144] European expatriates such as Aldous Huxley, Christopher Isherwood, Jules Romains, and Thomas Mann were being rounded up to form a new "Literary Hollywood," whose aim was to "weaken morally the Western European

[138] "S kem vy, amerikanskiye mastera kultury?" *Literaturnaya gazeta*, September 20, 1947, p. 1.

[139] Romanova and Rubin, "Protiv marshallizatsii kultury," *op.cit.*, p. 210.

[140] Romanova, "Cho takoye 'best-seller,'" *op.cit.*, p. 4.

[141] Romanova and Rubin, "Protiv marshallizatsii kultury," *op.cit.*, p. 213.
[142] *ibid.*, p. 215.

[143] Yel. Romanova, "Mrachniye perspektivy," *Novy mir*, No. 3 (1955), pp. 200-204.

[144] Sergei Lvov, "Perspektivy 'Perspektiv S Sh A,'" *Literaturnaya gazeta*, October 31, 1953, p. 4.

intelligentsia," and thus to bring about a "spiritual occupation of Europe, a denationalization and decomposition of European culture." Although their "social-political and philosophical views" varied, these "cosmopolitans" agreed on the "theory of 'uniting' the peoples of Europe under the aegis of the United States of America."[145]

The concept of "cosmopolitanism" was devised shortly after the war to embrace a cluster of actual and fancied heresies and disloyal attitudes during the nightmarish latter years of Stalin's rule. As applied to Soviet citizens it took a heavy toll as a weapon of intellectual terror. Under the accusation of "cosmopolitanism" numerous writers, critics, and scholars, and particularly the Jews among them, were silenced or imprisoned, and many of them were destroyed. For Soviet intellectuals who continued to function in the face of its rigors, the specter of "cosmopolitanism" effected a grim discipline, inhibiting all inclinations toward the expression, direct or indirect, of admiration for the West. The liberal intellectual circles of Western Europe and America were of course a major source of "cosmopolitanism." In 1947 Huxley, W. H. Auden, Richard Aldington, and Somerset Maugham were portrayed in the Soviet press as having entered the service of black reaction and as being merely lesser versions of such authentic wartime Fascist collaborators as Knut Hamsun and Ezra Pound.[146] In 1953 the term "literary Quisling" was applied to Stephen Spender, Koestler (also a "Fascist cosmopolitan"), and Raymond Aron.[147]

Among the ideological sins loosely identified as "cosmopolitan," one of the most heinous was to overestimate the role of foreign influences in the formation of Russian and Soviet culture. Accordingly, Soviet critics were obligated to play down West-to-East cultural influences. When in 1949 the

[145] R. Miller-Budnitskaya, "Kosmopolity iz literaturnovo Gollivuda," *Novy mir*, No. 6 (1948), pp. 282-96.

[146] Aleksandr Leites, "Sovetskaya literatura na mezhdunarodnoi arene," *Novy mir*, No. 3 (1947), pp. 154-56.

[147] Romanova and Rubin, "Protiv marshallizatsii kultury," *op.cit.*, pp. 218-19. A similar indictment is in D. Zhantiyeva, "Kosmopolity—vragi svoevo naroda," *Literaturnaya gazeta*, August 6, 1949, p. 4.

first volume of a Soviet history of American literature appeared, its authors were excoriated for "bourgeois cosmopolitanism" in "exalting American literature in every possible way, bowing and scraping before the third-rate writers of capitalist America."[148] Among other misdemeanors, these unfortunate authors had found instances in which Russian writers had been influenced by Americans! A Soviet anthology of English and American literature, designed as a textbook for students of the English language, was criticized for implicitly flattering American culture by such devices as calling Benjamin Franklin the "American Leonardo" without mentioning his "bourgeois limitations."[149]

In Soviet practice, lines of reasoning which are invalid when they seem to diminish the glory of the Soviet state become entirely legitimate when they appear to increase its stature or to discredit its enemies. Although the critics, for fear of being suspected of subversive sympathies, were forced to pretend that Russia had never been influenced by America, the poisonous center of cosmopolitanism, they were entirely free to push inflated claims of influence in the reverse direction. And in their insistence on the autonomy and originality of Russian and Soviet literature on the one hand, and on the dependence of Western literature on the other, the critics often overstated their case to a ridiculous degree. The critic Mendelson published in 1948 a lengthy article, based on considerable scholarship, detailing with much validity Russian influences on American writers.[150] In that same year, however, the critic Motyleva devoted twenty pages of tortured argument to the thesis that the "leading" writers of the West had been profoundly inspired by the example of Soviet cultural growth.[151] Pointing, correctly, to works in which Upton Sinclair had expressed admiration of the Soviet Union or its

[148] "Protiv burzhuaznovo kosmopolitizma v literaturovedenii," *Literaturnaya gazeta*, March 19, 1949.

[149] M. Mendelson, "Politicheskaya slepota," *Literaturnaya gazeta*, May 22, 1948, p. 4.

[150] M. Mendelson, "Sila pravdy," *Znamya*, No. 1 (1948), pp. 149-74.

[151] Tamara Motyleva, "Sovetskaya kultura i zarubezhnye pisateli," *Novy mir*, No. 1 (1948), pp. 198-218.

policies, she conveniently ignored his current and publicly expressed abhorrence of the Soviet example. She likewise embraced as a beneficiary of Soviet inspiration Sinclair Lewis —an outspoken enemy! The cold war had ushered in a new, heightened chauvinism, unprecedented in its insularity.

Since, in terms of the prevailing Party line, the best of American literature was largely derived from Russian sources, since so many writers who before the war had been deemed congenial were now thought to have degenerated, and since most of American literature was now involved in an enormous conspiracy to corrupt and enslave the world and remake it in the Fascist image, the choice of contemporary American writing open to Soviet publishers had become narrow indeed.

The critics have been cited at length to show that Soviet abuse of American literature and culture in the years 1946-1955 was as indiscriminate as it was thorough. With the picture of the recent enemy, Fascist Germany, still fresh in their imaginations, Soviet spokesmen readily shifted their attention to a newly identified adversary and directed against the United States the same bitter arsenal they had used against the Third Reich. The result was an appalling increment of misinterpretations and lies. More often than not, Soviet conclusions about American culture, based on the mechanical grouping together of the most diverse phenomena, were entirely devoid of logic. The only evident discipline behind the remarks of literary critics was a Party line that demanded universal condemnation of all American writing that was not clearly Communist in its orientation. For the critics had simply lost respect for, or at any rate had lost sight of, literary values. The road back to a literary criticism worthy of the name would be a long one.

CHAPTER VII

FROM 1955 TO 1960

⸙⸙⸙ BY THE END of World War II Soviet publication of American literature had reached a low ebb. In the following decade of painful recovery from the colossal devastation inflicted by Nazi Germany, the publishing apparatus was given high priorities. Hundreds of millions of volumes came out to meet a constantly increasing popular demand, and Soviet publication of books and periodicals of all kinds rose to new heights. Although translations of American literature played a relatively minor role in this growth, they did increase substantially.

Theodore Dreiser was by far the leading American author during this ten-year period, both in terms of editions and number of copies printed. Mark Twain remained a classic, and was second only to Dreiser. Jack London, who had reigned for a generation in Russia, descended to third place. Three other long-time favorites remained prominent: James Fenimore Cooper, Harriet Beecher Stowe, and O. Henry. Still enjoying their traditional respect from Russian readers were Bret Harte, Edgar Allan Poe, and Walt Whitman; each was published in two or three Russian editions. Other writers long familiar to Soviet readers continued to be printed modestly, among them Sinclair Lewis, Lincoln Steffens, Frank Norris, and Washington Irving. Of the fifteen authors published most extensively in Russian from 1945 to 1955, nine had been well known in the Soviet Union since at least the early 1920's, and of these nine, seven were nineteenth-century writers. In a time of cold war, Soviet publishing houses were by no means unwilling to bring out American works, but they were strongly disinclined to break new ground. The sole exceptions to this principle were a tiny group of "critical realists," of whom Mitchell Wilson was the most popular, and a larger group of writers of the extreme left wing, headed by Howard Fast.

In the light of the views of Soviet critics and publicists cited in the foregoing chapter, it is not surprising that the current American literature chosen for publication at this time was, on the whole, more critical of the United States than ever before. Also it was less representative of contemporary American writing than any preceding selection of translated works. Dozens upon dozens of writers who were scarcely known in the United States appeared in the pages of Soviet magazines, and many of these were printed in book form. Although some had literary talent, most of them had little. What they all had in common was the ability to contribute to a uniformly negative commentary on American life. By the same token, the most prominent contemporary writers of the United States were nearly all ignored. Soviet publishers boycotted not only such established authors as Hemingway, Faulkner, Hersey, and Steinbeck, but also a new group of promising postwar writers including Jones, Mailer, Saul Bellow, William Styron, J. D. Salinger, and others. The Soviet press acknowledged their existence by vilifying them, but they were not published.

A typical practice was the printing of anthologies that drew together stories, excerpts from novels, essays, and poems—frequently from the most diverse sources—all concentrating on a particular aspect of American life and painting it in the gloomiest colors. The favorite subject of these anthologies was the problem of race relations, under such titles as *The Literature of the American Negroes in the Fight for Freedom and Democracy*. At times the titles of Soviet anthologies were as fanciful as they were tendentious: *Panic in Washington* and *Worshipers of the Dollar*. The latter volume included items by Mike Quin, who was a regular contributor to the American Communist press and—Mark Twain.

Anthologies such as these were merely one aspect of the gallery of American horrors created by the carefully integrated machinery of Soviet literary propaganda. Soviet publications were assiduously propagating the myth that the United States was "going to fascism at a rapid rate," even if "in its details" the pattern was "somewhat different from

[171]

the German."[1] To support such contentions, Soviet commentators found the Fascist image, or facets of it, in such disparate figures as Harry Truman,[2] John Dewey,[3] Cardinal Spellman,[4] Billy Rose[5] and C. S. Forester's Captain Horatio Hornblower.[6] Periodicals such as *The Saturday Review of Literature*,[7] the *New York Times Book Review*,[8] and the *Saturday Evening Post*[9] were repeatedly caricatured as the lying organs of Fascist Wall Street. The weirdness of Soviet claims had no limits. The tragic suicide of Professor F. O. Matthiessen was ghoulishly and erroneously attributed to an organized terror that had, among other things, allegedly banished him from Harvard University.[10] The violent demise of Maxwell Bodenheim brought about a treatise on the manner in which American society crushes the free personality.[11] Less grim, but equally typical, was an article that appeared in 1954 under the title, "A Sermon on Cannibalism in the Guise of Folklore," in which a Soviet commentator dwelt at length on the inclusion, in a volume of folklore published

[1] Yu. Kovalev, "Tsena predatelstva," *Zvezda*, No. 1 (1952), p. 173.

[2] Boris Gorbatov, "Garri Trumen," *Literaturnaya gazeta*, September 20, 1947, p. 2.

[3] V. Brodov, "Filosofiya biznesa," *Literaturnaya gazeta*, October 22, 1948, p. 4.

[4] "Literaturnye uprazhneniya kardinala Spellmana," *Literaturnaya gazeta*, October 23, 1951, p. 4.

[5] Mikh. Bardin, "Karera gangstera Billa Rouza," *Literaturnaya gazeta*, November 26, 1947, p. 2.

[6] V. Khmelevski, "Portret voyennovo geroya burzhuazii," *Novy mir*, No. 2 (1949), pp. 243-48.

[7] Vl. Rubin, "Krizis sovremennoi amerikanskoi literatury," *Zvezda*, No. 8 (1948), p. 193; M. Mendelson, "Amerikanskaya progressivnaya literatura poslednikh let," *Zvezda*, No. 11 (1949), p. 168; Ye. Romanova, "Teoriya i praktika literaturnykh biznesmenov," *Novy mir*, No. 11 (1951), pp. 268-70; A. Belskaya, "Amerikanskaya pochta," *Novy mir*, No. 12 (1955), pp. 112-15; R. Orlova, "Ody biznesmenu," *Novy mir*, No. 5 (1956), pp. 231-34.

[8] Rubin, "Krizis . . . ," *op.cit.*, p. 193; A. Yegorov, "Ethics of 'The New York Times Book Review,'" *Soviet Literature*, No. 5 (1952), pp. 148-51.

[9] A. Belskaya, "V sakharnoi oblatke," *Novy mir*, No. 7 (1955), pp. 224-28.

[10] Sergei Lvov, "Ideinost i masterstvo," *Literaturnaya gazeta*, April 9, 1955, p. 3.

[11] N. R., "Sudba amerikanskovo pisatelya," *Literaturnaya gazeta*, February 11, 1954, p. 4.

in New York, of stories and jingles about the sadistically precocious Little Audrey and Little Willie. Their publication, the critic claimed, illustrated "the morals of shopkeepers who aspire to world domination."[12]

Soviet propaganda is capable, however, of reversing its direction swiftly and completely whenever the need arises. The notion that there have always been "two Americas" has made it possible for Russian commentators to draw diametrically opposite conclusions about the United States, depending on whether a positive or a negative image is required at a given time. In 1953, for example, there appeared in the magazine *Znamya* an article that listed, with card-file precision, uniformly derogatory opinions of the United States written by great Russian authors over the past two centuries. Lomonosov's "Ode to Glass" of 1752, the article pointed out, had "told about the bitter lot of the Indians, who fell in bondage to the colonizers," and ever since, for two hundred years, Russian writers had been "summoning people of good will to bar the path to the plunderers and murderers, to cut short the cannibalistic schemes of Wall Street."[13] But the summit conference at Geneva in the summer of 1955 brought a different Soviet card file into use. Another America emerged—one which had been deeply admired and celebrated by Russian men of letters (including some of those cited in 1953), and one to which the "spirit of militarism" was alien.[14]

Even in the most hostile years of the cold war, the frightfully repetitious and steadily vituperative Soviet denunciation of American culture had been punctuated, at rare intervals, by friendly pleas to United States artists in the name of peace.[15] Now that the heads of government had struck a more amiable note, the Soviet technique of threats and promises, of ranting interlarded with an occasional smile, was to be

[12] E. Shlosberg, "Propoved lyudoyedstva pod vidom folklora," *Znamya*, No. 7 (1954), pp. 191-92.

[13] A. Lyubarski, "Velikiye deyateli russkoi literatury razoblachayut amerikanskovo lzhedemokratiyu," *Zvezda*, No. 2 (1953), pp. 157-66.

[14] Boris Lavrenev, "Perelistyvaya stranitsy istorii . . . ," *Literaturnaya gazeta*, July 23, 1955, p. 4.

[15] Ilya Erenburg, "Otkrytoye pismo pisatelyam Zapada," *Literaturnaya gazeta*, April 5, 1950, p. 1.

replaced for a time by a more circumspect approach. In July and August of 1955 numerous articles in the Soviet press argued the need for more extensive cultural relations with the United States. Typical was a story in *Literaturnaya Gazeta* deploring the obstacles which the cold war had put in the path of the American, Arthur Voyce, in gathering materials for his architectural history of the Kremlin. The story concluded: "What rich perspectives are opened before the scholars of all countries, if their noble work will be supported in a spirit of mutual understanding and trust."[16] To the accompaniment of statements like this, the Soviet press began printing, for the first time in years, more accurate and less biased news of the American cultural scene.[17]

Simultaneously, Soviet criticism of American literature assumed a more objective, reasonable, and sympathetic tone. Although the traditional ideological standards and critical themes remained in force, a wider variety of writing came to be of legitimate interest, and many more works whose political implications were considered harmful were nevertheless found to have literary value.[18] Such American publications as *The New York Times Book Review*, which had been a favorite target for abuse, now received a calmer, more comprehensive, and even, at times, complimentary treatment.[19] The vast increase of official interest in cultural exchange that followed the Geneva conference, however, was merely the most spectacular sign of a revised attitude toward American culture and literature that had already become manifest, modestly, in the preceding year.

The death of Stalin in 1953 brought about a gradual, partial relaxation of the terror that for decades had governed the attitudes of the Soviet populace, and particularly the intelligentsia. At the height of the cold war, Soviet isolation

[16] "Amerikanskiye ucheniye o russkom iskusstve," *Literaturnaya gazeta*, July 30, 1955, p. 4.

[17] "Khronika kulturnoi zhizni S Sh A," *Literaturnaya gazeta*, August 9, 1955, p. 4.

[18] Yel. Romanova, "Zametki o novykh knigakh amerikanskikh pisatelei," *Literaturnaya gazeta*, September 3, 1955, p. 4.

[19] R. Orlova, "Koye-chto o vzaimnosti," *Novy mir*, No. 2 (1956), pp. 246-48.

from the West had been so complete and Soviet doctrine so rigid that genuine cultural contacts with America were virtually impossible. Intellectual activity that led to any kind of overt admiration for American culture had been dangerous in the extreme. Now the Soviet Union was once more emerging from isolationism, and as her intelligentsia gained release from their enforced timidity, their long-frustrated interest in things Western was given limited rein.

A restrained and tentative appeal for renewed, broadened, and bolder activity in the criticism of foreign literatures was published in *Literaturnaya Gazeta* in June 1954. The call for increased liberalization, stated tactfully in a spirit of self-criticism, pointed out that "sometimes schematic notions hinder the work of critics, which are rooted occasionally in our insufficient knowledge," and continued: "In other works there is evident a simplified conception of the literatures of capitalist countries—a conception according to which there exist only two kinds of writers: either active fighters for peace and democracy or arrant enemies, the henchmen of imperialism. But indeed the arrangement of forces is much more complex." The author of this appeal pointed out, euphemistically, that many specialists in the field were not "working to the full measure of their powers," had "lost the taste for independent contributions," and were "busying themselves by editing translations, compiling anthologies, and the like."[20] In point of fact, this was undoubtedly a timid, veiled reference to the numerous gifted critics who had weathered the terror by taking up safer work, or who had been silenced through imprisonment.

At this same time articles about American literature began to exhibit, occasionally, a higher proportion of objective literary analysis. These were the tentative beginnings of a criticism in which sober literary judgment, albeit with a strong sociological tinge, would be at least as prominent as political polemics.[21] By July 1955, clear, frank, and unmis-

[20] T. Motyleva, "Vazhnaya zadacha kritiki," *Literaturnaya gazeta,* June 15, 1954, p. 3.
[21] Yel. Romanova, " 'Filosofiya' mistera Steinbeka," *Literaturnaya ga-*

takable proclamations of the inadequacy of Soviet criticism of the literature of capitalist countries were in vogue. In that month the critic Romanova argued that criticism had been restricted to just the "most progressive" and the "most reactionary" writers, and emphasized that "many phenomena of literature have plainly fallen outside the field of vision of the critics." This, she declared, had "inevitably restricted our conception of foreign literatures."[22]

These remarks were published in the first issue of the monthly magazine *Inostrannaya Literatura* (Foreign Literature), which became the chief periodical for the publication and criticism of non-Soviet literature. In many respects this journal was reminiscent of *Internatsionalnaya Literatura* (International Literature), which had been founded in the Popular Front period and had died in the early forties, but in other respects it was different from its predecessor and far superior. It was, first of all, an organ for Soviet readers alone, whereas *Internatsionalnaya Literatura*, designed for a worldwide readership, had been published in several different languages. Although the new magazine performed a task of domestic propaganda, it did not undertake to be the oracle of a global revolutionary movement. Its primary aim was simply to acquaint the Russian reading public with literary developments abroad—of course in the proper ideological perspective. It was a vastly more informative, cultured, and sophisticated journal than the Russians had seen in years, and it made an instantaneous and enduring hit with Soviet readers. The editorial policies of *Inostrannaya Literatura* reflected a liberalized attitude toward the literature of the West, and specifically of America. In the first six years of its existence, it published works of William Faulkner, Ernest Hemingway, and Langston Hughes three times each; Steinbeck, Saroyan, Caldwell, Mitchell Wilson, Fast, and Carl Sandburg twice each; and printed one work from each of the following: Archibald Mac-

---

zeta, July 10, 1954, p. 4; Yel. Romanova, "Mrachniye perspektivy," *Novy mir*, No. 3 (1955), pp. 200-204.

[22] Yel. Romanova, "O nekotorykh yavleniyakh v poslevoyennoi literature S Sh A," *Inostrannaya literatura*, No. 1 (1955), p. 191.

Leish, John O'Hara, Arthur Miller, Tennessee Williams, Robert Bowen, William DuBois, Anna Louise Strong, Dexter Masters, Longfellow, Albert Maltz, J. D. Salinger, Jack Kerouac, Jay Deiss, Lorraine Hansberry, and Walt Whitman. While this selection was by no means eclectic, and while it was larded with many familiar names, it contained not a few surprises.

The choice of translated works in book form was somewhat more conservative, but here too the Russians achieved a broader range than they had since the twenties. Hemingway, Caldwell, Sherwood Anderson, Sinclair Lewis, Steinbeck, and Upton Sinclair, all of whom had been under dark clouds for a decade, now came out in new editions. The old favorites, such as Dreiser, Mrs. Stowe, London, Cooper, O. Henry, Mark Twain, and Bret Harte continued to be printed widely, and the publishers paid fresh attention to other American classics—Poe, Longfellow, Whitman, and Nathaniel Hawthorne. Herman Melville's *Moby Dick*, which had heretofore been the most significant work to be neglected by the Soviets, was published in Russian for the first time in 1960. Langston Hughes continued to be the Russians' favorite contemporary American poet, but a collection of Carl Sandburg was also published. Books by other contemporary Americans —Faulkner, Dorothy Parker, Arthur Miller, Ray Bradbury, Robert Sylvester, and Mitchell Wilson among them—were issued for the first time. It is true that whole schools of new American writing—including the freshest and most experimental—were excluded in the still severe Soviet process of selection, and that Soviet readers, without an opportunity to judge for themselves, still had to take the critics' word for it that many prominent American writers were not worth translating. On the whole, however, the situation had vastly improved since the somber days before the thaw.

The treatment of John Steinbeck's novella *The Pearl* illustrates the change of climate. In 1953, when it was fashionable, if not compulsory, to paint Steinbeck as a degenerate misanthrope, this touching, sensitive parable from the life of a Mexican Indian village was described by a Soviet critic as a typical attempt to "stupefy, to make a jackass of the reader, to poison him with the venom of pessimism, to inoculate him with scorn and hatred for man." The critic thought that the story "broaches, it would seem, a pointed social theme—the hard life of the Indian people—but with only one aim: to show the complete uselessness of the hopes of man to attain happiness."[23] But in 1956 this very same story was printed in *Inostrannaya Literatura*, complete with the original illustrations of Orozco, and in 1958 the translation appeared in book form together with a Soviet commentary that stressed the author's "reverence for simple people." The novella aroused "huge anger against injustice and oppression."[24] To be sure, the critics still mentioned Steinbeck's shortcomings of recent years. The preface to a reprint of *The Grapes of Wrath* (informing the reader, incidentally, that the United States had not changed fundamentally in the twenty years since it was written!) pointed out that the author's talent had slipped since this masterpiece.[25] While praising *The Pearl*, Soviet criticism still noted the pessimism, excessive sexuality, and lack of proper social protest in such works as *Cannery Row, Sweet Thursday, The Wayward Bus,* and *East of Eden*.[26] Nevertheless, the complete reversal of opinion about *The Pearl*, and the fact of its publication in Russian, testified eloquently to altered times.

A mellowed attitude was also evident in the comments that accompanied the revival of Erskine Caldwell. During the years of wholesale hostility to American culture it was easy to dismiss him as just another formerly promising writer who had sold his talent to Wall Street for the purpose of perverting and demoralizing the public. When the critics began to treat him more kindly, his inadequacies were cast in a different light. Two stories printed in an early issue of *Inostran-*

---

[23] I. Tikhomirova, "V borbe protiv reaktsionnovo mrakobesiya, za mir, demokratiyu i sotsialism," *Zvezda*, No. 11 (1953), p. 163.

[24] D. Zhantiyeva, "Poslesloviye," in Dzh. Steinbek, *Zhemchuzhina*, Moscow, 1958, p. 74.

[25] B. Izakov, "Predisloviye," in Dzhon Steinbek, *Grozdya gneva*, Moscow, 1957, p. 8.

[26] Zhantiyeva, "Poslesloviye," *op.cit.*, pp. 73-74.

naya Literatura were found to be morbid and written with a dispassionateness that approached indifference, but the author was praised for his courage in raising important issues of social injustice even though he did not know how to resolve them.[27] At about the same time a critic wrote that although sexual preoccupations often drowned Caldwell's themes of social criticism, his humanitarian penchant for writing about the poor and underprivileged was a saving grace.[28] In 1956 his *Georgia Boy* was reprinted, with a Soviet preface that stressed his "love of life and humanity."[29] The highest compliment, however, was an impressive collection of his translated stories published in 1956 with an aesthetically interesting, acute, and analytical introduction by an erudite and sensitive critic, Ivan Kashkin.[30]

Hemingway's restoration to grace was accomplished by way of *The Old Man and the Sea*, which enjoyed an enormous success with Soviet readers. In the lively discussion of this work it became clear that Hemingway could now be fully talked about and that in spite of continuing ideological strictures against his work, very nearly every aspect of his art was of legitimate interest.[31] Sinclair Lewis, whose *Gideon Planish* and *Kingsblood Royal* had been exploited in 1947 and 1948 as a form of cold-war propaganda, but who otherwise had shared in the studied neglect accorded contemporary American non-Communist writers, was revived in 1956 with the republication of *Arrowsmith*. In 1957 "Willow Walk" was printed in book form despite the fact that, as its Soviet preface noted, the story's "social-satirical motifs" were not

[27] Sergei Lvov, "Mesto cheloveka v zhizni," *Literaturnaya gazeta*, October 27, 1955, p. 2.

[28] Romanova, "Zametki . . . ," *op.cit.*, p. 4.

[29] M. Nolman, "Erskin Kolduell," in Erskin Kolduell, *Malchik iz Dzhordzhii*, Moscow, 1956, p. 8.

[30] I. Kashkin, "Erskin Kolduell," in E. Kolduell, *Povesti i rasskazy*, Moscow, 1956, pp. 5-15.

[31] Ivan Kashkin, "Perechityvaya Khemingueya," *Inostrannaya literatura*, No. 4 (1956), pp. 194-206; Ivan Kashkin, "Alive in the Midst of Death," *Soviet Literature*, No. 7 (1956), pp. 160-72; Ivan Kashkin, "Kheminguei na puti k masterstvu," *Voprosy literatury*, No. 6 (1957), pp. 184-204.

as highly developed as in the author's more mature works.[32]
There was now at least some room for Lewis the storyteller.

Perhaps the most radical departure from all previous Soviet
patterns was the attempt to introduce William Faulkner to
Soviet readers. Two stories of Faulkner had been published
in the middle thirties, but they had passed unnoticed, and
for twenty years the critics had stigmatized him, on those
rare occasions when they bothered to mention him at all, as a
decadent reactionary who displayed an unhealthy interest in
degeneracy. Faulkner was a formidable challenge to Soviet
criticism, which was most unaccustomed to grappling with
such complex, and often subterranean, visions of life as he
presented. It is not surprising that the first serious treatment
of the author, in December 1955, was devoted to the comparatively obvious, and certainly timely and congenial, theme
of antimilitarism in his writings. In this brief article, Elena
Romanova traced Faulkner's attitude toward war from his
first novel, *Soldier's Pay*, and the early story, "Victory," to
his then latest published work, *A Fable*. She found that the
author had at first reacted to war with "unconscious terror,"
and that while he had treated ironically the popularly accepted
slogans of the First World War, he had portrayed the ordinary soldier as simply a "tragic victim" of an "all-powerful
elemental force." But in *A Fable*, published thirty years later,
Romanova found a more mature "protest against the cruel
and senseless bloodletting" of that same war. Although she
found Faulkner still somewhat naive politically, she noted
that he "accused and exposed those who are responsible for
imperialist war." His revulsion against militarism, the critic
felt, was dictated by his "inner need to find anew that belief
in man which he himself has lost at times." For, despite the
frequent morbidity of his writings, Faulkner aspired to "raise
the value of the human personality in the eyes of his contemporaries, to defend the right of man to personal inviolabil-
ity." Having introduced the author in these limited terms,

[32] A. Startsev, "Predisloviye," in Sinkler Lyuis, *Ivovaya Alleya*, Moscow, 1957, p. 5.

Romanova urged that Soviet critics embark on a serious analysis of his art.[33]

The critics were slow to respond. It was as if some doubtfully edible monster had been hauled from the sea. No one seemed willing to try him. Finally in 1958 another, lengthier article appeared, devoted primarily to *The Hamlet* and *The Town*, but also attempting to define Faulkner's art as a whole. Although this study, by Orlova and Kopelev, was more ambitious and broader in scope than that of Romanova, it was less successful because, in trying to come to grips with the author, it used the traditional Soviet technique of class analysis. It served therefore more as a restatement of timeworn Soviet prejudices than as an elucidation of the art of William Faulkner. In the eyes of these two critics, for example, one of the most significant things about *The Town* was that, although it covered the years from 1909 to 1927, it failed to pay sufficient attention to the fact that "these were the years when the First World War and the Great October Revolution took place, opening a new era in the history of mankind; years when the USA was becoming the richest and most powerful of the imperialist powers of the world." Faithful to the new spirit of tolerance, these critics argued that Faulkner should no longer be called "decadent." However, they insisted that in presenting Snopesism "as a monstrosity, an anomaly, as a biological, not a social thing," Faulkner was guilty of "naturalism." For Faulkner should recognize that a character like Flem Snopes was actually the embodiment of the basic elements of the bourgeois world, and the sultry, tragic Eula Varner Snopes was in reality just a victim—like Anna Karenina and Emma Bovary—of bourgeois marriage. Correctly pointing out that the author's moral notions "for all their obvious sincerity are indistinct, abstract," and noting the alternation of "leading humanistic ideas" with "stagnant retrograde patriarchal illusions" in his writing, these critics attributed his shortcomings to the fact that he did not know "the basic laws of social-historical development." In short,

[33] Yel. Romanova, "Antivoyennyie motivy v tvorchestve Uilyama Folknera," *Inostrannaya literatura*, No. 6 (1955), pp. 170-76.

the authors implied, a good course in Marxism would be just the thing for William Faulkner.[34]

Actually Orlova and Kopelev had tried to be generous and elastic in their interpretation of the author. Their adherence to the rigid categories of Soviet literary political science was probably the result more of habit than of intent. But what is most interesting about their study is the reaction of other critics to it. Samarin, for example, objected to their claims that Faulkner knew and respected the Negro national character and culture. How could this author be portrayed as a "seeker of the truth and champion of justice" when only recently he had proclaimed a gradualist position on the question of civil rights for Negroes? These two critics, Samarin sternly noted, made the grave mistake of separating the author's art from his political views![35] Although the critic Kashkin agreed that Faulkner was a "reactionary in his attitude to Negroes and, it seems, to humanity in general," he argued that Orlova and Kopelev were simply wide of the mark. Kashkin wisely noted that Soviet criticism had simply "not begun to show Faulkner as he is."[36]

As of 1960 there was no way of knowing how Faulkner would fare in the Soviet Union. His short stories have continued to come out in Soviet periodicals, and a volume was printed in 1959. Certainly if the narrow political criticism advocated by Samarin were to prevail, the prospects for a genuine appreciation of the author would be dim. If, on the other hand, Faulkner could be studied as an *artist*, as Kashkin seemed to advocate, he would certainly find a permanent, though perhaps modest, place on Soviet bookshelves. In 1960 a Soviet observer noted that because Faulkner's "conception of good and evil" was confused and because his writing was "extremely gloomy," the Russian reaction to him thus far

[34] R. Orlova and L. Kopelev, "Mify i pravda amerikanskovo yuga," *Inostrannaya literatura*, No. 3 (1958), pp. 206-20.

[35] R. Samarin, "Ostreye, glubzhe, printsipalneye," *Literaturnaya gazeta*, May 24, 1958, p. 1.

[36] I. Kashkin in "Na puti k tretyemu syezdu," *Literaturnaya gazeta*, June 3, 1958, p. 4.

had been a mixed one.[37] To understand and appreciate Faulkner the critics would indeed have to display much greater ideological elasticity than they had heretofore shown in their judgment of American writing and would have to become receptive to moral subtleties and psychological and social interests which they have traditionally scorned.

For the time being it was clear that less complicated, more straightforward American writers, and particularly those engaged in direct, unambiguous social criticism, would continue to be favored. Even in the most frigid days of the cold war, the door had been left a tiny bit ajar for a few contemporary Americans who, although they were far from communism, exposed the dark sides of life in the United States. One was Sinclair Lewis, and another was Ira Wolfert, whose novel of the underworld rackets, *Tucker's People*, was translated late in 1947. Although the novel suffered from "exaggerated attention to instinct, to biological determinism,"[38] it was not just another gangster thriller,[39] for in depicting organized crime syndicates, Wolfert had shown that in the United States "the line between big business and gangsterism is obliterated."[40] The critics were quick to note, however, that there was an essential difference between Wolfert and "progressive" writers. Whereas authors such as Howard Fast and Albert Maltz foresaw the abolition of institutionalized corruption through revolution, Wolfert's novel argued the "unchangeability of the existing order of things, the fate of man consigned to eternal wandering in the circles of the capitalist Hell."[41]

The non-Communist writer who did provide the requisite amount of hope along with his social criticism, and who at the

---

[37] V. Belyayev, "Novye izdaniya amerikanskikh knig," *Inostrannaya literatura*, No. 1 (1960), p. 248.

[38] M. Shereshevskaya, "Tekker i drugiye," *Zvezda*, No. 6 (1948), p. 195.

[39] V. Nikolayev, "Business and Fear," *Soviet Literature*, No. 4 (1949), p. 124; V. Rubin, "Ben Tekker i drugiye," *Literaturnaya gazeta*, January 3, 1948, p. 3.

[40] Nikolayev, "Business and Fear," *op.cit.*, p. 124.

[41] Shereshevskaya, "Tekker i drugiye," *op.cit.*, p. 195.

same time struck themes that were especially appealing to the Russians, was Mitchell Wilson. His novel *Live with Lightning* was first published in the Soviet Union in 1952 and quickly went through several Russian editions. The first volume of a second novel, *My Brother, My Enemy*, came out in 1956 and the second volume in 1959. By early 1958 over a million copies of these books had been printed in Russia. Wilson was one of the few translated American authors currently being paid Soviet royalties and had enjoyed two extensive sojourns in the Soviet Union as an honored guest.

It is an interesting fact of cultural history that Wilson, a writer of fiction in the tradition of American critical realism, is much better known in the Soviet Union than in his homeland. It is true that his narrative method is direct, orderly, and devoid of stylistic innovation. Compared to the writers who are currently in vogue in the United States, he seems like a somewhat old-fashioned, although by no means stodgy craftsman. What sets him off from his American colleagues is his interest in science and, more specifically, the social role of the scientist. His treatment of this theme, more than any other single factor, has caused his immense popularity in the USSR.

Live with Lightning tells the story of a young physicist who works his way through graduate school at Columbia under difficult financial circumstances, serves on the faculty of a midwestern university, has a brief and disillusioning career as a researcher for private industry, becomes a key figure in the Manhattan Project, and, after the war, refuses a seat on the Atomic Energy Commission on moral grounds. Though sparing of complex scientific information, the novel is rich in detail about the psychology and drama of laboratory research, the intricacies of academic politics, the exploitation of scientists by the world of commerce and industry, and the political and ethical implications of the atomic bomb. The novel includes interesting portraits of the American scientific intelligentsia, and treats of anti-Semitism and incipient McCarthyism.

When *Live with Lightning* first came to the attention of

Soviet critics in 1951 it was mentioned, in the vituperative spirit of the times, as a document demonstrating "the process by which science is being mobilized to serve the criminal ends of the American warmongers. . . ."[42] When it was published in Russian in 1952 its propaganda potential was considered so great that David Zaslavski, Stalin's favorite poison penman, elected, or was delegated, to elaborate upon its message in the leading journal, *Novy Mir*.[43] To the critic Mendelson the book was an expose of the "militarization of science" and a "challenge to the robber band of imperialists."[44] Others emphasized that the novel illustrated the painful situation of American scientists who, in the words of one critic, are "compelled either to sell their talent for dollars or to lead a miserable, semi-impoverished existence."[45] The introduction to a 1956 edition repeatedly reminded the reader that the conflicts in the novel are of a uniquely capitalist nature.[46] In that same year two critics argued that it "showed those almost insurmountable obstacles which in America stand in the path of a scientist who strives to devote himself to the service of humanity" and "disenthroned the legend about freedom of science in capitalist society."[47]

The same was true of *My Brother, My Enemy*, whose first volume tells of the vicissitudes of two young inventors who discover the electron picture tube that paves the way for television. The novel deals prominently with difficulties between inventors and their financial backers and, in the opinion of one critic, illustrated the "basic conflict between people who

---

[42] E. Romanova, "In America," *Soviet Literature*, No. 3 (1951), p. 143.

[43] D. Zaslavski, "Yarki roman ob amerikanskikh uchenykh," *Novy mir*, No. 9 (1952), pp. 268-72.

[44] M. Mendelson, "Pod pyatoi imperializma," *Znamya*, No. 9 (1952), pp. 190-91.

[45] A. Belski, "Amerikanskaya progressivnaya literatura v borbe za mir," in *Sovremennaya progressivnaya literatura zarubezhnykh stran v borbe za mir*, Moscow, 1954, p. 168; Yu. Kovalev, "Zhizn vo mgle," *Zvezda*, No. 8 (1952), pp. 185-86; E. Guseva, "Roman ob amerikanskikh uchenykh," *Oktyabr*, No. 1 (1953), pp. 179-82.

[46] O. Pisarzhevski, "Predisloviye," in Mitchel Uilson, *Zhivi s molniyei*, Sverdlovsk, 1956, pp. 5-15.

[47] V. Rubin and P. Toper, "Poslesloviye," in Mitchel Uilson, *Brat moi, vrag moi*, Moscow, 1956, p. 421.

create genuine, permanent value for humanity and those who put these values to commercial use."[48] Another found that the book affirmed the fact that in bourgeois society, the inventor is "a lone person who is compelled to sell himself. . . ."[49]

The critics recognized at the outset that Wilson could not be regarded as a truly "progressive" writer, or even a fellow traveler. A certain "immaturity of world-view" prevented him from "understanding the laws of social development,"[50] so that his position was "far from revolutionary."[51] Since he was unable to see America's social contradictions in "all their fullness,"[52] he was inclined to attribute an "eternal, timeless character"[53] to the struggle of the scientist against bourgeois society. Nevertheless, he had taken up issues of urgent concern to all humanity in a serious but calm and responsible fashion, and he persistently sought an understanding of the "role, place, and future of science in the life of mankind."[54] Too many writers, the critics argued, indulged in cheap sensationalism, preying on fears of an atomic cataclysm.[55] Wilson refused to contribute to nuclear hysteria.

No people in the world are as conscious of science and technology as those of the Soviet Union. As members of a society which has not only staked its future on the rapid development of scientific resources but also, in fact, claims to be a new civilization based on scientific principles, they are urgently concerned over the ethical and cultural implications of science. A Soviet citizen reacts more intimately to a novel about scientific endeavor than, say, an American who, in accepting scientific achievement as a matter of course, fails

[48] A. Dudinskaya, "Sudba bratyev Mellori," *Oktyabr*, No. 8 (1956), p. 189.

[49] P. Toper, "Dve knigi Mitchela Uilsona," *Inostrannaya literatura*, No. 7 (1957), p. 202.

[50] Kovalev, "Zhizn vo mgle," *op.cit.*, p. 186.

[51] Pisarzhevski, "Predisloviye," *op.cit.*, p. 6.

[52] Guseva, "Roman ob amerikanskikh uchenykh," *op.cit.*, p. 179.

[53] Toper, "Dve knigi Mitchela Uilsona," *op.cit.*, p. 198.

[54] *ibid.*, p. 198.

[55] Rubin and Toper, "Poslesloviye," *op.cit.*, p. 421; Toper, "Dve knigi Mitchela Uilsona," *op.cit.*, p. 197.

to see it as a source of drama, excitement, or moral perturbation.

The obstacles faced by Wilson's scientist-heroes—the greed of entrepreneurs, the jealousy and intrigue of rival scientists, the difficulty of obtaining financial assistance, the indifference of the public, and the competing demands of theoretical and applied science—were all attributed to capitalist maladjustments. Of the section in *Live with Lightning* in which the hero fights a losing battle against unscrupulous and powerful financial interests, one critic remarked: "For a Soviet reader, and more so a Soviet scientist, who are used to seeing the cooperation of science and industry—one of the most important conditions for the development of both—it is strange to see this."[56] Both of Wilson's books derive their narrative interest to a considerable extent from the conflict between the aims of the theoretical scientist and the practical engineer, of science on the one hand and technology on the other. This elicited the comment that "to a Soviet reader this opposition seems absurd, but for Americans . . . it has an entirely definite, living meaning."[57] It was also noted that Wilson's heroes work independently, rely on their own resources, and, particularly in *My Brother, My Enemy*, are not strongly concerned with the potential social utility of their labors. The critics affirmed that the lone-wolf scientist who is indifferent to the social implications of his investigations was typical of the capitalist world. But, they insisted, no scientist has the right to such disinterest, and they criticized the author for failing to find fault with such individualism.[58] Even the hero in *Live with Lightning*, who gravely jeopardizes a brilliant career by refusing to participate in the AEC, was found by one critic to be inadequate because he failed to get into politics and thus to carry on the battle.[59] Most critics, however, thought that in this respect *Live with Lightning* was stronger

[56] Kovalev, "Zhizn vo mgle," *op.cit.*, p. 185.
[57] Toper, "Dve knigi Mitchela Uilsona," *op.cit.*, p. 200.
[58] D. Granin, "Roman Uilsona 'Brat moi, vrag moi,'" *Novy mir*, No. 6 (1956), p. 257; Toper, "Dve knigi Mitchela Uilsona," *op.cit.*, p. 206.
[59] Mendelson, "Pod pyatoi imperializma," *op.cit.*, p. 191.

than Lewis' *Arrowsmith*, since Wilson's hero becomes more actively involved in the vital issues of his time than Martin Arrowsmith, who simply repudiates the world of affairs and flees to pure science.[60]

Accounts of laboratory research are essential to both of Wilson's novels, and the Russians found them deeply meaningful. Daniil Granin, himself the author of a widely acclaimed Soviet novel of science, admired the way in which Wilson made "the most complicated physical processes . . . come alive in graphic poetic images which any reader can grasp." As a result, Granin wrote, *"My Brother, My Enemy* was dear and close to us precisely in its disclosure of the poetry and heroism of creative work."[61] The critic Toper saw in Wilson's books a "unique hymn to the glory of work," and argued that they occupied an "exceptional place in the literature of the West, in which, as is well known, work—the eternal theme of life—has not become and could not become, an eternal theme of art."[62]

The point about Wilson's novels, however, was not that they described scientific work as such, but that they showed how this work is sullied by the capitalist conditions under which it is conducted. Frustrated by these conditions, Wilson's heroes aspire to the freedom of "pure science." But Toper argued that, whether the author realizes it or not, the notion of "pure science" is a harmful illusion which, under the circumstances of Soviet society, is "reactionary and senseless."[63] Socialism, he insisted, has created the conditions for absolute harmony between the research laboratory and the production line, between the search for truth and the demands of social utility.

But all is not harmony in the Soviet Union. Despite their spectacular achievements, Soviet science and technology face impediments that are remarkably similar to those on which the tension of Wilson's novels is based. In such novels as

[60] T. Motyleva, "Predisloviye," in Sinkler Lyuis, *Erousmit*, Moscow, 1956, p. 18; Toper, "Dve knigi Mitchela Uilsona," *op.cit.*, p. 199.
[61] Granin, "Roman Uilsona . . . ," *op.cit.*, p. 258.
[62] Toper, "Dve knigi Mitchela Uilsona," *op.cit.*, p. 206.
[63] *ibid.*, pp. 199-200.

Granin's *Those Who Seek*, and Vladimir Dudintsev's *Not by Bread Alone*, there is abundant evidence that vested interests, venal political careerists and bureaucrats, intriguers and controllers of academic empires all hinder the development of Russian science and technology. A continuing conflict between theoretical and applied science is also plain to see. This is in part the reason why Wilson's novels are so popular in Russia. For the Soviet reader does not view with pitying detachment the troubles of the American scientist, fighting to capture his own individual vision of the truth. The reader's own experience has taught him to recognize these troubles, and to feel a close sense of identification with them.

Contemporary American plays have been translated and produced on the Soviet stage, selectively, ever since the revolution. But from the 1930's, when the left-wing theater of the United States excited considerable interest among the Russians, to the middle 1950's, the choice of American plays on the Soviet stage was sparse. During World War II several plays by Lillian Hellman were produced and they have appeared quite frequently on the Soviet stage ever since. A one-volume collection of her plays was published in 1959. The plays of Howard Fast and Albert Maltz, and some adaptations of their prose works, were performed in the forties and fifties. Around 1956, however, there were indications of a broadening Soviet taste for American drama. Clifford Odets' *The Big Knife* was translated, even though Odets had long since ceased to be identified as a fellow traveler. In 1957 the current hit by Jerome Lawrence and Robert E. Lee, *Inherit the Wind*, came out in Russian, Richard N. Nash's *The Rainmaker* was on the Moscow stage in 1958, and by 1960 Saroyan's *The Time of Your Life*, Lorraine Hansberry's *A Raisin in the Sun*, and several plays of Arthur Miller had been added to the Soviet repertoire. By far the greatest success, however, was that of Miller.

America's two most prominent postwar playwrights—Miller and Tennessee Williams—were not received in Russia with equal warmth. Miller has been known in the Soviet Union since the translation of *All My Sons* in 1948, whereas

[189]

Williams, whose plays have not yet been performed on the Soviet stage, was discovered by the critics—in a rather gingerly fashion—a decade later. At the outset Miller was recognized as a sharp social critic with, however, "bourgeois limitations" that kept him "very far from communism."[64] On the other hand, Williams was first described, in 1958, as a cynical decadent whose "scorn for the intellect, will, breeding, [and] social restraints," together with his Freudian proclivities, had made him, in the West, "as fashionable as he is odious."[65]

The really lively interest in Miller began in 1955 with the Russian publication of *The Crucible*, which was followed in 1956 by *Death of a Salesman* and in 1957 by *A View from the Bridge*. His plays were found to be "permeated with democratic ideas" and a "belief in the future."[66] However, Miller's frequent interest in purely psychological problems, a certain social and political ingenuousness, and an inclination toward "conciliation" often softened the social bite of his dramas. In *All My Sons,* "abstract justice" triumphs in the suicide of a remorseful war profiteer, but the social problems posed by the play are not "resolved to the end." By showing the "touching and pitiful . . . fate of a petty businessman" in *Death of a Salesman,* the author emphasized the "very illusory quality of the celebrated freedom of private enterprise." In his emphasis on flashbacks to explore the past of Willy Loman, however, Miller had tended to "replace social problems with psychological problems." Miller's next play, *The Crucible,* which employed the Salem witch hunts as the setting for an allegorical attack on McCarthyism, displayed a tendency to reduce all social conflict to ideological struggle alone. It implied that "the world today, just as before, is in the vise of two opposing absolutes in the form of the capitalist and Communist ideologies"[67] which could somehow be reconciled—a notion which, to the Soviet way of thinking, was

[64] G. Munblit, "Zapreshchennaya pyesa," *Novy mir*, No. 9 (1948), p. 292.

[65] V. Gayevski, "Tennessi Vilyams—dramturg 'bez predrassudkov,'" *Teatr*, No. 4 (1958), p. 181.

[66] G. Zlobin, "Surovoye ispytaniye," *Inostrannaya literatura*, No. 8 (1957), pp. 188-89.

[67] *ibid.*, p. 187.

naive and obviously impossible. Nevertheless, the play was regarded as a strong one, and one critic called it "not only an exposure of reaction, but also a passionate summons to struggle with it."[68] *A View from the Bridge* erred in treating social problems as if they were timeless, removing them from any immediate political context. But it was most important that Miller was devoid of "pessimism" and "skepticism" and his art was "healthy, life-affirming."[69]

Fewer positive qualities were found in the art of Tennessee Williams, but by 1960 at least one critic had decided he was worthy of serious attention. This critic pointed out that despite his "romantic protest," "in his best plays and episodes" Williams succeeds in "digging his way through to realism" and deals with "the problems of his country, although not the most important ones."[70] Like Miller, Williams avoided the "mysticism and irrationalism" of such "decadent moderns" as T. S. Eliot, Samuel Becket, and Eugene Ionesco. It was to his credit that he did not gloss over the ugliness of the capitalist world,[71] although his "naturalistic" emphasis on hopeless loneliness and depravity was exaggerated and in bad taste. A rich and intriguing field of investigation was suggested in the following summary of Williams' qualities: "An unbearable longing for justice, purity—and a disbelief in their attainability; an almost sentimental tenderness toward the unfortunate, the defenseless—and a celebration of sensuality, primitivism; a naturalistic sharpness of sight—and social blindness. These complicated traits, woven into a tight knot of contradictions in the world-view of T. Williams also determine the eclecticism of his artistic method, the dramaturgical form of his plays, the mechanistic mixture of the most varied stylistic means and devices."[72] Clearly it would be difficult if not impossible for Soviet critics to endorse numerous aspects of Ten-

---

[68] N. Balashova, " 'Salemski protsess,' " *Teatr*, No. 6 (1955), p. 138.

[69] Zlobin, "Surovoye . . . ," *op.cit.*, p. 189.

[70] G. Zlobin, "Na stsene i za stsenoi," *Inostrannaya literatura*, No. 7 (1960), p. 210.

[71] G. Zlobin, "Orfei s Missisipi," *Inostrannaya literatura*, No. 5 (1959), p. 259.

[72] Zlobin, "Na stsene . . . ," *op.cit.*, p. 209.

nessee Williams. But the very fact that he could be discussed dispassionately and attentively was an indication of increased liberalism.

The relaxation in the attitude toward American writers was further illustrated in the criticism of William Saroyan. In 1949 the critic Mendelson, avidly pursuing the fashionable policy of popping indiscriminately at American writers as at so many little iron ducks in a carnival shooting gallery, argued that early in his career, Saroyan had decided to sell himself to American capitalism by "trading in illusions," and, through purveying a special kind of "decadent optimism," to serve the aims of imperialist propaganda. Masking himself as a democratic lover of humanity and believer in the essential goodness of life, he continued to write about the dregs of society, "eagerly relishing all sorts of filth and perversion." His aim was to "console" the reader, to convince Americans of the "necessity of becoming reconciled to the capitalist order, since no matter how monstrous it is, everything in the bourgeois world is for the best." His protagonists were those who "accept with an idiotically silly smile the pitiful life to which they are doomed by capitalism."[73]

In 1954 the stories of Saroyan began coming out in Soviet magazines. They have continued to appear with increasing frequency. In 1958 a volume of the stories was published, and in that same year *The Human Comedy* came out in 150,000 copies. His visit to the Soviet Union in the fall of 1958 was heralded on the front page of *Literaturnaya Gazeta*, and he was given a reception at the Writers' Union. American imperialist propaganda was making amazing headway in the land of the Soviets!

Without the slightest exertion on his own part, and without even being aware of it, this "patently decadent writer"[74] had been transformed by the magic of Soviet criticism into a "very kind, philanthropic artist" whose "sincere and lively sympathy" for the sufferings of humanity had impelled him

[73] M. Mendelson, "Dekadent-uteshitel," *Literaturnaya gazeta*, January 5, 1949, p. 3.
[74] *ibid.*, p. 3.

"to disclose the bright and even the joyful sides of the darkest and saddest situations." The identical characters who in 1949 had looked on life's misfortunes with an "idiotic smile" had become "happy-go-lucky" by 1958, and were a source of "life-affirming art" with their "courage, humor, spiritual sturdiness."[75] The critics had decided that Saroyan genuinely loved mankind and that his optimism was based on deep knowledge of and respect for the ordinary American.[76] To be sure, he had his bourgeois limitations. It did not even occur to him that "there exist laws of historical development, laws of the class struggle," and that the sorrows he wrote about were caused by capitalism. But he was not cynical. Rather, in his attempts to reconcile the little man with reality, he was just politically naive. The critics had come to regard him as a talented, interesting, and often humorous writer somewhat on the order of O. Henry.[77] Indeed he was a sentimental, socially naive "consoler,"[78] but by now Soviet readers were being permitted at least a modicum of consolation.

Although turns-about in the published attitude toward individual American writers were fairly typical of the period from the death of Stalin through 1960, and although this practice was accelerated after the Geneva conference of 1955, the process was by no means smooth or uninterrupted. The hectic developments both on the international scene and in Soviet domestic affairs in these years had confusing effects both on literary doctrine and on publication policies. De-Stalinization continued in general, but it hit many snags, and at times it was scarcely possible to distinguish the reformed Soviet cultural policies from the old ones.

The events of 1956 and 1957 illustrate the confusion of the times. In 1956 there was great literary ferment in the Soviet

[75] R. Orlova and L. Kopelev, "Grustnyi i bespechnyi, dobryi i nasmeshlivyi uteshitel," in Uilyam Saroyan, *60 mil v chas*, Moscow, 1958, pp. 8-10.

[76] N. Vetoshkina, "Predisloviye," in Uilyam Saroyan, *Chelovecheskaya komediya*, Moscow, 1958, pp. 6-7.

[77] *ibid.*, p. 12; Vetoshkina, "Predisloviye," *op.cit.*, p. 7.

[78] V. Nedelin, "Smert, ne khodi v Itaku," *Inostrannaya literatura*, No. I (1959), pp. 253-54.

Union. Tasting new liberties, Soviet writers began publishing poems, plays, stories, and novels that were not disloyal to the regime but expressed a hunger for still larger amounts of freedom. At the same time, a number of political developments disturbed the Soviet scene. Khrushchev's admission of some of the crimes of the Stalin period, made at a Party congress in February, had a profoundly unsettling effect on Russian public opinion. When revolts against the Soviet power in Poland and Hungary took place in the autumn, it turned out that the most ardent supporters of the uprisings—and in many cases the instigators—were intellectuals, often writers, whose aspiration to freedom could be associated with their fondness for Western culture. From the point of view of Soviet political leaders, engaged in their own domestic power struggle and worried over the possible defection of their Eastern European satellites, thrusts toward freedom on the part of Soviet writers seemed to be part of the same equation as the increased respect for Western culture. Consequently, in the winter of 1956-1957 the old Stalinist ideological discipline, never moribund but recently on the wane, was partially revived, and a new term "revisionism" was coined as a tag for the sins that seemed to emanate from excessive regard for Western libertarianism. A tension—perhaps an age-old one with an altered visage—developed between those Soviet intellectuals who valued the newly won but still modest freedoms and those who longed for a return to the strait jacket of Stalinist times.

This tension was reflected in the Soviet attitude toward the publication of American works. In the summer of 1956, the Soviet publishing world was alive with plans for new ventures in the field of American literature. A volume of Faulkner was in preparation. Several separate novels of Hemingway were scheduled for printing, along with a big edition of an omnibus volume containing most of his novels and many of his short stories. Critics and editorial boards were eager for the names of new Americans to try out with the Russian reading public. Within a matter of months, it seemed, a substantial renaissance of American literature in Russia might

take place. But the events of that autumn nipped these sanguine plans in the bud. Many of the proposed editions were
published only after delays of as much as three years. It became clear that any real revival in the publication of current
American literature in the Soviet Union would have to be a
slow and cautious one.

Contemporary American literature faced a prolonged and
complicated battle for recognition in the Soviet Union. In
1958 the influential and reactionary critic Roman Samarin
accused the magazine *Inostrannaya Literatura* of favoring
American literature over those of other nations and specifically criticized the editors for printing two articles on William Faulkner.[79] In reply, the editor in chief defended his policy of printing foreign works of critical realism, but confessed
to insufficient ideological vigilance and promised that any future translations would be accompanied by a larger number
of corrective articles and editorial comments.[80] Nevertheless,
the magazine did continue to publish a wider variety of
American authors. In 1959 it printed Tennessee Williams'
Orpheus Descending—a feat that would have been unthinkable two years before. Equally startling were the appearance
in 1960 of excerpts from Jack Kerouac's *On the Road* (printed, however, as an example of the decadence of the "beat
generation")[81] and the entire text of J. D. Salinger's *Catcher
in the Rye*. At the same time, *Inostrannaya Literatura* printed
occasional pleas for even wider Soviet publication of American authors. It was suggested that "the social novels of Sinclair Lewis deserve Russian editions, all without exception."[82] (The same critic complained also that Melville,
Thoreau, and Edward Bellamy had been neglected.)[83] The
question was asked: ". . . does the Soviet reader get an understanding of the literature of the USA today by reading only

[79] Samarin, "Ostreye . . . ," *op.cit.*, p. 1.

[80] "Na puti k tretyemu syezdu," *Literaturnaya gazeta*, June 3, 1958,
p. 3.

[81] "Molodoi chelovek serediny xx veka v zhizni i literature," *Inostrannaya literatura*, No. 10 (1960), p. 294.

[82] Ivasheva, "Chto my perevodim," *Literaturnaya gazeta*, April 12,
1958, p. 4.

[83] *ibid.*, p. 3.

one novel of Maltz, only one or two plays of Miller?"[84] As if in answer, the critic Romanova recommended the translation of two authors whom Soviet critics had bitterly abused less than a decade before—Norman Mailer and James Jones.[85]

So long as the social and political systems of America and Russia remained poles apart, however, no real degree of Soviet liberalism could be expected. The Russians complained, and with some justice, that not only American publishers, but book reviewers as well, neglected Soviet literature. (Dozens of American books, without being translated, are nevertheless reviewed in Soviet newspapers and journals every year, but, as one critic pointed out, *The New York Times Book Review* printed only one review of a Soviet book in 1955.)[86] Just as American publishers pounced with glee upon and made best-sellers of books like *Doctor Zhivago* and *Not By Bread Alone* and continued to ignore works more complimentary to the Soviet system, so also would Soviet publishers continue to favor Maltz and Miller.

There would also continue to be general abuse and misunderstanding of American culture. Blatant chauvinism, such as that exhibited by the critic Orlova in 1955 when she argued that "the very existence of Soviet literature . . . helps to define the true paths, serves as a prop for American artists,"[87] would probably crop up less frequently. But there would still be such outrageous nonsense as the following, written in 1956: "Is book-burning really a fiction? No, bonfires of books blazed in the squares not only in the Middle Ages, not only in the times of the lunatic Hitler. With their stinking kerosene soot they have befouled the air of American cities even in our day, when at the command of obscurantists in pressed suits, driving in luxurious Cadillacs and Buicks, the deathless creations of Marx, Heine, Gorky, Twain have been

---

[84] *ibid.*, p. 4.

[85] Yel. Romanova, "Perspektivy otkryvayutsya," *Inostrannaya literatura*, No. 1 (1960), p. 206.

[86] Orlova, "Koye-chto o vzaimnosti," *op.cit.*, 248.

[87] R. D. Orlova, "Obraz kommunista v amerikanskoi literature 30-kh godov," *Uchenye zapiski*, Moskovski Oblastnoi Pegadogicheski Institut, Tom XXXIV, vypusk 2, 1955, p. 47.

burned. . . ."[88] There might be occasional protests by the
Soviet press itself against excessive usage of anti-American
cliches,[89] but the comfortable old habits would be hard to
break. In 1958, for example, these things were done: When
the school officials of New York City, in a clumsy attempt
to protect minority sensitivities, removed *Huckleberry Finn*
from school libraries because of its portrayal of Jim, the runaway slave, which these authorities mistakenly thought to be
uncomplimentary to the Negro race, *Inostrannaya Literatura*
proclaimed that the book had been suppressed because this
was the age of Little Rock and McCarthyism, and Twain
had been a fighter for racial equality.[90] Joe Hill, the famous
IWW poet, was identified, through a short-circuiting of political wires peculiar to the Soviet mind, as a Negro.[91] A review of the American edition of Paul de Kruif's *A Man
Against Insanity* became the occasion for pointing out that
American social conditions, war hysteria, and witch-hunting
were the cause of psychoses.[92] The appearance of Mickey
Spillane's Mike Hammer on television (indeed a sorry testament of American taste) was attributed to the strain of thinking about United States foreign policy that advocates a "position of strength."[93] The phenomenon of the "beat generation" began to attract increasing attention from Soviet critics,[94] who considered the beatniks mildly lunatic but never-

---

[88] A. Kazantsev, "Predisloviye," in R. Bredberi, *451° po farengeitu,*
Moscow, 1956, p. 7.

[89] Max Frankel, "Anti-West Drama Mocked in Soviet," *The New
York Times,* April 27, 1957.

[90] " 'Gek Finn' pod zapretom," *Inostrannaya literatura,* No. 2 (1958),
p. 281.

[91] Ivasheva, "Chto my perevodim," *op.cit.,* p. 4.

[92] S. Navashin, "Novaya kniga Polya de Kraifa," *Inostrannaya literatura,* No. 3 (1958), pp. 247-49.

[93] N. Vladimirov, " 'Molotom' po golove," *Literaturnaya gazeta,* March
8, 1958, p. 4.

[94] A. Belskaya, "Pokoleniye bez budushchevo," *Literaturnaya gazeta,*
April 24, 1958, p. 4; "Kto oni—'serditye'? 'poverzhennye'? 'zlye'?"
Inostrannaya literatura, No. 11 (1958), pp. 240-43; M. Tugusheva, " 'Razbitoye pokoleniye' Ameriki," *Literaturnaya gazeta,* December 20, 1958,
p. 4.

theless lauded their repudiation of "farcical bourgeois morality."[95]

This lingering predilection for glib, ill-informed, dogmatic,
and irresponsible disparagement of the United States made
tenuous any improvements that had taken place in the general
temper of Soviet literary criticism. But improvements there
were. A new restraint, subtlety, and regard for literary values
had become evident. The critic Romanova was one of the first
to demonstrate that it was possible for a Soviet critic to review American left-wing, even "progressive" writers without
resorting to hackneyed phraseology and political preach-
ments,[96] and to show that even ideologically inimical works
could be criticized with refinement, intelligence, and sensitivity.[97] In an interview in January 1957, Alexander Anikst,
a leading Soviet authority on Western literature, pointed
hopefully to "considerable progress" in this respect and stated
that "our critics do not confine themselves to analyzing merely
the ideological and sociological aspects of literary works but
are giving more and more attention to artistic and aesthetic
problems." Although he added that "true, this cannot be
said of all critics," he argued that "it is definitely the predominating tendency."[98] The writings of some of the most active
critics—such as Ivan Kashkin, Elena Romanova, Pavel Toper,
and Inna Levidova—did bear him out, and other, less prominent critics seemed to be using the new approach as well.[99]
The stubborn survival of the narrow, obtuse socio-political
view of American literature was evident in a Soviet study
published in 1957 under the title, *Progressive Negro Literature in the U.S.A.*[100] But an indication of the onset of the new

[95] Tugusheva, " 'Razbitoye pokoleniye' Ameriki," *op.cit.*, p. 4.

[96] Yel. Romanova, "Antologiya amerikanskykh rasskazov," *Literaturnaya gazeta*, July 17, 1956.

[97] Yel. Romanova, "Zametki o sovremennom amerikanskom romane,"
op.cit., pp. 210-16.

[98] "Soviet Studies of Foreign Literature (Interview with Alexander
Anikst)," *Soviet Literature*, No. 1 (1957), p. 180.

[99] I. Zheleznova, "Gonimyi sovestyu," *Znamya*, No. 2 (1957), pp. 209-
10.

[100] M. Bekker, *Progressivnaya negrityanskaya literatura S Sh A*,
Leningrad, 1957, 232 pp.

"tendency" was Levidova's review of this book, in which she pointed out that it was fairly strong on political, but weak on aesthetic analysis. Levidova argued that in the criticism of any given writer: "We want to understand not only his ideas, feelings, attitude toward life (in this sense he is in no way distinguishable from a philosopher, publicist, sociologist), but also that originality of artistic perception of the world that transforms him into a writer."[101]

Ultimately the success of any movement to raise the aesthetic level of Soviet criticism would depend on the degree to which Soviet ideological commitments could be unfrozen. For the Communist Party would continue to define monolithically the ideological boundaries within which the critics could operate, and these boundaries, in turn, would determine the degree of aesthetic latitude permitted. During the three years from 1956 through 1958, two ideological developments—one encouraging broader aesthetic horizons in criticism of American literature and one discouraging them—took place. The first of these was the move to make legitimate the study of a wider variety of Western "critical realists." In 1956 the critic Motyleva pointed out that textbooks on modern foreign literature, emanating from Moscow University, were rife with "vulgarizing schemes and dogmas." She complained that these textbooks "evaluated the literature of critical realism not in terms of the degree to which it is consistently democratic but in terms of how consciously revolutionary it is," and insisted that "in the twentieth century there have been and still are writers in whose works the living truth is manifest in spite of their own political prejudices."[102] At about the same time, others were complaining that in its eagerness to attack the ideology of Western critical realists, Soviet criticism had neglected to study the "artistic methods" of these writers. This error was explained in terms of the "general deficiencies in the development of the social sciences [*sic*]

[101] I. Levidova, "Kniga o progressivnoi negrityanskoi literature S Sh A," *Voprosy literatury*, No. 7 (1958), p. 227.

[102] T. Motyleva, "Tak li nado izuchat zarubezhnuyu literaturu?" *Inostrannaya literatura*, No. 9 (1956), pp. 212-13.

which arose under the influence of the cult of the personality of J. V. Stalin."[103] As a result of this baneful influence, Soviet literary theoreticians had been too quick in sounding the death knell of critical realism: "The correct thesis (that the sphere of the literature of socialist realism would broaden and, correspondingly, the sphere of the literature of critical realism would shrink in proportion to the growth of the world socialistic system) has often been interpreted dogmatically."[104] The terms under which the critical process would operate in the future were suggested in the following remarks of Anikst: "Aesthetics cannot be severed from philosophy, from the writer's social views. There are cases, of course, when there is not only a divergence, but a direct contradiction between a writer's subjective intentions and the objective message of his book. It is our task to understand such contradictions, explain them, and correctly evaluate the given writer's achievements without closing our eyes to the complexity of his work."[105]

The second ideological development in these years, one bound to vitiate much of the newly won freedom to study American works as aesthetic entities, was the above-mentioned campaign against "revisionism." It was clear that the leadership of the Communist Party would not tolerate any explorations in the realm of aesthetic theory that threatened the absolute supremacy of the principles of socialist realism. Any critic whose aesthetic curiosity tempted him to stray openly into paths of ideological heterodoxy was likely to be brought up short by such chilling statements as the following, from a *Pravda* article by the influential authority on Western literature, Anisimov: "It is a well-known fact that in Hungary the rabid attack on socialist realism was undertaken by the enemies of the people simultaneously with the preparation of the counterrevolutionary uprising. And this is of great

[103] I. K. Zhuravlev, "K voprosu o razvitii kriticheskovo realizma v amerikanskoi literature XX veka," *Uchenye zapiski* (Dagestanski universitet) vypusk 1, Makhachkala, 1957, p. 66.

[104] *ibid.*, p. 66.

[105] "Soviet Studies of Foreign Literature . . . ," *op.cit.*, p. 180.

significance: socialist realism is inseparable from the ideals of the socialist revolution."[106] It was permissible to display an interest in critical realism. But certain discipline awaited anyone whose interest in critical realism led to detectable political inattentiveness, conciliatory notions, or undue affection for the predominating modes of Western art.

The reforms that followed the death of Stalin had brought a degree of tolerance and objectivity to the Soviet attitude toward American literature. Even so, this attitude was much less liberal and receptive than it had been in the twenties. In the first decade of the Soviet regime, when the Russians were only beginning to assimilate the ideas implicit in the Revolution, the allowable margin for error in the evaluation of the literature of the capitalist world was relatively wide. A considerable diversity of tastes was permitted. When Soviet ideology solidified in the thirties and political controls became tighter and more efficient, literary criticism became forcibly constricted. In the course of the following two decades, Soviet attitudes became more and more thickly encrusted with official prejudice. An entire new generation had adopted ideological fears and inhibitions that made it impossible to see literature in its own terms, or to apply any standards of value but those of socialist realism. Although by 1960 the scope of interest in American literature had become a little wider, literary criticism would still be strictly subordinate to the foreign policy and ideology of the Soviet state.[107]

[106] I. Anisimov, "Sotsialisticheski realizm i sovremennaya literatura," *Pravda*, August 27, 1958, pp. 3-4.

[107] An interesting account of recent Soviet printings of American literature, based largely on unpublished Soviet sources and containing valuable statistics for the Soviet period as a whole, appeared after the present book was completed. See Melville J. Ruggles, "American Books in Soviet Publishing," *Slavic Review*, October 1961, pp. 419-35.

CHAPTER VIII

UPTON SINCLAIR

᪤᪤᪤ UPTON SINCLAIR seems to have been made to order for Russian readers in the early years of the Soviet regime. Always topical and sharply provocative, and catholic in his interests, he labored to expose the seamy side of American life, constantly hammering away at moral, social, economic, and political evil. Ever sympathetic toward the underprivileged, and perpetually shocked by social injustice, he made his writing a fervent protest against America's inadequacies. His works often graphically supported the generalizations about American life which appeared in the Soviet press, for his opinions coincided closely with those which were being fostered in the Russian public. His moral indignation, conveyed in furious satire, made his message convincing, and the Soviet reader, who was being indoctrinated to look for sharp contradictions in America, probably found much truth in what Sinclair said.

Political relevance alone, however, does not explain Sinclair's popularity in Russia, for, in addition to opinion, he also presented great quantities of documentary facts about America. His books provided a sense of involvement in the contemporary life of a country that was otherwise remote. In his preoccupation with social struggle, Sinclair has been accused, and justly so, of a lack of literary finesse. But his world-wide reputation is largely a tribute to his knack of providing his readers with a feeling of participation in the turbulent, newspaper-headline events of his books. And in a very real sense, Sinclair "dramatized the news" of America for Soviet Russians.

Sinclair is the only American author now living who has enjoyed a Russian audience both before and since the Revolution. The novel which introduced him to the Russian public, *The Jungle*, was translated shortly after its American publication in 1906 and achieved three editions within a year.[1] It was praised by no less a personage than Leo Tolstoy, who nevertheless disapproved of the author's socialist bias.[2] Despite this flurry of interest (by 1914 six of his novels had been translated),[3] Sinclair did not make a lasting impression at this time, for he fell under the shadow of the sensationally popular Jack London.[4]

In view of the decline of his Russian reputation by the time of the Revolution, the flood of 1,900,000 copies of Sinclair's books that appeared in the Soviet Union from 1921 to 1931 was indeed spectacular. In 1924 and 1925 his works, together with those of London, comprised seventy percent of the American titles published in Russia,[5] and in 1925 alone over 500,000 copies came out.

Yet the Soviet reaction to Sinclair was almost always a mixture of delight and annoyance. His intellectual and ideological development, self-chronicled in a steady flow of novels, pamphlets, and proclamations, was subjected to constant and anxious scrutiny. At times he was hailed as a literary hero; at times he was scorned. Although he always proclaimed his stand, he seldom gave his Russian followers time to define him, and for the critics his approach to the affairs of his time was elusive. Sinclair has been greatly loved and esteemed in the Soviet Union, and this warm acceptance by the reading public has made the periodic bursts of anger and disappointment from the critics all the more intense.

Over the Soviet period as a whole, there have been four

[1] "Knigi Sinklera na russkom yazyke," *Internatsionalnaya literatura*, No. 9 (1938), p. 170.

[2] A. Startsev, "Amerika i russkoye obshchestvo," *Internatsionalnaya literatura*, Nos. 9-10 (1941), p. 217.

[3] "Knigi Sinklera . . . ," *op.cit.*, p. 170.

[4] A. Aksenov, "Upton Sinkler. *Debri*," *Pechat i revolyutsiya*, No. 3 (1924), p. 256. In 1916 there were indications that his popularity was in decline (Abraham Yarmolinsky, "The Russian View of American Literature," *The Bookman*, September 1916, p. 48) and in 1920 *The Jungle* was only "fairly popular." S., "Albert Edvards. *Tovarishch Yetta*," *Kniga i revolyutsiya*, No. 2 (1920), p. 53.

[5] Lev Vaisenberg, "Perevodnaya literatura v Sovetskoi Rossii za desyat let," *Zvezda*, No. 6 (1928), p. 116.

general responses to Sinclair's writing. One was warm gratitude for his partisan picture of American society, which Soviet critics accepted as an affirmation of their own anticapitalist theses. A second response, however, was frequent disapproval of his interpretation of current political and social issues: his diagnoses of the ills of the United States were accurate, but the remedies he prescribed were often thought to be vague or incorrect. Third, the critics were often dissatisfied over his lack of "revolutionary psychology," for he was unwilling to interpret American social tensions in terms of class war, and as a result was inclined to compromise, to vacillate, and to preach reform, eschewing violent revolution. The fourth response was utter denigration, and was confined to the period from 1949 to 1955.

Before 1949, the most frequent response was the first. Sinclair's cumulative study of most of the burning questions of his era amounted to a comprehensive indictment of capitalism. Although his analysis was not Marxian, his observations were socialist, and he did criticize American society in terms of class injustice. His novel *Jimmie Higgins* which was published in no less than nineteen Soviet editions, was the first by an American to express sympathy for the Bolsheviks. It was so popular that it was made into a Russian film,[6] and as late as 1939 one critic warmly recalled that "in the days when fourteen capitalist powers fell upon the young Soviet republic, Upton Sinclair created the figure of Jimmie Higgins, brave little Jimmie, who died for the cause of the international working class."[7] The critical, or negative, aspect of his writing was bound to gratify Russian observers. *The Jungle*, for example, was lauded for its exposure of the "horrifying situation of several elements of the working class in America,"[8] and

---

[6] For early opinions of this novel, see V. Friche, "Ot voiny k revolyutsii," *Krasnaya nov*, No. 2 (1921), p. 209; V. Friche, *Korifei mirovoi literatury i Sovetskaya Rossiya*, Moscow, 1922, p. 25; and Valeri Bryusov, "Bernard Kellerman. 9-e noyabrya," *Pechat i revolyutsiya*, No. 7 (1922), p. 310.

[7] Anna Karavayeva, "Ob Eptone Sinklere i Lengstone Khyuze," *Internatsionalnaya literatura*, Nos. 7-8 (1939), p. 368.

[8] S., "Albert Edvards. *Tovarishch Yetta*," *op.cit.*, p. 53.

one critic asserted that "there is not a single production, in any literature, where the helplessness of a man before his exploiters has been shown more sharply and tormentingly."[9] *King Coal* was praised lavishly for its political acuteness[10] and for its portrayal of the "disintegration of the capitalist class and the departure of the younger generation from it."[11] *The Brass Check* was cited as proof that freedom of the press did not exist in America.[12] In its dramatization of the class struggle, the novel *100%* was "broad, gloomy, stimulating," as it "inflicted a shattering blow" on the "legend" of "democratic America."[13] *Boston* was a "monument to the fury and crimes of capitalistic justice,"[14] and *Little Steel* was a "remarkably realistic portrait of those reactionary circles of the American bourgeoisie who are today the bulwark of the imperialist policy of finance capital."[15]

Much of the grist that Sinclair supplied for the anticapitalist mill required reworking, however, for his critique of America nearly always fell short of Soviet requirements. In 1915 Lenin himself struck the keynote in Russian criticism of Sinclair's ideology when he wrote: "Sinclair is an emotional socialist without theoretical grounding. He attacks the question 'simply'; he is indignant over the approaching war and seeks refuge from it in Socialism . . . he is naive because he ignores the half-century-old development of mass Socialism, the struggle of currents within it; because he does not see that an objectively revolutionary situation as well as a revolutionary organization are prerequisites for the growth

---

[9] Aksenov, "Upton Sinkler. *Debri*," *op.cit.*, p. 256.

[10] P. S. Kogan, "Sovremennaya literatura za rubezhem," *Krasnaya nov*, No. 2 (1923), p. 322.

[11] S. Dinamov, "Epton Sinkler," *Pechat i revolyutsiya*, No. 5 (1928), p. 131.

[12] Sergei Sredinski, "Upton Sinkler o svobode pechati," *Molodaya gvardiya*, Nos. 4-5 (1922), pp. 283-94.

[13] Yu. Sobolev, "Epton Sinkler. *Sto protsentov*," *Pechat i revolyutsiya*, No. 8 (1922), p. 239.

[14] Yu. Danilin, "Kniga o Sacco i Vantsetti," *Novy mir*, No. 6 (1930), p. 199.

[15] T. Rokotov, "Sumerki amerikanskovo liberalizma," *Izvestiya*, March 5, 1940.

of an active revolutionary movement. This cannot be replaced
by 'sentiment'. . . ."[16] Like Lenin, Soviet critics in the twenties
and thirties did not question Sinclair's sincere desire for socialism, but also like Lenin and, no doubt, prompted by his
opinion, they consistently found fault with his ideology.[17]

In the early twenties, Soviet gratitude for his moral support, and delight in his exposé of capitalism, caused the critics
sometimes to overlook, and sometimes to excuse, the "hereti-
cal" character of his socialism. The attitude was one of friendship, tolerance, and hope. When in 1922 a critic noted a dangerous utopian tinge in Sinclair's socialism, he was quick to
add that the author was, nevertheless, a "deeply honorable,
steadfast, and aware person."[18] By 1925, however, the critics
had become markedly uneasy about his ideology. "Sinclair
is not a revolutionary," one article began in that year: "In
the peaceful intelligentsia-socialism of Sinclair, in which it is
often not difficult to observe a feeling of pity and a motif
of oversimplification, recently there has been ringing a quite
audible note of religiosity. More and more in his works there
glimmers the image of Jesus, the first Socialist. The communism of the Galilean had nothing in common with contemporary communism—that was communism not of production,
but of consumption. But for Sinclair He was the originator
of the American Socialist Party."[19] Thorough sarcasm appeared in 1927, when a critic wrote of the novel, *Oil!*: "The
'good will' of the author in this connection is unquestionable
—everything in the novel, so to say, is flooded with the sweet
sauce of beautiful feelings and is full of the spirit of optimism.
The quarrels of labor and capital can be resolved, must be

[16] V. I. Lenin, "English Pacifism and Dislike of Theory," *The Imperialist War, Collected Works*, New York, 1930, XVIII, 165-66.

[17] The critics in the thirties and forties were well aware of Lenin's
opinion. See A. Startsev, "Epton Sinkler," *Na literaturnom postu*, Nos.
20-21 (1931), pp. 165-66 and A. Yelistratova, "Mezhdu dvukh mirov,"
Literaturnaya gazeta, March 3, 1948.

[18] Sredinski, *op.cit.*, p. 284.

[19] V. Friche, "Tri amerikantsa," *Novy mir*, No. 5 (1925), pp. 120-22.
For Friche's comments on Sinclair's literary criticism, see "Iskusstvo
Mammony," *Novy mir*, No. 2 (1927), pp. 202-5.

resolved, in the private apartment of a good-hearted proprietor, somehow reminiscent of Santa Claus."[20]

By 1928 a period of greatly increased political stringency
in the criticism of Sinclair had set in. The critic Dinamov
contended that the author, who had been born in Baltimore
of a prominent but impoverished family, was, by class origin,
a member of the decayed Southern aristocracy, and that his
socialism was the protest of a declassed feudal aristocrat
against the bourgeois world. Consequently, he could not understand the psychology of the proletariat. His radicalism was
tainted, for "by his creative nature, Sinclair is not an artist
of great social phenomena, of class conflicts, of social shocks,
of historic periods."[21] In 1930, a review of *Boston,* Sinclair's
novel of the Sacco-Vanzetti case, accused this "spiritual de-
scendant of the repentant nobility of the nineteenth century"
of "depicting the proletariat by a method of idealization and
sentimentalism." Had he been a truly proletarian writer, he
would not have portrayed Vanzetti as an emotional and childlike figure, devoid of fighting qualities and "earthy, full-
blooded traits." Despite its insistence on the innocence of
Sacco and Vanzetti and its denunciation of their prosecutors,
the novel was politically naive: "Sinclair, who has long since
come to socialism, still cannot overcome the old idealistic
survivals of humanism, he still lingers outside the boundaries
of scientific socialism and a genuinely revolutionary world-
view."[22]

By 1931 he was merely a "socialistically inclined intellectual," nothing more than a temporary and dangerous ally.[23]
The novel *Mountain City* was a veiled apology for free enterprise; the single tax, which the author treated sympatheti-
cally, was a utopian panacea.[24] In *The Wet Parade,* "instead

[20] K. Loks, "Epton Sinkler. *Neft,*" *Pechat i revolyutsiya,* No. 1 (1927),
p. 206.

[21] Dinamov, *op.cit.,* p. 135.

[22] Danilin, *op.cit.,* pp. 201-2.

[23] A. Startsev, "Epton Sinkler i Amerika. 'Rimski prazdnik'—roman
krizisa," *Na literaturnom postu,* No. 34 (1931), p. 24.

[24] A. Startsev, "Epton Sinkler i Amerika. 'Maunten-siti' roman 'prots-
vetaniya,'" *Na literaturnom postu,* No. 33 (1931), pp. 22-26.

of using the class inequality involved in the enforcement of prohibition as a means for ruthless criticism of bourgeois democracy in general," Sinclair had tried to "appeal to this very democracy to do away with the inequality."[25] Now, his social apostle was a federal prohibition enforcement agent, and "the gospel of the new social order" was the Eighteenth Amendment.[26] In 1933 a review of *Roman Holiday* deplored his "misty hope for bloodless replacement of capitalism by socialism in America."[27] In 1935 he was dismissed as a "petty bourgeois dreamer."[28]

Meanwhile, publication of Sinclair had dropped sharply in Russia. Nearly two million copies of his books had been issued from 1921 to 1931; in the following decade less than 400,000 copies came out, and in 1934, 1935, and 1936 nothing of his was published.

Sinclair had gone under a cloud. The chief reason for this temporary fall from grace was his reaction to the American Depression when, instead of becoming a militant revolutionary, he joined the Democratic Party and ran for governor of California in 1934 under its banner. These developments led a critic to contend that "the last few years for Sinclair have been a period of profound artistic stagnation . . . in the sense of a castration and vulgarization of the social content of his work," and to conclude that, "as in former moments of historic crisis, naive 'socialism of sentiment' and a reactionary fear of revolutionary activity are again playing an evil joke on Sinclair."[29] From 1928 through 1936 all of his new works and many of his old ones were sternly scrutinized. Occasionally the former friendly warmth toward him was reasserted, but few of the books which he wrote during these years

[25] A. Elistratova, "Upton Sinclair's New Novel," *International Literature*, Nos. 2-3 (1932), p. 135.

[26] *ibid.*, p. 134.

[27] Tamara Khmelnitskaya, "Novaya kniga Eptona Sinklera," *Literaturny kritik*, No. 6 (1933), p. 136.

[28] Al. Abramov, "Molodost veka," *Internatsionalnaya literatura*, No. 6 (1935), p. 142.

[29] A. Yelistratova, "Literatura sovremennoi Ameriki," *Internatsionalnaya literatura*, No. 5 (1933), p. 106.

were ever published in the Soviet Union. And by 1936 the tone of his Russian critics had become almost elegiac: "The 'accusatory' novel of Sinclair played, in its time, of course, a certain progressive role. . . . In the period when American prose was governed by the sugary trend of 'tender realism' and when social themes were carefully banished from the pages of literature, such works as *The Jungle* had great progressive significance. But the lack of precision of Sinclair's own political position, his constant vacillation between the Socialist and Democratic parties, his insufficiently bold approach to the solution of social problems—all this has seriously hampered his genuine artistic growth."[30]

After five years in which not a single new work of Sinclair was published in Russia, a translation of *No Pasaran!*, his novel in support of the Spanish Loyalists, appeared in 1937. Soviet reviewers joyfully hailed it as the "fiery" work of an "implacable artist-accusor,"[31] and it was printed in 260,000 copies. At last, it seemed, the author had made his way out of the morass of "pacifism," "utopianism," and "gradualism"; hatred of fascism and understanding of its threat had enabled him to "escape the limitations of hackneyed, toothless Christian socialism."[32] Although, unfortunately, he had not lost hope of "resolving capitalist contradictions" by the "path of reform," nevertheless, ". . . life itself, the lessons of the class struggle, are convincing him: not words, not declarations, not reforms, but active revolutionary struggle and only this, can defeat fascism."[33]

It was as if Sinclair had arisen from the dead. By 1938, he had been entirely rehabilitated, and on his sixtieth birthday feature articles appeared in numerous newspapers and magazines, the most important of them, the *Literary Gazette*, de-

---

[30] O. Nemerovskaya, "Sovremennaya amerikanskaya literatura," *Sovetskoye studenchestvo*, No. 6 (1936), p. 83.

[31] N. M., "Epton Sinkler—'No pasaran!,'" *Internatsionalnaya literatura*, No. 12 (1937), p. 178.

[32] A. Mingulina, "'No pasaran!' Novaya kniga E. Sinklera," *Literaturnaya gazeta*, April 20, 1937.

[33] P. Balashov, "Epton Sinkler v zaschchitu svobody," *Literaturny kritik*, No. 9 (1937), p. 169.

voting half of one issue to warm testimonials.[34] Once more he was a leading political and social novelist in the eyes of the critics. In 1939 his new novel, *Little Steel*, was found to be "permeated with profound sympathy for the fighting workers of America,"[35] and a year later *Izvestia* declared that he had lost his distaste for violent revolution.[36]

Meanwhile, Europe had again gone to war, and the Soviet Union remained officially neutral, while condemning the conflict as an imperialist one. Sinclair's first Lanny Budd novel, *World's End* (in a review of the American edition), was found to be valuable in its contention that World War I had been promoted by big business, since the Russians claimed that the current war was of similar origin. Otherwise, however, the novel was "not distinguished by any profundity."[37] When Russia entered the war, excerpts from the Lanny Budd novels continued to be published in periodicals. In 1945 Sinclair was called a "leading novelist and publicist, widely known in the USSR, a fighter against reaction and fascism," and the possessor of a "profound knowledge of American reality."[38] When *World's End* was published in book form in Russia in 1947, a reviewer pointed out that Sinclair still had many "bourgeois-democratic illusions and prejudices," and seriously questioned the wisdom of showing crucial world events through the eyes of Lanny Budd, who, as a representative of the "idle rich," was merely a "pink."[39] Nevertheless, publication of the book and of its sequel *Between Two Worlds* in 1948 indicated that the author was still in high favor.

Then in 1949 Sinclair became a casualty of the cold war. Discovering that he had come out in support of the Atlantic Pact, the Russians revealed that he had "long been well

[34] *Literaturnaya gazeta*, November 20, 1938.

[35] Vl. Rubin, "Novy roman Eptona Sinklera," *Internatsionalnaya literatura*, No. 2 (1939), p. 182.

[36] Rokotov, *op.cit.*

[37] M. Mendelson, "Novy roman Eptona Sinklera," *Literaturnaya gazeta*, June 26, 1940.

[38] "Epton Sinkler," *Sovremenniye angliskiye i amerikanskiye pisateli*, Moscow, 1945, p. 47.

[39] A. Yelistratova, "Mezhdu dvukh mirov," *Literaturnaya gazeta*, March 3, 1948.

known as a careerist and businessman of literature, who at one time flirted with 'socialist' ideas." The following summary of his career ensued:

"The novels of Sinclair have always been fiery and timely, but, reacting to the evils of the day, Sinclair has been governed chiefly by the tendency to place salable goods on the literary market. A mercenary flair has been the distinguishing characteristic of his creative personality.

"These self-interested careerist goals have been served by the novels of Sinclair, which brought him fame by means of their 'accusatory' tone. We have in mind *The Jungle, 100%, Jimmie Higgins.* In issuing them to the world, Upton Sinclair extracted a double profit: earning himself popularity as a shield, achieving a fundamental designation in American literature, he preached errant reformism and conciliation, excused imperialist aggression, advertised the king of the newspaper gangsters Hearst, earnestly admired the philanthropy of billionaire-cannibals, defended Henry Ford's 'industrial peace,' and in every way came out against the class struggle."[40] This was merely the opening gun. In 1950, he became a "lackey of American imperialism," an atom bomb–waver and a warmonger. The Lanny Budd series was a "direct and unvarnished falsification" of history, as seen through the eyes of "stockbrokers and merchants, political profiteers, homeless cosmopolitans."[41] When in 1951 Sinclair suggested that working conditions in the United States were now improved over those which he had portrayed in *The Jungle* in 1906, he was met with a howl of derision.[42] The Russians knew better!

The crudely abusive tone of these Soviet remarks on Sinclair can be understood only in terms of bitter ideological warfare. Before 1949 he had often been called misguided, shortsighted, and poorly oriented toward the class struggle, but he had never been accused of opportunism, mercenari-

---

[40] P. Pavlenko, "Epton Sinkler—karyerist i klevetnik," *Literaturnaya gazeta,* April 20, 1949.

[41] L. Kislova, "Epton Sinkler—podzhigatel voiny," *Literaturnaya gazeta,* March 25, 1950.

[42] L. Kislova, "Epton Sinkler vysluzhivayetsya," *Literaturnaya gazeta,* April 3, 1951.

ness, or lack of sincerity. Above all he had been regarded as a realist, dedicated to utilitarian, socially constructive art. With the onset of the cold war in 1946 and 1947 an abrupt change had taken place in Soviet pronouncements on practically everything American, and Soviet criticism became almost exclusively a medium for political polemics. When Sinclair declared his stand on the cold war, a particularly vindictive explosion was bound to result.

In Russia the boundary line between art and journalism has always been vague and controversial. By establishing the principle that art is a weapon, the Soviet regime reinforced a long-standing tradition of civic tendency in Russian letters. Accordingly, Sinclair's works, despite their political inadequacies, might at least have been expected to satisfy Soviet aesthetic demands. He was by no means universally accepted as an artist, however, and many critics considered him essentially a pamphleteer. The term most frequently applied to him was "publicist." In Soviet parlance, "publicistics" is defined as: ". . . that section of literature which has as its subject actual social-political problems, solving them from the point of view of a specific class with the aim of immediately influencing society and therefore containing sharply expressed judgments, appeals, etc." This would seem to fit Sinclair. But a basis for aesthetic judgment is also suggested: ". . . one must distinguish those literary works in which tendentiousness protrudes and does not flow out of the situation and action . . . from those works in which publicism is an organic part of the system of ideas and images. Publicism of the first sort can arise from the inability of the artist to express his world vividly, an inability caused by the artistic weakness of the author."[43]

The Russians seem never to have decided which of the above two classifications best fits Sinclair. Seldom able to accept him as a novelist of stature, the critics were inclined to qualify their aesthetic judgments by placing his works in a special category reserved for Sinclair alone, a kind of no-

[43] M. Dobrynin, "Publitsistika, *Literaturnaya entsiklopediya*, Moscow, 1935, IX, 355-56.

man's-land, lying somewhere between the regions of journalism and art. Most Soviet reviews contained adverse comment
on the structure of his novels and stories, the flights of rhetoric, and the untidiness of the prose. In most cases, however,
these faults were deemed secondary, because the critics felt that
what Sinclair said was more important than the way in which
he said it. The following comment on *The Metropolis* is typical: "Undoubtedly, this great task which Sinclair took on his
shoulders demands a huge outlay of strength and time. Therefore, we do not dare to reproach him for the insufficient
'artistry' of the work: the fundamental problem and tendency
of the writer must stand before his obligation to art."[44]

While many felt that his method of combining documentary
fact, frank opinion, and fiction frequently produced crudities
of style, the great majority agreed with the critic who wrote
in 1923 that "this awkward crudity can compete with the
finest craftsmanship."[45] Comparing his "fierce realism" to that
of Zola, another critic argued that he even surpassed the
Frenchman in his "agitational qualities."[46] "Agitational literature," whose function is to "influence the feelings and will
of people, inciting them to definite deeds, to action,"[47] has
been especially prized throughout the Soviet period,[48] and
while Russian critics have apparently developed no formal
criteria for measuring the agitational novel, as distinct from
novels with a less immediate and hortatory purpose, it is clear
that Sinclair is credited with having made an important contribution to the genre.[49]

[44] B. Leontyev, "O novykh knigakh Uptona Sinklera," *Rabochi zhurnal*,
No. 2 (1924), p. 151.

[45] Kogan, "Sovremennaya . . . ," *op.cit.*. p. 322.

[46] Aksenov, "Upton Sinkler. *Debri,*" *op.cit.*, p. 256.

[47] E. Lunin, "Agitatsionnaya literatura," *Literaturnaya entsiklopediya*,
Moscow, 1929, I, 45.

[48] The *Encyclopedia* cites such novels as Furmanov's *Chapayev*, Libe-
dinski's *The Week*, and Gladkov's *Cement*.

[49] P. S. Kogan, "Sovremennaya literatura za rubezhom," *op.cit.*, p. 322;
P. S. Kogan, "O sotsialnoi drame 'Ad.'" *Krasnaya nov*, No. 5 (1923),
pp. 342-43; Leontyev, *op.cit.*, p. 149; Yevg. Lann, "Probeg po sovremennoi amerikanskoi literature," *Novy mir*, No. 10 (1930), p. 200. In 1939,
for example, a novel by B. Chetverikov, on an American theme, was

Although the critics were inclined to view Sinclair's books as something unique, they still criticized them as novels. In this light, his works suffered from several fundamental deficiencies. The most common complaint was against the "endless"[50] and "completely irrelevant"[51] details in his books. His writing was frequently "tedious";[52] he was excessively rhetorical; his dialogue was prolix; and his novels gave evidence of hasty, desultory composition.[53] Significantly, a critic found that abridgment did less damage to his works than to those of any other novelist. A cut version of *The Jungle* retained "all the power" of the original.[54] The charge of weakness in character delineation was prominent. Often, the critics contended, Sinclair's heroes were nothing more than social symbols and played a purely mechanical role. The hero of *Manassas* was merely a "peg on which are strung descriptions of historical events."[55] In *The Jungle*, "the author 'drags' Jurgis along the links of the social system, using him as a means of purely external splicing of a collection of facts."[56] The characters in *Roman Holiday* are mere "mannequins."[57] Particularly wooden are Sinclair's proletarian characters: Jurgis behaves as if he were in a "fixed orbit," and is portrayed as a martyr isolated from the life of his class. For *The Jungle* shows "the conditions of work, but not the workers, not the

---

subjected to a scathing review for being a poor imitation of Sinclair. The critic called the book a "second-rate pamphlet," and contended that Sinclair's works, in contrast, were *artistic* and thus could be called novels. He did not specify the qualities, however, which distinguished Sinclair's writing from mere pamphleteering. B. Yemelyanov, "Pamflet i yevo imitatsiya," *Literaturnaya gazeta*, August 15, 1939.

[50] I. O., "E. Sinkler. *Chetyresta*," *Zvezda*, No. 5 (1924), p. 278.

[51] E. Braudo, "U. Sinkler. *Zamuzhestvo Silvii*," *Pechat i revolyutsiya*, No. 4 (1924), p. 285.

[52] I. A. Aksenov, "Epton Sinkler. *Ad*," *Pechat i revolyutsiya*, No. 1 (1924), p. 287.

[53] L. Rozental, "Upton Sinkler. *Yug i sever*," *Pechat i revolyutsiya*, No. 4 (1925), p. 288.

[54] L. Rozental, "U. Sinkler. *Chashcha*," *Pechat i revolyutsiya*, No. 5 (1923), p. 298.

[55] Rozental, "*Yug i sever*," *op.cit.*, p. 288.

[56] Dinamov, *op.cit.*, p. 133.   [57] Khmelnitskaya, *op.cit.*, p. 137.

proletariat as a class, and not a proletarian as one of the members of this class."[58]

There were critics, however, who contended that since the distinguishing characteristic of Sinclair's novels was the social element, detailed characterizations would be superfluous. One wrote: "Critics point out that this straightforwardness of Sinclair, this purity of ideology, constitutes the weak side of his art. His works are lacking in living people; collectives, unions, boards of directors and syndicates predominate, and there is no diversity in his representation of man. This is a profound error. Sinclair's novels are read with rapt interest by that reader who is already fully conscious of the fact that without resolving the basic problem of our epoch, not a single problem can be decided."[59] This critic concluded that "the question of the 'humanness' of Sinclair's heroes is actually a question of world-outlook, not an aesthetic one." In brushing aside the question, however, this critic represented merely the extreme of the tendency to forgive Sinclair's aesthetic sins in the light of other considerations.

We have seen that Soviet enthusiasm for Sinclair was in direct proportion to his agreement with current official ideology. In his works the critics have sought documentation in support of their own preconceptions about America. Much that he wrote served their purposes, but when the evidence of his works ran counter to their prejudices, they remained unpersuaded. His books provided the Communist Party with an auxiliary form of propaganda, but whenever they failed to harmonize with the Party line, the latter unquestionably proved to be the authority. It is true that the critics sometimes disagreed about Sinclair, but the diversity was much greater in the period before 1928 than afterward. To some extent the variation that existed in the early and middle twenties came from the critics' ignorance of twentieth-century America. Another source of variety, however, was the relatively broad latitude of interpretation which Soviet Marxism permitted in its formative stage. The Communist Party itself had not

[58] Dinamov, *op.cit.*, p. 133.
[59] Kogan, "O sotsialnoi . . . ," *op.cit.*, p. 342.

yet established a uniform doctrine, and governed literary criticism with a fairly light hand. After 1928, through increased Party interference, literary criticism became more standardized, and in the following decades Sinclair's books were evaluated almost exclusively in terms of their agreement with the current Party line.

During the early years of the Depression, when Soviet criticism postulated an abrupt leftward movement in American culture and demanded that increasing numbers of radical writers become revolutionaries, Sinclair did not become a revolutionary. On the other hand, he did not drift to the right, as the critics contended. By joining the Democratic Party, he achieved a kind of New Deal respectability, but his change of position was only relative, for the political center of gravity in America had moved to the left. Nevertheless, his popularity with the critics dropped sharply, and publication of his books was curtailed. When the Soviet Union developed its Popular Front policy, Sinclair, as an ardent anti-Fascist, could once more be praised—however, with the usual qualifications. Later, during the brief period of the Hitler-Stalin pact, he met approval as an enemy of "imperialist" war. When the United States entered World War II and came to the aid of the Soviet Union, he was lauded as the writer of an allied nation. Then, in 1949, when his stand on the cold war became clear, he was denounced with unprecedented vehemence.[60]

[60] Mr. Sinclair has kindly provided for the present study a general statement of his views on the Soviet Union and its ideology: "I had high hopes of the Russian Revolution in the beginning; all liberal-minded men did. I accepted the thesis that the state would wither away; and I spent a long time waiting for that to happen. What first shook my hopes were the purges of 1935-36. At first I was inclined to accept the Soviet explanation that these represented the putting down of a counter revolutionary conspiracy, but the weight of the evidence convinced me in the end and, of course, in 1939 the deal between Stalin and Hitler put an end to my hopes forever. When Hitler made his attack upon Russia I, of course, agreed with Roosevelt and Churchill in accepting Russia as an ally, and I thought that there would be some kind of friendly settlement after the war. But, as you doubtless know, Roosevelt was disillusioned before his death, and I learned of his disillusionment. I realized then that Russia had become an imperialist nation, and the attempt at blockading Berlin

By 1956, when the second edition of the *Great Soviet Encyclopedia* reached the name of Sinclair, the virulence of Soviet commentary on American personalities had diminished, in keeping with the spirit of the Geneva Conference. The article on Sinclair merely repeated the interpretation of his ideology that had become standard over the years, noted dispassionately that recently he had "occupied a hostile position" in relation to the USSR, and added that his "best" works were being reissued in the Soviet Union.[61] Confirmation of this came in 1957, with the quiet announcement of a new edition of *The Jungle*.

The changes in Sinclair's fortunes in Russia illuminate particularly well the political content of Soviet criticism, since the critics' approval or disapproval of the author depended as much on the political climate at any given moment as it did on what he actually wrote. Novels such as *Jimmie Higgins* and *The Jungle*, for example, could provide a constant source of anti-American propaganda in Russia. Yet the publishers ceased printing even these books—and the critics disparaged Sinclair's entire corpus—in the two periods when the author's *current* political views were anathema in the Soviet Union. Aesthetic considerations were clearly secondary in Soviet evaluation of Sinclair. Soviet critics, like most Americans, were willing to accept him on his own terms as a combination of journalist and artist and to excuse, although not to overlook, his aesthetic deficiencies. On the other hand, unlike their American opposite numbers, Soviet critics found him to be a much better artist when his political message was congenial

---

seemed to me an act of war. Of course we couldn't resent it because we had disbanded our armed forces. Ever since that time I have been heartily supporting the Truman-Acheson policies, with the result that I am now in the eyes of the Russians a 'Wall Street's lackey.' The fact is that my stand has never brought me a single dollar so far as I know. My position is exactly what it has always been; my formula is 'the social ownership and democratic control of the instruments and means of production.' I use the word 'democratic' in the true American sense, and not in the fraudulent Russian sense." Letter from Upton Sinclair to Deming Brown, March 10, 1952.

[61] "Sinkler, Epton," *Bolshaya sovetskaya entsiklopediya* (2nd ed.), Moscow, 1956, XXXIX, 96.

and relevant to their needs than when it was not. When, in their eyes, Sinclair's political views were "correct," he was "growing" as an artist. When his politics were "incorrect," he was in artistic decline. The story of Sinclair in the Soviet Union, then, serves to emphasize the simple, naked obligation that underlies all Soviet criticism: to respect, first and foremost, the political line of the Communist Party.

CHAPTER IX

JACK LONDON AND O. HENRY

꙰꙰꙰ LIKE Upton Sinclair, the two writers to be treated in this chapter have enjoyed mass popularity in Russia. Their greatest vogue, like that of Sinclair, was in the twenties. Together with him, they provided Russians a kind of literary enjoyment that was peculiarly suited to their national demands.

Until the 1950's, Jack London was by far the most popular American author in Soviet Russia. Over thirteen million copies of his works have been printed since the Revolution. Even today he continues as a popular classic, and it is probable that over the Soviet period as a whole he has been read more widely than any other non-Russian author.[1]

At the time of the Revolution, London had already been the favorite American writer in Russia for a number of years. He had been introduced shortly after the Revolution of 1905,[2] and by 1916 his vogue was described as "truly extraordinary."[3] In 1941, recalling London's influence on the pre-Revolutionary generation, the poet Ilya Selvinski wrote that "whoever has not passed through this view of life cannot be a real man.... This is the first cigar we smoke in our youth."[4] More solemnly, a critic contended that London had served the Russians as an antidote for the "gloom" and "despondency" of literature in the years just before World War I.[5]

Despite the curtailment of printing under War Communism, London's books continued to come out. Only in 1921,

[1] "Publication of Fiction in the U.S.S.R.," *Soviet Literature*, No. 11 (1954), p. 209.

[2] G. Lelevich, "Frants Yung. *Dzhek London kak poet rabochevo klassa*," *Pechat i revolyutsiya*, Nos. 5-6 (1925), p. 511.

[3] Abraham Yarmolinsky, "The Russian View of American Literature," *The Bookman*, September (1916), p. 48.

[4] Ilya Selvinski, "Obrazi Ameriki," *Internatsionalnaya literatura*, Nos. 9-10 (1941), p. 239.

[5] V. Kirpotin, "Nashi simpatii k amerikanskoi literature," *Internatsionalnaya literatura*, Nos. 9-10 (1941), pp. 615-16.

when almost all book production ceased, did a work of his fail to appear. With the revival of publishing in 1922, he quickly jumped to the leading position among Americans. The new burst of enthusiasm for London, however, was not all salutary. The best of his writing had already been translated before the Revolution, and by the middle twenties critics were protesting against the indiscriminate printing of everything he had signed.[6] His name had become a magic word among the enterprising publishers of the NEP, guaranteeing sure sales for even the trashiest of his potboilers. This over-exuberance among the publishers explains in part the decline of interest in the author at the beginning of the next decade.[7]

The nature of London's appeal for Soviet Russians is clear. They deeply respect the elemental vigor of his writing, his hearty temperament, and his love of violence and brute force. Particularly fascinating are the primitive settings of many of his stories, in which man must pit his naked strength against the hostile forces of nature. In fact, the Russian taste for stories of hardy adventure in remote and uncivilized territories was cultivated largely through his works.[8] In the twenties critics even complained that his books had produced in the Russian mind a distorted image of America—a land of mysterious adventure instead of a country of industrialization and highly developed capitalist contradictions.

Less tangible, but equally charming for the Russians, is a quality which the critics have described variously as "love of life," "manliness," "a healthy attitude toward hardship," or "the will to live." London's ability to dramatize simple, fundamental virtues such as courage, perseverance, and strength of will is repeatedly extolled. It was natural for Soviet readers

[6] Boris Anibal, "Dzhek London. *Igra,*" *Novy mir,* No. 5 (1925), p. 156; L. Vasilevski, "Dzhek London. *Lunaya dolina,*" *Zvezda,* No. 5 (1924), p. 279.

[7] Lev Vaisenberg, "Perevodnaya literatura v Sovetskoi Rossii za desyat let," *Zvezda,* No. 6 (1928), pp. 110-22.

[8] The critics considered London's influence to be responsible for the interest in James Oliver Curwood in the middle twenties. Curwood was soon found to be a pale imitation. R. Culle, "American writers and literature in Soviet Russia," *Russki golos,* November 6, 1927; Vaisenberg, *op.cit.,* pp. 116 and 121.

to identify themselves with this "singer of the strong man who struggles with and conquers nature."[9] In 1927 a critic explained the current enthusiasm for London by pointing out that the Russian people "themselves have had bitter experiences in life."[10] The virile mood of his writings probably harmonized with the feeling of limitless power and accomplishment through struggle which, by all accounts, millions of Russians were experiencing at the time.

Running through the whole body of Soviet commentary on London is a refrain of respect for his hardihood, expansive love for humanity, largeness of heart, forthrightness, and healthy aspiration. His strongest trait, the critics feel, is his optimism. Not a reasoned, philosophic position, but an emotion, a mood which dominates the action of his stories, this optimism springs from a feeling of human energy and power, and is based on faith in the strength of man. The bearers of this optimism are his heroes—cheerful, bold, purposeful fighters whose iron wills have been toughened in tense struggle. The potential hortative value of these heroes was great, for they exemplified traits which, theoretically, were being imbued in the new Soviet man himself. And there is evidence that London did provide Russians with a kind of inspiration. Here are excerpts from remarks made by three presumably typical Soviet readers, as quoted by a critic in 1933:

"London generates heroism in people, he writes about those who seek adventure in life."

"London's books give you energy. . . ."

"After every book of London you are cheerful for a long time, you have a thirst for movement, for activity."[11]

The fullest expression of admiration in this respect came in 1935, when the critic Nemerovskaya wrote: "London is strongest and brightest where he places man face to face with nature, where he reveals his physical power, increased a hundredfold by the exertion of his will and by the superiority of

[9] Olga Nemerovskaya, "Sudba amerikanskoi novelly," *Literaturnaya uchyoba*, No. 5 (1935), p. 79.

[10] Culle, *op.cit.*

[11] S. Dinamov, "Zametki o Dzheke Londone," *30 dnei*, No. 9 (1933), pp. 53-54.

the human intelligence. Closeness to nature and the struggle with nature ennoble man, create their own special moral principles in the personal relationships of people and in the organization of the social collective. . . . A strong and active volition, and an inexhaustible thirst for life and a faith in victory over obstacles—this is the fundamental characteristic trait of London's heroes. . . ."[12] The critics' endorsement of London, however, has always been severely qualified. The defect most frequently mentioned is his all-pervasive individualism. His bold, aggressive heroes seek purely personal victories. They brave the Klondike and roam the seas solely in search of wealth or adventure. The heroes of *The Valley of the Moon* want only "independence, well-being, and cosiness,"[13] and Martin Eden is motivated by a "thirst to rise on the capitalist ladder."[14] Furthermore, they combat adversity single-handedly. While some of them display mitigating virtues of comradeship and self-sacrifice, most of them prefer a solitary to a collective struggle against their environment. London prefers sails to steamships. He writes a perpetual hymn to self-reliance, and while the heroes are fascinating on a purely emotional level, their rugged individualism militates against the idea of social cooperation.

Another aspect of London's heroes is even more disturbing, the critics feel, because it places the author squarely in the camp of social and political reaction. His typical hero is a "blond beast," an Anglo-Saxon morally and physically superior to the members of other races. Frequently this racial chauvinism is tied to a glorification of imperialism, for he sends his heroes on rapacious colonial adventures in which they subjugate and exploit primitive peoples. An apt summary of the critics' reaction is the remark of Startsev in 1938: "Indeed, all of Jack London is in this contradictory combination of hybrid elements: heroics, the pathos of struggle with

[12] Nemerovskaya, "Sudba . . . ," *op.cit.,* p. 80.

[13] Vasilevski, *op.cit.,* p. 279.

[14] B. Pranskus, "Dzhek London," *Literaturnaya entsiklopediya,* Moscow, 1932, VI, 574.

nature and human bravery which are close to us, and bourgeois individualistic motives which are alien to us."[15]

Such estimates are typical of the Soviet period as a whole, for the critics have noted many paradoxes in the ideological makeup of London. The author consciously identified himself with the world proletariat, studied Marx, was a politically active Socialist, and wrote passionately about the class struggle. On the other hand, he squandered much of his talent in writing for the bourgeois market and was charmed by the capitalist fleshpots. His outlook on the class struggle was profoundly influenced by Nietzsche, whose individualism attracted him no less powerfully than the collectivism of Marx.

Contradictions such as these, however, could be tolerated by critics in the early and middle twenties, for the Soviet ideological mold had not yet hardened.[16] Some critics insisted that many of his writings were genuinely proletarian; others felt that he was little more than a mercenary of the bourgeoisie; and still others indulged in the temporary luxury of refraining altogether from ideological judgments. But the de-

[15] A. Startsev, "K voprosu ob O. Genri," *Internatsionalnaya literatura,* Nos. 2-3 (1938), p. 353.

[16] Prior to 1927, his faults were viewed as aberrations and not as organic deficiencies in his outlook. Thus, a reviewer in 1923 found many flaws in the novel *Hearts of Three,* but mildly concluded that "lovers of light and diverting reading will read it with great enthusiasm." (K. Loks, "Dzhek London. *Serdtsa tryokh,*" *Pechat i revolyutsiya,* No. 6, 1923, p. 250.) Another found the novel "empty," but refrained from relating it to the rest of London's works. (Sergei Bobrov, "Novyie inostrantsi," *Krasnaya nov,* No. 6 [1923], p. 252.) In this same year a critic complained of the "banal images," "absence of powerful dramatic action," and "unskillful composition," of *The Iron Heel,* but merely added that the novel "does not belong among the author's best works." (L. Rozental, "Dzhek London. *Zheleznaya pyata,*" *Pechat i revolyutsiya,* No. 5, 1923, p. 298.) A thoroughly scathing review of *The Valley of the Moon* in 1924 made no attempt to generalize about his total product. (Vasilevski, *op.cit.*) Also in 1924, *The War of the Classes* was criticized simply as the unfortunate attempt of an artist to write as a sociologist. (Ch., "Dzhek London. *Borba klassov,*" *Zvezda,* No. 5, 1924, p. 283.) The tone of disappointment with an old friend, and of surprise at the extent of his error, continued in 1925. See Anibal, *op.cit.*; Sergei Obruchev, "Dzhek London. *Za kulisami tsirka,*" *Pechat i revolyutsiya,* No. 4 (1925), p. 287; and Lelevich, *op.cit.*

[*223*]

mand for definitive ideological analysis of established writers was growing, and the question of London was a particularly nagging one. His works were being read by precisely those broad Soviet masses who were supposed to be the true audience of a genuine writer of the people. However, Soviet theory already held that a writer who is popular with the proletariat is not necessarily "proletarian." Many opposing elements were present in his writing, but such complexity did not preclude Marxist classification.

A special inducement for establishing a consistent view was Lenin's own opinion of the American. As recorded by his widow, Lenin's reaction was the following: "Two days before his death I read to him in the evening a tale of Jack London, *Love of Life*—it is still lying on the table in his room. It was a very fine story. In a wilderness of ice, where no human being had set foot, a sick man, dying of hunger, is making for the harbour of a big river. His strength is giving out, he cannot walk but keeps slipping, and beside him there slides a wolf—also dying of hunger. There is a fight between them: the man wins. Half dead, half-demented, he reaches his goal. That tale greatly pleased Ilyich. Next day he asked me to read him more Jack London. But London's strong pieces of work are mixed with extraordinarily weak ones. The next tale happened to be of quite another type—saturated with bourgeois morals. Some captain promises the owner of a ship laden with corn to dispose of it at a good price; he sacrifices his life merely in order to keep his word. Ilyich smiled and dismissed it with a wave of his hand."[17] The critics have cited these episodes frequently—in each case an appeal to authority. But this authority had approved of one aspect of London and had disapproved of another, and it was still necessary to reconcile these views in terms of a single concept.

The year 1927 marks the turning point in interpretation of the man and his works. A completely damning article by an American, Joseph Freeman, appeared in Russian translation. Less a criticism of London's writing than of the man him-

[17] Nadezhda K. Krupskaya, *Memories of Lenin*, New York, 1930, pp. 208-9.

self, this article described him as a complete political and moral bankrupt. He had begun as an honorable writer, and had ended by selling sexual novels to the Hearst press. He wrote for money and hated what he wrote. This was merely a symptom of his petty bourgeois nature. London's life had been a tragedy of internal paradoxes, since "everywhere we find in him contradictions between the word and the deed."[18] Later in that same year a Russian critic referred to London's "compromise."[19] From then on the critics agreed that he was *not* a proletarian writer, harbored no illusions regarding the "proletarian" content of his writing, and explained everything he had written in terms of his petty bourgeois ideology. Whether or not this indicates the establishment of a "line" on London, it seems evident that Soviet enthusiasm had indeed been disproportionately great in terms of his worth as a purveyor of Marxist values.

Adoption of the proposition that London was fundamentally oriented to the American petty bourgeoisie *in all that he wrote* finally enabled the critics to develop an elaborate rationale to explain his apparent ideological inconsistencies. Briefly, the analysis of London's ideology that has obtained in Soviet criticism for the past thirty years goes as follows: He was neither a proletarian nor an apologist for the bourgeoisie. Rather, he was a typical "petty bourgeois rebel," who vacillated between adoration of the standards of the dominant capitalist class and a longing for reorganization of society through socialism. According to the *Literary Encyclopedia* in 1932, he was a victim of the "unstable position" of his class: "The socialism of London is merely a 'promised land' for which those who would save themselves from the misfortunes of capitalism yearn, while still dedicating themselves to the individualism of the petty bourgeois milieu."[20] He sympathized with the proletariat, had some understanding of its psychology, and viewed social change as a process of class

---

[18] Dzhozef Frimen, "Dzhek London kak revolyutsioner," *Na literaturnom postu*, No. 2 (1927), pp. 46-51.

[19] V. Solski, "O. Genri," *Na literaturnom postu*, No. 7 (1927), p. 46.

[20] Pranskus, *op.cit.*, p. 577.

struggle. But his preoccupation with the strong individual and his fascination with the primitive "dog-eat-dog" element of economic and social conflict impelled him to portray the proletarian masses as an "abysmal brute," incapable of organized, decisive political action. Because he lacked faith in the strength and volition of the proletariat, his attitude toward the cardinal question of social revolution was defeatist.

An example of the change in interpretation is the critics' treatment of the novel, *The Iron Heel*. In 1925, the well-known Marxist critic Friche had cited the novel as evidence that a "healthy class instinct" had led London to revolutionary conclusions: ". . . compared with Sinclair, who believes in the possibility of peaceful installation of socialism . . . Jack London knows that the new society can be born only from the fire and blood of social revolution." His was "a laugh of triumph, in sympathy with the proletariat."[21] In that same year another critic, who contended that basically London was not a proletarian, nevertheless agreed that "such separate and relatively late works" as *The Iron Heel* could be considered proletarian.[22] By 1933, however, this was the prevailing opinion, as expressed by the critic Dinamov: *"The Iron Heel* is a continuous cry of despair, it is a retreat before the might of capitalism. . . . London, like Upton Sinclair now, tried to combine revolution with evolution . . . and it is clear that he could not understand the nature of revolution."[23]

In the past thirty years, Soviet criticism has adhered to

[21] V. Friche, "Tri amerikantsa," *Novy mir*, No. 5 (1925), pp. 126-28. Apparently, Friche changed his mind in later years. The *Literary Encyclopedia* cites him as an authority for the opinion that London was *not* proletarian, and quotes him as having written, "London was heart and soul with an entirely different social milieu than the working class. . . ." Pranskus, *op.cit.*, p. 578. The encyclopedia takes pains to specify that this opinion appeared in the third edition of Friche's *Ocherk razvitiya zapadnykh literatur* (1931), which may indicate that in the first two editions Friche expressed himself otherwise. His book *Ocherk razvitiya zapadno-yevropeiskoi literatury*, mentions London only in describing *The Iron Heel* as a "Utopian novel, which describes the coming socialist revolution in the United States." (p. 254) I have been unable to find a copy of any of the editions of *Ocherk razvitiya zapadnykh literatur*.

[22] Lelevich, *op.cit.*, pp. 511-13.

[23] Dinamov, "Zametki . . . ," *op.cit.*, p. 55.

the thesis that London was an ideologist of the petty bourgeoisie. As a rule, he concentrates either on characters who are being forced down from the petty bourgeoisie or on individuals who are trying to raise themselves up from the proletariat. Nearly all of them, however, are striving solely for personal independence. Their search can take any one of three forms: escape, compromise, or revolt. Those who seek escape leave the city and its frustrations in search of a simpler, more primitive existence, either on a farm or in the wilderness, where they undertake "imperialistic" adventures. Those who compromise seek economic independence by playing the game according to the rules of the existing order. Sometimes these heroes succeed, in which case the artistic results are considered deplorable. Others in this second group, however, either fail or, having attained wealth, become disillusioned with it. The third group of heroes—those who refuse either to escape or to compromise—is best exemplified by Ernest Everhard, the hero of *The Iron Heel*, a political leader militantly engaged in the class struggle. Finally, there is the semi-autobiographical hero, Martin Eden, who is torn between all three desires—escape, compromise, and revolt—and ends as a suicide. The *Great Soviet Encyclopedia* makes the following comment: "Idyllic or happy outcomes with London are presented most unconvincingly. On the other hand, the struggle, failure, and destruction of his favorite heroes are drawn with great brilliance."[24] The ability to show convincingly the failure of a hero in conflict with bourgeois society places London in the "main stream of American literature, the stream of petty bourgeois realism."[25] The paradox of this "petty bourgeois individualist" who is at the same time a socialist, is explained historically: "The unstable position of the American petty bourgeois of the end of the nineteenth and beginning of the twentieth centuries, the hopes of working one's way up in the world, which were generated by the rapid general ascent of capitalism in America, on the one hand, and the in-

[24] "Dzhek London," *Bolshaya sovetskaya entsiklopediya*, Moscow, 1938, XXXVII, 397.
[25] Pranskus, *op.cit.*, p. 578.

creasing engulfment of the petty bourgeoisie by big capital, its proletarianization, on the other hand—all this generated along with the idealization of personal success and power, along with the theory of inequality of people, along with the apologia of capitalism, also a certain inclination toward the perception of socialistic theory, the slogans of class struggle, and revolutionary reformation of capitalist society."[26]

After placing London in historical perspective, Soviet criticism became generally more lenient toward his ideological vagaries.[27] Typical was a remark made in 1941: "However naive and confused the social outlook of London may have been, he was subjectively honorable and his revolutionary convictions were deeply sincere. . . ."[28] Meanwhile, in the 1930's he remained a steady favorite, although the circulation of his books dropped to less than half of what it had been in the twenties. His stories of animals continued to fascinate young Soviet readers. (*White Fang* is his most popular book in Russia, and has been made into a movie.) And the critics, for all their ideological reservations, continued to admire his heroes. Dinamov, for example, felt that the stories of Alaska "teach firm comradely solidarity and give one a brisk zest for living."[29] In at least one instance, this kind of enthusiasm gave rise to wild excesses. One critic in 1937 was reported as feeling that the hero of *Smoke Bellew* was endowed with such qualities as socialists are made of. He is reported to have written that from such men as Smoke there emerge "people's heroes, fighters against social oppression, revolutionaries."[30] In response, another critic declared that Smoke in the role of a people's hero would be even funnier

[26] *ibid.*, p. 576.

[27] An exception was the critic Dinamov, who insisted bitterly that London's was the "ideology of a social traitor" ("Zametki . . . ," *op.cit.*, p. 58), who had been "bought and corrupted." (S. Dinamov, "Smeshnoye i strashnoye u Marka Tvena," *Izvestiya*, April 21, 1935.)

[28] G. Vainshtein, "Dzhek London (65 let so dnya rozhdeniya)," *Literaturnoye obozreniye*, No. 2 (1941), p. 83.

[29] Dinamov, "Zametki . . . ," *op.cit.*, p. 54.

[30] As quoted in A. Startsev, "K voprosu ob O. Genri," *op.cit.* (1938), p. 353. The quotation is from an article of P. Balashov in *Literaturnoye obozreniye*, No. 21 (1937), which I have been unable to procure.

than one of O. Henry's cowboys would be as a "bearer of revolutionary morals."[31]

During World War II, London's works were singled out for publication when most other Americans were dropped, and he remained in favor even during the cold war. However, his reputation did not remain unscathed. As a Westerner, he was automatically suspect. In 1949, for example, a writer portrayed a Soviet wrestler as "deriving faith in his own strength, a burning desire to win, resolution in the struggle, sober courage in a difficult moment," from reading over and over a story of London. Two alert critics construed this as an act of kowtowing before the bourgeois West: "[The author] impudently asserts that the excellent Soviet wrestler was inspired to victory not by love of his Fatherland, but 'by the well-worn pages' of a book by Jack London."[32] Then, in 1951, a chance comparison of Boris Polevoi's *The Story of a Real Man* with London's *Love of Life* brought about a re-examination of the London hero. It was discovered that London's protagonist—deserted by his partner, dragging himself painfully across the ice, and locked in a savage death struggle with a hungry wolf—was fighting only for life itself, and that it had not occurred to the author to stipulate whether it was a capitalist or a socialist existence which the hero had in mind as he struggled! The fact remained that Lenin had liked the story. But a critic suggested that Lenin had probably valued it chiefly as an illustration of capitalist morality, in which comrades desert each other.[33] If this increasingly meticulous and absurd insistence on doctrinal purity in London should continue, Soviet critics may soon argue themselves into an ideological dead end.

The fact remains that in spite of his loss of ideological respectability in terms of current official doctrine, London continues to be published. Such novels as *Martin Eden* and

[31] *ibid.*, p. 353.

[32] From B. Ivanov and E. Rodikov, "Bourgeois Cosmopolitans in Sports Literature," *Komsomolskaya pravda*, March 6, 1949, as translated and condensed in *Current Digest of the Soviet Press*, April 5, 1949, pp. 55-56.

[33] P. Skomorokhov, "Zhizn i literatura," *Znamya*, No. 5 (1951), pp. 158-61.

The Iron Heel have recently been reissued in large editions, and the latter novel, which is actually a negative utopia, has been strongly promoted as a picture of contemporary America. This would suggest that London is now published as a critical realist, rather than as the creator of supercharged heroes.

O. Henry's books first appeared in Soviet Russia in 1923.[34] In the next four years over 750,000 copies of his works were published in the Soviet Union. During the period of the NEP, only two other Americans—London and Sinclair—exceeded him in popularity. Although his reputation has diminished considerably since then, new editions of his stories continue to come out.

The remarks of highly enthusiastic Soviet critics of the twenties indicate four reasons for O. Henry's unique appeal in those years. The first of these was his interest in the effects of urban life on little people.[35] Anticipating the promised era of industrialization, in which Russia would have her own metropolises, Soviet readers sought a future image of themselves in O. Henry's elevator girls and stenographers.[36] One critic found that the author had captured "the 'soul' of the big city,"[37] and another called him the "Rousseau of New York."[38]

A second reason for his initial success was his exposition of American life itself. In O. Henry the critics saw a poet of the common man, who would tell them the truth about the "average American." The brisk tempo of his stories, they felt, reflected the pace of American existence.[39] He provided an antidote for the "spiritual boycott" of America which had been perpetrated by such writers as Gorky and Korolenko.

---

[34] There had been a Russian edition of *The Heart of the West* in 1916, but the book had gone virtually unnoticed.

[35] I. A. Aksenov, "O. Genri. *Dusha Tekhasa*," *Pechat i revolyutsiya*, No. 5 (1923), p. 304.

[36] Sergei Bobrov, "Sinkler Lyuis. *Mister Bebbit*," *Krasnaya nov*, No. 5 (1924), p. 322.

[37] Friche, "Tri amerikantsa," *op.cit.*, p. 123.

[38] Bobrov, "Novyie inostrantsy," *op.cit.*, p. 353.

[39] Boris Anibal, "O. Genri. *Novy Bagdad*," *Novy mir*, No. 6 (1925), p. 157.

For, as one critic put it, this writer "does not curse the 'kingdom of the dollar,' he meanders in it like a tadpole in a puddle. . . ."[40]

The third cause of O. Henry's spontaneous acceptance by Soviet readers was the style and structure of his stories. Some critics were particularly impressed by his language, which Chukovski called "laconic, rich in intonation, original, muscular, and fresh."[41] Even more attractive were his innovations in the form of the short story. In 1925, the prominent formalist critic Boris Eikhenbaum remarked that the Soviet reader "values in him that which is lacking in our own literature—adroitness of construction, a diversity of plot situations and denouements, compactness, and swift action."[42] There were dissenting voices, it is true. Some complained that his stories were "prepared by machine methods" whose "monotony" was "almost tormenting."[43] Likewise, he relied excessively on the surprise ending.[44] Nevertheless, the critics repeatedly urged that Soviet writers try to emulate his devices,[45] and there are indications that he did find imitators in the twenties.[46]

The fourth, and probably the most important source of his appeal was his ability to divert and amuse. Several critics in

[40] Sergei Bobrov, "O. Genri. *Rasskazy*," *Pechat i revolyutsiya*, No. 4 (1923), p. 273.

[41] K. Chukovski, introduction to "Koroli i kapusta," *Sovremenny zapad*, No. 1 (1922), p. 17. Similar estimates are in V. Solski, "O. Genri," *Na literaturnom postu*, No. 7 (1927), pp. 44-46 and B. Eikhenbaum, "O. Genri i teoriya novelly," *Literatura: teoriya, kritika, polemika*, Leningrad, 1927, pp. 166-209. This chapter had been published previously in 1925.

[42] Eikhenbaum, *op.cit.*, p. 170.

[43] Bobrov, "O. Genri. *Rasskazy*," *op.cit.*, p. 274.

[44] V. Veresayev, "O knizhnom pyli, o komplimentakh Ruzvelta i o dvukh velikikh russkikh revolyutsiyakh," *Novy mir*, No. 12 (1927), p. 211; Anibal, *op.cit.*, p. 158.

[45] K. Loks, "O. Genri. *Shumi-gorodok nad podzemkoi*," *Pechat i revolyutsiya*, No. 1 (1925), p. 291; S. Zh-ko, "O. Genri. *Koroli i kapusta*," *Oktyabr*, No. 2 (1924), p. 211; Eikhenbaum, *op.cit.*, p. 185; Solski, *op.cit.*, p. 46.

[46] O. Nemerovskaya, "Roman kino-lenta," *Na literaturnom postu*, No. 2 (1928), p. 26. The critic did not identify any specific imitators.

the twenties were frank to point out his "escapist" value.[47]
As one of them remarked, ". . . it is so pleasant after a boring
and unhappy life to drink in strange joys."[48] There was some
disagreement, however, concerning the Russian reader's motivation. Eikhenbaum stressed the intellectual charm of the
stories, and suggested that Russians read them chiefly for
the sheer enjoyment of their convolutions of plot.[49] Others,
however, felt that while the author's narrative tricks were
refreshing and entertaining, the basis of his appeal was mainly
emotional, since his twists of plot served to convey a lightly
ironic or sentimental message.[50] All agreed, however, that O.
Henry offered the Soviet reader a release, a temporary escape
from his grim worldly cares.

But even in this period of greatest enthusiasm, the critics
paid close attention to the social implications of the stories.
And from the very first, he was found lacking both in breadth
and depth of social understanding. As early as 1923, a critic
regretted that O. Henry was "not one iota a contemplator."[51]
It was true that his stories frequently touched upon situations
of social pathos, that he often concentrated on small tragedies
in the lives of ordinary people, and that he showed a partiality
for poor and obscure individuals caught in the web of adverse economic circumstances. It was easy to read a note of
social protest into his writing, and many critics attempted to
do so. But they were almost always disappointed. One critic
wrote that while the author obviously perceived much that
was "false and hypocritical" in America, "he does not have
enough meanness to spit upon it. He speaks either with pain
or with forgiveness."[52] Another remarked: ". . . he does not
see that the country is split into two warring camps, that
around him there is unfolding a very great social drama. If
one is to believe his stories, all is well in the bosom of Ameri-

---

[47] Loks, *op.cit.*, p. 292; Sergei Obruchev, "O. Genri. *Volchki,*" *Pechat
i revolyutsiya,* No. 7 (1925), p. 283; Ya. Frid, "O. Genri. *Chetyre mil-
liona,*" *Novy mir,* No. 7 (1925), p. 156.

[48] Obruchev, *op.cit.*, p. 283.   [49] Eikhenbaum, *op.cit.*, pp. 182-201.

[50] Obruchev, *op.cit.*, pp. 281-83.

[51] Bobrov, "O. Genri. *Rasskazy,*" *op.cit.*, p. 275.   [52] *ibid.*, p. 275.

can democracy. There are no class contradictions, no exploitation. Under the shadow of the Star Spangled Banner social tranquillity reigns."[53] He was the slave of the bourgeois milieu about which he wrote; he accepted its standards and had no intention of objecting to them.[54] The critics noted that millionaires fascinated him, and that he saw no particular social danger in them. The proletariat was entirely absent from his stories.

On the other hand, they felt, he was not altogether insensitive to the evils of bourgeois society. At times, almost unwittingly, he was possessed by a feeling of boredom in dealing with the "triviality" of life under capitalism. As an antidote to this boredom, he chose humor. But, according to the critic Friche, ". . . this is the humor of a man of an intermediate class, for whom there is no other conclusion but just such a half-bitter smile with which to endure a life without perspective and horizons, a life in which there is neither content nor meaning."[55] Others felt that his humor was the traditional "laughter through tears,"[56] and indeed there were those who called him the "American Chekhov."[57] But the majority agreed with the critic who wrote that his art was a "retreat in the face of the terrible problems of life, from which you can hide only in a sentimental story."[58] He wrote only to please the dominant bourgeoisie, his sole desire was to entertain, and he had categorically refused to take part in the "struggle for a better life."[59]

Practically everything that has been written about O. Henry in the Soviet Union since 1927 follows this same line. An article in the *Great Soviet Encyclopedia* in 1929 contended

[53] Friche, *op.cit.*, p. 124. [54] Frid, *op.cit.*, p. 156.
[55] Friche, *op.cit.*, p. 126. [56] Solski, *op.cit.*, p. 44.
[57] S. Zh-ko, *op.cit.*, p. 211. This critic objected to the practice.
[58] Obruchev, *op.cit.*, p. 283.
[59] Solski, *op.cit.*, pp. 42-46. The appearance of translations of Al Jennings' *Through the Shadows with O. Henry* and Upton Sinclair's play *Bill Porter*, both in 1926, occasioned attempts to show that the author's experiences in prison had brought strong elements of social protest into his writings. This line of argument was soon dropped. See A. Tsingovalov, "Novinki amerikanskoi literatury," *Molodaya gvardiya*, No. 7 (1926), pp. 170-71 and Veresayev, *op.cit.*, p. 212.

that "all of his technique was directed toward external, purely formal, and therefore superficial effects," and that he "studiously avoids the contradictions of life. . . ."[60] In some respects he was distinctly antisocial: "He has been correctly named . . . the 'great consoler.' Yes, he is a 'consoler,' since he sows illusions, he gives vain hopes, he deceives his readers into believing that everything will be all right, that the beautiful life can be built without the slightest effort or struggle. It is false, this art of O. Henry, it is dangerous like opium, since it diverts one from life and struggle."[61]

In 1937, however, there were attempts to rehabilitate the author as a social critic of sorts. It was suggested that underneath his apparent sentimentality there was a deep sense of the tragedy of life in bourgeois society. The essential quality of an O. Henry plot was not its fortunate outcome, but the element of surprise. For the optimism of his happy endings was purely sham. Perceiving the shallowness of capitalist culture, he had slyly developed his narrative innovations as a means of protesting against it: "Every story of O. Henry is a malicious mockery of trite notions about the ordinary American, a sharp polemic against the authors of bourgeois tales, against the editors of cheap newspapers and magazines, who cultivate banal language and trite plots. . . . With his tricks of plot, O. Henry protested against the arithmetical-mean approach to the ordinary American."[62] There were even more ambitious claims. He possessed a "firm belief in man, in the tremendous power of the human will," and his chief goal was the "exposure of bourgeois individualism." In contrast to most of bourgeois literature, his art was a "burning moral sermon," since he was "organically connected with the life of urban and rural poverty, of working people crushed by need and sorrow."[63]

[60] S. D., "O. Genri," *Bolshaya sovetskaya entsiklopediya*, Moscow, 1929, XV, 215-16. The author of this article is probably Sergei Dinamov, who also wrote on O. Henry for the *Literary Encyclopedia*. See S. Dinamov, "Genri," *Literaturnaya entsiklopediya*, Moscow, 1929, II, 462-64.

[61] "Peredovaya," *Internatsionalnaya literatura*, No. 5 (1933), p. 3.

[62] A. Leites, "Skovanny smekh," *Izvestiya*, September 10, 1937.

[63] N. Ch., "O. Genri (75 let so dnya rozhdeniya)," *Literaturnoye obozreniye*, No. 16 (1937), p. 60.

A reply to claims such as these was not long in coming. The critic Startsev emphasized that O. Henry had been essentially a humorist, denied him any social value, and accused him of purposely distorting the facts of life. He had known the darkest sides of America, but had refused to write about them. As a result, his stories, though fascinating to read, were "sugary and absurd."[64]

Despite ideological strictures such as these, O. Henry is still published in the Soviet Union. In fact, the Russians probably think better of him than do his compatriots, for he obviously continues to answer some special need in the Soviet reader. Certainly, the factors of style and genre are important in this respect. Brevity, racy patter, the surprise ending with its lightly ironical or sentimental twist—O. Henry's stock-in-trade—are not common in Russia's own literary tradition. With the possible exceptions of Chekhov and Zoshchenko, no Russian has his flavor. This suggests that he continues to be popular because of the piquancy of his narrative method.

A more important source of his continuing attractiveness may be ideology itself. The stories of O. Henry, despite their evident sympathy for the underdog, their frequently satirical tone, and their preoccupation with life's disappointments, can all be classified as light entertainment. Soviet literature, on the other hand, does not often display a light touch. The obligation to instruct has been a guiding principle of the Soviet arts since the inception of the Five Year Plans. Not only does Soviet Marxist literary theory condemn stories which are merely diverting; it also demands a didactic element in harmony with the principles which constitute the basis of Soviet culture. Soviet humor, for example, is expected to be based on social satire much stronger and sharper than that of O. Henry. Likewise, such devices as the fortuitous happy ending and the melancholy coincidence, which the author uses

[64] A. Startsev, "K voprosu ob O. Genri," *op.cit.*, p. 351. The tendency to regard the author primarily as a humanist and moralist, however, lingers to the present. See A. Anikst, *Poslesloviye*, in O. Genri, *Izbrannye proizvedeniya v dvukh tomakh*, Moscow, 1955, pp. 558-79 and A. Anikst, "O. Genri," in O. Genri, *Rasskazy*, Moscow, 1957, pp. 539-50.

so frequently, are in fundamental conflict with the official Soviet literary doctrine which insists that man must not be portrayed as a pawn of fortune. Finally, the sentimentality of which Soviet critics accuse the author is purported to spring from a false standard of values in which righteous social indignation is displaced by pity.

But it is safe to assume that vast numbers of Russian readers fail to share the ideological prejudices of the critics. Constant strictures against the unreality of O. Henry's happy endings probably fail to impress the Soviet reader, for that reader is himself sentimental and enjoys short flights into a world of whimsy and gentle irony. The comments of the critics have frequently contained a note of caution, an implicit warning to the general reader lest he be seduced by the harmful moral and social values and the message of "consolation" which O. Henry's stories are purported to contain. Now the fact is that this writer *is* sentimental, glib, and superficial, albeit clever. No doubt, most students of American literature would agree with the distinguished writer, V. Veresayev, who characterized his stories as "magnificent railroad reading."[65]

Russians, however, probably have as great a potential appetite for "railroad reading" as other people. Significantly, Soviet publishers under the NEP issued this type of literature in great quantities. O. Henry was the most prominent among the Americans represented, but there were dozens of others. In 1928 the importation of this kind of writing ceased. While American popular magazines still print thousands of stories whose style and quality is comparable to that of O. Henry, Soviet publishers have continued to shun them. The sole exception is O. Henry himself. A huge stream of light fiction, the truly "mass" literature of twentieth-century America, is represented in the Soviet Union by this author alone.

This brings us to the question of why both O. Henry and London, whose views of the world are woefully inadequate in terms of Soviet Marxist ideology, continue to be published in Russia. The reading public alone could not have caused new printings of these authors, particularly in the period after the NEP. Party control of publication was increasingly firm after 1928. Foreign works were issued only after the most careful consideration of their ideological values and their probable immediate political effects on Soviet readers. On the other hand, the power of the Party had become so firmly established after the early thirties that it probably saw no danger in permitting a limited circulation of foreign "bourgeois" works. But this is probably not the whole story.

Continued tolerance of London and O. Henry after the NEP may also involve more practical considerations. Sheer political expediency may have prompted the Party to foster the publication of a small quantity of "escape" literature in an effort to bolster popular morale. Further, it should be remembered that both authors wrote at the very beginning of the century, and that their picture of American life was outdated. Their anachronistic image of the American standard of living may have aided Party propagandists in creating a distorted impression of the United States. Also it is obvious that both authors did offer criticisms of the United States which corresponded, in some respects, with those of Soviet propagandists. Finally, London and O. Henry had become "classics" in the USSR, and the public was anxious to continue reading them.

But why have they become "classics"? There are probably a number of reasons. London and O. Henry are excellent storytellers, whose tales move swiftly and are full of suspense and excitement. For Russians, whose native literature traditionally does not possess these qualities, they provide a kind of narrative refreshment. Also, Russian literature, particularly in the Soviet period, has been closely bound to contemporary reality. In the Soviet world of discipline, hardship, and iron effort, these two authors undoubtedly provide a welcome relief from everyday tensions. It should further be noted that the Soviet reading public has been chiefly a newly literate one, relatively lacking in literary sophistication. London and O. Henry, who can interest readers without making intellec-

tual demands on them, provide ideal material for such readers. The following characteristics of both writers should also
be noted: they are good psychologists, but they are not subtle;
they are moralists, but they do not engage in refined moral
speculations, nor do their stories, as a rule, involve moral
complexities; the standards of personal and social good and
evil are clear-cut and stable in their writings. The gropings,
doubts, and searching psychological and moral explorations
which have so far characterized the main stream of American
literature in the twentieth century, and which Soviet criticism
classifies for the most part as "decadent," are absent from
their works. Any lingering on questions of abstract social
justice, the psychology of sex, or personal ideologies, is precluded by the rapid movement of their narration. Taken for
granted are the simple moral and psychological truths and
human ideals which the masses of mankind have accepted as
basic in the twentieth century. For this reason, London and
O. Henry are particularly suitable to the general Soviet
reader, whose environment is such that he has neither the
leisure nor the inclination to indulge in delicate intellectual
or emotional probings. The values and standards of these
writers must seem "sound" to the Soviet reader, despite their
political backwardness from the Marxist point of view. This
accounts for the pronounced inclination of many critics to
value O. Henry as a poet of the "little man," despite the
simultaneous insistence of other critics that the author ran
away from real social problems. Likewise, it would account
for the fact that so many Russians see an inspirational quality
in London, despite the incorrectness of his ideological conclusions. For obviously these two writers have struck simple,
basic human chords which transcend ideology.

CHAPTER X

SINCLAIR LEWIS

AND THEODORE DREISER

〜〜〜 WHEN Sinclair Lewis received the Nobel Prize in 1930, eleven of the twelve novels he had written were already in Russian print. *Main Street* had achieved four Soviet editions, while *Babbitt, Arrowsmith, Mantrap*, and *Elmer Gantry* had run to three each. Several others had appeared in more than one edition, and only *Dodsworth* had not been translated. Next to Upton Sinclair, Lewis was the most popular contemporary American novelist in the USSR.

Lewis' novels had begun to appear in Russian translation in 1924,[1] and had achieved an instant success. The critics hailed *Babbitt* as a magnificent document of bourgeois life and praised its precision and abundance of detail.[2] One of them likened the novel to *Madame Bovary*.[3] Another drew from it revolutionary conclusions: "Setting his Babbitt to quarreling with the world, Lewis . . . finds no way out. The premise of the Babbittesque existence inevitably leads to the destruction of this existence. . . ."[4] These were the deductions of the critic, however, and were not attributed to Lewis himself. For already the critics were contending that his accurate portrayals were more a product of method than of ideology.[5]

In 1925 *Arrowsmith, Our Mr. Wrenn*, and *The Trail of*

[1] *Main Street* (two editions), *Babbitt*, and *Free Air.*

[2] B. Leontyev, "Novinki inostrannoi literatury," *Rabochi zhurnal*, Nos. 3-4 (1924), p. 219; Sergei Bobrov, "Sinkler Lyuis. *Mister Bebbit*," *Krasnaya nov*, No. 5 (1924), p. 324.

[3] G. Aigustov, "Sinkler Lyuis. *Mister Bebbit*," *Pechat i revolyutsiya*, No. 3 (1924), p. 255.

[4] Bobrov, *op.cit.*, p. 324.

[5] The critics were greatly dissatisfied with the translation of the first edition of *Babbitt*. One of them considered it "beneath criticism" (Bobrov, *op.cit.*, p. 325) and another wrote: "This book, by some misunderstanding attributed to Lewis, is written in the jargon of the Odessa black market, so peculiar that what has been printed must first be translated into Russian" (Aigustov, *op.cit.*, p. 255).

the Hawk were published. Again Lewis was compared to Flaubert in his depiction of the "haughty, pedantic, mundane, and comical bourgeoisie." In contrast to Upton Sinclair, Jack London, and O. Henry, Lewis showed how Americans "feel" —their "psychology."[6]

By the end of 1926 *Mantrap* and *The Job* had been translated, and the critics began to consider his work as a whole. He was a "penetrating master," who compelled attention "not only to the intrigue of the action, but also to trifles, details of life, which mold and modify the psychology of humanity in correspondence with its social development."[7] Particularly new and valuable for Russians was his treatment of *provincial* America.[8] His central theme was middle-class rebellion, the struggle of the average American against society to gain some kind of personal success.[9] But unfortunately he was not a socialist like Upton Sinclair, and "you do not meet an ordinary working man among his heroes. His attention is devoted wholly to democracy, its intelligentsia, skilled labor."[10] Politically, he was a reformer, and not at all a revolutionary.[11] He was merely a recorder of events, trying to catch the spirit of the times.[12] *Arrowsmith* was his best novel, but it did little more than suggest that socialism would be best for America.[13]

Nevertheless, Lewis' popularity continued to mount. In 1927 a critic could write that he ". . . carries on his shoulders

[6] Boris Leontyev, "Sinkler Lyuis. *Glavnaya ulitsa; Polyot sokola,*" *Novy mir,* No. 2 (1925), p. 154.

[7] Nikolai Aseyev, "O Sinklere Lyuise," *30 dnei,* No. 5 (1926), p. 87.

[8] *ibid.,* p. 88.

[9] Yak. Benni, "Sinkler Lyuis. *Una Golden,*" *Pechat i revolyutsiya,* No. 7 (1926), p. 218.

[10] Aseyev, *op.cit.,* p. 88.

[11] *ibid.,* p. 88.

[12] R. Kulle, "Sinkler Lyuis. *Mentrap,*" *Pechat i revolyutsiya,* No. 8 (1926), p. 213.

[13] Aseyev, *op.cit.,* p. 88. The "socialist" ideas in the novel were attributed to Lewis' collaborator, Paul de Kruif, whose books were translated in the thirties. See A. Yelistratova, "Sinkler Lyuis," *Literaturnaya entsiklopediya,* Moscow, 1932, VI, 648; S. Dinamov, "Sinkler Lyuis," *Pechat i revolyutsiya,* No. 1 (1928), p. 120; and T. Levit, "Istoriya odnovo optimizma," *Literatura i iskusstvo,* Nos. 2-3 (1931), p. 178.

the whole burden of the contemporary American social novel, presenting, in book after book, an extremely full and broad picture of America, which is swollen with wealth and entangled in prejudices."[14] Such works as *The Trail of the Hawk* and *Mantrap* had by now shown the critics that he was not entirely a social novelist, and one of them described the latter book as a "complicated amalgam of high tragedy, satire, comedy, lyric poetry, and adventure novel."[15] The popularity of these novels shows, in fact, that Lewis' escapist value was not lost on the Soviet public. His criticism of bourgeois morals and manners may not have been ideologically "sound," but it was bright, informative, and entertaining. This, however, was not what the critics were looking for.

As early as 1927 Soviet critics began a close ideological scrutiny of Lewis. By 1933 they had defined limitations in his works which, according to their standards, were decisive. First of all, they traced his career in perspective, and devised an interpretation of his artistic and ideological development.[16] His work was divided into three periods. The first began in 1914 with *Our Mr. Wrenn* and included *The Trail of the Hawk* (1915), *The Innocents* (1917), and *Free Air* (1919). These novels were "standard, diverting" literature, in which the author showed his heroes struggling upward to success against the opposition of capitalist society but preferred to view this conflict as an "extrasocial" problem. A partial exception was *The Job* (1917), which lacked the "exoticism" and "romanticism" of the other novels in this group.

The second phase of Lewis' development, the critics contended, began with *Main Street* (1920), which marked a "qualitative change" in his art. Now, the "revolt of Lewis' characters from their social surroundings" acquired "social tendentiousness." This was his period of "petty bourgeois

---

[14] R. Kulle, "Khudozhestvennaya proza sovremennovo zapada," *Sibirskiye ogni*, No. 1 (1927), p. 128.

[15] Yevg. Moravski, "Sinkler Lyuis. *Mentrap*," *Zvezda*, No. 1 (1927), p. 183.

[16] This scheme was followed by Yelistratova, Dinamov, and Levit and appears in all other Soviet evaluations of Lewis that I have been able to find for the years 1927-33.

protest" in which he began to rid himself of illusions by discarding his "romanticism" and "dreams of an unreal world." The reasons were historical: "The postwar crisis of American economics, which brought about a change in the apparent 'enlightenment' of the epoch of imperialist war, called forth a movement of protest in the circles of the American urban petty bourgeoisie, and particularly of the American farmer. Economically impotent, this movement flowed out into the radical stream of the American petty bourgeois intelligentsia and moved into the foreground of literature a whole pleiad of writers, who entered literary history under the name of the 'people of the twenties.' Lewis belongs to this group, along with Sherwood Anderson, Ben Hecht, Floyd Dell, and others. Thus he belongs in the general stream of American radical petty bourgeois literature, which was founded by Garland, Crane, and Norris—the first radical writer-realists, who stepped forth at the end of the last century. The direct predecessor of Lewis in this scheme is Masters, whose *Spoon River Anthology* laid out the path for *Main Street*. Like the author of the *Spoon River Anthology*, Lewis in *Main Street* rises up against the hypocrisy, narrowness, and intolerance of provincial America."[17]

This is a conventional enough interpretation of the literature of the twenties, since it differs from that of most American critics only in its strong emphasis on Marxist economic and social categories. But it does illustrate the importance which Soviet criticism attributed to the historical determinants in Lewis' development. The other books associated with this period of his "highest flowering" and "singular social protest" were *Babbitt* (1922), *Arrowsmith* (1925), *Elmer Gantry* (1927), and *The Man Who Knew Coolidge* (1928).

The third stage of Lewis' development, as it was interpreted in Soviet criticism from 1927 through 1933, was a period of ideological and artistic decline. This decline was first indicated in 1926, with the publication of *Mantrap*.[18] Here the au-

---

[17] Yelistratova, *op.cit.*, p. 647.

[18] Diar, "Sinkler Lyuis. *Elmer Gantri*," *Na literaturnom postu*, No. 1 (1928), p. 83. This anachronism did not disturb the critics.

thor reverted to his original "globe-trotting, sporting genre," and returned to the "trivial coin of empty amusement."[19] This new "crisis" became clearest with the appearance of *Dodsworth* (1929), which proved Lewis' "inner powerlessness to exceed the limitations of petty bourgeois 'radicalism.'" The reasons were again historical: "The temporary stabilization of American capitalism and the ebbing of the radical petty bourgeois movement which ensued established the basis for Lewis' departure from the position of accusatory realism. A way out of this creative crisis lies beyond the boundaries of those methods of struggle which have been used by his class until now, beyond the boundaries of spontaneous petty bourgeois sedition."[20]

By the early thirties, Soviet criticism, which had never expressed confidence in Lewis' ability to become anything more than an irritant to the members of his own class, had decided that there was little hope for leftward development in the author. It was noted that in 1929 he had "taken a step in the direction of friendship with the revolutionary movement" in his brochure *Cheap and Contented Labor*, devoted to the Marion textile workers' strike. This indicated that "to a certain degree" he had recognized that "only a transition to the position of a revolutionary fellow traveler of the proletariat could infuse a fresh stream into his art."[21] However, this pamphlet, and the author's unfulfilled intention of writing a labor novel, were all that came of his brief flirtation with the left, and his next work, *Ann Vickers*, produced only a "painful impression."[22]

Soviet critics explained Lewis' disappointing performance in terms of the source of his social ideology. They thought him a kind of capricious rebel against the society in which he lived. Irritated by the hypocrisy and banality of the middle class of which he was a member, he found relief from this

---

[19] Dinamov, "Sinkler Lyuis," *op.cit.*, p. 121.
[20] Yelistratova, "Sinkler Lyuis," *op.cit.*, pp. 648-49.
[21] *ibid.*, p. 649.
[22] A. Yelistratova, "Literatura sovremennoi Ameriki," *Internatsional-naya literatura*, No. 5 (1933), p. 107.

irritation in exploding the myths of his own class. The source of his art was therefore an egocentric reaction of discomfort, so that his writing took the form of a vigorous if superficial and personal rebellion. But his urge to rebel, the critics argued, was relatively easily gratified, since he was content with isolating the immediate source of his irritation—the "contradictions" of middle-class life. He was too easily satisfied: "A subjectively enraged opponent of bourgeois narrowness, he has not emerged objectively from its vicious circle. Lewis has tried to resolve the contradictions while remaining inside himself."[23]

Nevertheless, the critics felt, Lewis was best when he was most rebellious, for in this mutinous mood he was most alertly observant and his glance was most penetrating. His impulse to negate heightened his comprehension of the contradictions operating in bourgeois society. But even in its extremes, his insurrection was a limited one. He was tied too closely to the very civilization which was the object of his attack, and in the end he was always forced to compromise and conform. His strength was the strength of negation, but he lacked consistency. Soviet critics asserted that Lewis failed to carry out his indictment of American capitalist society to its logical conclusion, and this resulted, in their eyes, in compromise which tended to emasculate his work, both ideologically and artistically. The Russians concluded that Lewis was a rebel and not a revolutionary. He wanted to object, not to overthrow.[24] He was too fascinated with examining individual rotten trees to see that the whole forest was doomed. Consequently, though he was inclined to espouse by implication an "abstract and somewhat naive socialism,"[25] they concluded that he lacked the kind of social understanding that makes a revolutionary.

[23] Dinamov, "Sinkler Lyuis," *op.cit.*, p. 122.

[24] The critics treated H. L. Mencken in much the same terms as Lewis, although at times Mencken, unlike Lewis, was considered politically "fascistic." Mencken was published in Russia only twice (in periodicals in 1928), but the critics recognized his importance and devoted many pages to him.

[25] R. Kulle, "Sinkler Lyuis," *Novy mir*, No. 5 (1927), p. 177.

In spite of the shortcomings they observed in his approach to America, Soviet critics admired the thoroughness with which Lewis characterized the American bourgeoisie. One of them found that George F. Babbitt "is not only a type, Babbitt is the whole intermediate middle class, observantly and profoundly painted with the masterful brush of a great artist."[26] In this connection, however, another critic spotted a paradox. For the ridiculous and pathetic middle-class Babbitt is given a million dollars, elevated a few rungs on the social ladder, and transformed into the noble capitalist Sam Dodsworth. Where *Babbitt* indicted American society in its picture of the middle class, *Dodsworth* glorified capitalism in the person of its industrialist hero. Furthermore, *Dodsworth* replaced the social protest of *Babbitt* with optimistic affirmation and expansive American chauvinism.[27] Russian critics could only conclude that such glaring inconsistency indicated grave ideological weaknesses.

Generally, the most severely criticized aspect of Lewis' writing in Russia was his heroes and heroines. The most popular of his books with the critics were *Main Street, Babbitt, Arrowsmith*, and *Elmer Gantry*. The first three have as protagonists characters who rebel against their environment, and in so doing expose for the reader a number of the chronic defects of society. But each of these three resolves his rebellion by compromising. Carol Kennicott of *Main Street* challenges the bigotry and provinciality of Gopher Prairie, but succumbs to it in the end. She is unbroken but tamed; what she considers to be a strategic retreat actually turns out to be a negotiated peace. A small flame of rebellion is also kindled in George Babbitt, who resorts momentarily to a flirtation with "radical ideas" in his vague visitation of disgust with himself and his middle-class milieu. But Babbitt cannot bear the threat of ostracism from his class, and rapidly finds his way back to complete conformity. Martin Arrowsmith's rebellion

---

[26] Dinamov, "Sinkler Lyuis," *op.cit.*, p. 120.

[27] N. Eishiskina, "Iz amerikanskoi literatury. O novom romane Sinklera Lyuisa 'Dodsvort,'" *Novy mir*, Nos. 8-9 (1929), p. 301. This review was based on the American edition, since *Dodsworth* was never published in Russian.

is more sustained in that he never arrives at a position of acquiescence. But Arrowsmith's resolution of his rebellion is one of escape, since he takes refuge in a hermit-like existence as a pure scientist.

To Soviet critics it seemed that none of Lewis' heroes faced squarely the "evils" of capitalism, since none of them was able to transform his rebellious impulse into revolutionary action. They were ideologically deficient, since they were unable to perceive and act upon the "logical necessity" for a fundamental change in the structure of the society whose contradictions were apparent to them.

A more basic criticism of Lewis' protagonists was directed at their class origin. In 1927 a critic complained: ". . . indeed not everyone in America is a Babbitt. Were this class to die, the country would live on, new elements would force their way to the proscenium, preparing the way for a new, fresh class. . . . Sinclair Lewis does not yet know representatives of another class, coming to replace the decayed one, or, perhaps on purpose, will not show them until he is able to draw a complete picture of contemporaneity."[28] Another pointed out that a negation of capitalism must be accompanied by an affirmation of socialism in its place. He contended that in Lewis' novels there can be found the kind of protagonists required—such men as Miles Bjornstam in *Main Street*—but that Lewis neglected them. He saw his logical hero, but he did not recognize him.

In the final analysis, the critics decided, Sinclair Lewis was merely annoyed with bourgeois society. His passion for accuracy of detail often created an illusion of deep insight. But his inability to draw socially accurate conclusions and his frequent lapses into sentimental affirmation of bourgeois America betrayed a lack of understanding. His meticulous realism of detail often masked Philistinism and triviality.

This was the picture of Lewis that had evolved by 1933. Meanwhile, his novels had stopped coming out in Russia. From 1924 through 1929 there had been twenty-two printings of his separate books, totaling 140,000 copies. During

28 Kulle, "Sinkler Lyuis," *op.cit.*, p. 179.

the six years after 1929 not a single volume of his was published, although he was represented twice in periodicals. The explanation is clear. Russia had embarked on the era of the Five Year Plans. Private publishing houses were closed down and the importation of foreign literature of "bourgeois" orientation was sharply curtailed. Under increasingly tight Party supervision, the state publishing houses paid close attention not only to the broad ideological content of the foreign works they issued, but also to their immediate political significance in terms of the current Party line. In the perspective of official Party ideology in the thirties, Lewis' criticism of American life was relatively mild. Further, he was unmistakably anti-Communist, and was of little potential value as a political figure. There was no practical incentive to publish his works, from the Party standpoint. By 1936, however, the Party was once again allowing the publishing houses wider latitude in the selection of foreign works. A third edition of *Arrowsmith* came out in that year, and *Ann Vickers* was translated. In 1937 *It Can't Happen Here* appeared.

From 1933 to 1937 there had been little mention of the author in Soviet criticism, and what was written about him was, on the whole, derogatory. In 1936, for example, a critic complained of his "artistic departure from realism," and concluded that in comparison with his work of the twenties, "his latest things stand on a lower level in both artistic and ideological respects." Lewis was classified with a group of contemporary Americans who, "moved by an unconscious terror before the possibility of the approach of social revolution, blunt the satiric sharpness of their sting and move over to less risky themes and situations."[29] *Ann Vickers* was reviewed in that year without the slightest enthusiasm; its only source of interest was its description of American prison conditions.[30]

It Can't Happen Here, however, was greeted as a new and praiseworthy development in Lewis' art. The novel's anti-Fascist theme was timely, and the book could be con-

[29] O. Nemerovskaya, "Sovremennaya amerikanskaya literatura," *Sovetskoye studenchestvo*, No. 6 (1936), p. 84.
[30] N. Eishiskina, "Dve knigi Sinklera Lyuisa," *Literaturnaya gazeta*, July 10, 1936.

strued, in part, as a plea for United Front action. This, no doubt, accounts for the party's decision to make it available to the Soviet public at that time. The American nightmare it portrayed was subjected to thorough analysis by the critics. Lewis was generally lauded for having written a bold, if somewhat naive, indictment of fascism. The critics were delighted to find a certain militancy in the novel. One wrote: "The merit of Sinclair Lewis is in the fact that he is interested most of all not in those intellectuals who submissively bear the yoke of fascism, but in those who struggle against fascism."[31] Despite their hearty approval of the novel's intent, however, they found essentially the same faults that they had found in his previous works. The Vermont newspaper editor, Doremus Jessup, who is the hero, was a nobler and wiser Babbitt, but a Babbitt, nevertheless.[32] He sees and understands the signs of coming fascism, but his middle-class inertia renders him powerless to act. He vacillates before the twin specters of fascism and communism, clinging to what the critics thought to be an increasingly nebulous ideal of democracy. While Lewis recognized the guiding role of capital in his hypothetical Fascist regime, he did not show it with sufficient prominence.[33] He did not accord the labor movement its rightful place as the most important anti-Fascist political element, and as the source of the logical hero of such a novel.[34] Having selected Jessup as his hero, Lewis was realistic in delineating his attitude toward the political forces which surrounded him. But it was unfortunate that Jessup, and presumably the author who created him, were not entirely aware of political reality: "Jessup does not see that the Communists, carrying out a policy of a single popular front, are now precisely the prop of democracy, and that communism is the most democratic doctrine. The people and democracy are insepara-

---

[31] S. Dinamov, "Novy roman Sinklera Lyuisa," *Internatsionalnaya literatura*, No. 2 (1937), p. 86.

[32] I. Sats, "Sinkler Lyuis o sudbakh chelovechestva," *Literaturny kritik*, No. 11 (1936), p. 166. The review was based on an Amsterdam edition.

[33] V. Romm, "Roman Sinklera Lyuisa o fashizme v Amerike," *Izvestiya*, Nov. 26, 1935. This was based on the American edition.

[34] *ibid.*

ble things, but indeed the Communists are the party of the people. Jessup here steps forth as a typical petty bourgeois intellectual. . . ."[35] (Two years after this comment was published, the USSR formed its alliance with Fascist Germany.)

Following the brief period of interest occasioned by this novel, Lewis once again declined into relative obscurity in Russia. For ten years there were no new printings of his books. In 1945 he was not mentioned in a bibliographical index of English and American authors published by the State Central Library of Foreign Literature.[36] In 1946 his literary career was reviewed in detail as an illustration of the decadence into which, it was contended, American literature had fallen. Reiterating the deep Soviet respect for *Main Street, Babbitt, Elmer Gantry*, and particularly *Arrowsmith*, a critic nevertheless repeated the verdict of the thirties: Lewis, always bourgeois in his sympathies, had never been able to develop beyond the ideology of his class. When faced with the threat of fascism he had been startled to action, since he was indeed democratic in his sympathies. But, this critic continued, Lewis typically had refused to ally himself with the "proletariat," since he was fundamentally afraid of the socialism of which that class was the standard-bearer. This, among other things, had led him to calumny of the Soviet Union in *It Can't Happen Here*.[37]

But Lewis was to prove useful to Soviet propagandists in the next two years. The program of vituperation against the "decadent" West had begun, with special emphasis on the United States, and he unwittingly provided ammunition for the campaign. *Gideon Planish* was translated in 1947, as a document of corruption in American high circles. *Kingsblood Royal* came out, with considerable fanfare, in 1948. The reviews[38] were complimentary; once again he had found his

[35] Dinamov, "Novy roman . . . ," *op.cit.*, p. 185.

[36] *Sovremenniye angliskiye i amerikanskiye pisateli*, Moscow, 1945.

[37] Igor Sats, "A Controversy on Literature with Our Foreign Friends," *Soviet Literature*, No. 12 (1946), pp. 40-47.

[38] A. Startsev, "Rasshifrovannaya biografiya," *Znamya*, No. 3 (1948), pp. 184-88; N. Kozyura, "Kingsblad—potomok korolei," *Znamya*, No. 11 (1948), pp. 142-45; A. Startsev, "Soyedinyonniye linchuyushchiye

way back to limited grace. He was still unable to conquer the illusion that the "corruption of American social life" was transient and could be cured by "edifying laughter."[39] And despite his "terrifying picture of race persecution in the USA," he was neither brave enough nor wise enough to see that capitalism was the root of the evil and must be destroyed.[40] Also, unlike Sinclair and Dreiser, he had "never broken with the ruling class."[41] But it was to his credit that, in contrast to such writers as Hemingway, Sherwood Anderson, and Steinbeck, he had "never submitted to the temptations of decadent modernistic tendencies" in his art. He was "one of the last Mohicans of bourgeois critical realism."[42]

These remarks, however, have the flavor of token compliments for services rendered. *Gideon Planish* and *Kingsblood Royal* were published because of their topical quality and their timeliness in terms of the cold war.[43] To be sure, this was critical realism, just as it was the critical realist in Lewis that had originally brought him to the attention of Soviet Russians, had sustained interest in him in the twenties, and had twice rescued him from obscurity in the thirties and forties. Above all, however, these books, like *It Can't Happen Here*, were relevant to the Party line.

The criticism of the twenties, although antibourgeois in its premises, gave evidence of an ardent curiosity about American civilization and respected Lewis for the light he shed on it. In the thirties and forties, however, curiosity was replaced by a didactic insistence that Lewis prove Soviet theses. His books were judged in terms of their value in documenting the generalizations of current official propaganda. Yet it is significant that Soviet critics, despite their schematic

---

shtaty," *Literaturnaya gazeta*, March 7, 1948; T. Motyleva, "Put Sinklera Lyuisa," *Literaturnaya gazeta*, Dec. 1, 1948; Tamara Khmelnitskaya, "Roman o belom negre," *Zvezda*, No. 1 (1949), pp. 202-4.

[39] Startsev, "Rasshifrovannaya . . . ," *op.cit.*, p. 187.

[40] Kozyura, *op.cit.*, p. 145.　　[41] Motyleva, *op.cit.*　　[42] *ibid.*

[43] T. Motyleva, "Predisloviye," Sinkler Lyuis, *Gideon Plenish*, Moscow, 1947, pp. 5-16; O. Nemerovskaya, "Pamflet o politicheskikh gangsterakh," *Zvezda*, No. 9 (1948), pp. 205-7; I. Anisimov, "Predisloviye," Sinkler Lyuis. *Kingsblad, potomok korolei*, Moscow, 1948, pp. 5-14.

and oversimplified interpretation and the obvious element of political opportunism in their judgments, have usually favored the very same books of Lewis which American critics have preferred. The Russians, like most Americans, have contended that Lewis' greatest contribution to American letters was his social criticism.

Soviet critics were correct in deciding that Lewis' social criticism was not politically revolutionary and that around the beginning of the Depression his writing lost force and significance that it never regained. But the critics were right for the wrong reasons. It is true that Lewis' position in the history of American literature is grounded in his achievement of the 1920's and that his stature was scarcely enhanced by anything he later wrote. Occasionally he reasserted his satiric power and gift of trenchant social commentary, but for the most part he wrote mild sequels, even parodies, of his best novels of the twenties. Soviet critics in the thirties perceived accurately that Lewis was in decline, but, contrary to their claims, the cause of this decline was not the social cowardice of one who fears an incipient revolution. For reasons that were psychological and personal, he had simply written himself out. Lewis had already said nearly everything he was capable of saying.

In 1951 the State Literary Publishing House invited subscriptions to a twelve-volume edition of the collected works of Theodore Dreiser, to be printed in a total of 900,000 copies. Within a few days after the announcement, the subscriptions were sold out. The numerous editions of Dreiser's separate works that appeared during the next few years failed to satisfy the demand, so that in 1955 the twelve-volume edition was reprinted. And still the numerous printings of Dreiser's works continued. He had become, since World War II, the most popular twentieth-century American writer in Russia. At the same time he became the favorite subject of literary studies. Several books and monographs were published about him, and more dissertations for advanced degrees were devoted to Dreiser than to all other American writers combined.

The publishers' willingness to print Dreiser in large quantities in the 1950's, and the critical adulation as well, were in large measure a response to the author's political development, which culminated in his joining the Communist Party of the United States shortly before his death in 1945. But although his most spectacular success with Soviet readers took place in the 1950's, he had been well known in Russia since his first translation in 1925. The critics had always admired his "kaleidoscopic" picture of American society, with its "painstaking completeness" and "documentary accuracy."[44] One of them observed in 1937 that, like Upton Sinclair, Dreiser "acquaints us, who have never been in America, with the actual life of that country," and added that "thanks to the books of such writers as Dreiser, I feel this truth just as if I had seen it myself."[45] Another found Dreiser to be an "encyclopedia of American life" and, referring specifically to Frank Cowperwood's complicated financial operations in *The Financier* and *The Titan*, argued that his novels were an invaluable aid in studying "the internal and external life of that insatiable monster which is called the capitalistic exchange."[46] Still another called Dreiser's books "monuments, in which historians will study the epoch which has passed . . . before the eyes of this indefatigable observer."[47]

It was easy to find in Dreiser a thorough indictment of capitalism. In *The Color of a Great City*, one critic noted, the author stops the machinery of capitalism for a moment to observe it more closely, and there arises "the grinning image of the contemporary American, dying from overstrain; the mutilated fate of a man who is ripe for a new social tenor of life, enslaved, crushed by the present order of things. . . ."[48]

[44] Yanka Kupala, "Greetings across the Ocean," *International Literature*, World's Fair Issue, 1937, p. 47.

[45] I. Rapoport, "Romantika i realizm v amerikanskoi literature," *Internatsionalnaya literatura*, Nos. 7-8 (1937), pp. 286-87.

[46] Olga Nemerovskaya, "Draizer—romanist," *Literaturnaya uchyoba*, No. 9 (1936), p. 97.

[47] R. Kulle, "Po stranitsam mirovoi literatury,"*Sibirskiye ogni*, No. 2 (1928), p. 210.

[48] Yak. Benni, "O romanakh Teodora Draizera," *Novy mir*, No. 9 (1928), p. 241.

The book was compared to Dante's *Inferno* in its picture of a hell.[49] To a critic in 1928 it was gratifying that Dreiser portrayed not only "millionaires and skyscrapers," which already "bored" Soviet readers, but also the poverty of New York's proletariat, which had too often been neglected.[50] Similarly, *An American Tragedy* "torments, shakes, and infects one with pain for a man dying in the nightmare conditions of American reality."[51] The fate of Clyde Griffiths—"a tragic sacrifice of American everyday life"—showed how a man could be trapped in the bourgeois machine of law and morals.[52]

An American Tragedy has always been Dreiser's most widely read book in Russia. A report of a public discussion of it in 1952 came to the conclusion that the social conditions it described were so typical of capitalist America that "the book has lost nothing of its urgency in the 27 years since its publication."[53] (In 1958, the novel still left "not the slightest doubt of the fact that the crime of Clyde Griffiths was born of the monstrosity of the capitalist order.")[54] Additional excerpts from this report indicate how Dreiser's books served the interests of Soviet propaganda. The discussion was reported to have come to the conclusion that "naturally, in the Soviet Union, where a man's standing is won by free and honest labor and where no barriers frustrate the strivings of young people to attain useful careers and happiness, Dreiser's picture of the conditions of capitalist society cannot but arouse the indignation of readers." One such "indignant" reader was reported to have reacted to *An American Tragedy* in this manner: "Justifiable pride rang in his voice when he

[49] Diar, "Novyie amerikanskiye perevody," *Na literaturnom postu*, Nos. 13-14 (1928), p. 110.

[50] Yu. Danilin, "Teodor Dreizer. Nyu York," *Oktyabr*, No. 1 (1928), p. 242.

[51] Diar, *op.cit.*, p. 111.

[52] Yu. Danilin, "Teodor Dreizer. Amerikanskaya tragediya; Finansist," *Oktyabr*, No. 8 (1928), p. 210.

[53] "Library Discussion on Dreiser's Works," *Soviet Literature*, No. 7 (1952), p. 150.

[54] I. Anisimov, "Put, prolozhennyi Draizerom," *Inostrannaya literatura*, No. 11 (1958), p. 224.

[253]

spoke of the difference between the conditions in which he and his fellows live in the Soviet Union, and those of young American workers. As he said, the existence of such people [as Clyde Griffiths] beyond the pale of a decent life is inconceivable in a Socialist society."

Of *Sister Carrie,* another reader was reported to have said: "The degrading position of working girls in America evokes the sympathy of Soviet readers. Soviet people accept as natural the complete equality of the sexes; Soviet ethics preclude the slightest possibility of a woman being reduced to the plight in which Dreiser's heroines find themselves." Sanctimonious, ingenuous, and crudely transparent as this attempt at propaganda may be to an American observer, it does show the special utility of Dreiser's books in Russia. For, as the report stated: "Books which portray the realities of the capitalist world are, naturally, appraised by Soviet readers from the standpoint of their own experience. From that standpoint they can see how far they have progressed in material, cultural, and social respects compared with the working people in capitalist countries."[55] It was safe, and profitable as well, to compare Dreiser's America to the Soviet Union. This was done both explicitly, as in the above "discussion," and implicitly, as in an essay accompanying a 1955 edition of *The Genius,* which argued that the novel demonstrates that "genius is incompatible with the American way of life."[56]

The critics called Dreiser a realist, but they also often called him a naturalist. In Soviet usage "realism" is a very broad term that has undergone constant redefinition. Naturalism, on the other hand, refers to the "decadent" school of Emile Zola. With its emphasis on complete "scientific detachment" and "objectivity," naturalism is thought to be a negation of the writer's responsibility for pointing the way toward human progress—a capitulation to the *status quo.* The naturalist, it is contended, is too preoccupied with examining the processes of human conduct to understand the

[55] "Library Discussion . . . ," *op.cit.,* pp. 150-54.
[56] I. Anisimov, "Poslesloviye," in T. Draizer, *Genii,* Vilnyus, 1955, p. 691.

principles of social progress. Because he is unselective in the materials he takes from reality he allows that which is dead or passing from the social scene to choke out that which is living and growing. In striving to be apolitical, for example, the naturalist actually becomes a bulwark of political reaction.[57]

It would follow that in calling Dreiser a naturalist, the critics were judging him negatively, but this was not the case. He was criticized for some of the same shortcomings as naturalists are, but his art was considered to be closer to Balzac than to Zola.[58] For what Soviet critics meant when they referred to Dreiser's naturalism was his exactitude and completeness in handling physical and psychological detail—his method of writing, and not its broader ideological implications. Naturalism was a positive quality that sprang from his urge to tell the whole truth, and therefore, to portray as many facets of reality as possible. The critic Elistratova explained it this way: "For Dreiser, the artist, there was no such thing as uninteresting people or insignificant lives. Nor did this attitude spring from the same source as that of the naturalistic and decadent writers who regarded baseness and mediocrity as the normal condition of human nature. Quite the contrary—and this is the source of the lyrical warmth that pervades his invariably 'objective' and stark narration—Dreiser measured people by a high standard, by the standard of man's latent capabilities, even if the opportunity to realize these capabilities was lacking."[59] The critics of the 1950's were particularly, almost militantly, anxious to distinguish between what they thought was the social indifference of Zola and the special naturalistic method of Dreiser, which they described as a device for showing the unvarnished truth.[60]

[57] "Naturaliszm," *Literaturnaya entsiklopediya*, Moscow, 1934, VII, 612-21.

[58] S. Dinamov, "Teodor Draizer. Nyu York," *Pechat i revolyutsiya*, No. 2 (1928), p. 205; Diar, *op.cit.*, p. 110; Danilin, "Teodor Dreizer. Amerikanskaya tragediya . . . ," *op.cit.*, p. 212.

[59] Anna Elistratova, "Theodore Dreiser," *Soviet Literature*, No. 12 (1955), p. 179.

[60] *ibid.*, p. 179; Ye. Kornilova, "Sbornik statei o Draizere," *Voprosy literatury*, No. 6 (1958), p. 235.

One of the most attractive traits of Dreiser's realism, all Soviet critics agreed, was his "painstaking exactitude"[61] in assembling "huge quantities of documentary facts."[62] His writing had the "precision of a sensitive camera, which omits not a single detail, not a single feature." Another argued that "his novels are not an outcry, not pamphlets, not startling disclosures. His novels are a system."[63] He was an equally thorough psychologist. This same critic noted that he "seems to conduct an unfailing and continuous patrol around his heroes, he looks at them from above and from below and on a level with them," so that "everything is valuable for him, everything is important."[64] His interest in social themes did not hinder him as a psychologist, since in dealing with social problems he "intermixes them on the plane of the individual psyche, showing on the whole the psychological-individual aspect of large social phenomena."[65] Furthermore, he maintained an attitude of psychological objectivity, and did not try to beautify or ennoble his characters or to "make them better or more significant than they are in fact."[66]

Although Dreiser's works were always freighted with moral problems, the critics pointed out that his psychological detachment kept him from judging his characters morally. The introduction to a 1954 edition of *Jennie Gerhardt* noted that unlike Hawthorne, who treated the problem of the "fallen woman" on a predominantly moral plane, Dreiser sought to understand the problem of private immorality in terms of social conditions.[67] The ability to avoid the intrusion of moral judgments, the critics felt, heightened the objectivity of his approach to the sources of human conduct and at the same time increased the social breadth of his works.

The Russians were no less attentive to the inadequacies

---

[61] Nemerovskaya, "Draizer—romanist," *op.cit.*, pp. 99-100.

[62] Diar, *op.cit.*, p. 111.   [63] Benni, *op.cit.*, p. 241.

[64] *ibid.*, p. 241.

[65] S. Dinamov, "Teodor Draizer," *Literaturnaya entsiklopediya*, Moscow, 1930, III, 419.

[66] Nemerovskaya, "Draizer—romanist," *op.cit.*, p. 95.

[67] A. Anikst, "Teodor Draizer i yevo roman *Dzhenni Gerkhardt*," in T. Draizer, *Dzhenni Gerkhardt*, Moscow, 1954, p. 9.

of Dreiser's style than American critics are, but these deficiencies bothered Soviet critics less than they did Americans. One critic remarked that his novels were "unusually difficult in language, heavy in style, complicated in composition, and rather boring as a consequence of their fabulous bulk."[68] Dreiser was called "tedious and old-fashioned,"[69] "clumsy,"[70] "uneven," and even "quaint."[71] However, every adverse comment on his style was immediately followed by a qualification to the effect that these sins were not fundamentally important, and were far outweighed by other considerations. Although Olga Nemerovskaya, for example, found that he "loses his sense of proportion, rendering in superfluous detail that which is unessential," she argued that his novels contained a "huge inner power, truth of psychological analysis, ability to penetrate the depths of things, and especially an artistic veracity that shows the real face of America without ennobling makeup and the patriarchal wig."[72]

Dreiser's novels attracted the critics mainly because they probed the economic and social weaknesses and sore spots of America. As the Russians interpreted him, however, most of Dreiser's creative writing had been accomplished while he was still under the influence of petty bourgeois notions, and these attitudes accounted for a number of important defects in his picture of America. First of all, he was inclined to attack "bourgeois morals" instead of the "socio-economic foundations of American reality." In mistaking the effects for the cause he failed to get to the heart of the matter. This failing was typical of American social critics, who often lashed out blindly at the external manifestations of social evil because they did not understand that this evil was actually rooted in an eradicable economic system. In the Soviet view, the "petty bourgeois radical" typically perceives the connection between social evil and economic injustice, but somehow

---

[68] Kulle, "Po stranitsam . . . ," *op.cit.*, p. 210.

[69] Diar, *op.cit.*, p. 111.

[70] Danilin, "Teodor Dreizer. Amerikanskaya tragediya," *op.cit.*, p. 211.

[71] Yevg. Lann, "Probeg po sovremennoi amerikanskoi literature," *Novy mir*, No. 10 (1930), p. 202.

[72] Nemerovskaya, "Draizer—romanist," *op.cit.*, pp. 95-96.

fails to come to the "obvious" conclusion that the situation requires a socialist revolution. *Jennie Gerhardt* was a case in point. In this novel, Dreiser was a "severe indicter of the existing order," but his blindness to "the possibility of escape and salvation for a woman in living struggle" gave rise to "social pessimism."[73]

Other fundamental traits in Dreiser's outlook, which Americans might associate with his naturalism, Soviet criticism preferred to call petty bourgeois as well. One of these traits was his individualism, which appeared most clearly in Dreiser's admiration for the strong, conquering, amoral Cowperwood, an admiration that arose despite the author's obvious awareness of the social evil which his hero represented.[74] This "Nietzschean worship of the strong man," the critics understood, had its sources in Dreiser's early fondness for the writings of the "bourgeois materialists of the nineteenth century"—Darwin, Huxley, and Spencer, who had encouraged him to look upon life as a fierce, blind fight for existence.[75] (It was contended that by 1925, when *An American Tragedy* was published, he had largely outgrown this influence.)[76] On the other hand, it was characteristic of his "petty bourgeois radicalism" that, while harboring this concept of society as a coarse, brutal, elemental struggle, Dreiser could at the same time express "unconscious protest against the barbarous ferocity of capitalism." This failure of focus, this "typical vacillation and confusion of the petty bourgeois intellectual," the critics contended, was chronic in sensitive and socially conscious American artists, who were inclined to construct wrong (i.e. non-Marxist) theories of a religious, mystical, or pseudo-scientific nature to explain social facts which repelled them but which they felt themselves powerless to alter. Despite their attempts to rationalize outrageous facts, these artists nevertheless could not control the urge to object

[73] *ibid.*, p. 96.
[74] Danilin, "Teodor Dreizer. Amerikanskaya tragediya," *op.cit.*, p. 212.
[75] Nemerovskaya, "Draizer—romanist," *op.cit.*, p. 97; Ya. N. Zasurski, *Teodor Draizer: pisatel i publitsist*, Moscow, 1957, pp. 66, 73; Anikst, "Teodor Draizer i yevo roman . . . ," *op.cit.*, p. 8.
[76] Anisimov, "Put . . . ," *op.cit.*, p. 224.

against them by means of wistful appeals, subjective narrative coloration, and subtle expressions of frustration and despair. (In deploring these idiosyncrasies, Soviet criticism perforce ignored the fact that the very variety of American responses was a source of richness. Had American writers reacted with the ideological uniformity of Soviet writers, much of the freshness and inventiveness that come with personal coloration would have been eradicated from our literature.)

Another manifestation of Dreiser's individualism was his central theme of the struggle of the individual against society, which a critic outlined this way: "Selecting as his hero an ordinary fellow, showing the customary rhythm of his life, the usual circle of his activities, Dreiser then shows how this fellow suffers as his will is violated, when he is suddenly compelled to do something he does not want to do, but which is demanded of him by bourgeois society or his surroundings."[77] The feeling that the aspirations and welfare of the individual are in direct opposition to those of society led the author into the danger of concluding that organized humanity and individual happiness are incompatible, *even under socialism*. In 1928, in fact, a critic remarked that "we do not doubt that this writer will always stand in defense of the individual against the collective, whatever the nature of the latter."[78] Another aspect of the author's "individualism" came to the attention of the critics even after his conversion to socialism. Reviewing *Tragic America* in 1932, Sergei Dinamov recalled a "heated discussion" he had had with the author in 1927, in the course of which Dreiser had seemed to assert that society could be governed by a "narrow group of intellectuals." Now, on the basis of *Tragic America*, Dinamov contended that Dreiser still felt that "the world must be ruled by the aristocracy of mind."[79] This interpretation of *Tragic America*, incidentally, is greatly at variance with the one that became fashionable in the 1950's.

[77] Danilin, "Teodor Dreizer. Amerikanskaya tragediya," *op.cit.*, p. 211.
[78] Diar, *op.cit.*, p. 110.
[79] S. Dynamov, "Theodore Dreiser Continues the Struggle," *International Literature*, Nos. 2-3 (1932), p. 113.

The closing pages of *An American Tragedy*, where Clyde Griffiths becomes a penitent Christian before his execution, were also interpreted by one critic as evidence of the author's individualism. According to this critic, by concluding the novel in this fashion, "Dreiser the individualist, who had scorned established ethical conventions, became a moralist."[80] After having "condemned bourgeois justice, bourgeois law, and bourgeois retribution," the writer had advocated a spiritualistic approach to the solution of social evil. This tended to negate the conclusion, derived from all of the book's preceding pages, that the present organization of society was ultimately responsible for the crime of which Clyde was convicted. Other critics, however, seem to have realized that Dreiser's picture of Clyde's "conversion" did not indicate the author's *advocacy* of a spiritual solution. Zasurski, for example, saw the novel's ending as the indictment of a hypocritical conspiracy between religion and bourgeois justice, and called it a polemic against the Christian message of Dostoevski in *Crime and Punishment*.[81] Still another view was that of Anisimov, who, without citing the book as evidence of Dreiser's individualism, nevertheless found that the preacher's "unctious sermons" tended to "drain off the militant force of the work."[82]

Whatever the nature of Dreiser's individualism, the critics understood that it was not simple, and that it was closely related to a more deeply ingrained idea—his "biologism." This "petty bourgeois idea," which also had its source in the nineteenth-century materialist philosophers and scientists, held that human conduct is governed by instincts, such as sex and the urge to power, over which men ultimately have no control. One critic described it as Dreiser's "representation of man as a product of biology and chemistry, his firm conviction of the eternal, inevitable, hostile contradiction between the instincts of this 'biochemical' man and the laws of morals and public opinion which have not the slightest internal relation-

---

[80] Nemerovskaya, "Draizer—romanist," *op.cit.*, p. 100.
[81] Zasurski, *op.cit.*, pp. 127-29.
[82] Anisimov, "Put . . . ," *op.cit.*, p. 224.

ship to him."[83] Preoccupation with man as a creature of biological necessity explained the author's partiality for sex as a
motivating force in his stories. Although the critics frequently
felt that his emphasis on sex was excessive, they recognized
that, as in *An American Tragedy*, a presentation of the opposition between sexual expression and bourgeois morals was
a fruitful device for exploring society.[84] On the other hand,
this emphasis often detracted from the realism of his works,
particularly in his portrayal of women, which tended to be
"superficial and primitive." His women were lacking in intellect, took "no active part in the social and spiritual life of
humanity," and merely dreamed of "hearth and home, the
satisfaction of their physiological demands, and complete pos-
session of husband-and-lover."[85] The notion of biological determinism warped his understanding of social cause and effect,
so that in his narratives the individual tended to become a
creature of blind sex instinct and the movement of society
an enthralling but purposeless struggle for the survival of the
fittest. Since it doomed man and society to eternal enmity,
the strain of biologism in Dreiser was considered a source of
dangerous fatalism.[86]

By 1950 Soviet criticism had decided that Dreiser's image
of America was the truest and most profound that had been
created in the twentieth century. In the enthusiasm that surrounded his new status, there was a strong tendency to soft-
pedal allusions to his individualism, biologism, and other
ideological errors. Buttressed by the incontrovertible fact that
he had publicly and categorically applied for membership in
the Communist Party a few months before he died, Soviet
criticism could, with confident hindsight, describe his career
as a relentless process of ideological growth, culminating in
the flash of illumination of this final political act. By 1958
Dreiser's career, like the careers of Lincoln Steffens and

---

[83] Diar, *op.cit.*, p. 110.

[84] Danilin, "Teodor Dreizer. Amerikanskaya tragediya," *op.cit.*, p. 211;
Nemerovskaya, "Draizer—romanist," *op.cit.*, pp. 101-2.

[85] Nemerovskaya, "Draizer—romanist," *op.cit.*, p. 98.

[86] Danilin, "Teodor Dreizer. Amerikanskaya tragediya," *op.cit.*, p. 210.

John Reed, was assuming the proportions of a heroic Communist folk legend in the Soviet Union. It is interesting, therefore, to see what the critics of the 1920's and 1930's, writing without benefit of hindsight, thought of him at a time when there was no comforting assurance of his eventual conversion to communism.

In the twenties, the Russians felt that while Dreiser's works were implicitly critical of capitalism, he accepted it as an institution. He visited Russia in the fall of 1927, just as his works were becoming known there. In the spring of that year, he had expressed a "neutral, naive attitude" toward the country.[87] On his return from this trip, however, he wrote *Dreiser Looks at Russia*, showing heightened enthusiasm for the Soviet way of life. Nevertheless, the Russians were skeptical. One critic in 1928, praising the author's boldness in braving "the displeasure of the bourgeoisie" through being "apparently, more or less objective" about the Soviet Union, added that "one can be sure that Dreiser . . . is against the dictatorship of the proletariat."[88]

However, in the early thirties the Russians discovered, to their delight, that this "petty bourgeois radical" had become one of their staunchest friends and allies among the intelligentsia of the West. He had developed into a "revolutionary publicist . . . a sharp critic of the capitalist system and ardent defender of the USSR."[89] The trip to Russia, it was contended, had enabled him to see, by comparison, defects in American society which he had formerly overlooked or had failed fully to understand. With warm approval Soviet observers noted his growing involvement in left-wing literary activities, his steady flow of outspoken letters to newspapers on a variety of topics close to the hearts of American radicals, his contributions to the *Daily Worker* and his battles with the "reactionary press," his active support of crucial labor strikes, and his leadership in the League of Professional Groups for

[87] S. Dinamov, "Teodor Draizer idet k nam," *Literatura mirovoi revolyutsii*, No. 10 (1931), p. 98.

[88] Diar, *op.cit.*, p. 110.

[89] S. Dinamov, "Teodor Draizer idet k nam," *Literatura mirovoi revolyutsii*, No. 10 (1931), p. 98.

Foster and Ford in the presidential election of 1932. His *Tragic America*, published in 1931, was deemed a "complete attack on American capitalism, social-fascism, religion, and the dictatorship of banks and trusts."[90] The Soviet press reported on his various public quarrels and lawsuits,[91] watched anxiously in 1935 as he defended himself against charges of anti-Semitism, and breathed an editorial sigh of relief as he cleared himself of the charges.[92] Dreiser became one of the most prolific contributors to Soviet periodicals in the thirties, often writing political articles solely for translation and publication in Russia. In fact, since he had largely ceased to publish works of fiction in those years, the Russians in the thirties regarded him more as a militant publicist than as a working artist.

But even in 1930, when the author's leftward political trend was evident, a critic could write that although he did not "accept the system of the bourgeois world in all its parts," he still did not "threaten the foundations of contemporary capitalism," and added: "He approves of the principle of 'free play of economic forces,'—he loves his Frank Cowperwood. . . ."[93] The critics were never satisfied with anything short of complete ideological conformity from him, and this they never observed. In 1932, after the publication of *Tragic America*, a critic complained that he "still conceives unclearly the path and method of revolutionary overthrow of capitalism. . . ."[94] In 1933 another pleaded for patience toward the author, commenting that "from an artist constituted like Dreiser, whose creative tradition extends over three whole decades, one could scarcely expect a rapid fundamental crea-

[90] S. Dinamov, "Teodor Draizer prodolzhayet borbu," *Marksistsko-Leninskoye iskusstvoznaniye*, Nos. 5-6 (1932), p. 135.

[91] For example, see M. Umanskaya, "Teodor Draizer protiv Dzhessi Laski," *Literatura mirovoi revolyutsii*, Nos. 8-9 (1931), pp. 206-208.

[92] "Draizer i yevreiski vopros," *Internatsionalnaya literatura*, No. 7 (1935), p. 142.

[93] Lann, "Probeg . . . ," *op.cit.*, p. 202.

[94] A. Startsev, "Vseobshchi krizis kapitalizma i novaya volna soyuznikov proletariata v literature Ameriki," *Marksistsko-Leninskoye iskusstvoznaniye*, Nos. 5-6 (1932), p. 54.

tive rebuilding."[95] The Soviet literary world by 1936 had considered Dreiser a friend and collaborator for several years, and still there were deficiencies in his attitude. A critic summed up his position in that year in this fashion: "Dreiser has not yet remade himself once and for all. In his theoretical discourses there is still much that is confused and unclear. In his utterances there can still be felt the halfway policy of petty bourgeois ideology that has not yet been completely conquered. But Dreiser has already decided where he stands in the class struggle which is moving ahead, just as the best representatives of world artistic thought have decided this question."[96]

The difference between Dreiser and so many of these "best representatives of world artistic thought" was that in his case the ever-sanguine Soviet predictions of the thirties did eventually come true. Many writers in the thirties, including some of the authors treated here, seemed to be, or proclaimed themselves to be, in sympathy with the Soviet outlook. Others committed themselves suddenly and completely, and then, with varying degrees of speed, repudiated the commitment. Dreiser's evolution was painfully slow, but, from the Soviet viewpoint, positive to the end when he wrote in 1945:

"These historic years have deepened my conviction that widespread membership in the Communist movement will greatly strengthen the American people, together with the anti-fascist forces throughout the world, in completely stamping out fascism and achieving new heights of world democracy, economic progress and free culture. Belief in the greatness and dignity of man has been the guiding principle of my life and work. The logic of my life and work leads me therefore to apply for membership in the Communist Party."[97]

This application has been made the culminating episode in a beguiling Communist success story. It is not our purpose here to analyze or reconstruct Dreiser's motives in joining

[95] A. Yelistratova, "Literatura S A S Sh," *Literaturnaya gazeta*, November 29, 1933.
[96] Nemerovskaya, "Draizer—romanist," *op.cit.*, p. 107.
[97] *New Masses*, August 7, 1945, p. 4.

the Communist Party, but it is important to note that had he not taken this formal, confirming step, the Soviet interpretation of his career would probably have had quite a different flavor. (It is also quite possible that had he lived long enough to experience Party life and Party discipline, or to learn more about the post-war Soviet regime, he would not long have remained a Communist.) At any rate, Soviet critics in the 1950's took full advantage of this final circumstance of his life, by reviewing his whole career as a gradual triumph of the inevitable truth. Dreiser is now pictured as a writer who meticulously accumulated mountains of evidence over half a century, studied it carefully and deliberately, painfully overcame deep-seated bourgeois preconceptions, involved himself more and more actively and completely in the affairs of his time, and in the end experienced a total beatific revelation.

The Russians have been particularly irritated (at times even infuriated) by the suggestion of American critics that Dreiser's application for Party membership was an act of his dotage. For the Russians the possibility that Dreiser opted for communism out of intellectual fatigue and bewilderment is unthinkable. The novelist Vera Panova, usually a temperate writer who seldom referred to American literature, violently denounced Robert Elias' biography of Dreiser for suggesting that the Party episode had been "accidental."[98] Furthermore, Soviet critics in the 1950's repeatedly accused American criticism of trying to blacken Dreiser's reputation, dilute his revolutionary message, and destroy his stature as an artist.[99] Just as often, they charged that Dreiser's works were being suppressed by American publishers, "withheld from the public," and surrounded by a conspiracy of silence.[100] The special object of this "conspiracy," significant-

---

[98] Vera Panova, "V zashchitu pamyati Draizera," *Literaturnaya gazeta*, February 25, 1950.

[99] Anisimov, "Put . . . ," *op.cit.*, pp. 219-32; Kornilova, *op.cit.*, pp. 233-39; N. Samokhvalov, "Predisloviye," in *Rasskazy amerikanskikh pisatelei*, Moscow, 1954, p. 4.

[100] I. Anisimov, "Theodore Dreiser's Political Legacy," *Soviet Literature*, No. 1 (1949), p. 146; I. Anisimov, "Dreiser's American Gallery," *Soviet Literature*, No. 12 (1950), p. 165.

ly, was supposed to have been the "publicistic" work, *Tragic America*, written in 1931.

In the Soviet scheme for Dreiser's career that was perfected in the fifties, *Tragic America* played a different role than it had in earlier years. It will be recalled that Soviet reviewers in the thirties, while generally approving its anticapitalist spirit, had nevertheless maintained that the book contained strong elements of individualism and displayed the author's political confusion. But the critics of the fifties assigned it a central, pivotal position in his career.[101] They contended that two events immediately preceding its writing—Dreiser's trip to the Soviet Union and the onset of the Depression—had made a convinced revolutionary of the author, so that the book did not contain "a trace of thought about the stability of the bourgeois order." In it Dreiser broke the "circle of irresolution that constricted" *An American Tragedy*, published six years earlier. The book opened "a new page both in his own art and in the history of American literature," since it "came to a revolutionary conclusion, merciless to the end."[102] Incidentally, although *Tragic America* has been published several times in the USSR, it has never been printed there in its full text.

In the Soviet analysis of the fifties, it was unimportant that nearly all of Dreiser's creative writing had been finished before 1931 and that thereafter he had occupied himself mainly with political journalism. (His two posthumously published novels, *The Stoic* and *The Bulwark*, had been largely completed before 1920.) Once they decided that he had in fact "come to communism" with the writing of *Tragic America* (although postponing his formal affiliation for fourteen years), the critics devoted their efforts to tracing his ideological evolution up to that point and to showing that he had become a "socialist realist." In respect to Dreiser's great novels and stories, all of them written before he became a

---

[101] Zasurski, *op.cit.*, pp. 163-80; V. Nikolayev, "Draizer obvinyayet amerikanski imperializm," *Kommunist*, No. 13 (1952), p. 71; Anisimov, "Put . . . ," *op.cit.*, pp. 226-27; P. Toper, "Gnevnoye slovo pravdy," *Znamya*, No. 11 (1952), p. 188; "Library Discussion . . . ," *op.cit.*, p. 153.
[102] Toper, *op.cit.*, p. 188.

Marxist, the critics' major concern was to prove that, whether he realized it or not, the author had always been *essentially* a "progressive." All evidence to the contrary was placed in the category of transient, incidental impurities from which, through experience and stubborn honesty, he steadily purged himself. This practice gave rise to excesses which even the critics themselves sometimes recognized. For example, Zasurski, in his enthusiasm to prove that Dreiser had "entered American literature believing in the power of the popular masses and summoning them to active struggle against the rulership of the magnates of Wall Street," claimed that "an extremely important aspect of Dreiser's realism is his depiction in *The Titan* of the popular masses, their struggle." The critic Motyleva, realizing that "the masses" are scarcely evident in this novel, took Zasurski to task for this claim, pointing out that at this stage in his career the author was just a critic of the bourgeoisie.[103]

The most interesting, if depressing, aspect of the criticism of the fifties, however, was its attempt to weave Dreiser into the fabric of socialist realism. To do this it was necessary, first of all, to describe as art the overwhelmingly journalistic writing, such as *Tragic America* and *America is Worth Saving*, in which he engaged during the last fifteen years of his life, and to evade the question of why he did not embody his newly embraced ideology in significant works of fiction.

The critics never attempted to persuade themselves that Dreiser's major works of fiction were anything but critical realism. However, their analysis of these works stressed qualities that are normally ascribed to socialist realism. Elistratova, for example, emphasized Dreiser's "deep and tender love for the common people," his hatred of "social injustice in the lives of ordinary men," and his "enthusiasm for the energy of man—the worker, the creator, the builder." Comparing him with his early contemporaries—Henry James, George Meredith, and Thomas Hardy—who were "each in his own way asserting man's impotence in the face of 'life's

---

[103] T. Motyleva, "Tak li nado izuchat zarubezhnuyu literaturu?" *Inostrannaya literatura*, No. 9 (1956), p. 216.

little ironies,' " she found that "Dreiser insisted on man's right to happiness" and added that "all his work is pervaded with that lofty idea."[104] The Whitmanesque faith in the powers of man and the possibility of happiness on earth that Elistratova ascribed to Dreiser is, of course, an ideological cornerstone of socialist realism.

The writings that were specifically designated as socialist realism were few indeed. (Zasurski implied that his unpublished scenario, "Tobacco" and the unfinished play "The Girl in the Coffin" would have fulfilled the prescription, but he did not really attempt to prove it.)[105] In fact, the only work of fiction the critics cited as fully meriting this definition is the story of the Communist "Ernita" from *A Gallery of Women*. The critics claimed much for this story which, they felt, displayed all the qualities of ideological maturity, even though it had been written as early as 1929. One of its distinctions was that it was the first "lifelike portrait of an American Communist,"[106] but its major achievement was that it featured a genuine, full-blooded "positive hero" with a "revolutionary perspective."[107] Clearly the case centered on his political convictions and not his aesthetic practice, although there were admiring attempts to analyze his style as a pamphleteer.[108] The chief point in support of the contention that his journalism of the thirties and forties was actually socialist realism was that the image of the "people," the "masses," had become more and more prominent in these writings.[109] Dreiser's failure to express his new convictions in fresh works of fiction was dismissed with double talk: "And if the aspiration to place the image of the people as the cornerstone of his art could not or did not succeed in flowing out

[104] Yelistratova, "Theodore Dreiser," *op.cit.*, p. 180.

[105] Zasurski, *op.cit.*, pp. 185-86.

[106] I. Anisimov, "Dreiser's American Gallery," *Soviet Literature*, No. 12 (1950), p. 168.

[107] Zasurski, *op.cit.*, pp. 153-58; R. D. Orlova, "Obraz kommunista v amerikanskoi literature 30-kh godov," *Uchenye zapiski*. Moskovski Oblastnoi Pedagogicheski Institut, Tom XXXIV, vypusk 2, 1955, p. 66.

[108] Zasurski, *op.cit.*, pp. 176-80.

[109] Anisimov, "Put . . . ," *op.cit.*, p. 227.

into congenial artistic creations, nevertheless with greater force it becomes a legacy to advanced American literature."[110] Thus, Dreiser had "laid out the path of American socialist realism."[111] But the critics could not bring themselves to admit frankly that his "legacy" to socialist realism was in his politics and not in his art.

Dreiser has appealed to Russian readers' overwhelming inquisitiveness about life in the United States by creating meticulously thorough and veracious portraits of his country and its people. It is important to note that both Soviet and American critics agree in their admiration of his accomplishment as a social historian. However, although Soviet critics recognize his faults of composition, they are more willing than Americans to excuse his clumsiness and prolixity. Curiosity as to just how the capitalist system works enables the Soviet reader to digest painlessly Dreiser's tedious masses of detail and to follow patiently his brooding examination of our social machinery. And of course his writing is particularly satisfactory to the critics because it is so negative and tendentious that it can easily be employed as anti-American propaganda.

Soviet critics insist on seeing Dreiser as a prophet—although usually an indirect one—of social revolution. They have either minimized or rationalized aspects of his art that are out of keeping with the image of a life-affirming and progressive thinker. In portraying him as a socially militant writer, for example, they have virtually ignored his posthumously published novel, *The Bulwark*, whose message is one of pietism and reconciliation. They have studiously avoided the fact that his ideas were nearly always confused and contradictory. The pessimism that marks his great novels is treated as an annoying petty bourgeois aberration that is not, however, fundamental to their structure. In point of fact, Dreiser in his most productive years was a profound fatalist whose pessimism was so all-pervasive and unrelieved that it became an entire aesthetic system for interpreting human

110 *ibid.*, p. 228.
111 *ibid.*, p. 228; Zasurski, *op.cit.*, p. 203.

existence. It is true that he had an ideal of human decency and justice and that he fought for this ideal, but as an artist he was primarily a determinist. The human tragedies on which his novels are based are attributable in part to the organization of society, but they are also built on combinations of circumstances and fatal coincidences that are independent of the social structure. Soviet critics were indeed correct in seeing Dreiser as the champion of the underdog, since he deeply sympathized with the victims of social neglect and injustice. But they were wrong in claiming for his major novels a feeling of hope and faith in the possibility of social progress.

Because he had a tragic view of the world about him and wrote on a large scale, Dreiser's interpretation of American society was more profoundly critical than that of Sinclair Lewis and his ultimate moral judgments cut deeper. Lewis was a witty and extremely telling satirist, but he was essentially a commentator who wrote without a large sense of history and confined his interest to the middle class. His social criticism, based on mimicry and ridicule of smug, shallow, contented, and generally affluent bourgeois Americans, was limited, topical, and somewhat ephemeral. Dreiser's examination of his society emanated from his sheer fascination with its machinery and his sensitivity to the pain and suffering of its victims. His attempt to understand the entire system of American life to its very foundations resulted in a more penetrating, thorough, and ultimately more hostile analysis. Although both writers have been regarded in Russia as welcome sources of uncomplimentary information about the United States, Dreiser has been more highly favored because he has portrayed greater depths of inequality and injustice. Whereas Lewis is regarded as merely a useful critic, Dreiser's books can be presented as a thoroughgoing attack on the whole structure of American life.

In the periods of their highest literary productivity, both Lewis and Dreiser criticized America in terms of her own standards, emphasizing the inconsistencies between her ideals (which both writers then affirmed) and her actual practices.

Both clung to the ideology of democracy—although they felt that it had been betrayed and corrupted—and neither conceived of embracing an alternative ideology. Even in the twenties, however, when there was no real evidence that either of them desired to do more than record American life critically, Soviet spokesmen were already demanding that both of them adopt a revolutionary perspective. In the case of Lewis, such a demand was patently impractical. Like the overwhelming majority of writers of the twenties, Lewis was assessing his country from a moral and cultural point of view, not a political one. Spiritually he was a critic from within, a member of the loyal opposition, and was in no need of a politically revolutionary standard. In the twenties Dreiser—although he was more restless and unsure of his ideological foundations—was also groping for an understanding, with little thought of an alien ideology. Both were classified by the Russians, for essentially the same reason, as petty bourgeois realists.

The commentary of the thirties, forties and fifties would indicate that in the Soviet view the major difference between the two writers was Dreiser's capacity for more powerful intellectual growth—a growth which enabled him ultimately to advance to a belief in communism while Lewis stayed mired in a morass of bourgeois prejudices. This conclusion is sufficient for the purposes to which Soviet criticism puts American literature and its authors. It is interesting, but beside the point, that the Soviet estimate of the art of Lewis and Dreiser corresponds closely to that of American critics in many respects. The agreement is largely vitiated by the political tendentiousness of Soviet criticism.

CHAPTER XI

HOWARD FAST

❧❧❧ THE Soviet image of American "progressive" writers after World War II was a brave one. A beleaguered group, constantly "persecuted, suppressed, thrown in jail,"[1] they courageously gathered around the magazine *Masses and Mainstream*—the spearhead of the counteroffensive against an "orgy of fascist reaction"[2] that was attempting to suppress all progressive writing.[3] The function of *Masses and Mainstream* was described by the critic Romanova as follows:

"The magazine spreads the truth among the multitudes of Americans who have not yet fully grasped the implications of the criminal policy pursued by the instigators of war, and still are being humbugged by the slanders and distortions of the reactionary press.

"The struggle against the unbridled propaganda of a new war is waged along with the struggle against the reaction raging within the United States. The war hysteria is invariably accompanied by an offensive against the standard of living of the toiling masses, intensified race discrimination and a further fascization of culture, and primarily the system of education, and by the persecution of progressive scientists and artists.

"Unwaveringly exposing the vile slanderous attacks of Wall Street's hangers-on, the magazine uses facts and concrete instances to prove convincingly the steady growth of the movement of protest against the fascist-minded obscurantists who do all they can to stifle everything living, courageous, new.[4]

[1] I. Anisimov, "Literature in the Service of Reaction," *Soviet Literature*, No. 10 (1948), p. 149.

[2] E. Romanova, "A Proud Record," *Soviet Literature*, No. 12 (1951), p. 160.

[3] I. Levidova, "Slander and Falsification Pillorized," *Soviet Literature*, No. 2 (1952), p. 177; M. Mendelson, "Amerikanskaya progressivnaya literatura poslednikh let," *Zvezda*, No. 11 (1949), pp. 167-82.

[4] E. Romanova, "Masses and Mainstream," *Soviet Literature*, No. 1 (1950), pp. 186-87.

For a number of reasons, not the least of which were the mounting revulsion against Soviet foreign policy and increased knowledge on the part of American radicals of the Soviet system of domestic repression, the Communist movement in the United States was rapidly losing strength. Yet the peculiar Soviet brand of wishful thinking led the critics, in the face of abundant evidence to the contrary, to insist that the Communist Party of the United States was "gathering more and more adherents among the working class and the leading intelligentsia of the USA."[5] Neither persecution by the "police regime" nor the "Fascist terror" could stem the tide.[6] In the face of "all the efforts of reaction to clamp down on freedom of expression" the movement of writers to the "progressive camp" continued,[7] with "unmistakable signs of nascence."[8] It was difficult, the critics occasionally admitted, for such publications as *Masses and Mainstream* to remain alive when "more and more brazen manifestations of fascism . . . are becoming common features of the daily life around them."[9] Nevertheless, they blindly maintained, the number of "progressive journals" was rapidly increasing in America.[10]

The four "progressive" writers who were published most prominently by Russia during this period were Albert Maltz, Howard Fast, and two writers who were scarcely known in the United States—Lloyd Brown and Alexander Saxton. While others, such as the venerable Michael Gold and the hallowed Lincoln Steffens and John Reed, were occasionally reprinted, the critics pinned their hopes for a vigorous new Party-line literature on relatively young and promising authors. They identified themselves closely with these Ameri-

---

[5] A. Anikst, *Progressivnyi amerikanski pisatel Govard Fast*, Moscow, 1948, p. 27.

[6] N. Zhulanov, "Progressivnye pevtsy Ameriki," *Zabaikale*, No. 6 (1953), p. 219.

[7] E. Romanova, "In America," *Soviet Literature*, No. 3 (1951), p. 143.

[8] P. Toper, "Pravda vostorzhestvuyet," *Znamya*, No. 7 (1954), p. 185.

[9] Romanova, "In America," *op.cit.*, p. 143.

[10] Yel. Romanova, "Golos pravdy," *Literaturnaya gazeta*, November 12, 1953, p. 4.

cans, and wrote of them with a familiarity and sympathy reserved for them alone, in the same spirit of patience and encouragement that had marked their attitude toward the
American proletarian writers of the 1930's. The critics used
the same critical standards and formulas (although sometimes with altered terminology) that had been employed with
earlier writers like Jack Conroy and Grace Lumpkin. Partly
because of the topics these writers chose and partly because
of the way in which they handled them, the critics used their
works as springboards from which to launch editorials on
the evils of life in the United States. Invariably in reviewing
the books of these "progressives," the critics vied with one
another in inventing dark epithets to describe America. One
often senses a feeling of gratitude in these reviews, as if the
critics, having exhausted their imaginations in fulfilling their
propagandistic duties, were pathetically happy that these
Americans had supplied them with fresh ammunition that
would break the monotony of their own deadly clichés. Very
often their reviews were merely gleefully slanted synopses of
the works at hand.

Only Albert Maltz had been known to Soviet readers before the war. He was first published in the middle thirties,
and by 1941 numerous translations of his stories had appeared, both in books and in periodicals. By 1954, according
to official Soviet figures, 750,000 copies of his various works
had been printed, in seven languages of the USSR.[11] Soviet
readers knew him best for his short stories, which one critic
called "a magnificent contribution in the history of the development of the novella genre."[12] The simplicity of his plots
and language, another critic argued, was illusory. Actually,
his stories were marked by "great depth" and "large perspective," so that "one short and laconic novella of Maltz provides immeasurably more for an understanding of the times
than an epos of the cosmopolite Sinclair spread out over a

---

[11] "Publication of Fiction in the U.S.S.R.," *Soviet Literature*, No. 11
(1954), p. 209.
[12] Yu. Chaplygin, "V tupike," *Oktyabr*, No. 4 (1954), p. 182.

thousand pages."[13] In the thirties he was recognized as "an artist who calls to struggle," although what impressed the critics most was his Gorky-like concern for the underdog. His stories were gloomy, but they strove to "find the human in man, no matter how deformed his life may be."[14] By the beginning of World War II, the Russians viewed him, together with Steinbeck and Richard Wright, as one of the most promising authors who had been nurtured by the Depression.[15]

After the war the critics found that, particularly in his first works, Maltz had shared the unfortunate tendency of many left-wing writers to view America's corruption with alarm and pity instead of belligerence. Even such a relatively late novel as *The Journey of Simon McKeever* (1949), the tender story of an impoverished old man in search of a cure for his arthritis, "provoked disappointment" in its failure to treat "the sharpest problems of contemporary American life, the struggle against reaction and the threat of war."[16] In 1952, however, his play *The Morrison Case*, in which a worker accepts blacklisting in preference to serving as an FBI informer, was praised warmly for showing the "fascistization of the U.S. government machine" and, at the same time, "the awakening of the average American, of the ordinary man whom the reactionaries have been duping and terrorizing."[17] The Russians were grateful, moreover, for Maltz's political activity. Not only was he a contributor to *Masses and Mainstream*, but also he was a member of the "Hollywood Ten,"

[13] S. Gansovski, "Ot imeni amerikanskikh trudyashchikhsya," *Zvezda*, No. 3 (1952), p. 181.

[14] P. Balashov, "Chelovek na doroge," *Literaturnaya gazeta*, June 30, 1939.

[15] Yuri Smirnov, "Molodye revolyutsionnye pisateli S Sh A," *Molodaya gvardiya*, No. 9 (1940), pp. 150-52; T. Rokotov, "Anglo-amerikanskaya voyennaya novella," *Internatsionalnaya literatura*, Nos. 11-12 (1941), p. 116; A. Kramskoi, "Internatsionalnaya tematika v 'molodoi gvardii,'" *Internatsionalnaya literatura*, No. 3 (1941), pp. 164-65.

[16] Mendelson, "Amerikanskaya progressivnaya literatura . . . ," *op.cit.*, p. 175.

[17] A. Elistratova, "Two Plays of Present Day America," *Soviet Literature*, No. 1 (1953), p. 173.

a group of screen writers who had been prosecuted by the Federal government for their Communist affiliation. Finally, his writings, despite their occasional ideological mistakes, provided excellent opportunities for the springboard technique of political journalism in Soviet criticism. In 1953, for example, a critic wrote: "With special love and sympathy Maltz writes about American children. They are deprived of a real childhood, of joys. Children are reared in such a way that they become bandits and murderers. It is precisely as such that the world has now seen the American soldiers in Korea. The psyche of children is mutilated by the beastly laws of capitalism, where man is a wolf to man, where man is an enemy of man."[18]

Maltz's most important contribution to the cold war was *The Underground Stream,* a violent novel which, against a background of labor strife in the Detroit automobile industry, focused on the struggle between the Communists and the Black Legion. Although the book had originally been published in the United States in 1940, the Russians found it extremely timely. In foreseeing that America was "going Fascist,"[19] Maltz had proved himself a profound political prophet.[20]

Another prophetic novel was Lloyd Brown's *Iron City,* the story of how a group of Negro Communists, imprisoned for their political beliefs and activities, band together to fight for the life of a fellow convict who has been unjustly convicted of murder. Unable to find aid from any other source—including Negro civil rights organizations—this victim of a judicial frameup discovers that only the Communist Party is willing to battle in his defense. The critics saw a microcosm of contemporary America in the book.[21] The time of the ac-

[18] Zhulanov, "Progressivnye . . . ," *op.cit.,* p. 228.

[19] R. D. Orlova, "Obraz kommunista v amerikanskoi literature 30-kh godov," *Uchenye zapiski,* Moskovski Oblastnoi Pedagogicheski Institut, Tom XXXIV, vypusk 2, 1955, p. 60.

[20] M. Mendelson, "Amerikanskiye smertyashkiny," *Novy mir,* No. 12 (1948), pp. 219-20.

[21] P. Toper, " 'Zheleznyi gorod' Lloida Brauna," *Novy mir,* No. 6 (1953), p. 269.

tion was 1941, but "in spite of the ten-year gap," Brown's novel was "linked vitally with today."[22]

In the opinion of at least one critic, however, "the most powerful attainment of American progressive literature in recent years"[23] was Alexander Saxton's *The Great Midland*. This novel of the railroad labor movement, set primarily in Chicago, chronicles the lives of a family of workers and their involvement in union activities, concentrating on the growth of one member of the family as a Communist. A leitmotif is the railroad itself, which becomes a monster through the brutality and corruptness of the actions of its management against labor.

The actions of *The Underground Stream, Iron City*, and *The Great Midland* take place before World War II, and none of the novels explicitly refers to postwar America. Yet it seems never to have occurred to the critics that even if, as they believed, these novels did give a faithful picture of the prewar United States, that picture might now be anachronistic. Committed to the assumption that the class war in the United States was reaching its most brutal final stage, and poorly equipped for refined analysis of the American scene, the critics could only proclaim the timely truth and relevance of the books of Maltz, Brown, and Saxton. Even had they recognized that these novels were out of date, however, political and ideological considerations would have compelled the critics to find special merit in them. In Soviet criticism of this time a fundamental proposition, derived from a generally exaggerated notion of the influence and importance of the American Communist Party, was that the logical, proper, and typical chief protagonists in the progressive literature of the United States would be Communists. The plea for Communist heroes, which had been strong in the thirties but fairly dormant in the forties, arose once more after the war. In one sense the demands of the critics were quite nat-

---

[22] I. Mikhailova, "A New Writer Comes to the Fore," *Soviet Literature*, No. 5 (1952), p. 141.

[23] A. Belski, "Amerikanskaya progressivnaya literatura v borbe za mir," *Sovremennaya progressivnaya literatura zarubezhnykh stran v borbe za mir*, Moscow, 1954, p. 171.

ural, for, ethnocentrically bound and impressed with the image
of their own omnipresent and omnipotent Party, they could
scarcely have been expected to comprehend fully an American
party as weak as it actually was.

Considered as a whole, the Soviet criticism of these three
novels gives an indication of the standards the Russians used
in judging the works of American "progressive" writers. At
the center of these works, the critics felt, should be heroes
who carry Communist Party cards. Maltz, who sometimes
failed to create adequate heroes, came up with the requisite
man of steel in *The Underground Stream*.[24] Moreover, he
was a "flesh-and-blood man you believe in, a fighter with an
indomitable will."[25] "For this advanced worker, closely bound
up with his class, participation in the revolutionary movement is not a matter of martyrdom or self-denial; on the
contrary, it is only in struggle that his personality finds full
expression, only fighting is he happy."[26] Communists, the
critics further insisted, should be shown to be completely
human. *Iron City* was praised for endowing its Communists
with a variety of personalities, and for avoiding idealization
of them.[27] A depiction of moral and ideological growth on the
part of Communist heroes was also highly prized. A particular virtue of *The Great Midland* was that "for the first time
in American literature [the author] tries to show the formation of the character of a revolutionary worker in his development through the historic stages of the revolutionary
movement of the USA."[28] The day-to-day work of Communists in organizing the working class should be shown.
Both Maltz and Saxton were criticized for failing to do this
in sufficient detail.[29] The Russians wanted to be shown that

[24] O. Nemerovskaya, "Borba prinimayet novye formy," *Zvezda*, No. 5
(1950), p. 187; Gansovski, "Ot imeni . . . ," *op.cit.*, p. 182.

[25] R. Orlova, "America's Progressive People," *Soviet Literature*, No.
5 (1950), p. 153.

[26] *ibid.*, p. 153.

[27] Mikhailova, "A New Writer . . . ," *op.cit.*, p. 143; Toper, " 'Zheleznyi
gorod' . . . ," *op.cit.*, p. 271.

[28] Al. Abramov, "Roman o chestnykh lyudyakh Ameriki," *Literaturnaya gazeta*, September 17, 1949, p. 4.

[29] *ibid.*, p. 4; Gansovski, "Ot imeni . . . ," *op.cit.*, p. 182.

American Communists were engaged in popular activity at the grass-roots level. Maltz was therefore lauded for taking his Communist characters from "the very heart of American life,"[30] and for portraying them as the "brain and heart" of the trade-union movement,[31] but he was also criticized for failing to give sufficient prominence to the "struggle of the masses" against the Fascist threat.[32] It was correct to show the Communists as leaders, but one must also demonstrate that they have enthusiastic followers! The unity and solidarity of Communists must also be shown, and *Iron City* was found to be especially praiseworthy in this respect,[33] although Brown was also criticized for having failed to show *white* Communists working with their Negro comrades.[34] Finally, the progressive novel must affirm unbounded faith in the ultimate triumph of Communist virtue, regardless of whether or not the novel itself has a happy ending. The hero of *The Underground Stream* is tortured to death by thugs in the employ of the Black Legion; nevertheless, the book was found to be optimistic, since it "shows by artistic means the motive force which clarifies the understanding of the masses and unites them."[35] One critic called the novel an "optimistic tragedy" because of the dedicated courage of its hero.[36] *Iron City* also, though lacking an "artificial 'happy end,'" left its reviewer with "a real feeling of the Communists' having won a victory."[37]

The prescription for a fictional portrayal of Communists in mid-century America was carried out in greatest detail, however, by Howard Fast in his novel *Clarkton*. Concerned with labor strife in a Massachusetts mill town shortly after World War II, this book might well have been a delayed answer to the prayers of the critics of the 1930's for a "prole-

[30] Mendelson, "Amerikanskiye smertyashkiny," *op.cit.*, pp. 219-20.
[31] Mendelson, "Amerikanskaya progressivnaya literatura . . . ," *op.cit.*, p. 175.
[32] *ibid.*, p. 175.
[33] Toper, " 'Zhelezny gorod' . . . ," *op.cit.*, p. 271.
[34] *ibid.*, p. 172; Mikhailova, "A New Writer . . . ," *op.cit.*, p. 143.
[35] Nemerovskaya, "Borba prinimayet . . . ," *op.cit.*, p. 186.
[36] Elistratova, "Two Plays . . . ," *op.cit.*, p. 175.
[37] Mikhailova, "A New Writer . . . ," *op.cit.*, p. 142.

tarian literature." Its warm reception by the critics of the 1950's is a good measure of the essentially unchanging quality of Soviet literary formulas and ideological criteria over the years. The novel was gratifying, first of all, because it showed the "growing influence of the Communist Party."[38] Furthermore, it portrayed its Communist characters as plain, average, but politically acute Americans. Although they were clearly "the leading force of the working class," they had emerged from a broad variety of American backgrounds and represented an extensive spectrum of the populace.[39] (One critic observed that "perhaps [Fast] even exaggerates somewhat the 'ordinariness' of their characters to score his point.")[40] Fast had "countered the calumny of the reactionary press,"[41] and had proved that these true Americans were not agents of a foreign government.[42] The novel's most pleasing feature, however, was its display of Communists *in action*,[43] and the climax of the book—a bloody strike episode—was considered so powerful that it was published separately in Russia as a booklet. In this respect, *Clarkton* was superior to *The Underground Stream,* since "Fast to a much greater extent than Maltz shows the activity of Communists on a background of the broad workers' movement."[44]

Clarkton is actually one of the weakest things Howard Fast ever wrote. And although the Soviet critics, for their own peculiar reasons, praised the novel unanimously, they were obliged to find fault with certain features. (There were, of course, the typical fine points of political interpretation: Fast had erred in implying that the relations between labor and capital during the war had been amiable.)[45] Just as they

[38] Anikst, *Progressivnyi amerikanski pisatel Govard Fast, op.cit.,* p. 27.
[39] *ibid.,* pp. 26-27.
[40] Orlova, "America's Progressive People," *op.cit.,* p. 156.
[41] *ibid.,* p. 156.
[42] Anikst, *Progressivnyi amerikanski pisatel Govard Fast, op.cit.,* pp. 27-28.
[43] R. Miller-Budnitskaya, "Kniga o prestupleniyakh amerikanskovo fashizma," *Oktyabr,* No. 10 (1951), p. 180.
[44] Mendelson, "Amerikanskaya progressivnaya literatura . . . ," *op.cit.,* p. 178.
[45] M. Mendelson, "Chetyre dnya v Klarktone," *Literaturnaya gazeta,* April 21, 1948, p. 4.

had found that Maltz sometimes used decadent "bourgeois" devices of refined psychological analysis and, in his eagerness to show the depravity of the capitalist class, indulged too freely in erotic detail,[46] and just as Saxton had devoted too much space to the psychological problems of one of his female characters who vacillates between communism and Bohemianism,[47] so also was Fast guilty of "naturalism." The chief representative of capitalist iniquity in *Clarkton* is a spineless factory owner, an erstwhile "liberal" who, in his desperation, enlists the services of professional strikebreakers. In an effort to contrast this degenerate capitalist with his morally healthy workers, Fast makes him a voluptuary and involves him in a rape. This awkward device, involving "disgusting naturalistic details"[48] was repeatedly deplored by the critics.[49] The objections, however, were based not so much on aesthetic as on puritanical grounds.

The critics' willingness to praise *Clarkton* was a tribute to its ideological purity, but their approval was also to some extent a matter of course, because its author was currently the Soviet Union's staunchest American literally ally. No American writer has ever enjoyed more Soviet adulation in his own lifetime than Howard Fast. From 1948 to 1957, over 2,500,000 copies of his works were printed, in twelve languages of the USSR.[50] His novels, stories, essays, poems, plays, and editorials—seemingly his every utterance—appeared by the dozens in Soviet magazines and newspapers, and his works were required reading in universities and schools throughout the country. When Fast served a three-month prison sentence for contempt of Congress in 1950, the Soviet press hailed him loudly as a victim of Fascist terror and an indomitable fighter for the only truth. In 1953 he was

[46] Nemerovskaya, "Borba prinimayet . . . ," *op.cit.*, p. 187.
[47] T. Motyleva, "Cherty progressivnoi zarubezhnoi literatury," *Novy mir*, No. 5 (1950), p. 211.
[48] Mendelson, "Chetyre dnya . . . ," *op.cit.*, p. 4.
[49] Mikh. Urnov, "Khovard Fast i Amerika," *Zvezda*, No. 10 (1948), p. 176; Motyleva, "Cherty . . . ," *op.cit.*, p. 209; Mendelson, "Chetyre dnya . . . ," *op.cit.*, p. 4.
[50] "Publication of Fiction in the U.S.S.R.," *op.cit.*, p. 209.

awarded, and accepted, a Stalin International Peace Prize.

It is evident that many American authors whom the critics have recommended have not been accepted by the Soviet public. Not so with Fast. His was clearly a mass popularity, and for a decade he ranked next to Mark Twain, Dreiser, and London as a favorite. He stood head and shoulders above all other contemporary Americans, and Russian readers trusted completely in his picture of life in the United States. It seemed to the present writer, on a visit to the Soviet Union in 1956, that the name of Howard Fast was on the lips of nearly everyone he talked with.

Although a great many of Fast's writings were translated in the USSR, he was best known to Soviet readers for his historical novels, of which the two most widely published were *The Last Frontier*, the tragic story of how a band of Cheyenne Indians were dispossessed, betrayed, and penned in reservations by the United States government, and *Freedom Road*, which tells of a brutally suppressed attempt at interracial agrarian democracy in the Reconstruction South. The critics liked particularly the "materialist conception" of American history he infused into his novels. In portraying the past as a process of class struggle, his novels served as an antidote to bourgeois myths: "American propaganda abundantly used its resources to create a false impression of the special paths of development of capitalist America, as though it were able to avoid the fundamental contradictions peculiar to capitalism."[51] Fast's works, the Russians believed, counteracted the false "legend" of the "unique development of American capitalist society." Before Fast appeared on the scene, America's novelists had viewed her history sometimes as merely "biographies of statesmen," and sometimes as simply the "abstract collision of good and bad principles."[52] Usually they had perfumed the unsavory episodes of the past. Cooper, for example, had been an apologist of the white conqueror as he invaded the homeland of the Indian, and Mar-

[51] Urnov, "Khovard Fast i Amerika," *op.cit.*, p. 172.
[52] B. Smirnov, "Doroga svobody," *Zvezda*, No. 11 (1949), p. 189.

garet Mitchell had glorified the slaveholding South.[53] In an effort to "revive the most progressive revolutionary-democratic tradition of the American people,"[54] Fast's novels fought such romantic misconceptions.

Most American historical novels, the Russians argued, were a form of escape literature. Fast's works, on the contrary, were not a "flight from reality"[55] since they were taken up with "essential and burning questions" and expressed his "attitude to present-day reality."[56] From the Soviet point of view his books about the American past were constructively tendentious: "[He] turns to the history of his country not as a dispassionate chronicler of events long past: his narrative of the past is always inspired by the living breath of the present, helps one to understand better contemporary America, to see how the ancestors of the present-day American cannibals were already, in those far-away times, preparing the soil for the rise of fascism."[57]

Freedom Road was a case in point: "Despite the fact that the events of the novel relate to the past century, *Freedom Road* is a profoundly contemporary book, a book which summons to active struggle against the oppression of races and nationalities, a book which affirms the equality of people independent of nationality and color of skin, which indicts reactionary racial theories."[58] Fast's historical novels are peopled heavily with representatives of the masses, and this was regarded as an "innovation," since "he not only reconstructs genuine historical heroes but also the common people from whose surroundings they come."[59] These included the ordinary soldiers of the War for Independence in such novels as *Conceived in Liberty, The Unvanquished,* and *Citizen Tom*

---

[53] *ibid.*, p. 189; Anikst, *Progressivnyi amerikanski pisatel Govard Fast, op.cit.*, pp. 7-18.

[54] *ibid.*, p. 10.

[55] Zhulanov, "Progressivnye . . . ," *op.cit.*, p. 220; Toper, "Pravda vostorzhestvuyet," *op.cit.*, p. 183.

[56] Anikst, *Progressivnyi amerikanski pisatel Govard Fast, op.cit.*, p. 7.

[57] B. Galanov, "Doroga svobody Gideon Dzheksona," *Znamya*, No. 11 (1949), p. 189.

[58] Anikst, *Progressivnyi amerikanski pisatel Govard Fast, op.cit.*, p. 24.

[59] Smirnov, "Doroga svobody," *op.cit.*, p. 189.

Paine, and, even more important, representatives of the exploited races of America: the Indians of *The Last Frontier* and the Negroes of *Freedom Road*. One critic called *The Last Frontier* "the first significant artistic work to disclose the true fate of the Indian people." The author's particular achievement was this: "Without idealizing the Indians in the slightest, Fast nevertheless emphasizes poignantly the nobility of their conduct, characterizing their feeling for justice, their deeply ingrained love of freedom, their consciousness of their human worth, the feeling of comradeship deeply inherent in them, their mutual support. Fast is devoid of sentimentalism, he tries to evoke in the reader a feeling not of pity but of indignation, and he achieves this."[60] In *Freedom Road*, the critics noted, Fast had avoided both the bourgeois temptation to dwell on the exotic features of Negro culture[61] and the equally strong sentimental "Uncle Tom" tradition, which philanthropically depicted the Negro as merely a pitiful "victim of social injustice."[62] He had "created the image of a Negro hero, making him a Man in capital letters."[63] Fast's Negroes fought actively for their rights as human beings. Although *Freedom Road* concluded with a massacre perpetrated by the Ku Klux Klan, the book was another "optimistic tragedy," since "defeat is inevitable, but just as inevitable is the continuation of the struggle."[64] Ultimately the significance of the novel was that it "summons one to vigilance, inculcates one with revolutionary firmness, teaches one to hate the enemy."[65]

At times, the Russians felt, Fast's implicit protest against the present-day betrayal of the democratic tradition led him to "idealize the bourgeois democracy" of the American past. In general, his novels of the Revolutionary War exaggerated "the role and significance of the American bourgeois Revolu-

[60] Anikst, *Progressivnyi amerikanski pisatel Govard Fast, op.cit.*, p. 21.
[61] Smirnov, "Doroga svobody," *op.cit.*, p. 189; Anikst, *Progressivnyi amerikanski pisatel Govard Fast*, p. 21.
[62] Urnov, "Khovard Fast i Amerika," *op.cit.*, p. 172.
[63] Smirnov, "Doroga svobody," *op.cit.*, p. 189.
[64] Urnov, "Khovard Fast i Amerika," *op.cit.*, p. 173.
[65] Galanov, "Doroga svobody . . . ," *op.cit.*, p. 192.

tion" in shaping the character of the United States of today.[66] In *The Unvanquished* he correctly showed that Washington was named commander in chief of the "bourgeois republic" because he was the "richest landowner in North America," but he erred in "trying to convince the reader that Washington, despite his inner alienation from the people, nonetheless in the course of events became a people's commander." A critic noted that "it would be more correct in this circumstance to show not so much what united the Virginia planter with the New York artisans and Pennsylvania farmers as what divided them."[67] Similarly, in depicting General Anthony Wayne in *The Proud and the Free* as "the cruel hangman of a soldiers' uprising," Fast had served the truth, but he had also "preserved in him an aura of historic justice, which was not warranted in reality."[68] However, Fast wore his rose-colored glasses only occasionally. *Conceived in Liberty*, a novel of Valley Forge written from the point of view of the man in the ranks, disclosed the "class discord between the ordinary soldiers and the officers of Washington's army." And *Citizen Tom Paine* showed the "class contradictions in the camp of the American bourgeois Revolution" by demonstrating that the revolutionaries had to conquer not only the British but also "the opposition of rightist conservative elements." More important, this book argued that the Revolution had not created a just political and social order, and indicated that fundamental questions remained unsolved in the United States.[69]

Although the critics found contemporary relevance in Fast's historical tales, they especially prized his topical novels and stories of twentieth-century America, since every one of them contained a clear political message, provided commentary on useful cold war issues, and offered a stimulus for editorials

[66] Urnov, "Khovard Fast i Amerika," *op.cit.*, p. 175.

[67] Anikst, *Progressivnyi amerikanski pisatel Govard Fast, op.cit.*, pp. 12-13.

[68] P. Toper, "Rasskazy Govarda Fasta," *Inostrannaya literatura*, No. 4 (1956), p. 211.

[69] Anikst, *Progressivnyi amerikanski pisatel Govard Fast, op.cit.*, pp. 11-15.

in the form of book reviews. *Silas Timberman*, the novel of a liberal college professor who is hounded by legislative investigating committees, driven from his job and sent to jail, was a "fresco of American life today,"—a "realistic picture of the persecution, lawlessness, and intimidation that have come to be so dominant a part of life in latter-day America."[70] *The Passion of Sacco and Vanzetti*, though written in 1953— a quarter-century after the shameful events with which it is concerned—was considered timely partly because of its thematic similarity to the case of Julius and Ethel Rosenberg.[71] The collection of short stories, *The Last Supper*, was concerned with "the most stirring questions of the day: the danger of war and the opportunities for preventing it, the hydrogen bomb, the colonial yoke, the persecution by the FBI, political reaction and the struggle against it."[72] And *Peekskill, U.S.A.*, Fast's eye-witness account of the violent mob attack on a Communist-led peace rally, was a "document of the epoch of fascistization of the USA."[73]

The critics steadily insisted, however, that Fast was far more than a pamphleteer. One of them contended that "after Theodore Dreiser he is without doubt the most powerful representative of American realism."[74] The special nature of Fast's realism was its "organic fusion of the political and the personal theme," which enabled him to "show the full richness and complexity" of the lives of his characters.[75] The author's "richness and complexity" were of course restricted to an ideologically acceptable sphere. There is less than meets the eye in a statement like the following: "Howard Fast is one of those artists who in every way, in even the smallest experiences of life, try to disclose their connections with the

[70] V. Rubin, "Howard Fast's New Novel," *New Times*, No. 39 (1954), p. 28.

[71] L. Yakovlev, "Novy roman Govarda Fasta," *Literaturnaya gazeta*, March 23, 1954, p. 4.

[72] Toper, "Rasskazy Govarda Fasta," *op.cit.*, p. 212.

[73] Miller-Budnitskaya, "Kniga o prestupleniyakh . . . ," *op.cit.*, pp. 180-81.

[74] Smirnov, "Doroga svobody," *op.cit.*, p. 188.

[75] Sergei Lvov, "Ideinost i masterstvo," *Literaturnaya gazeta*, April 9, 1955, p. 4.

fundamental lines that permeate the motley variety of life phenomena." For such statements were invariably accompanied by qualifications like this one: "A naturalistic depiction of facts has never attracted him; he considers it his problem to discover their meaning from the point of view of great social destinies. . . ."[76]

Fast pleased the critics not only because of his Marxist view of American history, the bouquets he threw to the Communist Party, and the political inclination and relevance of his novels and stories of contemporary America, but also for the notions of aesthetics that governed his writing. They thought him to be, among other things, a genuine theoretician of "socialist realism." His book of essays *Literature and Reality* (1950) was hailed as a "major event in the history of American literature and an important achievement of the international progressive literary movement as well."[77] The book was translated into Russian, quoted, and paraphrased repeatedly in Soviet journals. Anna Elistratova pointed out that while reactionary critics had "tried repeatedly to represent Socialist realism as a trend that can exist only in the Soviet Union," Fast's study proved that "the rise and development of Socialist realism in the contemporary progressive literature of the capitalist world is firmly rooted in historical conditions."[78] Now, Fast had "defined a path for socialist realism in America."[79] Moreover, he led by example. Since the framework of the old "critical realism" was "confining for him," he could not limit himself to a mere indictment of capitalism, but must also show the "progressive democratic ideal," relying heavily, of course, on the experience of Russian classical literature and especially of Soviet literature.[80]

The fullest single assessment of Fast as a socialist realist came from Elistratova, who pointed out that: ". . . this striv-

[76] Toper, "Rasskazy Govarda Fasta," *op.cit.*, p. 213.

[77] Anna Elistratova, "Howard Fast—Writer and Critic," *Soviet Literature*, No. 5 (1955), p. 162.

[78] *ibid.*, p. 163.

[79] Toper, "Pravda vostorzhestvuyet," *op.cit.*, p. 188.

[80] Anikst, *Progressivnyi amerikanski pisatel Govard Fast, op.cit.*, p. 28.

ing to portray man's growth in the struggle with his social environment, to embrace reality with all its numerous and multiform relationships and contradictions, in whose development all historical progress is rooted, has enabled Fast to achieve in his writing an integrity and lyrical quality which were lacking in the American realistic novel for a long time. The details of the hero's surroundings and of his relations with other people are woven into the fabric and are deeply relevant to the logic of the story. Fast, one might say, overcomes the cult of accident which characterized the naturalistic trend in American critical realism. In his best works the accidental is no longer accidental in the real sense of the word. Specific details are charged with deep meaning; manifested in them are all the typical aspects of the people's life."[81] Like all other Soviet critics of Fast, Elistratova referred constantly to his heroes as the keystone of his socialist realism. She wrote that in his books, ". . . no matter how modest or insignificant a man's actions may seem, how tragic his fate may be or how much historical circumstances may restrict the social purport of his activities, if his actions coincide with the course of historical progress, with mankind's forward movement, nothing he has done has been done in vain."[82]

The critic Toper added that there was always an essential fiery nobility in Fast's protagonists: "No matter whom he writes about, whatever attracts his creative thought, he finds his favorite and most familiar heroes among those who honorably and uprightly, almost always in open battle, almost always with weapon in hand defend their human worth, their right to life, to freedom."[83] Most important of all, Fast apprehended his heroes as social beings, inseparable from the collective: "Fast achieves great depth of artistic generalization because he shows that his characters, despite the inimitable, distinctive features of their individual personalities, are part of the greater life of the people whose interests they come to represent and express. And it is an important feature of his

[81] Elistratova, "Howard Fast—Writer and Critic," op.cit., p. 171.
[82] ibid., p. 166.
[83] Toper, "Pravda vostorzhestvuyet," op.cit., p. 183.

realism that he strives to depict this process of the individual's growing unity with the struggle of the masses, his deepening comprehension and awareness of social interests which he at last comes to identify with his own."[84] The ability to project his characters on a social plane, the critics contended, sprang from Fast's deep knowledge of the psychology, behavior, and aspirations of the masses. This knowledge provided artistic strength, for he was able "in few words, without resounding phrases, without special plot contrivances, in clear and expressive language, with captivating pungency and sincerity, to transmit the thoughts and feelings of the workers, who struggle for freedom."[85] It also enabled him to discern "the creative and constructive energy latent in the masses," so that "for the first time in the history of American literature considerable attention is paid to the role of the masses in bringing about social changes."[86] Because his fiction portrayed them as feeling and behaving not as they actually do but as Soviet critics *wanted* them to, Fast possessed a "profound knowledge" of the American masses!

Positive heroes, the most essential ingredient in a work of socialist realism, were abundant in Fast's writings. Gideon Jackson of *Freedom Road*, a slave who becomes the leader of a racially integrated South Carolina farm community and a Representative in the United States Congress, was considered a masterpiece, since the author shows how "an illiterate Negro acquires knowledge, begins to see life not only on the scale of his little village, but also on the scale of the whole country."[87] *Silas Timberman*, which received the supreme compliment of being compared to Gorky's *Mother*,[88] contained a "brilliant and full-blooded image of a positive hero" that was without precedent in American literature.[89] At times the

[84] Elistratova, "Howard Fast—Writer and Critic," *op.cit.*, p. 167.

[85] Motyleva, "Cherty . . . ," *op.cit.*, p. 209.

[86] Elistratova, "Howard Fast—Writer and Critic," *op.cit.*, p. 168.

[87] Mendelson, "Amerikanskaya progressivnaya literatura . . . ," *op.cit.*, pp. 179-80; Smirnov, "Doroga svobody," *op.cit.*, p. 191.

[88] Elistratova, "Howard Fast—Writer and Critic," *op.cit.*, p. 170.

[89] Yel. Romanova, "Novy roman Govarda Fasta," *Literaturnaya gazeta*, October 2, 1954, p. 4.

author was guilty of slightly "idealizing" such "bourgeois democrats" as Washington, Tom Paine, John P. Altgeld in the novel *The American,* and even Gideon Jackson.[90] And in his play "Thirty Pieces of Silver," the account of a man who allows himself to collaborate with the FBI by falsely denouncing an acquaintance, one critic failed to find the requisite hero.[91] Another critic pointed out, however, that when the betrayer's wife learns of his act she breaks with him and thus, in her way, becomes a positive heroine by embodying the "awakening of the American people's latent forces of resistance to Fascist reaction."[92]

Clearly the Russians felt that in Fast they had found a writer who could clothe a correct ideology in aesthetically respectable and attractive garb. As in the case of many ideologically pleasing Americans who had preceded him in Soviet favor, however, he occasionally gave rise to aesthetic misgivings. One critic who praised him for his "brevity of exposition, dynamism of dialogue, and rapid development of plot" nevertheless added that "it cannot be denied that the thinker has occasionally outstripped the artist. . . ."[93] Writing of *Silas Timberman,* another critic paid him a left-handed compliment by noting, approvingly, that "Fast will not be daunted by reproaches of concessions to newspaper style."[94] *The Passion of Sacco and Vanzetti,* which is more a pamphlet than fiction, was "in many respects more convincing" than *Silas Timberman* for this very reason.[95] Without ever admitting it, several critics seem to have perceived that Fast was very similar to Upton Sinclair, since in the works of both it was often difficult to distinguish between art and journalism. They exhibited no more enthusiasm for his fiction, for exam-

[90] Anikst, *Progressivnyi amerikanski pisatel Govard Fast, op.cit.,* p. 28.

[91] Yu. Kovalev, "Tsena predatelstva," *Zvezda,* No. 1 (1952), p. 175.

[92] Elistratova, "Two Plays . . . ," *op.cit.,* p. 172.

[93] Toper, "Rasskazy Govarda Fasta," *op.cit.,* p. 213.

[94] Rubin, "Howard Fast's New Novel," *op.cit.,* p. 31.

[95] Toper, "Rasskazy Govarda Fasta," *op.cit.,* p. 213.

ple, than they did for *Peekskill, U.S.A.* in which "reportage becomes genuine art."[96]

The critic Toper observed that in *Peekskill, U.S.A.* and *The Passion of Sacco and Vanzetti* Fast had employed the weapon of satire to good effect, and suggested that satire might have improved *Clarkton*, in which the author had indulged in "such improbable and false psychologizing that it confused the composition and idea of the whole novel."[97] Other works of Fast were found to suffer, occasionally, from this same defect of "excessive naturalism." In dwelling on certain dark aspects of the behavior of underprivileged children in his early story "The Children," Fast had given evidence that he "unconsciously admires the forces engendered by the [social] jungles."[98] And in *Spartacus* he had given a "disproportionately large place" to the "morbidly drawn-out experiences of wealthy Romans."[99] For a writer as universally admired as Fast, however, such mistakes were considered as peccadilloes.

His only serious transgression, which seems to have been duly recorded by the critics and promptly forgotten for the time being, was the novel of ancient Judea, *My Glorious Brothers.* Tamara Motyleva called it a "false, entirely fictitious description," in which "the living truth is replaced by sentimental rhetoric." In portraying this community of Jews as an "idyllic patriarchal democracy" he had propagated "harmful notions of 'supraclass' bourgeois nationalism."[100] The critic Mendelson observed sarcastically that Fast had characterized the "yearning of the Hebrew landlords for peace and freedom as something completely unique in the ancient world."[101] In the light of the anti-Semitism and anti-Zionism

[96] Miller-Budnitskaya, "Kniga o prestupleniyakh . . . ," *op.cit.*, p. 181. See also N. Veniaminov, "Volya k borbe," *Zvezda*, No. 1 (1952), p. 177.

[97] Toper, "Rasskazy Govarda Fasta," *op.cit.*, p. 214.

[98] Urnov, "Khovard Fast i Amerika," *op.cit.*, p. 171.

[99] T. Motyleva, "Progressivnye pisateli—bortsy za mir," *Novy mir*, No. 2 (1953), p. 261.

[100] Motyleva, "Cherty . . . ," *op.cit.*, p. 210.

[101] Mendelson, "Amerikanskaya progressivnaya literatura . . . ," *op.cit.*, p. 180.

that were rampant in the USSR, it is not surprising that neither this work nor any other work of Fast primarily devoted to Jews was published in Russia.

On the whole the reservations in regard to Fast were quite minor and did not dampen either the critics' or the public's enthusiasm for him. The Russians should have been at least slightly prepared, however, for his bombshell announcement in February 1957, that "I am neither anti-Soviet nor anti-Communist, but I cannot work and write in the Communist movement."[102] Word of his resignation from the Communist Party by this, the leading "progressive" writer of the United States, was followed a month later by an article in *Mainstream* in which he attacked the Soviet system as "socialism without morality," described passionately his disillusionment with communism, deplored the absence of genuine civil rights and liberties in Russia, pointed to Soviet restrictions on freedom of artistic creation, and proclaimed his knowledge of anti-Semitism in the USSR.[103]

The ostensible Soviet reaction to Fast's dramatic defection was one of stunned silence. For seven months not a word was printed about his repudiation of the Communist faith; his books still circulated and his plays continued to be performed on the Soviet stage. (He ceased receiving mail from Russia, however, three days after his announcement.)[104] Clearly the Soviet government and its literary officials were shocked, for Fast had been a consistent and staunch apologist for the Soviet Union, had gone to jail for his beliefs, and had been celebrated in Russia as no other living American writer. His defection was not easily accepted. Finally in August 1957 came the long-delayed but inevitable denunciation. In an article entitled "Desertion under Fire" the *Literary Gazette* proclaimed that he had made a "malicious and slanderous attack on the Soviet Union," based on "borrowed false arguments and libelous methods."[105] Much more violent and deci-

---

[102] *New York Times*, February 1, 1957.
[103] Howard Fast, "My Decision," *Mainstream* (March 1957), pp. 29-38.
[104] *The New York Times Magazine*, June 9, 1957.
[105] "Dezirtirstvo pod ognem," *Literaturnaya gazeta*, August 24, 1957.

sive abuse came in January 1958, when the same newspaper devoted nearly one third of its space to a thorough hymn of hatred for the writer that alternated between lofty indifference, icy contempt, condescending sarcasm, and the bitter invective of the betrayed. The attack, obviously designed as a crowning blow, was totally political, and dismissed Fast as a "fellow not without talent in the realm of artistic work" who "never has been capable of strong, logical thought." As for the writer's personal ideology: "In the weakness of his faith, and also of his historical and social perception, Howard Fast decided to draw together, in a convenient but contradictory union, Karl Marx with Jesus Christ and Charles Darwin with the Gospel of St. Luke, tried to view the struggle of the working class through the smoky incense of Sunday services and to envisage its power in genuflexions and prayers." In the process he had become a "revisionist," a "right-opportunist," a "worshiper of the capitalist order," and a "deserter" who had sold out to Wall Street. The fact was that "Howard Fast is not a Marxist, not an internationalist, but a militant Zionist. . . ."[106]

Fast's own reply to this attack included the following remarks about the *Literary Gazette*: "For many years, this organ has been the craven and willing tool of the party leaders in their war against free expression in the arts and in their war to subjugate independent thinking among all writers of Russia."[107] The *Literary Gazette* had been for ten years the chief Soviet publisher of Howard Fast's journalism.

Fast's departure was merely one spectacular incident in the near-disintegration of the Communist Party of the United States that took place in the 1950's. This breakup was the result of a combination of developments that included severe repressive measures by the Federal government, sharp factional disputes within the Party itself, and the shocked reaction of American Communists to Khrushchev's speech before the 20th Party Congress in February 1956, in which

---

[106] N. Gribachev, "Govard Fast—psalomshchik revizionizma," *Literaturnaya gazeta*, January 30, 1958.
[107] *The New York Times*, February 1, 1958.

he admitted for the record many of the iniquities and weaknesses of the Soviet system. The distress of Communists in the United States was further complicated by the anti-Soviet uprisings in Poland and Hungary in the fall of 1956 and by the bloody suppression of the Hungarian revolt.

In a sincere but confused and rather pitiful testament, *The Naked God*, which he published in 1957, Fast detailed his honest disillusionment with communism and disclosed, far more authentically than any outside observer could, the motives of his defection. Nevertheless the Russians, unwilling to allow their former literary ally to sink quietly into oblivion in the Soviet Union, preferred to place the most dire interpretation on his career. In 1956, before Fast broke with communism, the critic Toper had noted, with sympathetic interest, the frequency of the image of Judas in his works.[108] In 1958 another critic alleged the existence in the Soviet Union of an unpublished manuscript of a novel, written in 1953, in which Fast told the story of a Communist writer who had sold out to become a hireling of capitalist reaction. The conclusion was obvious: Fast had realized years ago that he would eventually betray his comrades, had outlined his own Judas role in this novel, and was now performing it.[109]

It was impossible for the Russians to explain Fast's defection as anything but a betrayal. The Soviet literary world had made a heavy moral, emotional, and even financial investment in the author. (He was one of the few translated writers who received Soviet royalties, and his Stalin Peace Prize had been munificent.) The public adulation and official honors that had been given him, together with the wide publication of his books, constituted a serious commitment which could not be repudiated without great embarrassment and chagrin.

Since the early thirties Soviet critics had been urging Americans to create a militant literature that would inspire hatred for the enemies of communism and infect readers in the capitalist world with revolutionary sympathies. The class-

---

[108] Toper, "Rasskazy Govarda Fasta," *op.cit.*, p. 212.

[109] Boris Izakov, "Dve ispovedi Govarda Fasta," *Inostrannaya literatura*, No. 2 (1958), pp. 214-20.

conscious writers of the proletarian movement of the thirties, in spite of warm encouragement and advice from Russia, had been disappointing. Aesthetically the movement had accomplished little, and politically it had lost its impetus with the termination of the Depression and the onset of the Second World War. A few holdovers from the Depression period, such as Maltz, had continued to produce acceptable fiction of approximate ideological correctness. Not until their discovery of Fast, however, had the Russians found an American who conformed so closely to their political and aesthetic demands that they could embrace him wholeheartedly.

Except for a few annoying tendencies, Fast had all the qualities they desired in a contemporary writer. His historical novels and fictional biographies were based on Marxist concepts and followed closely the Soviet scheme for interpreting American history, and their contemporary relevance was clear and obvious. His novels, set in the present, involved precisely the topics which Soviet propagandists wanted most to exploit, and he treated these topics with close fidelity to the current Party line. Like the critical realists, he inspired indignation against a decadent capitalist world, but he went beyond them by featuring the progressive struggle against reaction. His works contained the requisite optimism. Although his protagonists suffered painful defeats, his narratives were infused with a faith in the ultimate triumph of the forces of revolution. Fast's practice of affirming a sense of inevitable victory through the portrayal of a heroic defeat followed the concept of "optimistic tragedy," which is one of the major propositions of socialist realism.

Fast fulfilled the prescription of socialist realism more exactly than any other American author. As a writer, however, he was not worthy of the extreme praise which Soviet critics heaped upon him in the period of his greatest popularity. He resembles many commercially successful writers of slick fiction in his talent for smooth and swift narration and deft, if superficial and schematic, characterization. His books have sold well in the United States, many of them in the juvenile market. The main quality that sets him off from dozens of popular but shallow contemporaries is his powerful social conscience. A skillful storyteller with a gift for political rhetoric, he was adequate to his task of conveying the Party message in a lucid, dramatic manner. As a result, his books were effective political vehicles, but they lacked psychological, intellectual, and ideological profundity. These very characteristics made Fast a fitting candidate for the schedule of literary activity which the Russians urged upon him. The fact that he could defect overnight, despite such careful cultivation and such precise adherence to the schedule, is an excellent illustration of the blindness and bankruptcy of Soviet literary policies of the 1950's.

CHAPTER XII

ERNEST HEMINGWAY

ᒫᒫᒫ ERNEST HEMINGWAY was first published in Russia in 1934. His rise to popularity was so rapid that in 1937, when the editors of a Russian literary magazine asked fifteen leading Soviet writers to name their favorite non-Russian author, nine of them named Hemingway. There were no new Soviet printings of his books from 1939 to 1955, and during the last ten years of this period, largely because of the tensions of the cold war, he was rarely mentioned in the Soviet press. Yet Russian readers have always ranked him high among Western authors, and today his works are once more openly and warmly lauded. His death in July 1961 was reported by the Soviet press with great sorrow and deep respect.

Prior to 1934, Hemingway had been practically unknown in Russia. A small circle of professionals had heard of his growing international reputation, and a few of them had read him in English. In the absence of translations, however, the general impression of him was vague, and he was usually cited merely as a symbol of "decadence" in contrast to the "revolutionary" Dos Passos. But by 1934, following the cultural famine of the First Five Year Plan, Soviet editors and publishers had decided that the time was ripe to expose the Russian reader to Hemingway.

This was done in three ways in that year. First, a work of his appeared in an anthology of American short stories. Second, his stories began to come out in magazines. Finally, a collection made up of selections from four of his books was published under the title *Death in the Afternoon*.[1] From then until 1939, his stories were printed with great frequency in Soviet magazines. *The Sun Also Rises* was published in 1935, and in 1936 the first of four editions of *A Farewell to Arms* came out. *To Have and Have Not* was translated in 1938, and was followed by a volume entitled *The Fifth Column and*

---

[1] This book had little in common with the American edition published under the same title.

the First Thirty-Eight Stories in 1939. There were also several serial publications of the novels in these years.

The sudden publication of Hemingway in 1934, several years after his American reputation had been established, indicates that the Russian discovery of the author was calculated. Hemingway was an active anti-Fascist, and the Soviet Union was particularly anxious to lend a helping hand to those whom it considered its potential friends. Although he was certainly aware of their interest in him, and corresponded with one of their best critics, Ivan Kashkin, Hemingway remained immune to the Russians' blandishments. Nevertheless, the Russians stated their case with extreme thoroughness. Not only did Soviet editors turn out carefully translated editions of Hemingway; they also encouraged literary critics to examine him meticulously. In the course of six years, in dozens of articles, these critics devised an interpretation of his career which was intended both to explain his deficiencies and to encourage his leftward growth.

According to the tenets of socialist realism, a writer must approach his art as a materialist, a rational optimist, and a collectivist. He must be firmly anticapitalist in his political convictions, and must dedicate his writing, either implicitly or by direct appeal, to revolutionary socialism. Consequently, his themes must be clearly social, and his heroes must be socially engaged. These "positive heroes" must act upon the conviction that man, and not some external force, shapes the collective destiny by understanding his physical and social environment and by reshaping it. Examining Hemingway from this point of view, Soviet critics found that his most notable characteristic was a development away from individualism, pessimism, and the aimless cultivation of artistic craftsmanship—toward collectivism, optimism, and the dedication of his art to socially constructive ends. According to their scheme, his attitudes were first of all a product of his experiences in the First World War. Here was the genesis of the themes which were to run through most of his works to 1936: an obsession with death, and a consequent feeling of hopelessness, fatalism, and passivity; an attitude of disillusionment, characterized by a hurt, defensive mistrust of ideals and a general skepticism; an attitude of political and social indifference, in which the only values are individual values; and concentration on the various means of flight from reality.

Soviet critics were particularly fascinated by his treatment of death. Comparing him to Ambrose Bierce in this respect, the critic Nemerovskaya wrote: "War impregnated him with hopeless pessimism, war prompted in him a terror in the face of death. . . . Despair before the impotence of life is interwoven with despair before the all-powerfulness of death. War is not an arena for heroism, for the snatching of glory for self and country; it is a struggle for the preservation of one's life, for the overcoming of one's own fear of death."[2] And the critic Miller-Budnitskaya found that "fear of death is the key to Hemingway's entire personal and creative biography, to his whole system of images and style."[3] This fixation drove the artist to fruitless self-laceration, a kind of grim game in which he sedulously sought out situations, both in his life and in his art, in which to face the horror of death and to struggle with it. This accounted for his passion for bullfighting, big game hunting, and violent sports, and for exploring the details of the death process, as in "The Snows of Kilimanjaro" and *To Have and Have Not.*[4]

But the obsession with death was only part of a larger composite of desolation in Hemingway. Accompanying this morbid, vigorous probing at the ultimate terror was a feeling of futility, an all-embracing attitude of indifference and passivity. The critic Abramov pointed out that his "rough, athletic style" and the "masculinity" of his themes were a mask covering a "weariness, skepticism, spiritual and artistic impotence."[5] Kashkin argued that his tremendous mental and

[2] Olga Nemerovskaya, "Sudba amerikanskoi novelly," *Literaturnaya uchyoba*, No. 5 (1935), p. 102.

[3] R. Miller-Budnitskaya in O. Berestov, "Vecher E. Khemingueya," *Rezets*, No. 7 (1939), p. 24.

[4] Olga Nemerovskaya, "V poiskakh geroizma," *Znamya*, No. 6 (1938), p. 277.

[5] Al. Abramov, "Molodost veka," *Internatsionalnaya literatura*, No. 6 (1935), p. 141.

physical energy, in combination with his emotional and intellectual pessimism, had created the peculiar synthesis of a full-blooded zest for the acts of living within an omnipresent consciousness of morbid futility. And as this attitude continued to develop, Kashkin declared, "It has become increasingly clear that his vigor is pretended, that it is dissipated by him and by his heroes little by little. Hemingway's sharpness of sight has led up to this, that as the most deformed and terrible qualities in man appeared in his writing, it became all the more clear that his vigor is the aimless vigor of a man trying in vain not to think, that his virility is the aimless virility of a despair, that Hemingway all the more inexorably seizes upon the temptation of death, that again and again he writes only of the end—the end of relationships, the end of life, the end of hope and everything. . . . Strength itself, unapplied and unnecessary, becomes a weakness and a burden. . . . Action turns into its reverse, into the passive pose of the stoic, into the courage of despair."[6]

The war affected Hemingway even more strongly, the Russians felt, by shattering his personal and social beliefs. Perceiving the senselessness of the war, he was shocked by the human degradation it involved—the destruction of the dignity of the individual and the feeling of moral and intellectual emptiness it left with those who had experienced it. An equally important shock was his return, with heightened sensitivity, to the spiritually empty bourgeois world. The necessity of returning to life in these decadent surroundings, so the Soviet interpretation goes, solidified the feeling of moral devastation in the author. Acutely perceiving the ugliness and purposelessness of existence under the conditions of capitalism, he became the prey of a chronic and bottomless skepticism, denying all ideals, and insisting on the futility of value judgments. In his writing this feeling took the form of a pose of ironic indifference, of an unwillingness to go beneath the surface of things, a mistrust of emotions, passions, and speculative thought. Endowed with an appetite for

[6] I. Kashkeen, "Ernest Hemingway: A Tragedy of Craftsmanship," *International Literature*, No. 5 (1935), p. 75.

the joys of living and an acute sense of beauty, he had become spiritually stupefied in perceiving the hollowness of the
postwar world. ". . . he passionately loves life, because life—
for all its deformity and unhappiness—is nevertheless beautiful and gives man an inexhaustible source of delight and
joy. But these pleasures are poisoned, since bourgeois society is a rotten swamp, in which natural feelings and aspirations become putrefied."[7] As a result, his outlook was one of
tense reluctance to give himself up to pleasure and healthy
emotion, for fear that it was all a lie, that through it he
might become a prisoner of the general slow death about him.
This had its effect on the development of his writing technique: "The unique objective manner of Hemingway, his
conscious dispassionate fixation of facts and his stinginess of
detail, which he has brought to the level of a high technique,
arose from the soil of his disillusioned, skeptical consciousness. This is characteristic of the crisis of contemporary bourgeois thought in general, which is more inclined toward the
empirical stating of facts than to their explanation and generalization. Devoid of genuine pathos, unfulfilled by any personal emotional participation of the author in the world he
describes, it leads to spiritless, passionless, artistic glitter,
which does not move or infect the reader and impresses one
only by its splendid craftsmanship. But behind this craftsmanship is heard the voice of a despondent skeptic, weary of his
own skepticism, but knowing no means of overcoming it."[8]

Kashkin pointed out that the feeling of hopelessness in
Hemingway was not accompanied by a loss of ideals or integrity. Instead, it had driven him to individualism: "Not to
save the world, but to see it and to remake at least a tiny part
of it, that's what Hemingway wants and calls upon others to
do. *Il faut cultiver notre jardin*, he seems to repeat after Can-
dide, and as his aim he selects the attainment of craftsmanship."[9] Within this narrowed perspective which Hemingway
defensively set for himself, he had become preoccupied with

[7] Nemerovskaya, "V poiskakh . . . ," p. 276.
[8] Nemerovskaya, "Sudba . . . ," p. 104.
[9] Kashkeen, "Ernest Hemingway . . . ," p. 78.

problems of literary style. He had developed a passion for simplicity, but in the process of simplification his writing had grown capricious and cynical. He had begun presenting death, horror, and perversion in such primitive tones that his pseudo-simplicity had developed into a desperate complication. He had devoted his energies to art for art's sake, and had reached the point of frustration and perpetual floundering.

A corollary of this stunned suspension of belief and emotion was his indifference to political and social problems. For the author had purposely constricted his field of vision to protect himself from the possibility of further shocks. As a realist, he could not avoid reflecting the objective facts of twentieth-century civilization in his writing. There was a backdrop of war, revolution, and social unrest in his stories. These phenomena, however, were not important in themselves, but served merely as devices for underlining the feeling of personal disillusionment which he sought to project. Of his treatment of war in *A Farewell to Arms*, Nemerovskaya writes: "Hemingway perceived war through separate military episodes, through the single persons with whom he came into direct contact. He did not and did not want to look into the reasons for the rise of war, he did not look for the real hero of military action—the massed millions of soldiers who were transformed into cannon fodder."[10] And the critic Dinamov complained that the love story occupied too large a place in the novel, since it did not permit the author "to turn to more significant phenomena."[11]

Another sign of Hemingway's fundamental lack of concern with large social problems was his concentration on the theme of isolation and flight. His heroes all repudiated society, considering themselves as something apart from the world about them. They refused to relate their problems to those of the rest of humanity, and tried to solve them as individuals. Of the hero of *A Farewell to Arms* the critic Mingulina complained that ". . . Fred Henry is an enemy of im-

[10] Nemerovskaya, "V poiskakh . . . ," p. 275.

[11] S. Dinamov, "Roman Khemingueya o voine." *Internatsionalnaya literatura*, No. 7 (1936), p. 165.

perialist war, but he does not stop to consider the possibility of fighting against it. Henry is a 'passive' pacifist. He deserts not only from the front, he deserts from society and tries to win from fate only his own personal happiness."[12] Another critic pointed out that Hemingway's heroes flee from thought itself: "Behind the insistent attention of Hemingway's heroes to little, everyday details there hides a fear of everything that is important, fundamental, and decisive. People are afraid to recall anything grave or terrifying; they fear thought as they would fear an unbearable pain."[13] Even the "healthy" tendencies in his writing sprang from the urge to escape, since "the proclivity for nature, for sports—has led him along the path of severance from the world which surrounds him."[14]

Despite their distress over these motifs of pessimism, disillusionment, fear, and flight, Soviet critics saw many good things in Hemingway's art of this period. In the blackest, most despairing and passive of his attitudes, they perceived strong strains of hardihood, honesty, courage, and clear vision, and a passionate longing for truth and beauty. They admired his deep, persistent, unchanging honesty in facing the problems with which he tortured himself. His heroes might try to run away from reality, but the tragic dispassionateness with which the author comprehended their fruitless attempts to escape bespoke a firm resolve not to delude himself. Beneath the skepticism and seeming indifference, the critics observed a moral bravery and integrity, and an intellectual perseverance that compelled admiration. As one critic stated it: "The force of all of Hemingway's works is precisely in the bravery which is welded to his despair, in the fact that he does not give in to his despair, but finds within it the ability to struggle against it."[15] Another wrote: "Depicting even the most tragic moments in human life, he is able to show the health

[12] A. Mingulina, "Ernest Kheminguei," *Kniga i proletarskaya revolyutsiya*, No. 8 (1937), p. 125.
[13] Ya. Frid, "Rasskazy Khemingueya," *Literaturnoye obozreniye*, No. 18 (1939), p. 49.
[14] Nemerovskaya in Berestov, *op.cit.*, p. 24.
[15] Adimoni in Berestov, *op.cit.*, p. 24.

in man, his belief in the worth of humanity, of which there is so little in Western European literature."[16]

Allied to these qualities of courage and integrity was a largeness of soul. With his vigorous love of life and his haunting dread of death, he understood well the dignity and nobility of human passions and suffering. This quality led the critic Startsev to remark with deep respect on his treatment of the love story in *A Farewell to Arms*,[17] and caused the writer Kaverin to observe that he was "one of the most tender of writers," although his prose was genuinely masculine.[18] Others remarked on his democratic sentiments and his thirst for justice.[19] And even Dinamov, who was particularly fond of accusing American authors of "selling out," found that Hemingway, though "a victim of the bourgeois world," was nevertheless an honorable writer.[20]

In this period of his writing Hemingway was considered the prisoner of a destructive ideology. Yet he had a strong insight into the nature of bourgeois society. Thus, *A Farewell to Arms* was "not a patriotic bourgeois book," since it demonstrated the folly of imperialist war.[21] Likewise, his high intelligence and instinctively healthy sense of human values prevented him from becoming a party to the decadence of the "lost generation." Kashkin asserts that he was "at one and the same time a part of the lost generation and above it,"[22] that he was "internally hostile" to it, despised its Bohemianism, and after a period of experimentation, had even repudiated the decadent influence of its literary gods.[23] Another critic pointed out that his interest in nature and sports was

---

[16] A. Korneichuk, "Literatura velikovo amerikanskovo naroda," *Internatsionalnaya literatura*, Nos. 7-8 (1939), p. 236.

[17] A. Startsev, "Novoye dekadentstvo," *Literaturnaya gazeta*, October 20, 1936.

[18] V. Kaverin in Berestov, *op.cit.*, p. 23.

[19] Konst. Fedin, "O knigakh Khemingueya," *Internatsionalnaya literatura*, Nos. 7-8 (1939), p. 217.

[20] Dinamov, "Roman Khemingueya . . . ," p. 169.

[21] *ibid.*, p. 167.

[22] I. Kashkin, "Ernest Kheminguei," *Internatsionalnaya literatura*, Nos. 7-8 (1939), pp. 319-20.

[23] *ibid.*, p. 322.

in itself a repudiation of bourgeois society: "Hemingway likes to write about people who justify their lives in struggle, in stubborn daily competition. Despising the 'competition' of the bourgeoisie, the struggle of capital with capital, and of capital against poverty, Hemingway passionately studies those rare events in bourgeois society when only the naked abilities of people compete, their wills, intelligence, strength, skills, and sharp-sightedness. . . ."[24]

Finally, and perhaps the most important of the "positive" qualities which shone through the ideologically uncongenial works which Hemingway wrote before the middle thirties was the charm of his prose. Commenting on "The Killers" in 1934, Kashkin wrote: "The stinginess and reticence of Hemingway, which force the reader to complete the saying of that which inevitably flows out of what the author has told, his tendency to sharpen the perception of the reader, to teach him alertness, to focus his eyes to unaccustomed angles—all this demands thoughtful, creative reading. And Hemingway deserves this."[25] There were almost no objections to the effort which Hemingway demands of his readers. His disciplined, laconic, and economical narrative technique was consistently praised, by critics and writers alike. At various times he was compared to Tolstoy, Chekhov, Mayakovsky, and even Pushkin. Kashkin, who made the most thorough study of his style, stressed the variety of his verbal gifts, which made it possible for him to suggest depths of emotion and a wide range of psychological shadings through change of pace and rhythm, and through the manipulation of purely objective detail.[26] Others stressed his precision and simplicity. The writer Kaverin remarked: "In the artistic manner of Hemingway one is struck by one point—accuracy, not only the astonishing accuracy of description, but the unusual faithfulness of intonation in the transmission of the most intimate things."[27] His seemingly reticent, dispassionate manner was

[24] Frid, p. 49.
[25] Ivan Kashkin, "Dve novelly Khemingueya," *Internatsionalnaya literatura*, No. 1 (1934), p. 93.
[26] Kashkin, "Ernest Kheminguei," pp. 321-22.
[27] Kaverin in Berestov, *op.cit.*, p. 23.

found to be capable of extraordinarily sharp and powerful dramatic effects. Perhaps the greatest tribute to Hemingway as a craftsman was made by the critic who said, simply: "Hemingway describes descending a mountain on skis with amazing plasticity—not a single contemporary prose writer has told about movement with such precision, energy, grace, and simplicity."[28]

It might be concluded, despite the obvious fondness for Hemingway, that Soviet critics would consider him hopelessly mired in a doomed ideology, destined to end his days as a prisoner of his own sensitivity. But when Soviet criticism saw worth in a writer, it was always eager to prescribe solutions for his psychological and ideological problems. So it was in the case of Hemingway. In spite of their distress at his subjectivity and his passive attitude toward the social, economic, and political problems of the world he so loathed, they saw hope in his freedom from bourgeois ideals. The key to his dilemma, they contended, was his self-absorption. The prescription was clear. He must cease his personal brooding over insoluble problems and employ his marvelous energy and intelligence and his high sensitivity to questions which *were*, in Soviet opinion, capable of solution. He must transform his concern over individual destiny into a concern for social destiny.

The critic Grinberg discussed the tragic lovers of *A Farewell to Arms*, with their dream of simple, sequestered happiness, and remarked that Hemingway should understand that "besides these little and unattainable dreams there exists a large dream which will be attained, a large dream which will win out in battle."[29] Miller-Budnitskaya wrote that: "The tragedy of Hemingway the artist is in his huge longing to create an epic art and his inability to find genuine material for it in his surroundings. . . . The epic art of the twentieth century cannot be built on the material of the imperialist war of 1914 or of future wars of the peoples of the capitalist world. This is because one of the indispensable prerequisites

[28] Frid, p. 48.
[29] I. Grinberg, "Chto zhe dalshe?" *Zvezda*, No. 3 (1937), p. 190.

of a great epos and the great theme of the most powerful epic creations of the past is the struggle for social revolution."[30] Dinamov felt that one of Hemingway's chief difficulties was the inability to find a positive hero, since the class which he stubbornly persisted in writing about—the bourgeoisie—was incapable of supplying such a hero.[31] Again, the solution was obvious: "A remarkable master of detail, a fine observer of particulars, an attentive investigator of the little lives of empty people—Hemingway in the name of art must tear himself away from the bourgeois world."[32]

Soviet critics first saw the symptoms of ideological change in Hemingway in activities that were not precisely literary. In 1935 he wrote a bitter article for *New Masses*, concerning the responsibility of the United States government for the deaths of unemployed war veterans whom it had sent to the Florida Keys in hurricane months. The article was immediately translated and printed in the Russian edition of *International Literature*, with the following editorial footnote: "We insert the article by Ernest Hemingway as one of the most important documents of the development of revolutionary literature in America. Hemingway—the most powerful American writer—has never taken part in any sort of social action of writers and has consciously stood aside from the revolutionary movement."[33] The critic Silman remarked approvingly that Hemingway was beginning to release himself from the shackles of "absolute neutrality" by seeking ways of effective protest against bourgeois society.[34]

The first artistic evidence of fundamental change in Hem-

[30] R. Miller-Budnitskaya, "Ernest Kheminguei," *Internatsionalnaya literatura*, No. 6 (1937), p. 219. For a discussion between Edmund Wilson and the Russians on this point, see Kashkeen, "Ernest Hemingway . . . ," *op.cit.*, and Edmund Wilson, "Pismo sovetskim chitatelyam o Khemingueye," *Internatsionalnaya literatura*, No. 2 (1936), pp. 151-54.

[31] Dinamov, "Roman Khemingueya . . . ," p. 169.

[32] *ibid.*, p. 170.

[33] Footnote to title of Hemingway's "Kto ubil veteranov voiny vo Floride?" *Internatsionalnaya literatura*, No. 12 (1935), p. 56.

[34] T. Silman, "Ernest Kheminguei," *Literaturny sovremennik*, No. 3 (1936), pp. 181-82.

ingway, however, came in 1937,[35] with the American publication of *To Have and Have Not*. Soviet critics stressed that here, for the first time, the author had decisively come to grips with economic and social problems and had taken pains to point out sharp class contrasts,[36] although one reviewer felt that he had done this somewhat "mechanically."[37] All critics perceived that the hero of this novel, Harry Morgan, was less individualistic than Hemingway's previous heroes. Unlike his predecessors, Harry faces problems which are basically economic, brought on by the depression in the America of the thirties. The critic Platonov felt that Harry displayed most of the traits of a real proletarian hero, and Nemerovskaya tentatively suggested that he might even be considered a "positive hero."[38] There was a major shortcoming, however: "He lacks the ability to seek his salvation in cooperation with other proletarians. . . . He does not have enough of that which cognizant proletarians have—an understanding that one must ally oneself with all workingmen."[39] Kashkin insisted that Hemingway was still lost in his "pessimistic blind alley."[40] Nemerovskaya agreed: "To his general dissatisfaction with capitalistic reality, Hemingway has added a protest against the social order. But this protest, which discloses no perspective, remains sterile and merely aggravates the pessimistic character of his work. The novel *To Have and Have Not* belongs among his most gloomy and hopeless

---

[35] Two critics in 1939 looked back to the stories, "The Short Happy Life of Francis Macomber" and "The Snows of Kilimanjaro," both published in 1936, and found evidence of impending change. Kashkin, "Ernest Kheminguei," *op.cit.*, p. 330 and Frid, *op.cit.*, p. 51.

[36] V. Druzin, "V poiskakh nastoyashchevo cheloveka," *Rezets*, No. 18 (1938), p. 22; Nemerovskaya, "V poiskakh . . . ," p. 286; Kashkin, "Ernest Kheminguei," p. 329; Frid, p. 51.

[37] "Ot redaktsii," *Internatsionalnaya literatura*, No. 4 (1938), p. 23. This was the only reviewer who objected strongly to the book on aesthetic grounds. Druzin took issue with this review, and contended that "in the Soviet press this novel has received unanimously positive evaluation." Druzin, *op.cit.*, p. 22.

[38] Nemerovskaya, "V poiskakh . . . ," p. 278.

[39] A. Platonov, "Navstrechu lyudyam," *Literaturny kritik*, No. 11 (1938), p. 171.

[40] Kashkin, "Ernest Kheminguei," p. 329.

things."[41] Nevertheless, Kashkin felt that there was great collective significance in Harry's dying verdict that "no matter how, a man alone ain't got no bloody chance."[42] And the overwhelming number of critics shared the opinion of Kaverin: "Two points are distinctly visible in the creative path of Hemingway: *The Sun Also Rises*—this nonintervention in tragedy, and *To Have and Have Not*—an intervention in it. Gradually, just as gradually as his heroes approach the turning point in their understanding, Hemingway himself has come to an understanding of his obligation to the people, to world art."[43]

Hemingway's departure for Spain shortly after the beginning of the civil war was widely heralded in the Soviet Union. It was decided that at last he had accomplished a decisive political act, which in turn might bring about a reshaping of his art. Upon learning that he was writing a book on Spanish themes, one critic wrote: "We believe that this book will tear Hemingway away from his devastated, confused heroes. We believe that Hemingway will understand that heroism consists not in fearless single combat with bulls in a circus arena or in pursuing wild beasts in Africa. Because if Hemingway recognizes that in the present moment the duty of every honorable man, of every writer, is to raise his voice against the unbridled might of world reaction, then he will find the answer to the question which torments Jake Barnes: how to live in this world."[44]

The chief product of his experiences in Spain to reach Soviet readers, aside from his ardently anti-Fascist reportage of the conflict, was the play *The Fifth Column*. The critics reacted to this work with complete and unanimous enthusiasm.[45] One of them stressed Hemingway's understanding of

[41] Nemerovskaya, "V poiskakh . . . ," p. 286.

[42] Kashkin, "Ernest Kheminguei," p. 330.

[43] Kaverin in Berestov, *op.cit.*, p. 23.

[44] Nemerovskaya, "V poiskakh . . . ," p. 287.

[45] B. Pesis, "Pyataya kolonna," *Literaturnoye obozreniye*, No. 11 (1939), pp. 33-36; M. Bleiman, "Poeziya borby i gumanizma," *Iskusstvo i zhizn*, No. 5 (1939), pp. 15-17; A. Abramov, "Novoye v amerikanskoi dramaturgii," *Teatr*, Nos. 2-3 (1939), pp. 39-50; I. Grinberg, "Geroi

the complicated psychology of a fighter, and his appreciation of the fact that a positive ideology can be molded in a man in the process of struggle. Another wrote: "... the experiences of the past two years have taught Hemingway much, have compelled him to make a definite conclusive choice, have forced him to understand that humanity, in the face of attack by the Fascist barbarians, has, in the words of Hemingway himself, only one path—'fight, fight for the right to a life worthy of humanity.' "[46] Kashkin concluded that "the problem of the personal and the social, the anarcho-individualistic and the pacifistic, which he treated a decade ago in *A Farewell to Arms*, has taken a 180-degree turn, in correspondence with Hemingway's changed view of a new, just war. In *A Farewell to Arms*—flight from the social to the personal, here —from the personal to social duty."[47]

For Whom the Bell Tolls had not been published in the Soviet Union as of the time when the present study was completed. The novel was by no means unknown in Russia, however. The manuscript of a Russian translation had been widely circulated in the Soviet literary world, literary critics cited it with familiarity, and a few copies of the American editions could be found in public libraries. One can only speculate on the reasons for withholding its Russian publication for more than two decades. Certainly, there are serious ideological deficiencies in the book, in Soviet eyes. Its hero, Robert Jordan, has found a social cause in the fight for the Spanish Republic against fascism, and he pursues the fight with the usual Hemingway vitality. But in spite of this the feeling of cosmic purposelessness remains dominant in his nature, and Kashkin has pointed out that his death is a meaningless act of stoical sacrifice, dictated by a purely subjective code.[48] Further, the novel's pronounced disparagement of certain

---

beryotsya za oruzhiye," *Rezets*, Nos. 9-10 (1939), pp. 28-30; introduction to "Pyataya kolonna," *Internatsionalnaya literatura*, No. 1 (1939), pp. 99-100.

[46] Abramov, "Novoye . . . ," *op.cit.*, p. 39.

[47] Kashkin, "Ernest Kheminguei," *op.cit.*, p. 333.

[48] Ivan Kashkin, "Perechityvaya Khemingueya," *Inostrannaya literatura*, No. 4 (1956), p. 200.

highly placed Comintern figures would be enough to prevent its issuance in Russia. A few remarks made by the critic Mendelson in 1947 help to explain its suppression. Mendelson complained that Hemingway had proved incapable of dealing with "advanced ideas," and that he had "perverted the meaning of many of the most important events of the Civil War in Spain." He had made Jordan the protagonist of the "American ideals of agrarian democracy of the middle of the past century." Hemingway's only genuinely positive characters, according to Mendelson, were his Spanish partisans. And his treatment of André Marty and other "international fighters" was "absolutely distorted."[49]

In 1955, after a period of sixteen years in which there were no new translations of Hemingway and no reprintings, *The Old Man and the Sea* was published in the magazine *Inostrannaya Literatura*. The story created a sensation among Soviet readers; once more Hemingway was their favorite living American author. No doubt he had never lost first place in the hearts of many of them, but now the official sanction of an appearance in print made it possible to admire him openly again. Clearly this story, with its message of rugged courage and quiet, dogged heroism, held something special for them. There was disagreement, however, on what that something special was. Three students of Moscow University, presumably representative of the reading public, were inclined to accept the story primarily as a parable of unflagging bravery in the face of adversity. In an open letter to Hemingway in *Inostrannaya Literatura* they gave it this interpretation: "Everywhere people struggle for happiness, for a life worthy of man. They do not always win: they must experience both misfortune and defeat. But he who, like the old man, is capable of daily feats, who *knows how* to seize victory, does not despair after the most grievous failure. He does not despair—and continues the struggle."[50]

[49] M. Mendelson, "Amerikanskaya literatura v poiskakh obraza nastoy-ashchevo cheloveka," *Znamya*, No. 3 (1947), pp. 176-77.

[50] V. Agrikolyanski, A. Krasnovski, and D. Rachkov, "Pismo studentov Ernestu Khemingueyu," *Inostrannaya literatura*, No. 1 (1956), p. 233.

Like these students, all the critics agreed that the author
had shown deep sympathy and respect for the dignity of Santiago, his simple fisherman hero, and that Santiago's solitary
exploit against nearly impossible odds was inspiring. What
disturbed them, however, was that both Santiago's symbolic
victory in triumphing over the giant marlin and his defeat
in losing it to sharks took place in a tenuous social context.
In the words of the critic Lvov, the story contained "all the
winds of the sea," but lacked "a feeling of the winds of history."[51] The critic Drobyshevski clumsily provided an historical ingredient by reading the story of Santiago as a tragedy of man's loneliness in the capitalist world. It was an
"optimistic tragedy," since the old man, in "all the beauty
of his healthy soul and healthy body," is the kind who "will
not submit to the dollar and will not lower his head before
the cannon's mouth."[52] Lvov replied, however, that a man's
lone struggle, however valiant, is not a source of optimism:
"It seems to me that one must seek conflict in those causes
which turned the life of Santiago into a mortal combat face
to face with the elements and beasts of the sea. One must seek
conflict in the social sphere. And however the struggle ends,
this conflict will not be removed. The very circumstance that
the old man has no sort of other perspective than a naked,
primitive struggle for existence—this is the sum total of his
life. And that is the dramatic conflict between the magnificent
human qualities of Santiago and the inhuman life he lives.
Hemingway senses the existence of this conflict, but he does
not know a way out."[53]

In a retrospective article on Hemingway in 1956, Kashkin
pointed out that in this story, as in the novel *Across the River
and Into the Trees*, the writer had reemphasized his early
personal themes of fate and death. Formerly, however, he had
explored the weaknesses and vulnerability of strong people;

[51] Sergei Lvov, "Mesto cheloveka v zhizni," *Literaturnaya gazeta*, October 27, 1955, p. 2.

[52] Vladislav Drobyshevski, "Nepobedimy," *Zvezda*, No. 5 (1956), p.
166.

[53] Sergei Lvov, "Replika kritiku Vladislavu Drobyshevskomu," *Zvezda*,
No. 8 (1956), p. 189.

now he wrote of the "moral strength of a decrepit old man," and in doing so had asserted "more faith in man and respect for him." Kashkin thought it significant that although Santiago is physically defeated by circumstances of fate, his moral victory does not cost him his life. Nevertheless, there was fatalism in the old man's words to the fish: "Come on and kill me. I do not care who kills who." Brooding and closely identified with his hero, Hemingway had "directed life itself into the narrow, immediate surroundings of a lonely old man." Although he deeply admired the story, Kashkin still felt that, like the unsuccessful novel that had preceded it, this was a "muttered conversation," a fragment, an etude, an attempt to work out a limited problem—"scarcely the sum of Hemingway's reflections on postwar reality." For the writer had attempted to evade the "postwar contradictions" of the capitalist world by taking up a "pan-human theme." He still refused to write about America, and this was a silent protest against his own, now alien culture. But as long as he continued to fight shy of contemporary social problems, "his attempt to avoid looking at much, and thinking about much, limits and impoverishes his creative possibilities."[54]

Although the critics continued to deplore his isolation from social themes, his stature in Russia continued to increase. In 1960 one Soviet spokesman said that he had the "firmest and highest reputation" of all contemporary American authors in the USSR.[55] The magazine *Ogonyok* published an interview between Hemingway and one of its correspondents in Cuba,[56] and the magazine *Neva* announced its intention to publish *For Whom the Bell Tolls* in serial form.[57] Hemingway's death in July 1961 was widely mourned in the Soviet Union.

[54] Kashkin, "Perechityvaya . . . ," *op.cit.*, p. 194. These sentiments are repeated in Viktor Shklovski, "Kheminguei v yevo poiskakh ot yunosti do starosti," *Khudozhestvennaya proza: razmyshleniya i razbory*, Moscow, 1959, pp. 597-605.

[55] V. Belyaev, "Novye izdaniya amerikanskikh knig," *Inostrannaya literatura*, No. 1 (1960), p. 248.

[56] Genrikh Borovik, "U Ernesta Khemingueya," *Ogonyok*, No. 14 (April 1960), pp. 26-29.

[57] *New York Times*, February 20, 1960, p. 11.

Pravda published a tribute from the novelist Leonid Leonov,[58] and Ilya Ehrenburg, who called Hemingway his "favorite writer," appeared in a memorial broadcast on Moscow television.[59] *Izvestia* eulogized him as a "great writer and a great man."[60]

Well over a million copies of Hemingway's works, in book or periodical form, have circulated among the Soviet public. It is obviously impossible to measure accurately his impact on Russian readers as a whole. Certainly his influence extends far beyond the small circle of writers and critics whom I have cited here. Russian readers may view him from a perspective quite different from that of the professional critics, who are influenced by the ideological discipline of socialist realism and must respect the political realities of the Party line. The judgments of the critics, while interesting in themselves, may in fact present a distorted picture of the general Russian reaction to Hemingway.

Despite the critics' disapproval of his preoccupation with themes of desolation, it is probable that many readers have appreciated him precisely because he offers a forlorn picture of life. Although there has been a concerted attempt to exorcise attitudes of pessimism, disillusionment, hopelessness, and skepticism from the Soviet scene, these emotions undoubtedly exist in abundance in Russia. Particularly in the twenties, but certainly continuing to some extent even to the present, Russia has had her own "lost generation," intellectual and spiritual casualties of the Revolution who must feel a strong affinity for Jake Barnes and Brett Ashley. Paradoxically, Hemingway's morbid picture of life in the "decadent" West may also appeal to yet another group of Russians—those who ardently support the Soviet regime—by reinforcing their feeling of cultural superiority.

On the other hand, Hemingway's realism lacks the documentary quality which is so prominent in such realists as

[58] Leonid Leonov, "Pisatel s mirovym golosom," *Pravda*, July 4, 1961, p. 4.

[59] *Saturday Review*, July 29, 1961, p. 20.

[60] "Bolshoi pisatel," *Izvestiya*, July 4, 1961, p. 4.

Sinclair, Dos Passos, and Theodore Dreiser. In general, his writing is much more philosophical and psychological than sociological in its emphasis. Despite his marvelous ability to reconstruct the world of people and things, he is much more concerned with eternal, abstract problems than with those of immediate social, political, or economic interest. Ultimately to like Hemingway, one must sympathize with his approach to the large personal issues which trouble and will continue to trouble everyone, everywhere. This would suggest that in insisting that he cease exploring the problem of death and de-emphasize the element of love, the critics were subscribing more to official doctrine than to their own feelings. For Russians are still awed by death, and Russians still fall in love.

Other aspects of Soviet criticism probably indicate the reader's response more accurately. For one thing, readers must admire Hemingway's narrative gifts. If his style conceals, as Kashkin suggested, a "desperate complication," it is nevertheless simple and intelligible. It moves swiftly, and it is exciting. In this respect, the Soviet reader probably appreciates him for the same qualities that have made him a best seller in America. Likewise, his vigorous love of nature, sports, combat, and adventure must appeal to the Russians. This clean, rugged outlook on life (despite its elements of bravado, of which the critics took due note) strikes the same chord in the Russian heart as do the stories of London. In the Russians there is a strong love of the primitive, and a comparable distaste for the sophisticated, which amounts at times to a puritanical attitude toward the "decadent" trappings of civilization. The unmistakable longing for a simpler, purer, and more elemental life which rings in Hemingway's stories must find response in this part of the Soviet reader's nature. Ultimately it is Hemingway's profound understanding of the natural aspirations of men which appeals to the Russian public.

CHAPTER XIII

CONCLUSION

ᘏᘏᘏ IN THE first four decades of the Soviet regime more than fifty million volumes of translated works of American literature were published in the USSR. Roughly half of this total represented authors—such as Mark Twain, Jack London, and Harriet Beecher Stowe—who had been popular in Russia before 1917. Although the high proportion of nineteenth-century works reflects an unquestionably genuine and permanent affection for their authors among Russian readers, it also reflects political policy. From the standpoint of Party and government, it was safer to print works that described an antiquated America than to print contemporary works, which often depicted conditions of life far superior to those in the Soviet Union.

The proportion of older works was high also because of the difficulties that attended the publication of contemporary American writers. Soviet publishing houses had not only to exclude works complimentary to the United States, but also to seek out works which actively promoted, or at least harmonized with, Kremlin policies. Since American literature was constantly changing, and since Soviet cultural policy was subject to shifting political demands, the task of choosing for translation living authors who could serve the needs of a given moment and at the same time prove enduring political allies, was precarious. Even Howard Fast, on whose loyalty the Russians counted extremely heavily, let them down. The political criteria of Soviet publication also created other complications. Many writers who were printed for their political attractiveness—such as the "proletarians" of the thirties and their successors of the forties and fifties—did not succeed with Soviet readers. By the same token, many contemporary Americans who might have gained a following among Soviet readers were excluded for political and ideological reasons.

The Russians have often complained that the quantity of contemporary American literature published in the USSR is greater than the quantity of Soviet literature printed in the United States. Although this complaint is based on accurate information, it is beside the point, since the proper question is not one of quantity but of quality. Had Soviet literature proved generally attractive to American readers, the publishing houses of the United States would gladly have satisfied the market, whereas American works, in order to reach the Soviet public, had first to pass through the thick filters of official censorship. Soviet readers have never been really free to choose among contemporary American works, and it is a tribute to the vitality of American writers that with even a limited choice, the Soviet public maintained an affection for them. The point is that, had official shackles been removed, contemporary American writing would have been much more popular than it was.

The Soviet choice of translations contributed abundantly to a distorted impression of America. The high percentage of politically biased works of left-wing, and often Communist, orientation, simply misinformed the Russian public about the political climate and tendencies of the United States. Although domestic tranquillity and social harmony were indeed a rarity from 1917 to 1960, the country was not ripe for revolution, nor was it stratified in such viciously antagonistic social and economic groupings as the Soviet choice of our literature suggested. Yet millions of the most gullible Russian readers, looking to this American writing for a documentary picture, must have harbored rather constantly the lurid image of a sick and highly explosive society. Moreover, this image was badly outdated. In the 1950's, for example, the works of Dreiser became for Soviet readers the highest American authority on the details of life in the United States—the workings of its social system, the operation of its economy, the psychology of its classes—whereas in actuality the country had changed profoundly in many respects since Dreiser's time. Sinclair's *The Jungle*, describing a situation that had existed half a century ago, continued to be published as a valid and timely document. In passing off such works as true descriptions of contemporary America, the publishers performed a twofold service to Soviet propaganda. First, they helped to perpetuate the image of a mythical America that was totally vulnerable to the classic nineteenth-century Marxist critique of capitalism, and, second, they showed the America of the days of the horseless carriage, thus obscuring the improvements in her standard of living and the increasingly equalitarian distribution of her wealth.

Many translated works provided a more up-to-date picture of the United States, but even among these the dominant note was critical realism. Such writers as Lewis and Steinbeck emphasized the failures, discords, and sorrows of American life much more heavily than its successes and social accomplishments. *Kingsblood Royal* and *The Grapes of Wrath* were novels of protest that described extremely serious but nevertheless limited social evils. They were written to inform and arouse an American audience that was already well aware of the fundamental strength of its own society. But Soviet readers, who lacked any familiarity with the United States, might well have concluded that Lewis and Steinbeck had drawn universal portraits.

For opinions of the American literature that was made available to the Soviet public, the present study has relied almost entirely on professional literary critics. The opinions of ordinary readers, which are much more elusive and difficult to come by, have been cited only occasionally. In any country critics tend to form a special caste whose views of literature are not necessarily shared by the public, and in the USSR the gulf between the critics and the rest of the populace is easily as great as it is in other societies. What the critics, operating on strict and narrow ideological assumptions, find in an American work is probably quite different from what many Soviet readers find.

Most often the critics wrote not as individuals striving to contribute personal insights to the study of literature, but rather as inspectors of ideology, presumably endowed with a special knowledge of the public taste and the authority to determine what works could legitimately satisfy it. Their task, in large measure, was to make the reader want to read

[318]

what the Party thought he needed to read. As they commented on American writing, there seemed to loom before them the image of an ideal Soviet reader whose greatest aspiration was to find the one and only correct view of a given work of literature and who eagerly clung to Party-inspired pronouncements as a guide to his reading. Their account of American literature was therefore colored by a peculiar blend of wishful thinking and exhortation.

Frequently the critics were impelled to misinterpret American works in their attempts to make them conform to set ideological patterns or to give an ideologically "respectable" explanation of an author's popularity among Soviet readers. In treating of O. Henry, for example, many critics began with the make-believe assumption that Soviet readers are uninterested in the portrayal of life's little ironies, that they do not look to literature for comfort and consolation, and that they want most of all to read about the class struggle. From there these critics proceeded to reason that since Soviet readers *do* like him, O. Henry must indeed be a writer whose main interest was the class struggle. This kind of reasoning led in many different directions. Starting from the assumption that the Soviet reader *should not* be interested in gloomy or erotic literature, the critics proceeded to pretend that he *was not* interested, and they used this pretense to justify their disparagement of fundamental tendencies in Sherwood Anderson, Faulkner, Dos Passos, Hemingway, and others. Likewise, when confronted with the fact that London's immensely popular heroes are not only laudably self-reliant but also distressingly individualistic, and that these two qualities are frequently inextricable in them, the critics lamely attempted to decontaminate the reader by separating the inseparable.

Although some of the critics were genuinely erudite and had the privilege of reading, in English, numerous works that were kept from the public at large, none of them had more than a secondhand knowledge of the United States— the kind that comes from books. Despite their scholarship (which was sometimes truly impressive) they remained essentially ignorant of the United States—her real political processes, her way of life, her material conditions, her freedoms and liberties. Even their most sincere attempts to understand American culture were hampered by ethnocentric assumptions on the basis of which they projected Soviet mores and the facts of Soviet political life to the United States. They believed, for instance, that it was possible for the financial interests of Wall Street to control the output of American literature, and, moreover, to control it to the same degree that the Party apparatus controlled Soviet literature. Lacking an authentic comprehension of the free play of ideas, they assumed that the contemporary American literature they read represented efficiently mobilized, monolithic cultural forces. Bewitched by their own historic Russian image with a latter-day Marxist-Leninist tint, they also accepted uncritically the notion that the American working class was a separate, sharply defined social and economic unit, with its own distinct and individual customs, ideals, and living conditions. With little understanding of the mobility of classes in the United States or of the broad influence of middle-class culture, they were the easy victims of a doctrine that told them that the ranks of the American proletariat were constantly swelling and that a separate proletarian ideology was developing and triumphing in the USA. Their search for this mythical ideology in contemporary American literature was benighted and futile, but stubborn.

The elements of genuine literary criticism did emerge from time to time throughout the whole Soviet period. Many critics of American writing had a deeper interest in literature than their narrow tasks permitted them to demonstrate. Many of them, moreover, had good taste, high literary standards, and the ability to read wisely and perceptively. Occasionally their sound judgment, quite independent of the ideology that constricted them, shone timidly and even deviously through their writings. Usually, however, their political and ideological obligations prohibited them from expressing their love for good writing, except in passing. The Party line at any given time demanded that certain sets of ideas, with corresponding slogans and clichés, govern the writing of all critics, so that they had constantly to trim their sails to fit the prevailing winds. No doubt most of them willingly accepted these conditions of professional survival. In many instances, however, the moral costs must have been very great, for some of the worst, most narrowly doctrinaire, and obviously insincere criticism has at times been written by some of the most talented critics.

It is impossible to believe that the best informed of these critics were devoid of cynicism. Especially from the end of World War II to the death of Stalin, the comments of those who continued to write on American literature were so outlandish that, for a time, all of them seem to have become little more than calculating hacks. On the other hand, many of their most glaringly unfair remarks about American literature may well have been sincere. Sheer ignorance, in combination with the delusions fostered by a totalitarian regime, produces weird results among Soviet intellectuals.

Since politics, Party controls, and censorship prevented many critics from writing as they would have liked, any attempt to characterize individual critics on the basis of their published utterances is bound to produce inaccuracies. Nevertheless, certain groupings are discernible among them. The most influential group were the supermilitant Leninists who achieved prominence in the 1930's, accumulated power and authority in the following two decades, and became a strong force of reaction in the 1950's. These critics were simply not interested in literature. They used American works solely as documentation to support propagandistic attacks on the United States. By 1960 the pronouncements of these veterans, such as Ivan Anisimov and Roman Samarin, and of their younger adherents, such as Yasen Zasurski, were all designed to retard the liberalizing trend in the Soviet attitude toward American literature. Ossified, unable to discard the dogmatic habits of a lifetime, these men constituted a formidable barrier against increased understanding of American culture.

During the disastrous years from 1945 to 1955, the Soviet critical imagination became indolent. Even intelligent and potentially creative critics, reduced to the confining task of inventing ways of abusing America, allowed their talents to become stultified. After the liberalization that began in 1955, their attempts to write genuine literary criticism were often painful and humiliating. Some of them, such as Elena Romanova, Inna Levidova, and Pavel Toper, succeeded quite well in casting aside international polemics. Turning to humanistic criticism, they proved to be much more sensitive to literary values than they had appeared to be in the years before 1955. Others, such as Raissa Orlova, whose talent for purely political criticism had been nurtured in the darkest years before 1955, proved unequal to the task of writing aesthetic commentary.

Literary scholarship—although Marxist, heavily historical, and sociological—has always been carried on to some extent in the Soviet Union. Some persons wrote with a true knowledge of American literary history and a respect for its tradition. The critics Abel Startsev, Alexander Anikst, Anna Elistratova, and Tamara Motyleva undoubtedly belong in this category. Startsev, for example, ranged widely and wrote as frequently about the American literature of the eighteenth and nineteenth centuries as he did about contemporary authors. Although he dutifully subscribed to official dogma, he usually avoided the temptation to vulgarize and distort individual works to make them fit an official pattern. Likewise, Elistratova and Anikst based their opinions and interpretations on sound investigations and respect for the literary heritage of the United States.

The best Soviet critic of American literature has been Ivan Kashkin, who is an erudite, imaginative, aesthetically perceptive student of the prevailing modes of the contemporary West. An accomplished linguist and translator, he clearly admired the variety and technical proficiency he observed among American writers. Kashkin wrote as a convinced Marxist who completely shared the political opinions of his colleagues. What set him off from them was his aesthetic understanding and his ability to draw literary conclusions in situations where his colleagues confined themselves to political interpretations. Significantly, from 1945 to 1955 he wrote nothing about American literature.

Although he admired its virtuosity, Kashkin always viewed contemporary American literature as the product of misspent talent. He seemed to pity a nation of writers whose gifts were being expended in the portrayal of what he considered to be social decay. In his view, American authors were creatures alienated from their culture but spiritually imprisoned because they were blind to the possibility of social change. The same talents that were now being directed to morbid themes of capitalist decadence, Kashkin argued, would become more powerful and revealing if only they would turn to positive themes of social revolution. However, Kashkin's choice of authors for investigation belied this judgment: his favorite American author was Hemingway, and he completely ignored Howard Fast. Although he could never admit that the "negative" writing whose thematics he ostensibly deplored contained more aesthetic possibilities than the "positive" writing he advocated, this judgment is implicit in everything he wrote.

Because Kashkin wrote as a Marxist and adopted an acceptably condescending tone in commenting on the ideological values of current American literature, his criticism was published fairly consistently. There must have been others whose intelligence, breadth of interest, and gifts for criticism would have enabled them to publish perceptive comments on American literature had they been able to clothe their comments in the proper ideological garb. The forces of sophistication, wisdom, and balance, however, were suppressed fairly consistently throughout the Soviet period, so that persons whose intellectual integrity and sense of cultural decency demanded that they tell the whole truth about American literature were nearly always inhibited.

The overwhelming defect of Soviet criticism has been its insistence that there is only one correct way for the artist to perceive life. From this arrogant proposition ensues a dogmatic blindness to the multiple influences that intervene between the objective world and the printed page: the complexities of the creative personality, the strength and dignity of literary tradition, and the variety of aesthetic principles that are valid and applicable in our twentieth century of expanding knowledge. The belief that there is but a single path to the truth not only promoted intolerance of competing literary attitudes; it also provided the doctrinal justification for the subservience of Soviet criticism to the political policies of the Communist Party.

The narrow limitations of doctrine prevented Soviet criticism from recognizing and giving full value to many sources of literary insight that were discovered or developed by Americans during this period. The critics were forced, for example, to dismiss under the label of "naturalism" the growing American literary interest in psychological exploration and aberrant behavior, on the ground that such disclosures divest mankind of its nobility. A fixed and rigid view of human nature prevented them from understanding that *any* discoveries about human beings can be the legitimate material of literature, and that a knowledge of the truth, however unpleasant, is precisely what ennobles mankind. Moreover, even time-honored themes, such as fate, love, death, and the private destiny of the individual—whose validity the critics admitted in their comments on the literature of past ages—were patronizingly disparaged when they appeared in works of twentieth-century American authors.

At times an obsession with the social and political function of literature nearly obliterated aesthetic standards. Serious works of artistic merit were frequently treated as if they were on the same aesthetic level as inferior works whose only interest was political. Political evaluations so obscured artistic considerations that, judging from the critics' comments alone, one might easily have concluded, for example, that Michael Gold was as accomplished a writer as Ernest Hemingway. The Marxist-Leninist view of literature also forced the critics to postulate a much more direct and simple connection between social and economic conditions and the work of the individual American writer than actually exists. A fruit of this fallacy was the constant and imprecise use of the term "petty bourgeois." As applied to American writers, particu-

larly in the thirties, it became so indiscriminate and confusing as to be virtually meaningless. Originally an economic
term denoting the small proprietor with a disappearing stake
in the capitalist order, the expression "petty bourgeois" came
to signify, in contexts that really called for careful literary
discrimination, any theme, attitude, interest, or device that
in the opinion of the individual Soviet critic marred the ideological purity of a work, detracted from its political militancy,
directed the reader's attention away from society, or suggested the writer's cultivation of artistic form for its own
sake. It became a blanket device for obfuscation that enabled
many Soviet critics to avoid naming things precisely, reasoning out critical judgments, or investigating literary phenomena which they lacked either the intelligence or the taste to
deal with.

The notion that social utility was the only legitimate justification for literature became responsible for another Soviet
term—"formalism." The feeling that complexity and refinement of verbal expression are undemocratic because they make
literature difficult for common people to comprehend was
strong among many Russians long before the Revolution.
After 1917, there was a growing doctrinal intolerance of
experiments with literary form, on the ground that such
pursuits were esoteric and aristocratic. As Soviet criticism
developed, "formalism" became a term designating an artist's
excessive—and therefore politically harmful—preoccupation
with form at the expense of social message. Eventually it became a catchall term for the purpose of dismissing literary
considerations that were of no interest to the individual
critic or for evading questions that were too complex or too
pertinent to be handled without ideological compromise and
embarrassment. The abhorrence of formalism explains in
large measure Soviet critics' lack of interest in contemporary
American poetry, their indifference to much of the American
criticism that was written during these years, and the relative
sparsity and superficiality of their comments on the style and
structure of works of American fiction.

The notion that the Soviet Union held a complete monopoly over the pursuit of truth led also to a glaringly paradoxical attitude toward realism in literature. American critical realism was condoned because the social evils and sins of man it portrayed could be attributed by Soviet critics to the workings of the capitalist system. When similar evils and sins were mentioned in Russian works about Soviet society they were supposed to be portrayed as transitory phenomena that were undergoing eradication. Since the behavior, attitudes, and emotions typical of American society were considered to be untypical of and merely ephemeral in Soviet society, American literature was said to have very limited validity as an interpreter of common human experience. Because Soviet criticism pretended that one breed of mankind existed in the nascent world of communism and that an entirely different breed predominated in the effete West, the critics reduced the role of American literature to a kind of historical commentary on a people whose problems had only secondary relevance for Soviet readers. Until such time as the critics could discard the myth of Soviet exceptionalism and perfectibility, could be permitted to admit that the basic core of human nature is common to all societies, and could proclaim without qualification that literature communicates truths that are universally applicable, their efforts to understand American literature would be severely handicapped.

Although it indeed narrowed their horizons, the very rigidity of Soviet critics' adherence to simple political and ideological principles sometimes enabled them to make perceptions that were not characteristic of less dogmatic and absolutist bodies of criticism. Their fixed concentration on and defense of a single social ideology, for example, enabled them to discern that the diversity of literary devices used by Dos Passos sprang from his own ideological uncertainty and consequent inability to generalize about the life around him, and that his vital anxiety over the fate of the private personality in an increasingly organized society might—as it eventually did—turn him into a conservative foe of collectivism. Likewise, from their politically radical position they could see that such writers as Sinclair Lewis and Upton Sinclair, who have seemed dangerously leftist to many of their fellow Americans, were actually loyal critics of American society. The Russians were acutely gifted in the techniques of distinguishing liberals from Communists, and in this respect they provided insights which, ironically, are all too lacking in the United States.

Doctrinal opposition to the presence of certain themes in literature also made Soviet critics especially alert to their occurrence in American works. Had the critics been less opposed to the prominence of the theme of death in contemporary literature, they might have been less able to see and analyze the importance of its role in the writing of Hemingway. And having decided that the strength of Steinbeck and Caldwell was in their portrayal of social struggle, they were able to see clearly that the growing prominence of sex and degeneracy in their works was a source of weakness.

Soviet critics are not the only ones who have found fault with the American literature of the past fifteen years. American critics themselves are painfully aware of the fact that, despite its engaging variety and color, the literature of the United States since World War II—including that which was devoted to the war itself—has become fragmented and superficial, that confusion and aimless groping are chronic among American writers, and that none of them seems capable of grasping large and significant amounts of the current national experience and shaping it into a profound work of fiction. The Soviet indictment of our recent writing is deeply irritating in its smugness and patently wrong and unfair in its insistence that the present-day literature of the Soviet Union is superior to that of the United States. But the very self-righteousness of Soviet critics enables them to perceive with heightened clarity the fact that American writing today is unsure of its own ideological foundations.

Soviet literary criticism today is—as it has been for the past forty years—a mixture of national prejudice, Marxist-Leninist ideology, and timely attitudes dictated by political expediency. Maimed and groggy from repeated blows directed at it by the Communist Party, it continues doggedly to grope for formulas that make literary sense and are at the same time politically workable. In the past five years significant steps have been taken toward removing the curtain that prevents the Soviet people from knowing what the American literature of today is really like. The belated discovery of *Moby Dick*, the recent publication of William Faulkner after years of calumny and boycott, the translation of one of Tennessee Williams' plays, and the appearance of such works as *The Catcher in the Rye* do not at all promise a complete loosening of ideological bonds. But these events should aid Soviet critics in their labors over the dilemma that has been confusing them for decades: how to observe the Leninist imperative of judging contemporary literature first of all as an agent of social change, and at the same time to understand and appreciate the various elements that make up a work of American literature.